KV-050-219

Photographic Imaging and
Electronic Photography

Titles in the Technical Pocket Book Series

Photographic Imaging and Electronic Photography

Series editor: Sidney F. Ray

Focal Press
An imprint of Butterworth-Heinemann Ltd
Linacre House, Jordan Hill, Oxford OX2 8DP

ℛ A member of the Reed Elsevier plc group

OXFORD LONDON BOSTON
MUNICH NEW DELHI SINGAPORE SYDNEY
TOKYO TORONTO WELLINGTON

First published 1994

© Butterworth-Heinemann 1994

British Library Cataloguing in Publication Data
A catalogue record for this book is
available from the British Library

Library of Congress Cataloging in Publication Data
A catalogue record for this book is
available from the Library of Congress

ISBN 0 240 51389 4

Printed and bound in Great Britain by Clays, St Ives plc

Preface

The technical aspects of photography and imaging cover a wide range of ideas and topics drawn from optics, chemistry, engineering, electronics and visual perception that bring together the mature technology of silver halide systems in the form of photographic materials with the newer and fast evolving technologies of electronic imaging and digital photography. Common to all such knowledge however are the additional craft skills required to produce a successful image as previsualised, involving or including controlled manipulation of images at the camera, recording and post production stages.

This book, as one of a related series, presents a specific topic or subject in detail to provide a balanced overview of relevant theory, practice and applications.

To ensure authoritative, contemporary information and details, the format and material is drawn from the Focal Encyclopedia of Photography, third edition, edited by Leslie Stroebel and Richard Zakia, published in 1993. This massive volume has entries compiled by 90 contributors and gives extensive coverage of most aspects of photography, movie production, video, electronic and digital imaging. The selected extracts are largely unaltered but some have been further edited in content to suit the overall subject of the Pocket Book or possibly modified in details to conform to European practices as distinct from those in North America.

The topic of this Pocket Book is photographic imaging and electronic photography dealing with the principles and properties of electronic imaging devices and the practice of video production. Coverage includes still video and digital cameras, the conversion of images into digital form and the manipulation of those digital images. The basic features of computers for digital image processing are covered, together with some applications of electronic and digital imaging, especially relating to the printing processes.

Suggestions for further reading are included in some of the longer entries.

Companion volumes in the Pocket Book series include Photographic Chemistry and Processing, Photographic Data, Photographic Lenses and Optics, Photographic Printing and Enlarging, Photographic Technology and Image Science.

AERIAL PHOTOGRAPHY Improved imaging methods for aerial photography have significantly changed this technology area over the last several years. Before the introduction of real-time, digital imaging sensors, this field made nearly exclusive use of high resolution photographic products to collect imagery from aircraft and space-borne platforms. The imaging process consisted of preplanned flight paths with specifically identified locations to be photographed. Pilots would fly the route, and the camera would operate automatically to acquire the specified target regions. The plane would then return to its base, where the film was unloaded, processed, duplicated, and distributed as required. This process could take from several hours to as much as several weeks (or even months) before users of the imagery could gain access to the photographic product.

Recent advances in aerial imaging for reconnaissance applications have centered around the need for rapid transmission and exploitation of collected imagery. Real-time sensors that transmit digital imagery to the ground at the instant it is acquired have significantly altered the functions, uses, and applications for aerial imagery. Film cameras are still used to provide information to satisfy requirements when the timeliness or availability of image products is not critical to the information being sought. Film systems can usually be obtained for less initial cost than comparable electro-optical (EO) systems, provide good image resolution, and have the advantage of a long-standing base of technology and available equipment for film analysis. For real-time applications, however, EO, thermal, multispectral, and other digitally-based imaging sensors surpass film in their ability to provide important time-critical information.

EO sensors using linear or area-array charge coupled devices (CCDs) are rapidly becoming the replacement for panchromatic (black-and-white) film-based reconnaissance systems. Linear arrays containing 10,000 pixels are now available that can provide ground details and area coverage nearly equivalent to film systems. Digital sensors that acquire imagery in regions other than the visible spectrum include thermal, radar, and multispectral systems. Thermal sensors add the advantage of being able to collect imagery at night and locate sources of heat, which usually indicate some form of activity. Imaging radar sensors can be used to "see" through clouds, smoke, and haze. Space-borne multispectral cameras (such as the U.S. Landsat and French SPOT systems) have been used to assess natural disaster damage (e.g., the Chernobyl nuclear reactor explosion, Alaska oil spill effects, and oilwell fires in Kuwait). Each of these sensor types has been used for aerial photography missions to provide essential information not achievable with film systems.

Although real-time digital systems provide rapid transmission of imagery to ground-based receiving stations, they require computer-based image processing equipment to display and enhance the image. The image-processing technology associated with digital-image products has grown rapidly with the availability of faster and more powerful computers and image workstations. There are several technical societies currently emphasizing or specializing in image processing capabilities: SPIE, the International Society for Optical Engineering; SID, the Society for Information Display; and IS&T the Society for Imaging Science and Technology. Processing techniques range from simple manipulation of gray-scale reproduction and image sharpening to sophisticated image perspective transformations, sensor-fusion techniques, geo-positioning, and automatic object identification and recognition by expert system algorithms.

The field of aerial photography encompasses many diverse disciplines. The major categories related to aerial imaging and their associated technical specialties include camera and platform design (optical, mechanical, and electrical engineering); image transmission and receiving (electrical engineering, signal processing, computer science); image processing and reconstruction (computer science image science, image processing), and image display and hard-copy reproduction (image science, psychophysical, and vision research). Each user and application area also requires specialized training in order to best use the imagery products from these diverse sensors.

Commercial users and applications for aerial imagery include regional and urban planning, forestry, ecological and environmental studies, population surveys, crop production and vegetation studies, geology, mining, and natural resource exploration. The American Society for Photogrammetry and Remote Sensing (ASPRS) is the leading technical association that describes the uses, applications, and current processes related to aerial imaging products.

ALGORITHM In computers, an algorithm defines the number of steps or the extent of the process required to solve a coding problem. It is a structured step-by-step course of action.

ALIASING Low- and medium-resolution computer imaging systems display normally smooth edges as jagged edges. These *jaggies* are known as aliasing. It may result from undersampling the spatial frequency, or when the detail exceeds the display ability of the monitor.

ALPHA CHANNEL Unused 8-bit portion of a 32-bit image. It can be used as a mask to apply filters, colour changes, or overlay graphics on top of an image. The alpha channel can be used to control the opacity of the image.

ALPHANUMERIC TARGET A resolving power test object in which the target elements consist of block letters and numbers, each of which contains three parallel bars. Variability tends to be lower with alphanumeric targets than with conventional resolving power targets since the observer is required to identify the set of characters selected.

ALTERNATING CURRENT (AC, ac) Any electrical current that periodically reverses the direction of flow. When used to describe power sources, it refers to the sinusoidal variation of current that rises from zero to a maximum in one direction, falls to zero, rises to a maximum in the other direction, returns to zero, and continues to repeat this cycle. The abbreviation AC, or ac, is invariably used to describe a voltage that reverses polarity in a similar manner, for example, ac voltage.

AMERICAN NATIONAL STANDARDS INSTITUTE (ANSI) The national standardizing organization of the United States of America.

AMERICAN STANDARD CODE FOR INFORMATION INTERCHANGE (ASCII) This is a 7-bit encoding system that is capable of generating 128 characters. Every computer character, including control characters, is assigned a binary number according to the ASCII protocol. The translation of keystrokes into ASCII and then into binary allows the computer to read the data.

AMPERE (A, Amp) The basic unit of electric current intensity. The current is said to be 1 ampere when 1 coulomb of electric charge (6.25×10^{18} electrons) flows in a circuit in 1 second.

See also: *Electrical current*

AMPLITUDE (1) The size dimension of a waveform, usually represented graphically in the vertical plane. The size represents the strength of the unit being measured, for example, sound pressure level for sound.
(2) The strength of an analog signal. In computer imaging, it is the voltage level that represents a brightness of a given point in the image.

ANALOG Identifying a measuring instrument in which the value appears on a scale from which the user takes the result. Mercury thermometers are analog instruments. Contrast with *digital*.

ANALOG AUDIO Any signal representation of sound such as electrically, mechanically, magnetically, electromagnetically or by means of light, where the signal waveform is transmitted or stored in direct, 1:1 correspondence with sound. The amplitude dimension of the audio signal is represented by way of a direct analogy between a voltage, displacement of position (such as for the phonograph or an analog optical sound track), or strength of magnetic flux (analog tape recording), for example, and the signal. Analog systems may also employ modulation and demodulation such as frequency modulation (FM) where audio is imposed on a carrier frequency such as a radio frequency by way of modulation; despite the modulation/demodulation cycle the audio remains in analog form since no digitization has occurred.

AND/OR In computers, the logical operators are generally part of the arithmetic logic unit (ALU). It provides for the combining of two images pixel by pixel. The *and* function is used to mask off a portion of the image. The *or* function is used to add subimages into a composite output.

ANIMATION An approach to motion-picture or video production used most often to create screen realities that could not naturally exist—by making inanimate objects, such as cartoon drawings or puppets, appear to move of their own accord. Animation is frame-by-frame motion-picture or video production. While live action cinematography records actual events as a series of still pictures (frames) exposed rapidly one after the other (24 per second for film, and 25 per second for video), animation *creates* moving events by recording, one frame at a time, an organized sequence of still drawings or objects. In both cases, when the sequence is projected normally, the audience perceives, thanks to the phi phenomenon and persistence of vision, a continuous moving image.

When creating animation, each image is slightly altered from the one before, showing a change in position that corresponds to the change in position during a 24th (or a 25th) of a second for a similar natural movement. In creating the illusion of movement animated objects are also imbued with a sense of life and even personality, particularly when they interact and seem to respond to one another. While animation is a powerful story-telling tool, usually identified with cartoons it is also a regular part of most film productions, being used in the creation of special effects and titles. Its potential for visual expression, narrative uniqueness, and the creation of imaginary screen realities is limited only by the animator's imagination and the practical difficulty of creating thousands of individual coordinated images.

EARLY DEVELOPMENTS OF ANIMATION In 1824 at the same time work was being done that led to the creation of the first photographs, Peter Roget, Frenchman and author of *Roget's Thesaurus,* published his *Persistence of Vision with Regard to Moving Objects.* The popularization of this concept, that the eye will meld still images together if they are presented rapidly enough and with sufficient light, led to the development of a variety of very popular toys and novelty devices that successfully created the illusion of movement or combined images in an interesting way. The *thaumatrope* was a disc with a drawing on each side. When the disc was spun, the images appeared to combine—the animal appeared to be in the cage, or the ball became balanced on the seal's nose. The *zoetrope* and *phenakistiscope* were two of the most popular versions of a rotating drum device, in which a strip of drawings was placed on the inside wall of a shallow drum and viewed through vertical slits in the drum wall. The slits worked like the shutter in a modern motion-picture projector, interrupting the images to allow a sequence of different images to be seen in the same position. The *praxinoscope* also used a circular strip of drawings in a rotating drum. In this case however, the images were reflected from a central circular set of mirrors and viewed through a single opening. Also popular, and still common, was *the flipbook,* a bound sequence of drawings that gave the illusion of movement when rapidly flipped through. Projection systems were also developed using magic lanterns and rotating wheels mounted with a sequence of drawings on slides, and in one case a giant praxinoscope.

While these devices were limited in many ways, presenting little variety in one- or two-second segments of simple action, and depending for popularity on the novelty of seeing drawings move, they were an important part of the chain of experimentation and commercialisation that led to the development of motion pictures. In 1888 George Eastman made roll film available through his patented process of applying a light-sensitive emulsion to a flexible celluloid strip. In contrast to the previous techniques of using glass or metal plates for the emulsion, roll film allowed the photography of a rapid sequence of images over an extended period of time. In 1895, the Lumiére brothers presented in Paris the first theatrical projection of movies for a large audience. In 1899 J. Stuart Blackton and Albert E. Smith, founders of the Vitagraph company, successfully faked news footage of Spanish American War naval battles using animation techniques, cutouts, and some water, smoke, and gunpowder. In 1906 Blackton went on to produce The Humorous Phases of Funny Faces, generally considered to be the first animated cartoon film, with drawings done in chalk on a blackboard. Later in the same year, Emile Cohl, a French artist began working on a series of short animations using charming, though crude, white on black stick figures. A significant step forward in the development of character animation was made when Winsor McCay, a successful newspaper comic strip artist, produced Gertie the Dinosaur in 1914. Gertie possessed a distinct and endearing personality and demonstrated a smoothness of animation and elegance of drawing that is still impressive today. McCay used more than 5000 drawings for Gertie, and an assistant traced the backgrounds.

With both a commercial market and creative potential established, animation studies and techniques for more efficient production quickly began to develop. By 1915 peg bars for registering drawings, cel animation, and a system for rotoscoping had all been patented. Influenced by competition among studios, technological advances, and economic, social, and market factors, the history of animation has been one of continual evolution and change in style and technique and is today entering a new era as computer technology allows animators to deal with imagery or a complexity previously impractical or impossible to achieve.

ANIMATION TECHNIQUES Because of the extensive time and labour involved in frame-by-frame filmmaking and the variety of imagery and effects that can be achieved, many animation techniques have been developed to allow the greatest efficiency in producing the desired results. Some of the most common are described in the following paragraphs.

Cel Animation Drawings are made on clear sheets of cellulose acetate (called cels) that can be overlayed and combined when they are photographed. This technique, standard for cartoons since its invention in 1915, allows the separation of static and moving picture elements and requires the minimum amount of drawing and colouring. For instance, only one background drawing may be necessary to go with a long series of drawings for a complicated character movement, or only the moving parts of a character may be animated with separate drawings. This technique may also simplify production procedures, allowing different characters to be animated separately, and provides an image consistency frame by frame that would be difficult to achieve if the backgrounds had to be traced and redrawn for every frame.

Cutout Animation Instead of making individual drawings for each increment of movement, cutout figures, usually with jointed limbs, can be placed directly on the animation stand, photographed, and then moved slightly before exposing the next frame. This technique creates a unique visual style and requires a minimum amount of drawing or artwork preparation, making it particularly popular with students and others working without the aid of a large staff of animators.

Drawing on Paper While cel animation creates a look particularly suited to cartoons, animators might choose, for the sake of an alternative graphic style, to design each frame to be exposed from an individual complete drawing. This approach is most likely with very short films, abstract films, films exploiting a unique drawing style, personally expressive films, and stylized cartoons involving little background or character detail.

Three-Dimensional Animation Animation of puppets, clay models, or any real (as opposed to drawn) objects or people. Sometimes called stop-motion animation, the object is photographed for one frame, then its position is slightly altered and the next frame is exposed, followed by another slight object move and then another exposure, and on and on. A few seconds of stop-motion animation might take several hours to shoot. While two-dimensional animation is recorded on an animation stand, and changes in point of view, or lighting effect, are handled by changing the drawings, three-dimensional animation uses procedures more similar to that of live-action production. Shooting takes place on real location or with sets that must be built and dressed. The single-frame camera is positioned as it would be for live-action, changes in point of view are handled by repositioning the camera, and lighting techniques are the same as for live action.

Pixilation A three-dimensional technique involving the frame-by-frame shooting of live actors and normal sized props. Using this technique, a person could appear to glide, rather than walk, down a street, or appear to be dancing along a large variety of props.

Claymation Claymation is a trade name for a clay model technique capable of subtle lifelike expression and dramatic transformations. Layers of clay are built around a wire armature, allowing practical control of incremental change in both position and surface appearance of the clay models.

Scratch-off Starting with completed artwork, the animator scrapes off or erases part of the image between exposures. Scratch-off often is filmed in reverse, so that rather than seeming to disappear, the material appears to be growing into a finished image. This technique is also called wipe-off or scratch-back.

Special Techniques By combining and modifying standard techniques and developing unique approaches to the creation of the original images, animators are continually developing new techniques that reflect individual expressive goals and interests. The cameraless technique of painting directly on motion picture film is an interesting example. Pinscreen technique creates images from the shadows of thousand of steel pins whose configuration is altered between exposures. Animations have been created drawing with sand, glass beads, or modelling clay, spread across bottom-lit glass plates. Photokinesis is a technique of using static artwork that is moved beneath the camera between exposures, creating the illusion of movement. By recording a series of dissimilar static images, such as still photographs, for only two or three frames each, one after the other, animators can achieve unusual illusions of movement and image combination.

Computer Animation Animation using digital computers as the principal tool for the creation of the individual images is a quickly growing field that is beginning a new era of possibility for frame-by-frame production, providing a relatively rapid system for incrementally altering complex images in fine detail that would be impossible or impractical using traditional techniques. The computer deals with images as digital information describing each pixel (point of light) that makes up the image. A typical TV monitor uses more than a quarter of a million pixels for each image, while high resolution systems might use several million pixels. Photographs or drawings may be entered into the computer via a video camera, or frames may be grabbed directly from a videotape. One can also draw directly into the computer using a mouse, electronic pencil, and screen, or writing by directions through the computer's keyboard. The computer can then be directed to manipulate the image in any number of ways, which it does by altering each appropriate pixel. Once a final image is created, it can be fed directly to a frame-by-frame video recorder, or filmed off a CRT screen, or printed out on paper and photographed on a traditional animation stand. A dramatic application of this technology popular for the creation of special effects in live-action science fiction films and TV commercials, is called *morphing* and involves the apparent realistic transformation of a person or object into another person, creature, shape, or object.

Computers can also handle a great deal of the work that traditionally is accomplished by tedious hand drawing. Given two key images, the computer can create all the inbetween images necessary for smooth animation. Describe a light source and the computer can add proper shadow detail. Create a change in point of view, and the computer will redraw the image, maintaining proper perspective and object relationships. In accordance with programmed instructions, the computer will also combine images and add backgrounds, colour, and surface texture.

Computers have also been used effectively to enhance traditional animation techniques, as with programmable control systems used with stop-motion and animation stand photography, and automated ink and paint systems.

PRODUCTION PROCEDURES Because of the great amount of time and effort required for each frame, animation requires considerable planning, organizing, and checking throughout the production process. Major studios have established routines for assigning responsibility and guiding the production through their individual systems.

Starting from an initial idea, a script is developed, including all dialog and descriptions of action. Once approved, a visual presentation of the script, called a storyboard, is produced. Looking something like a comic strip, the storyboard presents a drawing of each shot within a scene, with lines of dialog or action descriptions written below. Presenting an overview of the film at a glance, the storyboard is a convenient format for modifying and improving the directorial and visual plan and becomes a useful guide throughout the production.

Unlike live-action production, where the sound is recorded during or after filming, with animation the sound is recorded before production begins. It is immediately transferred to sprocketed magnetic motion picture films, allowing an exact frame-by-frame analysis of the placement of each word, sound effect, or musical beat, which is written out on charts called *bar sheets,* which then become guides for the director or animator as to the timing and placement of mouth movements and actions. A frame-by-frame plan called an *exposure sheet* might also be developed at this time.

Before the final drawings are begun, animators will test their movement plan by making pencil tests, filming or videotaping rough sketches done on paper. Key animators will then make drawings for the extreme points of movement, and assistant animators, called in-betweeners, will make the intermediary drawings. Other artists might be drawing the background scenes, and inkers and painters will complete the drawings. A detailed exposure sheet is prepared to guide the camera operator through the frame-by-frame recording, which may involve moving or changing several cels and moving the camera for each frame.

Because of all the advance planning for every single frame, editing for animation is usually a matter of making minor adjustments and preparing the picture and sound for release printing, unlike live-action editing, which is a major creative part of the production process.

ANIMATION PHOTOGRAPHY Two-dimensional animation is generally filmed or taped on a specially built animation stand, which is a solidly built table-like platform for holding and moving artwork, with a vertical crane arm rising from the back for the camera. Camera and artwork registered in peg bars can be moved in small increments with great precision, and both must be protected from extraneous vibration or off-axis movement during exposure. A glass platen is usually used to hold the artwork in place on the surface of the platform called the compound. The image can be bottom-lit through the compound, or lit with a lamp placed on each side of the compound at 45 degrees to both camera and platform.

It is easier to create many movements such as tilts, pans, tracks, and fades during the filming stage than it is to do by drawing, so the animation camera operator often maintains several sequences of incremental change between every exposure. At 24 frames per second, a few seconds of screen time might take many hours to shoot.

Books: Laybourne, K., *The Animation Book*. New York: Crown Publications, 1979; White, T., *The Animators's Workbook*. New York: Watson-Guptill Publications, 1986; Hearn, D., and Baker, M. P, *Computer Graphics*. Engelwood Cliffs, N.J.: Prentice-Hall, 1986.

ANODE The positive terminal of an electrical load from which electrons flow in the external circuit. Inside the load device, however, the electrons flow toward the anode as in an electron tube. The negative terminal of a source, such as a battery, is its anode because it is the source of electrons for the external circuit.

ANTIALIASING A computer algorithm designed to smooth jagged edges in an image. This can be accomplished by blending an object with its background in a smooth transition. This technique is often used to accomplish the appearance of smooth, large text on a display.

ANTILOG See *Logarithms*.

ANTI-VIRUS A software designed to identify and or reject "diseased" software covertly placed into a computer. The virus is designed to disorient, slow down, or "kill" the computer's operating system or data files or the hard disk's directory.

APPARENT POWER In alternating current circuits, the product of voltage and current. Units are volt-amperes (VA) and kilovolt-amperes (kVA). True or actual power is equal to apparent power multiplied by the power factor of the circuit.

APPLICATION A computer program written for a specific purpose such as a drawing program.

ARCHIVE In electronic imaging, long-term storage of an image, typically on a magnetic tape or disk.

AREA PROCESSING See *Neighbourhood processing* .

ARITHMETIC LOGIC UNIT (ALU) A component found on the computer motherboard that performs multiplications, additions, or logical operations on data, including images.

ARRAY The holding of the image in a two dimensional (x, y) configuration. This structure or matrix on the y axis equals the number of lines that makes up the image. The x axis equals the number of pixels per line.

ARRAY PROCESSOR Specific computer hardware designed to hold the image in the form of a two-dimensional array. Such devices are "hung onto" the central processing unit (CPU). The device allows for fast image processing. Some array processors have built-in algorithms for specific image processing.

ASCII American Standard Code for Information Interchange, a byte coding for the standard character set used by most computers; used to transfer text files between computers.

ASTRONOMICAL CAMERA See *Camera types*.

ASTROPHOTOGRAPHY Astrophotography is the photography of the moon, planets, stars, and other celestial objects. Most modern astronomical discoveries are made photographically for two reasons: the camera provides a permanent record and, by making time exposures, it can record images that are too faint for the human eye to see. Many faint celestial objects, such as the Horsehead Nebula, are invisible to the human eye even with large telescopes but are easily photographed with proper equipment. Additionally, some photographic emulsions can "see" into the infrared and ultraviolet.

HISTORY The entire history of photography has been closely linked to astronomy. The word *photography* was coined by the astronomer Sir John Herschel in 1839; in the same year Louis Daguerre is said to have made the first astronomical photograph, a daguerreotype of the moon. With the advent of dry plates around 1880 came a flurry of astronomical discoveries, including the discovery of many faint nebulae, the spiral structure of galaxies, and extensive mapping of faint stars. An international project to photograph the entire sky, the *Carte du Ciel* project, was organized in 1887 but never completed.

The three main kinds of photographic observations took shape quickly: *astrometry* (position measurement for mapping), *photometry* (measurement of brightness), and *spectrography* (study of chemical composition as indicated by emission or absorption at particular wavelengths).

Observatories built since 1900 have been designed mainly for photographic work. From 1949 to 1956 the entire sky visible from Mount Palomar, California, was photographed with a 1.2 meter (48 inch)f/2.5 Schmidt camera, and prints of the resulting *Palomar Sky Survey* have been used by astronomers worldwide.

A second survey is being undertaken now, using better emulsions, and the southern sky is being surveyed with similar equipment in Australia and Chile.

In recent years there has been a shift toward electronic imaging rather than photography. Photometry has been done with photomultiplier tubes since the 1950s. Charge-coupled devices (CCDs) came into wide use for all types of work in the 1980s because of their sensitivity to faint light and their ability to deliver an image directly to a computer for analysis. Computers are also used to process images obtained photographically; the computer can enhance local contrast and bring out faint detail. Precision astrometry of wide fields continues to be done with photographic emulsions, often on glass plates rather than film in order to rule out shrinkage.

Book: Eccles, M.J: Sim, M.E.; and Tritton, K.P. *Low Light Level Detectors in Astronomy.* Cambridge: Cambridge University Press, 1983. (Theory of photographic and electronic imaging.)

AUDIOVISUAL COMMUNICATION

Audiovisual communication refers to the communication of information, concepts, and attitudes through audio and visual media. Photographic visual media include such things as still pictures, overhead transparencies, slides, filmstrips, and motion pictures.

HISTORICAL BACKGROUND Before 1950, photographic materials used for audiovisual communication consisted largely of still photographs, 3-1/4 X 4-inch lantern slides, filmstrips, and 16-mm motion pictures. Most of these were black-and-white and were used in schools, the military, and in business and industry settings. During the 1950s, high-quality 35-mm colour slides replaced lantern slides, colour largely replaced black-and-white for filmstrip and film production, and overhead transparencies assumed an important role. Technical developments resulted in slide projectors that could be controlled, first by punched paper-tape programmers and later by electronic control units, which made elaborate multi-image presentations possible. Typically, photography for audiovisual communications was done by photographers with a broad range of skills. The next two decades saw rapid technological advances. Electrostatic copying and other developments made it possible to reproduce photographs more easily and at lower cost. Fast high-quality colour films for slides and motion pictures became available. Electrostatic and thermal processes largely replaced the more complex dual-spectrum, diazo, and lithographic film processes for overhead transparency production. Computers assumed important roles in production and presentation. Such developments, coupled with the demand for effective instructional and motivational programs, led to an expansion of audiovisual communication in the 1980s.

CURRENT PRACTICE Still photographs for printed materials and for displays are widely used. Filmstrips are used, particularly in public schools. Motion pictures, although still viable, have been largely superseded by video, especially for classroom presentations. The demand for overhead transparencies for presentation purposes continues to increase. Computers are used to create masters, which are converted to transparencies by thermal or electrostatic methods and by peripheral printing devices. In some instances transparencies are made from art work by conventional colour reversal processes. Colour slides are used extensively for instruction and for a variety of motivational multi-image presentations.

Although a broad general knowledge of photography is needed by producers, there is need for persons who also have skills in the design of instructional materials and for persons with the complex skills required for creating multi-image presentations. In multi-image shows, the relationships among the images, both simultaneous and sequential, is of more importance than the individual images. Therefore, the skills of a motion-picture photographer, as well as the skills of the still photographer, are needed. In the laboratory, skills of creating quality duplicates, masked and multiple images, and seamless panoramic slides are necessary. An understanding of the use of computers is increasingly important to audiovisual communicators. The words and artwork for a large proportion of all graphic slides are created on a computer, and high-resolution, computer-screen images are photographed with a film recorder in house or by sending the computer disks to a service bureau via mail or over various networks including common carriers.

THE FUTURE The rapid changes in technologies that are taking place in all areas of our society will continue to increase the need for training and public-relation activities, which, in turn, will increase the need for effective audiovisual materials. Computers will play an even more important role in the production of both print and projection media. Digitized images that can be easily manipulated will increase in quality and will become easier and less expensive to produce. Electronic transfer of images, coupled with electronic clip-art systems and ultimately electronic multimedia databases, will change the role of the audiovisual photographer. In addition to creating original images, photographers will be called upon to choose and manipulate available images to create their audiovisual products.

Organizations of particular interest to the producer of photographic audiovisual materials are the Association for Educational Communications and Technology (AECT), the Association for Multi-Image International (AMII), the International Visual Literacy Association (IVLA), and the Society of Photographers in Communication (SPC).

Books: Bishop, A., *Slides: Planning and Producing Slide Programs*. Rochester, NY: Eastman Kodak, 1986; Kemp. J. and Smellie, *D., Planning, Producing, and Using Instructional Media,* 6th ed. New York: Harper and Row, 1989; Kennedy, M. and Schmitt, R., *Images, Images, Images,* 2nd ed. Rochester. NY: Eastman Kodak, 1981; Pettersson, R., *Visuals for Instruction: Research and Practice,* Englewood Cliffs, NJ: Educational Technology Publications, 1989.

BACKING-UP In the event of a system failure, a backup operating system and backup files are used to restart the system. Backing-up generally refers to making copies of the startup software (operating system) and important applications and data files.

BACK PORCH In video recording, a brief blackout period between the horizontal sync pulse and the start of picture data. This blackout period is considered to be blacker than black. The setting allows for the distinction between a picture signal that is black and the black resulting from no signal.

BALLISTIC VIDEOGRAPHY Ballistic synchro photography is based on the principle of synchronizing the rate of movement of an image of a projectile with the rate of film movement or the rate of sweep across static film. This produces a single detailed picture of the projectile as it passes across the line of sight of the camera lens. The analysis and measurement of a single ballistic synchro photograph will provide quantitative information on flight aspect (yaw), spin rate, sabot separation, and velocity. The same record will also show the condition of the projectile and any damage that has occurred.

Immediate access to ballistic instrumentation data is always desired in iterative development tests or in failure analysis of burst fired projectiles. The availability of gated intensified video cameras has provided a capability for shoot-look-shoot testing with near real time results and minimum delay between test firings.

A gated intensified video camera is a solid-state charge-injection device (CID) type chip camera with an image intensifier tube between the lens and the imaging chip. Light from the object of interest is imaged by the lens onto the photocathode of the intensifier. The intensifier amplifies the light and forms an image on its output phosphor screen. This image is transferred to the active area of the CID chip for normal video display. The intensifier can be gated (turned on) for very short intervals and acts as a shutter. Effective exposure times can be as short as 50 nanoseconds (nsec.). Recording asynchronous events is accomplished by inhibiting destructive readout of the image in the CID until the intensifier has been gated.

A typical use of this camera might be to image the attitude and position of a projectile immediately after leaving the gun muzzle. Assume that this projectile is small calibre, spin stabilized, with a velocity of 1000 m/sec and rapid-fired at a rate of 1000 rounds/min in groups of 50 or more.

Traditional instrumentation would include a 35-mm ballistic film camera with 135 meters of film running at 75 m/sec, providing a usable image size of 1.5 mm. However, this film

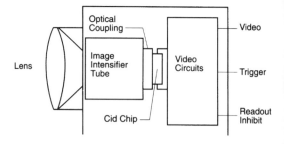

Ballistic videography. Block diagram of gated intensified CID camera.

velocity will provide an effective run time of just 1 sec during which only 16 of the 50 rounds will be recorded.

High speed film and high intensity lighting would be required to compensate for the short exposure time. The film camera would need to be reloaded after each burst, and data on any particular burst firing would not be available until the roll of film is processed, which could be as little as a few hours or, more likely, a few days.

Using a gated intensified video camera offers a cost-effective method for instrumentation of burst fired ballistic events that have a low statistical probability of occurrence. The image of each projectile is available in real time, exposures as short as 0.5 microsecond (µsec.) can be attained with only 150 W of incandescent lighting, the data are stored on videotape, which is available for immediate review, and hard copy prints can be produced in a timely manner.

BATTERY Technically, a battery is an assemblage of two or more electric cells, although a single cell is now commonly called a battery. Cells are frequently connected in series to increase the available voltage. An automobile battery consisting of six 2-volt cells connected in series has an output voltage equal to the sum of the cell voltages, or 12 volts. The output current capability of several (identical) cells connected in parallel is equal to the sum of the current rating of the cells. When current is drawn from a battery, the voltage measured at the terminals of a battery decreases. The drop in voltage is proportional to the current drawn because of a voltage drop across the internal resistance of the battery. With continued usage, the voltage (even without current flowing) will decrease because of the deterioration of the chemicals that generate the electromotive force. The two broad categories of batteries are primary batteries and secondary batteries. Primary batteries cannot be recharged and must be replaced when their voltage drops below a minimum working value. Secondary batteries can be recharged from an external power supply when they run down. Because some batteries may leak electrolyte, it is good practice to remove batteries from equipment whenever the equipment is not to be used for a couple of months.

Battery. Comparison of Cells/Batteries

System	Carbon–zinc (Leclanche)	Carbon–zinc (heavy duty)	Alkaline	Silver Oxide	Lithium	Nickel Cadmium
Chemistry Anode Cathode Electrolyte	Zn MnO_2 NH_4Cl and $ZnCl_2$	Zn Mno_2 $ZnCl_2$	Zn (powered) MnO_2 KOH	Zn Ag_2O KOH or $NaOH$	Li MnO_2 $LiSO_2$ with organic solvent	Cd $Ni(OH)_3$ KOH
Rechargeable?	No	No	No	No	No	Yes
Cell voltage	1.5 V	1.5 V	1.5 V	1.5 V	3.0 V	1.25 V
Energy density	Low	Low	Moderate	High	High	High
Shelf life	Fair	Fair	Good	Excellent	Excellent	Good
Cost	Lowest cost	Low	Moderate	High	High	High
Special characteristics		Designed for heavier output current	High energy and current capacity	Maintains a constant voltage	10-year shelf life; leakproof	Rechargeable; leakproof
Best suited for	Intermittent uses such as flashlights	General use performance better than regular zinc–carbon	Continuous heavy drain loads such as motor drives	Constant voltage applications; portable light meters, cameras, etc.	Still camera electronics, TV remote controllers, smoke detectors	Power packs for electronic flash, video cameras; portable tools
Limitations	Low energy density; prone to leak	Performance lower than alkaline batteries; prone to leak	More costly than zinc–carbon	Available in a limited number of sizes	Available in limited number of sizes	Does not retain its charge as well as non-chargeable batteries do

The quality and diversity of portable batteries available to the public have vastly improved in recent years. These advances have been in response to the increased popularity of transistorized electronic products, including photographic equipment. The uses of batteries in cameras include providing power for energizing the motors that advance film and automatically focus the camera, firing expendable flash bulbs or electronic flash units, and operating the automatic exposure control mechanism. In video camcorders and electronic still cameras batteries provide power for a multitude of electronic circuits.

Energy density is the energy stored in a fully charged battery and is typically measured in watt-hours per unit weight. Shelf life is the length of time a battery can be stored without an appreciable loss in service life.

BAUD In the transmission of data, a unit of measurement of transmission.

BAUD RATE The speed of data transmission, usually equivalent to bits per second. Most data transmission protocols support 300, 1200, 2400 to 9600 baud rates over standard telephone lines. Dedicated local area network lines can support baud rates at and about 19,200 baud. The higher the baud rate, the more data can be transmitted in the same time. A gray-scale, low-resolution image would transmit in approximately 2.2 minutes at 19,200 baud as compared to a transmission time of approximately 34.2 minutes at 1200 baud.

BINARY A number system based on exponents to the base 2. Thus with only two symbols, such as 1 and 0 (in electronic circuitry, *on* or off), any numerical quantity can be represented. Example: The number 105 can be written 1101001(on, on, off, on, off, off, on).

A)............2^7	2^6	2^5	2^4	2^3	2^2	2^1	2^0
B)............128	64	32	16	8	4	2	1
C)	1	1	0	1	0	0	1

Legend
A) Exponents to the base 2 from right to left continue beyond 2^7.
B) The numbers associated with the exponents to the base 2. Each number doubles, all numbers are even except for the number 1.
C) The *symbols* 1 and 0 in binary notation are indicators, *not* numbers. The symbol 1 in binary code means to add the number indicated; a 1 under 64 means to add 64. A 0 under 16 means to not add 16. It is an on-off code. The number 105 in binary code (1101001) is arrived at in the following "game-like" manner:

1. The goal is to find a *set* of numbers that will add up to 105.
2. By inspection, the largest number closest to 105 is 64. Begin with 64.   (1 - - - - - -)
3. The next largest number that can be added to 64 is 32, (64 + 32 = 96).   (1 1 - - - - -)
4. The next to be added, without exceeding 105, is 8, (96 + 8 = 104).   (1 1 0 1 —-)
5. Now add the number 1 to 104, and the result is 105.   (1101001)
6. The set of numbers, therefore, that add up to 105 are: 64 + 32 + 0 + 8 + 0 + 0 + 1 = 105. In binary form, the symbols   1101001 (1101001).

Shown as a vertical array:

Exponent	Factor	Binary	On-Off	Sum
2^6	64	1	on	64
2^5	32	1	on	32
2^4	16	0	off	0
2^3	8	1	on	8
2^2	4	0	off	0
2^1	2	0	off	0
2^0	1	1	on	1
				105 total

The same number in the *decimal* system, based on exponents to the base 10, would be:

...................10^3	10^2	10^1	10^0
................1000	100	10	1
	1	0	5

In the decimal system the *symbol* 105 is also the number 105, the sum of (1) hundred, (0) tens, and (5) ones.

BIPOLAR JUNCTION TRANSISTOR (BJT)

A three-terminal semiconductor device capable of amplifying current. It is also capable of amplifying voltage when used in a circuit with resistors. Bipolar junction transistors are available in two types—NPN and PNP. Each type transistor consists of two junctions between three layers of semiconductor material. N refers to n-type semiconductor; P to p-type semiconductor. The three terminals are emitter, base, and collector. Typically, a small current flowing from base to emitter of an NPN transistor will cause a hundred times that amount of current to flow from the collector to the emitter.

BIT

A contraction for binary digit. A bit is the smallest unit of data transfer. As a basic unit it represents an off (0) or on (1) state. In imaging, the more bits, the more tones that can be displayed in a digitized image. A 7-bit image can display 128 tones including black and white. A 3-bit image can only display a total of 8 tones.

BITMAP

A pixel-by-pixel description of an image, where each pixel is a separate element.

BIT PLANE

The storage of graphical images including text as a graphical representation. The image is stored in random-access-memory (RAM) as a pattern of bits in the sequence in which they are scanned (rastered), thus representing the image.

BLACK-AND-WHITE (B&W) (b-w)

Designation for a photograph, material, or process in which the resulting image contains only tones of gray. Toned prints are commonly included to distinguish them from colour prints made on colour paper. *Monochrome* would be a better term for toned prints, and perhaps for all black-and-white images.

BLACK LEVEL In setting a video camera to record at an optimal level, the camera recording system should be set so that the black level is 7.5 IEEE units above the no-signal level. This will ensure that black will image well within the contrast range of the system and will be distinguishable from no signal.

BLEED A term used by photographers and graphic artists to define an image that runs to the edge of the picture or page without any borders. (1) The edges of the surface act as borders incorporated into the structure. (2) To run a continuous tone or halftone image off the edge of the paper or support without a border. (3) To spread beyond an original or desired position, resulting in a loss of definition of an image, especially line and dye images.

BLEEDING A loss of image definition due to a spreading of the image-forming material, such as dye or ink, beyond the original or desired position.

BLOCK TRANSFER In computers, the movement of data in a group formation to achieve speed in the transfer. Often a preferred method for moving images from storage to the display monitor, this allows for rapid updating of the image as it is electronically edited.

BLUR Image unsharpness, such as that caused by inaccurate focusing or movement of the subject or the camera during exposure of the film.

BLURRING In computers, the attenuation of high-frequency information in the image through the use of neighbourhood averaging. The strength of the blur is determined by the size of the kernel. This technique may be used to remove patterned noise.

See also: *Low-pass filter*.

BOARD Generally, in the DOS world a board is a device that plugs into a bus slot to perform a specific task, such as accelerating graphics, driving the monitor, controlling hard and floppy disks, or digitizing video and sound. In the Macintosh world, boards are generally referred to as cards.

BOOT To *start up* a computer. If the computer is off, this is known as a cold boot. If the computer is on but not operating, a warm boot (restart) is performed.

BPS Bits per second. See *Baud rate*.

BRIGHTNESS RANGE (1) The visually perceived relationship between the lightest and darkest areas of a scene. (2) As commonly used by photographers, the ratio of luminances for the lightest and darkest areas of a scene. Preferably, *luminance ratio*. (3) A method of using a luminance (reflected-light) meter. Measurements are made of the darkest and lightest areas of interest and the calculator indicator is set midway between the two readings.

BRIGHTNESS RESOLUTION The luminance contrast range that a pixel is capable of providing. The higher the resolution, the greater the number of gray levels or tones that are capable of being reproduced. This is also referred to as pixel depth or number of bits deep.

See also: *Bit*.

BRITISH KINEMATOGRAPH SOUND AND TELE-VISION SOCIETY (BKSTS) A British-based professional group with interests in film, video, sound, and television.

BRITISH STANDARDS INSTITUTION (BSI) The national standardizing organization of the United Kingdom.

BRUSH In electronic imaging, the electronic equivalent of an artist's paintbrush, used to modify the colour, shape, or size of a computer image.

BUFFER In computers, a temporary storage area designed to hold data to enhance the performance speed of a particular component of the system. For example, a video buffer enhances the display speed of the video monitor; a CD-ROM buffer enhances the speed of a CD-ROM player.

BUG An error or malfunction in hardware or software that causes the computer to abort. The term results from the actual discovery of a moth in a Mark I computer's electronic relay. The removal of the moth gave rise to the term *debugging*.

BUS (1) An electrical interconnection among many points, so called since it can be viewed like a bus line, with stops (connections) along its way. Signal buses include main ones, often called mixdown buses; ones intended to send to a multitrack tape recorder, called multitrack buses; and ones to send signals from input channels to outboard devices, called auxiliary buses. Auxiliary buses may be named for their purpose: reverb send (signals sent to a reverberation process) and cue send (signals sent to performers in order to cue them). (2) A network or path within the computer that moves data to and from the central processing unit (CPU) and other input/output devices.

BYTE A group of eight bits. Bits are moved about the computer in groups. These groups may be 8 bits (a byte) 16 bits (2 bytes) or 32 bits (4 bytes). The greater the number of bits moved per cycle, the faster the computer.

CACHE In computers, a section of reserved memory designed to allow the central processing unit (CPU) to process data faster. Cache can also be used to speed video access and hard drive access.

CAMERA

DEFINITION A device for controlling light to form a visual record on light-sensitive material. The light is directed into a dark box by an opening in one end that allows only the rays of light from objects within the angle of coverage of the lens to enter. That light forms an inverted image on the opposite side of the box where a sensitized material or other light sensitive receptor records the image. The amount of light that enters is controlled by the size of the opening and the length of time the opening is left uncovered.

Over the past century and a half, there has been great improvement but little change in the fundamental concept of the camera. Today, the light is focused with computer designed lenses made with extra-low dispersion glass and recorded on superb emulsions. Extremely accurate electronic shutter systems have been created, and now, with the advent of electronic imaging, these systems have almost unlimited freedom to modify images. At no time in photographic history has the camera been more versatile.

AN EVOLUTION OF DESIGN One can better understand the workings of the camera by following the light path from an object to the film.

Light enters the lens and passes through a regulated opening in a diaphragm that provides control over the amount of light coming into the camera. That light is blocked, however, by the shutter, which can be placed between the lens, behind the lens, or at the back of the camera in front of the film. The shutter is controlled by a timing mechanism that is classified as mechanical, electronic or electromechanical (a combination of both), that opens the shutter for a specified length of time. These two devices, the shutter and the lens diaphragm, control the amount of light that exposes the film, or, in an electronic system, the light-sensitive receptors.

Framing and Focusing the Image On some simple nonfocusing lens cameras, a separate viewfinder works to approximately target what will appear on the film. These are the old point-and-shoot box cameras, and their successors, the instamatic and disc cameras. With lens systems that can critically focus on different distances, there has to be some way to determine if the lens is focused on the desired distance. If the back of the camera could be removed and replaced with a piece of ground glass, the projected image would be visible. In the case of view cameras, that is exactly what happens. When it is time to make an exposure, the film, kept in a light-tight holder with a dark slide covering it, is placed in the same plane of focus as the ground glass. The dark slide is removed and the shutter released. Another viewing system would require two identical lenses mounted in two separate chambers, one above the other, and operating on a unified focusing track. One of the lenses would be used for composing and focusing the image and the other, with a shutter and diaphragm, for exposing film. This would be a smaller system and continuous in operation without having to remove the film holder for focusing each time. Essentially, this describes a twin-lens reflex. The light path of the top viewing lens reflects upward from a 45-degree mirror so that the photographer can peer down into the camera, while the bottom lens with the shutter is directly in line with the film plane.

The camera could again be made smaller if the focusing chamber could also be used to expose the film. In the case of the single-lens reflex, the design is basically the concept of a twin-lens reflex condensed into one chamber. The mirror is in the same position, but is now movable. Just prior to exposure, the mirror is elevated to allow the light to expose the film, during which time there is no image in the viewfinder.

Some cameras, to be made even smaller, use a separate rangefinder focusing system that presents a split image or two superimposed images in the viewfinder. When the images align, the lens is focused on the selected object by means of a coupled focusing mechanism. This simple rangefinding system has become so advanced that it can provide automatic focusing by means of an infrared beam splitter. A microprism equivalent of the rangefinder is used in many single-lens-reflex cameras.

Camera Exposure Meters The amount of light entering the camera needs to be analyzed and controlled to prevent under exposure or overexposure. In earlier cameras, this was done with an independent hand-held exposure meter, which still has advantages for more critical work. With the advent of more self-contained camera systems, exposure meters were placed inside of the camera body. Contemporary electronic metering systems are sophisticated and extremely fast. Exposure analysis can be made and corrected while the actual exposure is being made by measuring light reflected from the film.

Four basic categories of contemporary general-purpose cameras are the simple point-and-shoot, the 35-mm and medium format single-lens reflex, the 35-mm and medium format rangefinder cameras, and variations of the view camera.

As the need grew for the camera to perform more sophisticated and specialized tasks, cameras were designed to fit those needs.

Cameras are becoming more computerized and more electronic in their exposure analysis, focusing, and shutter operations. The use of digital recording of images on electromagnetic discs, as opposed to traditional silver halide films, is becoming a realistic alternative. The technology exists to rival the resolution of traditional films, but currently only at a prohibitive cost. The trend is perhaps best marked by alternative backs on some cameras that allow for silver halide or digital recording systems on the same body, making the camera more adaptable.

Sony Mavica The Sony Mavica was the first commercial still-video camera that reproduced images on an electromagnetic disc. Still-video cameras have been accepted more rapidly in the field of photojournalism because there is no processing delay, images can be sent great distances by telephone, and the limited resolving power can be tolerated. The technology for still-video to rival conventional film resolution is available, but the cost is still prohibitive for most users.

CAMERA BACK

A camera back is the part of a camera that provides a light-tight seal for the film and commonly performs other functions, and is normally hinged, removable, or held in position with springs that allow for the insertion of a film holder. With most 35-mm cameras and some medium-format roll-film cameras, the back contains a pressure plate that holds the film in contact with guide tracks in the body of the camera. The backs for some roll-film cameras include the film-transport mechanism, and even a dark slide so that different types of film can be used and switched in mid-roll by changing backs. The backs for view cameras and other sheet-film cameras normally include a ground glass for composing and focusing.

Many cameras allow for the substitution of other backs or film holders to increase the usefulness or convenience of the camera. Bulk-film holders can be used with some 35mm and medium-format roll-film cameras to eliminate the need to change film frequently when doing large-volume production work. Data recording backs are available for some cameras, an important feature for certain types of forensic, technical, and research activities. Accessory backs that accept instant-picture film packs can be used with some roll-film cameras to obtain a proof print before exposing conventional film or to obtain a usable photograph quickly. Electronic-imaging backs can be used on some cameras to allow the photographer to display the image on a monitor as an aid in arranging and lighting a setup, to record the electronic image on a magnetic disc, to digitize the image for computer processing and recording, or even to transmit an image to a remote location for evaluation, approval, processing, recording, or reproduction. Alternative backs for modular view cameras include backs that accommodate larger or smaller sheet-film sizes or roll films, backs that include an exposure meter probe and meter holder, and backs that include functional and convenience features such as a device to close the shutter and stop the lens down to a preselected f-number when a film holder is inserted.

CAMERA TYPES

AERIAL CAMERA A specifically designed camera used to record topography from an airplane. Some aerial cameras are designed to be mounted to the bottom or side of a plane on a special mechanism that uses shock absorbing springs and to be fired by remote control. They are designed and calibrated to make a series of overlapping images along a selected flight path.

An additional camera may simultaneously photograph the instrument display of the airplane to indicate the height and tilt of the plane at the time of exposure. The film is held flat against the pressure plate by a glass plate with inscribed markings. These markings are placed at specific intervals and, when combined with data from the instruments about altitude and plane tilt (see instrumentation camera), yield the land distance between the two markings. If the overlap exceeds 50%, stereo three-dimensional images can be made. Aerial cameras have no bellows and the lens focus is locked on infinity since aerial images are seldom made below 300 feet. Shutters are focal plane rotating sector type to allow for speeds up to 1/4000th of a second. A frame finder is used as a viewfinder.

Films can be monochromatic, colour, or infrared, depending on the application, and they come in 70-mm rolls yielding 6 x 6 cm images or larger size film in 100-foot rolls yielding 23-cm square images.

Conventional cameras can also be used for aerial photography. Such cameras can be hand held at fast shutter speeds. Holding the camera against any part of the plane picks up the motor and air turbulence vibrations.

Aerial photographs are used for a variety of purposes, including mapping, military intelligence, and agriculture. Much of this work is now done by satellites (Landsat) using both radar and infrared sensors.

ASTRONOMICAL CAMERAS Large scientific telescopes with tracking mechanisms have photographic path options. Instead of the light being projected through to a viewer lens, the light path is diverted to a photographic recording apparatus in the focal plane of the telescope. Dimensional stability is also essential and glass plates or critically accurate film pressure plates are used. The advantage of using photographic materials in astronomy is that photography allows for weak light intensities to accumulate on film and thus become visible with prolonged exposure. With long exposures, the camera needs to be on a tracking system with the object observed to avoid streaking caused by the earth's rotation or orbital movement. Separate exposures made at different times can be used to track celestial placement. Some astronomical cameras make images that separate radiation wavelengths that yield information about the composition and velocity of the object.

Other cameras can be used with adapters to attach a Schmidt-Cassegrain design long telephoto mirror lens. If using a lens with a telescopic adapter, the normal lens for the camera can be removed, using the telescope's lens only for image formation.

CHARGE-COUPLED CAMERA A camera having an integrated circuit photoelectric detector charge-coupled device (a CCD silicon chip instead of film) and used for optical image recording. The CCD chip is located at the focal plane. When light strikes the silicon surface, it releases electrons, similar to what happens with traditional silver halide emulsions. The electrons are read out as pixels, which are small sections of the whole image. The electrical signal is then amplified and sent to a magnetic disc for storage.

DIGITAL-IMAGING CAMERA A camera that transforms visual information into electronic digital information (binary code of 0s and 1s). The information can then be recorded, read, enhanced, or manipulated on a computer.

ELECTRONIC STILL CAMERA A camera (with a conventional optical system) that captures the optical image with either a charged-couple device (CCD) or a metal-oxide semiconductor (MOS) device that converts light to an electronic signal that in turn is recorded on a 2-inch magnetic floppy disc, typically in analog form. Each disc can hold up to 50 images. The recorded images can be displayed on a monitor or can be digitized for computer processing or electronic transmission. Some newer electronic still cameras have built-in digitizing capability. Image resolution has not been as high as with silver-halide photography but is rapidly improving. Electronic still cameras were first used professionally by photojournalists because of the speed with which images could be transmitted by telephone and reproduced on the printed page. Electronic capture devices are now available as replacement backs on conventional view cameras and are being used, especially, for large-volume imaging for catalog production.

HIGH-SPEED VIDEO CAMERA A video camera designed to record images over very short exposure times either with a shutter or by applying a short-duration electric field to an image converter where exposure times as short as 1/200,000,000 second have been achieved.

IMAGE-CONVERTER CAMERA A camera/lens design using an image tube and a series of secondary emitter couplings (i.e. caesium coated mirrors) to multiply the electron gain, so that the light output is greatly increased over the original input. The light increase allows for exposures of millions of images per second. The image converter camera is used in high speed photography, because it has no moving parts and can be used for single, multiple, or streak recordings. The basic camera consists of a photocathode that projects an image toward a phosphor screen at the rear of the tube. The phosphor screen emits light similar in intensity to the photocathode. Thus, the original light input is turned into electrons, which are then excited further by a low voltage pulse. The electrons reaching the phosphor screen are greatly enhanced over the original light input. The screen then emits a respective increase in light output (as high as 1000x). The enhancement can take place many times over, allowing for extremely fast exposures.

INFRARED CAMERA A camera used to record heat images produced by infrared radiation. When infrared is absorbed, heat is radiated. The image is focused onto a nitrocellulose membrane carrying a gold layer on an oil film. The heat pattern from the infrared produces a pattern of thicknesses on the oil film. The pattern is then illuminated and reproduced on film as a visual image. This type of camera can be used to distinguish distances at night, to detect heat loss in buildings, and in medical applications to discern malignant from benign tissues by their temperature differences.

OSCILLOSCOPE CAMERA A camera used to photograph

the face of a cathode-ray tube (television screen) to document the image activity on the screen. One problem with photographing a cathode ray image is that the entire image is never completely present on the screen at any one time. Instead, the image is produced by a repetitive scanning pattern. The image exposure has to be long enough to include a complete cycle of two fields (one frame), 1/25 second. Shorter times will record a partial image. Between-the-lens leaf shutters are better for this type of photography because of the scanning movement of focal plane shutters.

SURVEILLANCE CAMERA A camera that can be transported and operated inconspicuously and yet have a long focal length lens that is capable of resolving small detail at great distances. It is used in research observation and evidence/investigative photography. In scientific research, the surveillance camera is commonly set up to function with an intervalometer that exposes a frame and advances the film at specific timed intervals designated by the photographer (i.e., once a minute, once an hour, once a week). A special data-recording back superimposes information about how and when the exposure was made.

Some surveillance cameras are meant to be seen to deter criminal activity. These are the wide angle cameras mounted on automated teller machines, in toll booths, and in banks. The cameras automatically make images of a subject and then advance the film. They can hold up to 800 frames.

The term *surveillance camera* also refers to a hidden video camera.

VIDEO CAMERA A camera that converts an optical image into an electronic image that can either be displayed on a monitor or recorded on magnetic tape to be replayed later. The system usually records both image and sound information. Video recording yields much lower production costs than motion pictures. Recording is instantaneous without further processing, but requires a video tape unit for viewing. Unwanted imagery can be magnetically erased from the tape and the tape reused. The term *video camera* has been used to relate to everything from a full television studio camera to a small portable camcorder.

Formats for video tape are Super 8 mm, Beta, VHS, VHS-C, 3/4 inch, 1 inch, and 2 inch. Video cameras can also be used to transmit an image to other electronic sources, such as computers.

CARD In the Macintosh and Amiga world, cards are analogous to boards.

CASCADING OF FUNCTIONS A procedure of combining the values of a characteristic of the individual elements of an imaging system, such as camera lens, film, projector lens, and printing paper, to determine the value of that characteristic for the entire system. The modulation transfer of a system is found by multiplying the modulation transfer functions of the individual elements.

CATHODE The negative terminal of an electrical load to which electrons flow. Although the cathode of an electron tube is the source of electrons within the tube, electrons flow to the cathode in the external circuit. The cathode of a battery, however, is the positive terminal because electrons in the circuit are attracted to it.

CATHODE-RAY TUBE (CRT) An evacuated glass tube used to display data in visual form by the use of a moving electron beam (cathode ray). In this device, a narrow beam of accelerated electrons passes through an electrostatic or magnetic deflecting field before striking a phosphor screen at the end of the tube. It has long been used as the display tube for television, radar, oscilloscopes, and video display terminals. Photographic equipment using the CRT includes video colour negative analyzers and electronic enlargers.

A CRT consists of an electron gun (heater, cathode, control grid, and accelerating and focusing anodes), deflection plates or coils, and a fluorescent screen, all enclosed in an evacuated glass bulb or tube.

ELECTRON GUN In an electron gun a cathode is heated indirectly by an incandescent tungsten filament. The elevated temperature releases electrons from the oxide coating of the cathode. The accelerating anodes are at a positive potential with respect to the cathode and attract the electrons. The control grid is held at a negative potential with respect to the cathode. It controls the number of electrons leaving the cathode and therefore the brightness of the display. Typically, between the two accelerating anodes there is a focusing anode that narrows the electron stream into a tight beam and prevents the electrons from striking the accelerating anodes.

DEFLECTING PLATES OR COILS Two methods of moving the electron beam are in current use: electrostatic and magnetic. With electrostatic deflection, two pairs of deflection plates are perpendicular to each other. The electron beam is deflected up and down by an amount determined by the magnitude and polarity of the voltage applied to the vertical deflecting plates. The beam is deflected left and right by an amount determined by the magnitude and polarity of the voltage applied to the horizontal deflecting plates. Typically, the beam moves from left to right with a displacement proportional to time. The beam of electrons is deflected in the direction of the more positive plate. With magnetic deflection, the deflection is determined by the magnitude and polarity of the current flowing through the vertical and horizontal deflecting coils.

FLUORESCENT SCREEN The inside of the end of the tube is coated with various phosphors. When the high-energy electron beam strikes the screen it will glow in a colour dependent on the chemical composition of the phosphor. The screen will continue to glow even after the beam has been removed. The afterglow, called *persistence*, can vary from a few milliseconds to several seconds, depending on the chemical composition of the phosphor used.

Cathode-ray tube (electrostatic deflection).

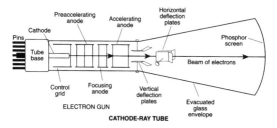

CATHODE-RAY TUBE

A narrow beam of electrons is displayed as a bright spot on a phosphorescent screen. The position of the spot depends on the voltages applied to the deflecting plates. Its brightness is determined by the voltage applied to the control grid.

THREE-COLOUR CRT The phosphor screen in a three-colour CRT consists of an array of tiny clusters of red, green, and blue phosphors. Three separate electron guns generate three beams, one each to excite the red, green, and blue phosphor. A shadow mask is positioned in back of the screen. Holes in the mask keep the beam from the red gun, for instance, in line with the red phosphors. The brightness of each colour is controlled by the voltage applied to the control grid in each gun.

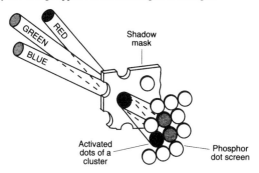

CATHODE-RAY TUBE

Shadow mask of a three-colour cathode-ray tube allows only the electron beam from the red electron gun to activate the red phosphor dots. Similarly, the green and blue electron guns are aligned to activate only the green and blue phosphors, respectively.

CCD ARRAY An electronic imaging device that uses many charge-coupled devices (CCDs) to convert a large amount of image information to digital values at the same instant.

CCD COLOUR SCANNER An optical scanner that uses a linear CCD array to capture a row of pixels simultaneously.

The array is then moved laterally to scan the image.

CENTRAL PROCESSING UNIT (CPU) The brain of the computer that performs all calculations and routes data via a bus to and from other computer components.

CHANNEL In electronic imaging, the holding of colour information in a separate location. Each component of the colour data, RGB, is held in a separate channel. In colour separation, four channels are used to hold the CMYK data. Channels can be likened to separation negatives or to printing plates.

CHARGE-COUPLED DEVICE (CCD) An array of photo sensors that detect and read out light as an electronic signal.

CHIP (ELECTRICAL) See *Semiconductor chip*.

CHROMA A characteristic of colour that varies with the saturation of hue, the extent to which a colour differs from a gray of equal lightness. In the Munsell system of colour notation, one of three attributes of colours, the other two being hue and value.

CHROMATIC COLOURS Colours exhibiting hue (as distinct from achromatic colours, those commonly called white, gray, black, neutral, and colourless).

CHROMATICITY An objective specification of the colour quality of a visual stimulus, such as a coloured light or surface, irrespective of its luminance. Defined in the CIE system of colorimetry either by the combination of the dominant wavelength and purity of a colour but excluding its luminance, or by two numbers, x and y, termed the chromaticity coordinates.

CHROMATICITY COORDINATES In colorimetry, the ratio of each of a set of tristimulus values to their sum.

CHROMATICITY DIAGRAM A rectangular diagram on which the composition of a colour stimulus is defined in terms of two of its three attributes: lightness or brightness is not shown because it would require a third dimension. A spectral locus, within which all real colours lie, represents hues in terms of wavelengths, and saturation is represented by the position of the colour between a white point and the spectral locus.

CHROMATICNESS (1) Natural colour system measure of the chromatic content of a colour. (2) An alternative term for colourfulness. (3) Perceptual colour attribute consisting of the hue and saturation of a colour (obsolete).

CHROMINANCE (1) In television, the part of the signal carrying the colour information, as distinct from the brightness information, which is carried by the luminous part of the signal. (2) In video, the colour hue and saturation information encoded into signal data by a video camera, later to be displayed by a colour cathode ray tube (CRT).

CIE COLOUR RENDERING INDEX A Commission Internationale de l'Eclairage (CIE) method of assessing the degree to which a test illuminant renders colours similar in appearance to their appearance under a reference illuminant.

CIELAB SYSTEM Colour space in which L^*, a^*, b^* are plotted at right angles to one another. Equal distances in the space represent approximately equal colour differences. $L^* = 116(Y/Y_n)^{1/3} - 16$, $a^* = 500[(X/X_n)^{1/3} - (Y/Y_n)^{1/3}]$. $b^* = 200[(Y/Y_n)^{1/3} - (Z/Z_n)^{1/3}]$.

CIELUV SYSTEM Colour space in which L^*, u^*, v^* are plotted at right angles to one another. Equal distances in the space represent approximately equal colour differences. $L^* = 6(Y/Y_n)^{1/3} - 16$, $u^* = 13L^*(u' - u'_n)$, $v^* = 13L^*(v' - v'_n)$.

CIE STANDARDS In colorimetry, internationally accepted standards for illuminants and colorimetric observers, established by the Commission Internationale de l'Eclairage (CIE).

CIRCUIT BREAKER A protective device that opens an electrical circuit when the current through it exceeds the current rating of the circuit breaker. Like a fuse, it is primarily used to protect equipment and wiring from damage due to an overload or a short circuit. Unlike a fuse, the circuit breaker can be reset and reused.

C LANGUAGE A high-level compiler language published by Ritche and Kernighan of Bell Laboratories. C links machine language to conventional, high-level programming languages. It is a concise code that is highly portable between platforms. C is widely used for image-processing programming.

CLOCK In computers, the regulator of the central processing unit (CPU). It is measured in cycles per second or hertz. Current personal computers may have clock speeds between 20 and 50 megahertz (MHz). Generally speaking, the faster the clock speed the faster the computer will execute the program; however, there are other factors that make it difficult to simply measure clock speed to determine overall computer efficiency. In image-intensive applications clock speed is important.

CLONE In electronic imaging, the function by which an exact duplicate of an image or part of an image is made.

C-MOUNT The standard screw-type lens mount for 16mm movie cameras. The major diameter is 1.0 inch with 23 threads per inch, the focal plane being 0.690 inch behind the seating face.

CMYK Cyan, magenta, yellow, and black, photomechanical reproduction and thermal dye transfer printing colours.

CODE The vernacular for any machine or higher–gauge instructions.

COLLAGE (from the French *coller;* to glue) The pasting together of torn or cut pieces of existing visual materials such as photographs, pictures in magazines and newspapers, newsprint, and the like to create a new image that can be displayed as it is or photographed and displayed.

COLOUR The word *colour* is used to mean both a perception in the mind and a stimulus that can produce that perception. Thus, when we say that a red car looks brown when seen in yellow sodium street lighting, *brown* refers to the perception in the mind, but *red* and *yellow* refer to the stimulus. In this article we consider mainly colour perception; in the article on *colorimetry,* colour stimuli are the main consideration.

THE SPECTRUM When white light is passed through a prism, or diffracted from a suitable grating, it is split up into the various colours of the spectrum. The different parts of the spectrum are identified by quoting the wavelength of the light (in air, or for the highest precision in vacuum). In colour science the unit used for wavelength is the nanometer, abbreviated nm (which is 10^{-9} meter). The colours seen in the spectrum change gradually from one to the next as the wavelength is changed, and their appearance depends on the viewing conditions, but the following colour names correspond approximately with the following bands of wavelength: violet: 380 to 450 nm; blue: 450 to 490 nm; green: 490 to 560 nm; yellow: 560 to 590 nm, orange: 590 to 630 nm; red: 630 to 780 nm. Radiation having wavelengths in the band below 380 nm is normally invisible to the eye and is called ultraviolet; that in the band above about 780 nm is also normally invisible and is called infrared. Because the sensitivity of the human eye to wavelengths below 400 nm and above 700 nm is very low, the wavelength range for light is sometimes considered to be 400 to 700 nm. When considering trichromatic concepts, the visible spectrum is usually regarded as consisting of a bluish third (up to about 490 nm), a greenish third (from about 490 nm to about 580 nm), and a reddish third (above about 580 nm).

THE VISUAL PHOTORECEPTORS When light is imaged on the eye's light-sensitive surface, the *retina,* it is absorbed by light-sensitive pigments. These pigments are contained in a random mosaic of very small receptors called *rods* and *cones*. Each eye has about six million cones and about a hundred million rods, and these receptors are connected to the brain by about one million nerve fibers from each eye. The rods contain a single light-sensitive pigment, *rhodopsin,* which absorbs most strongly at about 510 nm and less strongly at longer and shorter wavelengths. Although the rod response at one wavelength, say 600 nm, may be very different from that at another, say 500 nm, such responses can be made the same by adjusting the intensities of the stimuli appropriately. The rods cannot, therefore, distinguish between changes in colour intensity (saturation) and changes in spectral composition; hence, they do not provide colour vision but only colourless perceptions, such as white, black and shades of gray. This type of vision occurs at low levels of illumination, such as full moonlight and lower.

In the cones, however, there are three different types of pigments: one absorbs light mainly in the reddish third of the spectrum, another mainly in the greenish third, and the other mainly in the bluish third. We refer to these three different types of cones as ρ, γ, and β, the Greek letters rho, gamma, and beta, representing red, green, and blue, respectively.

Because the cones contain more than one type of pigment, they are able to distinguish between changes in intensity and changes in spectral composition. Taking again the example of stimuli of 500 and 600 nm, the 500 nm stimulus gives about half as much ρ as γ response, but the 600 nm stimulus gives more than twice as much ρ as γ response; and this difference in the ratio of ρ to γ response will remain for all intensities. Furthermore, the ratio of response to ρ and γ response is also different for different wavelengths. These differences in the ratios of the three types of cone responses throughout the spectrum provide the basis of colour discrimination.

The numbers of ρ, γ, and β cones are not equal. For every one cone there are about 20 γ and 40 ρ cones. The reason for the small number of β cones is that the eye is not corrected for chromatic aberration, so that blue, green, and red light are focused in different planes in the eye. The eye tends to focus on yellow light, so that the blue light image on the retina is not sharp. Hence, there is no need to sample the blue light image at a high spatial frequency, so the number of β cones is reduced.

THE VISUAL COLOUR SIGNALS Absorptions of light in the three types of cones generate electrical potentials, and these electrical signals are then coded into an *achromatic* and two *colour difference* signals for transmission through the optic nerve to the brain. Although, in the early stages, the signals are analog voltages, when they reach the ganglion cells they are transformed into a series of nerve impulses, all of the same voltage, and the strength of the signal is then represented by the number of nerve impulses per second.

The achromatic signal is produced by *nonopponent* cells summing the voltages produced by the ρ, γ, and β cones in the retina. This signal provides the basis for the perception of *brightness*, which is common to all colours. Because of the greater number of ρ cones and the very much smaller number of β cones, the cone part of the achromatic signal is probably approximately similar to $2\rho + \gamma + (1/20)\beta$, where ρ, γ, and β are the magnitudes of the voltages produced by the three types of cones. The rod signals are probably also transmitted along the achromatic channel to the brain, so that the complete achromatic signal is represented by $2\rho + \gamma + (1/20)\beta + S$, where S represents the rod signals.

At normal daylight levels of illumination, the rods play little

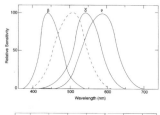

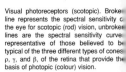

Visual photoreceptors (scotopic). Broken line represents the spectral sensitivity of the eye for scotopic (rod) vision, unbroken lines are the spectral sensitivity curves representative of those believed to be typical of the three different types of cones ρ, γ, and β, of the retina that provide the basis of photopic (colour) vision.

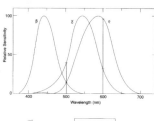

The spectrum. Light of wavelength 500 nm results in about half as much ρ response as γ response, whereas light of 600 nm results in more than twice as much ρ response as γ response. It is the differences in the ratios of the ρ, γ, and β responses that enable differences in spectral composition to be detected independently of the amount of light present, thus providing a basis for colour vision.

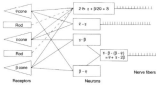

The visual colour signals. Greatly oversimplified and hypothetical diagrammatic representation of possible types of connection between some retinal receptors and some nerve fibers.

or no part, and, in colorimetry and colour reproduction, only the cones are considered. The spectral sensitivity of the achromatic channel is then given by adding to the spectral sensitivity of the γ cones twice that of the ρ cones and one-twentieth of that of the β cones (because of nonlinearities in the stimulus-response relationships in the receptors this simple addition is not strictly valid, but it provides a useful approximation). The resultant composite spectral sensitivity can be considered as the basis of the *spectral luminous efficiency function,* or V(λ) function; this important function is used to weight spectral power distributions for summation to obtain measures for photometry, such as luminance. The very much smaller number of β cones explains why power at the blue end of the spectrum makes only a small contribution to luminance.

The colour-difference signals are produced by *opponent cells* evaluating the differences between the voltages produced by the ρ, γ, and β cones. These colour-difference signals are probably approximately similar to ρ − γ and ρ + γ − 2β. If these difference signals are zero, this is indicated by the number of nerve impulses per second being at a *resting level;* increases above this resting level then indicate a positive signal, and decreases below it represent a negative signal. The ρ − γ signal is positive for reddish colours and negative for greenish colours; the ρ + γ − 2β signal is positive for yellowish colours and negative for bluish colours. These colour-difference signals explain the existence of four *unique hues* in opposed pairs: red and green; yellow and blue. The pairs are opposed in the sense that redness and greenness cannot be perceived together in the same colour, and yellowness and blueness cannot be perceived together in the same colour; but redness and yellowness, or yellowness and greenness, or greenness and blueness, or blueness and redness can be perceived together in the same colour. The situation can then be summarized as follows:

3 Cone Types

ρ sensitive to the reddish third of the spectrum
γ sensitive to the greenish third of the spectrum
β sensitive to the bluish third of the spectrum

3 Signal Types   *6 Unique Colours*

Achromatic $2ρ + γ + (1/20)β$ indicates whitish or blackish
Red-green $ρ - γ$ indicates reddish or greenish
Yellow-blue $ρ + γ - 2β$ indicates yellowish or bluish

4 Unique Hues

The existence of *four* unique hues when there are only *three* different types of cones presents an apparent paradox, but the achromatic signal provides two additional unique colours, black and white, so that, including the four unique hues, there are six unique colours. These six colours are in three opposite pairs, so that the trichromacy of the visual system is still present. The white-black pair of unique colours is different from the pairs of opponent hues in that it is possible to perceive both whiteness and blackness in the same colour; when no unique hues are present such colours are referred to as *grays*.

As light levels increase, the strengths of the achromatic signal and of the colour-difference signals increase, and this results in greater brightness and colourfulness. This is why scenes and pictures look brighter and more colourful at higher levels of illumination than they do at lower levels of illumination.

The degrees of amplification of the voltages produced by the cones, and the concentrations of the pigments, vary to reduce the effects of variations in the level and colour of illuminants. By these means the appearances of colours change much less than might be expected when changes occur in the level and colour of the illumination, a phenomenon often referred to as *colour constancy*.

The relationships between stimulus intensities and magnitudes of visual signals are not usually linear; this means that systems that attempt to represent the domain of different colours as a uniform distribution have to incorporate nonlinear components in their formulations.

CONTRAST The appearance of colours can be markedly affected by the conditions under which they are viewed. For instance, after prolonged viewing of a bright yellow area, colours tend to appear darker and bluer than normal, a phenomenon referred to as *successive contrast*. Similarly, when viewed with a bright yellow surround, colours tend, again, to appear darker and bluer, and this is referred to as *simultaneous contrast*. In these contrast effects, the colours generally become less like the preceding or surrounding conditioning fields, in the sense that the achromatic and colour-difference signals of the colour considered become less like those of the conditioning

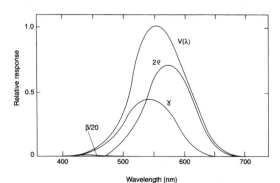

Visual photoreceptors (photopic). The sensitivity, $V(\lambda)$, of the eye to light at normal (photopic) levels of illumination. The contributions of the three different types of cone to this sensitivity are also shown, it being assumed that, compared with the number of ρ cones present in the retina, there are twice as many p cones and only one-twentieth as many β cones.

fields. A consequence of these effects is that if a reflection print is mounted on a white surround it will look darker than if mounted on a black surround; similarly, a yellow surround will make it look bluer, and a blue surround will make it look yellower, and similarly for other hues.

SUBJECTIVE AND OBJECTIVE COLOUR If a reversal transparency film that is balanced for daylight is exposed in tungsten light, the resulting pictures usually have a pronounced orange cast. This is because the tungsten light is orange by comparison with daylight, and the film simply records this orange bias. In the original scene, the eye is able to adapt to the orange colour of the tungsten light to largely offset its colour bias, but, when viewing the picture, its limited angular subtense results in only a small amount of adaptation taking place. To achieve correct results with the film, it is necessary either to use a bluish filter over the camera lens or to rebalance the film by increasing the speed of the blue layer and decreasing that of the red layer, relative to that of the green layer. When negative films are used, from which positive images are obtained by printing, it is possible to correct for any bias in the colour of the camera illuminant by altering the effective colour of the printing light; however, this does require the colour film to have sufficient exposure latitude to accommodate the bias of the camera illuminant. Another example of this type of situation can occur when photographing interior scenes; even though the film, or filtration, may be chosen for the normal illuminant, bias can be caused by the colour of the decoration in the interior. For instance, if a daylight balanced film is used in a room lit by daylight, the presence of pink walls and a red carpet can result in reddish pictures being produced, whereas the eye adapts to the pink bias of the lighting in the interior and tends to see the colours normally.

Books: Billmeyer, F. W., J., and Saltzman, M., *Principles of* .

Color Technology. 2nd edition. New York: Wiley, 1981; Hunt, R. W. *G., The Reproduction of Colour* 4th edition. New York: Van Nostrand Reinhold, and Surbiton, England: Fountain Press, 1987.

COLOUR ADAPTATION A process of adjustment of the visual system such that exposure to a given hue results in decreased sensitivity to that hue and an apparent increased sensitivity to the complementary hue. For example, when a person has fully adapted to the light source, either tungsten light or daylight may appear white despite the wide differences in the relative red, green, and blue content in these two sources.

COLOUR ANALYSIS Determination of the amounts of primaries or colourants required in a reproduction, as distinct from colour synthesis, the production of a colour in an additive or subtractive process.

COLOURANTS Typically pigments or dyes that selectively absorb light of various frequencies, such as cyan, magenta, and yellow dyes or filters that are designed to absorb red, green, and blue light respectively.

COLOUR ATLAS Collection of surface colours, usually in a systematic arrangement, used for choosing or specifying colours in practical applications. Colour atlases have the advantages of being easy to understand, easy to use, and adaptable in terms of the number and spacing of the samples. They also have the following disadvantages: the number of the samples is always limited, so that interpolation is often necessary; they always have a limited gamut of samples; there may be some variations between copies; they may deteriorate as a result of the samples fading or becoming dirty; there is no unique system for arranging the samples; different observers may make different matches between the samples and colours being checked; colour matches between the samples and colours being checked may be upset by changes in the colour of the lighting; and they cannot readily be used for light sources.

COLOUR BALANCE The average overall colour of a reproduction. The colour balance is dependent on the relative strengths of the three primaries in additive systems and on the relative strengths of the colourants in subtractive systems.

COLOUR BLINDNESS See *Defective colour vision*.

COLOUR CAST The average overall colour of a reproduction relative to some defined or optimum average overall colour. See also: *Colour balance*.

COLOUR CHART A panel of selected colours that is designed to be photographed for the purpose of evaluating colour reproduction quality.

COLOUR CHECKER A set of selected colours that approximate the colours of real objects. The gamut of colours is specified by the Inter-Society Color Council, National Bureau of Standards. Colour checkers can be used to make an evaluation of the colour reproduction qualities of a system such as video camera and monitor.

COLOUR CIRCLE Arrangement of colours in a circle according to hue, such as red, orange, yellow, green, blue, violet, purple, magenta, and back to red. In the Munsell system, red, yellow, green, blue, and purple.

Syn.: Hue circle.

COLOUR DEFICIENCY Colour vision that is deficient in the ability to see colour differences, compared to normal observers. About 8% of men have some colour deficiency, but only about 2% are seriously deficient. For women, the corresponding figures are about 0.5% and 0.03%. The colours confused, and the average incidence, for the different types of colour deficiency may be summarized as follows:

Type of Defect	Colours Confused	Incidence Men	Women
Protanopia	All reddish and greenish; reds dark	1.0%	0.02%
Deuteranopia	All reddish and greenish	1.1%	0.01%
Tritanopia	All yellowish and bluish	0.002%	0.001%
Protanomaly	Some reddish and greenish; reds dark	1.0%	0.02%
Deuteranomaly	Some reddish and greenish	4.9%	0.38%
Tritanomaly	Some yellowish and bluish	?	?
Rod mono-chromacy	All colours	0.002%	0.002%
Cone mono	All colours	Very rare	Very rare
Totals		8.0%	0.4%

Syn.: Colour blindness.

COLOUR DEPTH In electronic imaging, the number of bits per pixel that supports colour display. Eight-bit colour depth will support 256 colours, standard video graphics array (VGA). Fifteen-bit colour depth will support 32,768 colours, high colour, and 24 bits will support 16,777,216 colours, true colour.

COLOUR DIFFERENCE SIGNAL (1) Visual signal from the retina composed of differences between the cone responses. (2) In television, signals consisting of the differences between the red signal and the luminance signal and between the blue signal and the luminance signal.

COLOUR DIFFERENCE UNIT (ΔE) Unit of colour difference used in a colour difference formula.

8ee also: CIELAB system; CIELUV system.

COLOUR FRINGING A noise problem in colour video resulting from a registration error in the RGB images; the fringing is most noticeable at the vertical edges of images. Often this is manifested by the appearance of colours that did not exist in the original scene.

COLOUR GAMUT Range of colours involved in original scenes or in systems of reproduction. In additive systems. the colour gamut is defined in a chromaticity diagram by the triangle formed by joining the three points representing the reproduction primaries. In subtractive systems, the colourants usually have unwanted absorptions; these absorptions affect the luminance factors, and because luminance factors are not shown on chromaticity diagrams, it is more comprehensive to use colour spaces. Chromaticity diagrams or colour spaces used to show colour gamuts should represent the spacing of colours as uniformly as possible. Hence the u´, v´ chromaticity diagram, and the CIELAB or CIELUV colour spaces are usually used.

COLOUR GRAPHICS ADAPTER (CGA) In computers, the original standard for colour display on the personal computer. CGA was limited to spatial resolution of 320 x 200 pixels and 4 colours from a palette of 16 colours. In text mode, characters are formed from an 8 x 8 matrix at a resolution of 640 x 200.

COLOUR HARMONY An arrangement of colours that creates a pleasing affect and effect in the visual perception of an image. Expressive harmony can also be achieved through discordant colour combinations.

COLORIMETER An instrument for measuring colours. Visual colormeters are sometimes used in research work. but practical colorimetry is usually carried out with photoelectric instruments in which the light from the sample is passed through three filters onto a photoelectric detector.

COLORIMETRIC COLOUR REPRODUCTION
Reproduction in which the chromaticities and relative luminances are the same as those in the original scene.

COLOURIZATION The process of electronically adding colour to video versions of motion pictures originally produced in black and white.

COLOUR LOOK-UP TABLE (CLUT) CLUT's provide an algorithm that will allow for the translation of RGB colour into some other colour space, such as CMYK. If an area of the image that is displayed as red comprises 85% red, 10% green, and 10% blue, then a CLUT would be written to translate the RGB data into 5% cyan, 60% magenta, 35% yellow and 0% black. The CLUT exists as a predetermined set of values in tabular form, thus making it unnecessary to calculate the appropriate values for each change in display colour.

COLOUR MAPPING Colour mapping uses a colour look-up table (CLUT) for monitor display purposes.

COLOUR MATCHING (1) Procedure in the colourant industries whereby a sample is adjusted to be the same colour as a reference material. (2) In colorimetry, the processing of adjusting a mixture of colours until it matches a test colour.

COLOUR MEASUREMENT Colours can be measured in various ways, the most important of which are (1) by comparison with calibrated samples on a colour atlas; (2) by visual matching against calibrated amounts of red, green, and blue primaries in an additive mixture; (3) by computation from spectral power data using a set of colour matching functions as weighting functions; and (4) by photoelectric measurement through filters that, with the spectral sensitivity of the photodetector being used, generate a set of sensitivities that closely match a set of colour-matching functions.

For the calibrated atlas method, the atlas used could be, for instance, the *Munsell Book of Color* or the *Natural Color System Atlas*. This method is simple but is not very accurate. It requires interpolation and sometimes extrapolation, and it implies the use of an illuminating source that matches the illuminant used for calibrating the atlas, but such a source is not usually available.

The red, green, and blue colour matching method is the one that was originally used for setting up standard colorimetric measures, but it is now only used for research work, because it is very slow and of limited precision.

The computation from spectral power data method is the one that is regarded as standard for practical applications. It requires the spectral power distributions of the samples, and these are usually derived by multiplying the spectral reflectance factor, or the spectral transmittance factor, of each sample by the spectral power distribution of a chosen illuminant, at regular wavelength intervals throughout the spectrum.

The method of measurement with filtered photodetectors is convenient in that the equipment required is relatively simple, but it is not possible to match the required colourmatching functions exactly, so that accuracy is limited.

Books: Billmeyer, F. W., Jr., and Saltzman, M., *Principles of Color Technology*. 2nd edition. New York: Wiley, 1981; Hunt, R. W. *G., Measuring Colour*. New Jersey: Prentice and Schuster, and Hemel Hempstead, England: International Book Distributors, 1987.

COLOUR NOTATION Means of defining colours, for example, the CIE X, Y, Z system; the CIELAB and CIELUV systems; the Munsell system; the natural colour system (NCS).

COLOUR PROOFING Colour proofing is the process of making test colour reproductions of colour images to see how the final printed colour reproduction will look.

COLOUR PROOFS There are two main types of colour

proofs: press proofs and off-press proofs.

Press Proofs There are two types of press proofs: those made on special flat-bed proof presses and those made on rotary production-type presses. Most proofs made on flat-bed proof presses are made one colour at a time. Most rotary-type proofing presses are multicolour lithographic or letterpress presses in which proofs are made with wet trapping of inks similar to that on production presses. Press speeds may be different. Gravure proofs are made on slow production-type presses in one colour or multicolour. In lithography especially, speed differences are great, and this causes variations between proofs and press prints. The fact that proofs are made on presses with the same ink and paper as the printing press is no guarantee that the proof will match the print, as there are many variables in lithographic printing that can affect printing results.

Off-press Proofs There are two main types of off-press proofs: analog, which are made from separation films; and digital, which are made from digital data in computers or storage media. Analog proofs are of two types: overlay and single-sheet or laminated proofs. Digital proofs are also of two types: soft proofs, which are the colour displays on video terminals; and hard proofs, which are made on paper or other substrates. Digital hard proofs are in turn of two types: continuous tone and halftone or screened.

PROOFING MATERIALS AND PROCESSES

Overlay Proofs There are three types of overlay proofs: (1) individual plastic foils with photosensitive coatings overcoated with a pigmented layer corresponding to the colour of the separation or other printing colour; (2) individual photosensitive foils overcoated with dyes corresponding to the printing colours; and (3) foils coated with a photosensitive peel-apart layer. Overlay proofs are less costly than other analog proofs. They are useful as progressive proofs to show what the single-, two- and three-colour overprints look like in addition to the appearance of the four-colour print. They have the disadvantage of high optical-dot gain in highlight and middletone areas because of the many reflective surfaces in the combined layers.

Single-sheet or Laminated Proofs There are six types of single-sheet or laminated proofs: (1) photosensitive ink layers; (2) laminated photoadhesive layers that change in adhesivity on exposure to light and absorb pigmented dry toners in proportion to the adhesivity of the image areas; (3) adhesive peel-apart images pigmented with dry toners, laminated onto a reflective base; (4) laminated pigmented photosensitive layers; (5) multiple liquid-dispersed toner images transferred to the printing substrate from an electrophotographic photoconductor; and (6) images exposed onto colour photographic paper using multiple exposures to correct or contaminate the hues produced by the dye/emulsion layers in attempts to match the printing ink colours. Many of the single-sheet proofs are used as contract proofs which clients sign or approve as being representative of what the printed job should look like. The laminated adhesive toner and pigmented layer proofs suffer from excessive optical gain throughout the tone scale. The photographic proofs have difficulty matching the printing colours, especially the yellow, which is slightly orange in hue on the photographic proof.

Soft Digital Proofs Soft digital proofs have difficulty correlating the RGB (red, green, blue) phosphors of the video display terminal (VDT) to the CMYK (cyan, magenta, yellow, and black) of the printing colours. Also they cannot be used as contract or sign-off proofs.

Hard Digital Halftone Proofs There are two types of hard digital halftone proofs: electrophotographic and thermal dye sublimation transfer proofs. Both types produce good-quality proofs. They are, however, limited in size to two or four pages and are very expensive. Hard digital continuous tone proofs are of four types: (1) dye diffusion thermal transfer; (2) thermal dye sublimation transfer; (3) light valve technology; and (4) inkjet. The main objections to these proofing systems are the inability to simulate image structure (halftones) in printing, and subject moiré effects caused by interference patterns between the halftone screen image and patterns in the subject such as herringbone weave and lace textiles.

CQLOR REPRODUCTION OBJECTIVES The objective in a colour reproduction may be any one of a number of alternatives. Six objectives have been defined for different circumstances.

Spectral colour reproduction is defined as reproduction in which the colours are reproduced with the same spectral reflectance factors, or spectral transmittance factors, or relative spectral power distributions, as those of the colours in the original scene.

Spectral colour reproduction is the ideal aim for commercial catalogues in which it is desired to depict the colour of goods accurately. For accuracy to be achieved for viewing under a variety of light sources, spectral colour reproduction is required but can usually only be achieved by supplying samples of the actual goods.

Colourimetric colour reproduction is defined as reproduction in which the chromaticities and relative luminances are the same as those in the original scene. This is usually applicable to reflection prints.

Exact colour reproduction is defined as reproduction in which the chromaticities, relative luminances, and absolute luminances, are the same as those in the original scene. This is applicable to cases where absolute luminance levels are important.

Equivalent colour reproduction is defined as reproduction in which the chromaticities, relative luminances, and absolute luminances are such as to produce the same appearances of colours as in the original scene. This is applicable to cases where simulation of appearance is required.

Corresponding colour reproduction is defined as reproduction in which the chromaticities and relative luminances are such as to produce the same appearances as the colours of the original scene would have had if they had had the same luminances as those of the reproduction. This is generally applicable to many reproduction situations.

Preferred colour reproduction is defined as reproduction in which the colours depart from equality of appearance at equal or at different luminance levels in order to achieve a more pleasing result. This is applicable when departures from any of the other five objectives are required in order to achieve a more pleasant or more flattering result.

Books: Hunt, R.W. G., *The Reproduction of Colour* 4th edition. New York: Van Nostrand Reinhold, and Surbiton, England: Fountain Press,1987.

COLOUR SCIENCE Systematic knowledge about colour in all its aspects, including physics, chemistry, physiology, psychology, measurement, instrumentation, art, photography, television, printing, colourants, lighting, and displays.

COLOUR SEPARATION (1) The process of obtaining three (or more) monochrome images from a colour image or from a colour scene. Such images are used to produce printing surfaces. (2). 0ne of the monochrome images obtained in (1).

COLOUR SPACE Three-dimensional representation of colours.

See also: *CIELAB system; CIELUV system*.

COLOUR SYNTHESIS The process of producing a colour image from red, green, and blue components in an additive system, or from cyan, magenta, and yellow components in a subtractive system.

COLOUR TEMPERATURE (1) All light sources emit electromagnetic radiation, some of which is in the visible region between 400 and 700 nm in wavelength. The amount of radiation emitted at each wavelength, and the total amount of radiation emitted, varies from source to source. The most exact way to describe the radiation emitted is with a spectral energy distribution diagram, which specifies the amount of energy emitted at each wavelength. The total amount of energy emitted can then also be determined by integrating or summing over all the wavelengths. The fact that many types of sources approximate a blackbody in their spectral energy distribution, however, provides for a simpler means of specifying, at least approximately, the output of a source.

The spectral energy distribution of the radiation emitted by any blackbody, or source approximating a blackbody, is a function only of the temperature of the blackbody. This means that all blackbody sources will have the same spectral energy distribution if they are at the same temperature. (Such curves are frequently called blackbody radiation curves.) It is therefore possible to completely specify the spectral energy distribution of a blackbody type source by specifying the temperature of the source. By convention, this temperature is specified using the absolute, or Kelvin, scale. (This convention also results in zero emittance at all wavelengths at 0 K.) Because the spectral energy distribution of a visible source describes the colour of the source, the temperature of a blackbody light source is known as the colour temperature. It is important to remember, however, that the total amount of energy emitted by a blackbody source is dependent on the area of the source as well as the temperature.

Strictly speaking, the colour temperature of a real light source is defined to be the temperature (using the Kelvin scale) of the blackbody which most closely approximates the source. Colour temperatures for incandescent sources, however, do correlate fairly well with the actual temperature of the source. It is important to note that sources that do not approximately resemble a blackbody in output do not have colour temperatures, although they can be assigned *correlated* colour temperatures. The lower the colour temperature of a source, the longer the mean wavelength of the radiation emitted and, therefore, the warmer the colour of the light emitted. Lower colour temperatures also result in smaller amounts of radiation and light being emitted.

Colour temperature is particularly important in colour photography because colour films are designed to give optimal colour rendition only when exposed using light of a specified colour temperature. In particular, daylight colour films are balanced for 5500 K, type A tungsten films are balanced for 3400 K, and type B tungsten films are balanced for 3200 K. Colour temperature is also important in printing and projection systems because photographic materials are designed to be printed or viewed using specific types of illumination. Colour temperature can also be important in black-and-white photography because the speeds of photographic materials are frequently dependent on the colour temperature of the illumination.

Two relations that use (colour) temperature describe two of the key characteristics of blackbody radiation curves. The first is the Stefan-Boltzmann law, which was determined experimentally by Josef Stefan and later derived theoretically by Ludwig Boltzmann. This law states that the amount of radiation emitted by a blackbody source is proportional to the fourth power of the colour temperature: $E_{tot} = \sigma T^4$, where σ is the Stefan-Boltzmann constant equal to 5.67×10^{-8} W-m^{-2} - K^{-4}, and T is the temperature. The second is Wien's displacement law, which gives the wavelength of maximum emittance: $\lambda_{max} = 2.8978 \times 10^{-3}/T$. This law gives rise to an alternative way of expressing colour temperatures: the MIRED (micro-reciprocal-degrees) scale. The MIRED value of a light source is its colour temperature divided into 1,000,000. Thus a colour temperature of 5000 K corresponds to a MIRED value of 200. Because the MIRED value, like the wavelength of peak emission, is inversely proportional to the temperature, MIRED values are directly related to the wavelength of peak emission (in fact, the wavelength of peak emission in nanometers is approximately 2.9 times the MIRED value). MIRED values are useful in assessing the effect of colour temperature shifts and light balancing filters. When colour temperature is expressed using the MIRED scale, the change in the MIRED values when going from one source to another (the MIRED shift) is independent of the initial colour temperature. This is because the MIRED value is directly related to wavelength rather than to temperature. Colour temperatures and MIRED values can be read out on most colour temperature meters.

Colour Temperatures of Various Sources

Source	Approximate Colour Temperature
Standard tungsten bulb (below 100 watts)	2600 K
Standard tungsten bulb (100 watts and above)	2800 K
Sensitometric lamp (standard)	2848 K
Projector lamps	3200 K
Photoflood lamps (several hour life)	3400 K
Flash bulbs	4000 K
Electronic flash	5000-6000 K
Sunlight	5000 K
Daylight	5500 K
Overcast daylight	7500 K
North sky, blue	10,000-20,000 K

Of historical and physical significance is the absolute relation between the spectral energy distribution of a blackbody source and its temperature, given by Planck's radiation law: $E_\lambda = (8\pi hc/\lambda^5)$ $(1/(e^{hc/\lambda kT}-1))$, where E_λ is the energy emitted at wavelength λ, h is Planck's constant $(6.626 \times 10^{-34}$ joule-sec), c is the speed of light $(2.9979 \times 10^8$ m/sec), and k is Boltzmann's constant $(1.381 \times 10^{-23}$ joule/K). This law is of particular interest since in its derivation Max Planck invented the idea of quantization of energy, which led to quantum theory and our idea of the universe today.

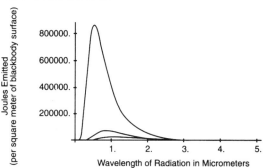

Color temperature. Plots of the spectral energy distribution as given by Planck's radiation law for various temperatures. *Top curve*, 5500 K; *middle curve*, 3400 K; *bottom curve*, 2800 K.

COLOUR TEMPERATURE (2) In computer imaging, colour temperature is supposedly a measure of the colour quality of the monitor image. It assumes that the monitor adheres to a heat-to-light relationship as does a blackbody radiator. This is not the case for video monitors. A more accurate term would be correlated colour temperature. Quality monitors generally allow for a 5000 K setting and higher. The purpose of such monitors is to approximate daylight viewing conditions for images so that matching can occur.

COLOUR TEST CHART A selection of colours assembled into a convenient array for testing the colour reproduction characteristics of a colour reproduction system. An example is the *Macbeth ColourChecker Colour Rendition Chart* of painted paper chips, in which 6 neutral colours and 18 carefully selected chromatic colours are mounted together on a cardboard base.

COLOUR VISION See *Vision, colour vision*.

COMB FILTER A filtering circuit on some colour monitors designed to give a better colour rendition and minimize distortion.

COMPACT DISC-INTERACTIVE (CD-I) A new standard for the use of CDs containing still images, moving image sequences, and audio tracks. A CD-I device will allow a user to *interact* with the program contained on the disc. It requires a CD-I player and appropriate monitor. The CD-I player has its own microprocessor and represents a higher-level of built-in intelligence than a standard CD or CD-ROM player.

COMPACT DISC READ-ONLY MEMORY (CD ROM) Discs that can hold text, images, and sound, and are a major means of data storage and distribution. Their storage capacity is in the region of 650 Mbytes of data. Since the throughput of CD-ROM players are standardized at 150 Kbytes per second, these devices are capable of playing audio CDs.

COMPILER A software type program that converts high-level programming language into machine language in preparation for execution. Compiled languages run faster than interpreter languages and can be complied into executable programs.

COMPLEMENTARY COLOURS (1) In colorimetry, two colour stimuli are complementary when it is possible to reproduce the tristimulus values of a specified achromatic stimulus by an additive mixture of these two stimuli. (2) Generally, complementary colours are those of the opposite hue: thus, red and cyan are complementary colours, as are green and magenta, and blue and yellow.

COMPLEMENTARY WAVELENGTH Wavelength of the monochromatic stimulus that, when additively mixed in suitable proportions with the colour stimulus considered, matches the specified achromatic stimulus.

COMPOSITE PHOTOGRAPH A photograph on which two or more separate images have been combined by any camera, printing, or postprinting technique.
See also: *Photomontage*.

COMPRESSION In electronic imaging, image data are compressed in order to achieve smaller files for storage and/or transmission. LZW and Huffman codes are two compression algorithms widely used on images. Video is often compressed using an interframe process whereby redundancy shared by two frames is ignored. In transmission of image data under this scheme only the differences between the frames are transmitted, thus decreasing the time necessary to transmit the data.

COMPUTER-AIDED DESIGN (CAD)
The use of computers to assist in design activities such as graphics, architecture, engineering, and page layout.

COMPUTER-AIDED MANUFACTURING (CAM)
The use of computers to assist in the design and monitoring of a manufacturing process.

COMPUTER ANIMATION
See *Animation, Animation techniques.*

COMPUTER-ASSISTED INSTRUCTION (CAI)
The use of computers in the classroom to advance teaching and learning. Almost any involvement of computers in providing instruction, questioning, or feedback in the teaching learning paradigm has been labeled CAI. Currently, CAI has come to mean the use of a computer in the control of multimedia for the purposes of instruction.

COMPUTER GRAPHICS
When personal computers were first introduced, they were seen as a mere novelty. It wasn't until the introduction of word processing and spreadsheet software that their use as an integral tool for communications was recognized. Even though programs that could create graphic elements soon followed, words and numbers remain the mainstay of most computer-generated communications. This was due in large part to several factors including the fact that programs were not only difficult to use, they failed to provide the user with a real-time display of what was being created, there was no efficient, inexpensive way of obtaining hardcopy output of graphic information, and there was no way to easily integrate graphics and text elements.

In the mid-1980s, several technological developments occurred that changed all of that and launched the visual communications revolution known as desktop publishing. The introduction of a graphic user interface and a concept embodied in the acronym WYSIWYG (what you see is what you get) made it possible for anyone who could use a *mouse* (a point-and-select device) to draw with a computer. At the same time the introduction of inexpensive, high-resolution output from laser printers made it possible to get graphic designs off the computer's display screen and into the hands of intended viewers. Finally, page layout software made it possible to integrate text, graphic elements, and photographs into a single document.

TEXT INFORMATION Today word processing programs not only allow users to enter and print out alphanumeric characters, they provide the writer with an opportunity to be a graphic designer as well. With thousands of type fonts available and the ability to apply any number of type styles to a document, designers can easily use text as a graphic design element. For many situations, a word processing program and a laser printer have totally replaced the need for typesetting.

GRAPHICS PROGRAMS There are two basic approaches that graphics programs take in representing information on screen and to output devices. These approaches give the programs two unique *feels* that not only affect how the artist creates elements but also what the final output looks like.

Bitmapped Programs Bitmapped graphics generated with *paint programs* use a work surface made from a grid of individual picture elements (pixels). Graphic line artwork is created by assigning black or white values to each pixel in the work area Gray-scale artwork is possible if the program supports assigning gray levels to individual pixels. The number of pixels contained in the work area determine the resolution of the file regardless of the potential resolution of the output device. For example, even though a drawing can be printed on a laser printer having a potential resolution of 300 dots per inch, if the paint program used to create the file only uses 72 dots per inch, the final output will only have a resolution of 72 dots per inch. The visible effect of graphics created with low-pixel resolution will be that curved elements in the design will exhibit stair-stepped artifacts referred to as *jaggies* or *aliasing*.

Vector-Based Programs Vector-based (sometimes referred to as object-oriented) graphics created with *draw programs* use mathematical expression (like those used in coordinate geometry) to describe graphic shapes. Shapes are dealt with as individual objects that may be grouped, layered, and superimposed to create graphic designs. Because the location of pixels needed to render an object are defined by those points that make the mathematical definition true, the resolution of the graphic will be determined by the capabilities of the output device, not by the number of pixels the program can address. In the case of a graphic object rendered to a laser printer having a resolution of 300 dots per inch, the mathematical definition will identify which 300 pixels should be activated for any given inch. The file size of a vector-based graphic will be substantially smaller than the file size of a similar bitmapped graphic because the vector-based program does not have to store information about each and every pixel.

DESKTOP PUBLISHING Desktop publishing has given personal computer users, working under short deadlines, the ability to inexpensively generate documents that use graphic design, photography, and text to effectively communicate. Page layout programs make it possible for a designer to perform many of the tasks that previously required the services of specialists, including such things as typesetting, halftone separations, stripping, and printing. The page layout program brings computer data that may exist in a number of formats together as one file. The other significant function that page layout programs provide is that once the data have been edited and assembled into one file, they are translated into a format that can be universally understood by a wide range of output devices, independent of the computer system used to create it. This is accomplished through the use of a page description language. Like other programming languages, a page description language generates a list of instructions that tells an output device how to render all the visual elements contained on any given page. The page description language that has essentially become an industry standard is called Postscript and many output devices will list one of their advantages as being Postscript compatible.

PRESENTATION PROGRAMS In addition to desktop publishing documents, computer graphics will be prominently featured in the production of images used to support presentations by live speakers. Generally distributed in the form of slides and overheads, these images represent a multibillion dollar segment of the communications industry. There are a number of software programs that, like page layout programs, help the designer organize, produce, and output the visuals that will be used in a presentation. In addition to a full range of graphic production tools, these programs also allow users to organize ideas with the use of an outlining feature, generate summary handouts, and produce scripts and storyboards for the speaker as well as import visual and text information from other programs.

MULTIMEDIA Depending on who you talk to, the term *multimedia* will be given a variety of definitions. A relatively new computer concept, multimedia uses the personal computer to bring together text, graphics, animation, photography, and sound. This digital information is organized into presentations that can exist as interactive packages delivered by the computer, self-contained programs presented on videotape, or visual support material used in live presentations.

COMPUTERS FOR PHOTOGRAPHERS

In recent years there have been a number of developments and trends in computer technology that have important implications for the photographer. Computers have traditionally been large, centralized devices requiring technical specialists to operate them. Their primary function has been computation. Unprecedented improvements in technology, however, have resulted in system efficiencies that have reduced size, lowered costs, and greatly expanded capabilities. As a result, the form and function of today's computer have changed radically. The advent of the personal computer has resulted in a decentralization of computing. A computer at every desk has become the norm in many organizations. The primary function of the computer has changed from computation to communication. Word processing, databases, spreadsheets, electronic mail, and desktop publishing are all examples of this change. Until recently, the tangible output of a computer's communications function has taken the form of text-based documents and graphic representation of data. This is rapidly changing, with computers playing an ever increasing role in the creation and distribution of both halftone and continuous-tone photographic images. Today computer technology represents a tremendous opportunity for photographers, as visual communicators, to express themselves in new and exciting ways.

COMPUTER SYSTEMS In discussing computers, there are many systems to consider. These systems can be as simple as the hand-held calculators that have replaced the slide rule, or as sophisticated as the supercomputers used by scientists and engineers to solve complex theoretical problems. Photographers will most likely find themselves working with a microcomputer or perhaps a workstation. Accordingly, this discussion will focus on these computers.

Computer systems, from simple to sophisticated.

Regardless of their sophistication, all computer systems are a combination of hardware and software components. These components can be functionally grouped into the three broad areas of input, processing, and output. Hardware includes all the physical (mechanical, electronic, electrical, magnetic) parts of a computer, as well as a number of peripheral devices. Hardware components are useless without appropriate software. Operating system software gives a computer its functionality by providing a set of instructions that direct hardware components to perform specific tasks. Utilities and applications are software programs that work in concert with the computer's operating system to perform specialized jobs such as word processing.

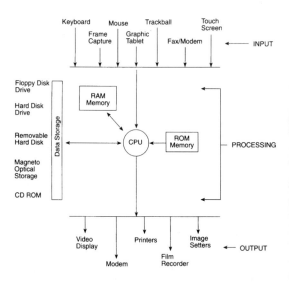

Computer system components: input, processing, and output.

The way in which the user interacts with the computer is referred to as user interface. In the past few years, this relationship has been the subject of much study and has resulted in new user-friendly environments, making computer use by neophytes much more common. There are currently two ways a user can interact with a microcomputer. The first is a command line, character-based interface, which requires the user to learn a set of commands (instructions) with very specific syntax. The computer waits for a command to be typed in with a keyboard and, if that command is in the software's vocabulary, tasks such as creating a file, saving a file, or printing a file are accomplished. Programs that use this type of interface can have a substantial learning curve associated with them because each new program may require learning a whole new set of commands. This is an example of a command line used in Microsoft's Disk Operating System (MSDOS): C> Format/4 a:. It represents, for a novice user, a fairly cryptic way of communicating.

The other approach uses a graphic user interface. The Apple Macintosh and Microsoft Windows are examples. In these systems, icons graphically representing files, storage devices, and other program and system components are used to create a somewhat intuitive visual work environment. All commands and actions that can be taken by the user are listed under a set of menus. In addition to the keyboard, the user also uses a pointing device called a *mouse*. Unlike the command line interface, which simply waits for an appropriate instruction, the graphic user interface provides closed-loop communications. The computer is continually checking and updating mouse positions and displays that position on the screen. Users are able to select and move visual elements on the screen. The system provides feedback when inappropriate actions are taken.

INPUT Computer input refers to any component, function, or action that provides the system with information. Human beings live in an analog world. We receive information using the senses of sight and sound. Light energy and the mechanical energy that constitutes sound are converted by the eyes and ears into a constant flow of fluctuating electrical voltages. The brain processes these electrical currents and provides us with the sensations of sight and sound. Unlike humans, a computer, which is nothing more than a collection of circuits that can be turned either on or off, requires that the information it receives be presented in a digital form (a series of ones and zeros representing the on and off states the computer can understand). Input devices and software therefore serve as the interrupter between man and machine.

Analog to digital (A/D) conversion is the process by which a flow of infinitely varying electrical voltages (analog information) is sampled at a given rate and the discrete values that are obtained are expressed as a string of binary (ones and zeros) numbers (digital information). Once converted these values can be used by the computer, manipulated, stored, and retrieved for later use. Many input devices are used with today's microcomputers.

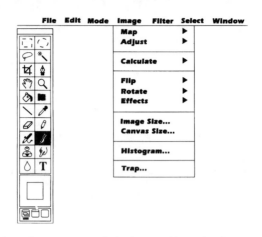

Input. Computer screen display for a graphic user interface

Keyboards Keyboards have provided the traditional way in which people interact with a computer and provide an efficient way of entering alphanumeric information. In addition to the keys found in standard typewriter layouts, most computer keyboards also contain a separate numeric keypad for easier number entry. Also, most computer keyboards contain a special set of *function keys* that provide shortcuts when using certain software programs. In some cases these keys can be programmed to perform special tasks.

Mouse While a keyboard is adequate for interacting with text-based programs, it doesn't provide the kind of input necessary to take full advantage of a graphic user interface or to interact with many graphic drawing programs. A mouse is a hand-held device that is moved along any flat surface. A pointer (cursor) on the display screen indicates the relative position of the mouse as its position changes. Buttons on the mouse allow the user to select, grab, and move objects, as well as make selections from various menus. In some cases, these buttons can be made to operate like the function keys found on most keyboards.

The mouse's location is tracked in one of two ways. The most common method uses a rollerball located in the bottom. As the mouse moves, the ball rotates against two variable resistors, which make voltage adjustments to signals representing x and y coordinates. While this design is adequate for most uses, it is somewhat inaccurate and susceptible to mechanical failures, dust, and dirt. The second method uses a special pad that has a very fine grid etched into its surface. The mouse shines a laser light source onto the grid. The reflected light is interpreted, providing very accurate mouse location information.

Trackball One of the drawbacks of a mouse is that it requires a minimum 8 x 9-inch area to operate. It also requires the user to develop a certain eye/hand coordination to use it efficiently. The trackball works on the same rollerball principle as the mouse. However, instead of being underneath, in a trackball the rollerball is located on top. Rather than dragging the ball around on a flat surface, users rotate the ball with their fingers. Many users find this gives them greater control and accuracy in moving the cursor on the screen. Also, the fact that the trackball remains stationary, requiring less space, makes this a popular alternative to the mouse.

Graphics Tablet While a mouse or trackball gives the user the ability to move a pointer (cursor) around on the screen and use the basic drawing tools found in many graphics programs, they are awkward to use for intricate drawings tasks. Most illustrations are created by artists who have developed their ability to render objects using pencils, brushes and similar hand-held tools. The digital graphics tablet provides the artist and designer with an input environment that closely replicates using such tools.

The graphics tablet is an electronic work surface containing a finely placed grid of sensors. A stylus, resembling a pencil or brush, is moved over the tablet's surface, activating the embedded sensors and causing the motion to be rendered on the screen as lines or brush strokes. The sensors will respond to either pressure or to magnetic flux being emitted by the stylus. In some graphics tablets the amount of pressure being applied to the stylus is also noted. This information, when presented to software programs designed to recognize it, provides the artist a realistic environment for working with tools such as air brush, pencils and charcoal.

Tablets are available in various sizes and can be programmed to respond as either absolute or relative devices. With absolute referencing, the tablet responds, point by point, to physical locations on the screen, (i.e. to a point 1 inch in from the left edge of the screen would correspond to a point 1 inch in from the left side of the graphics tablet. An 8 x 10-inch piece of artwork created on the screen would require and 8 x 10-inch graphics tablet.) In the relative mode, the distance moved is noted and rendered on the screen. In this way, a large piece of artwork can be manipulated using a relatively small graphics tablet. The stylus is simply picked up and repositioned on the tablet to continue drawing a line whose length exceeds the length of the tablet. (Most mice and trackballs use the same *relative distance* method being described here.)

Touch-Sensitive Screens Touch-sensitive screens are a type of interactive system in which the user is prompted to interact with the program by touching certain objects depicted on the screen. This system uses a pressure-sensitive film that is attached to the video display screen. These screens can eliminate the need for a keyboard or any other input device and are well suited for those situations in which a novice user must interact with a computer.

Scanners Scanners are computer input devices that can convert black-and-white or colour line art, halftone, and continuous-tone photographic images, into digital information. Although image scanners have been available for some time, the cost of these systems, and the computers needed to support them, have kept them out of the reach of the average photographer. The three basic designs available for use with microcomputers include flatbed, hand-held, and desktop film scanners. In each case these devices make use of a photosensitive integrated circuit chip called a charged-coupled device (CCD). A CCD contains thousands of transistors, made from light-sensitive semiconductors. When light energy strikes the CCD, it is converted to electrical current with voltages proportional to the illuminance of the light striking it. Analog-to-digital circuitry samples these voltages and converts them to binary numbers that can be used by the computer.

Flatbed scanners are designed for the reflective copy of print and photographic material as large as 11 x 17 inches. The original is placed face down on a glass platen, and, in much the same way as an electrostatic copy is made, an optical system focuses reflected light onto a CCD that is mechanically passed under the original in stepped increments. For coloured originals, three passes (scans)—one each for red, green, and blue information—are made.

Hand-held scanners work on the same principle as the flatbed; however instead of the scanner mechanically moving the CCD past the original, the user rolls the scanner over the original material. This is very useful for those situations where the original cannot be placed on the glass platen of a flatbed, or where portability is a concern. Hand-held scanners are fairly inexpensive and work reasonably well with small images. Larger originals can be difficult to scan because of the need to roll the device consistently over larger areas.

Film scanners are used to convert photographic negatives and transparencies into digital information. Like flatbeds, film scanners contain an optical system that focuses an image on a CCD. The CCD will either be moved through the projected image, or, in the case of scanners that use an area array CCD, be exposed to the entire image for a fixed interval without moving the CCD. Colour information will be scanned by making three passes (or exposures) through red, green, and blue filters. Film scanners are available for originals ranging in size from 35-mm to 4 x 5 inch. Some flatbed scanners can be fitted with a light source for transillumination and can be used to scan larger-sized negatives and transparencies. The overall image quality obtained from a scanner will depend on the scanner's spatial and brightness resolutions.

Frame Capture Cards Frame capture cards bridge the gap between electronic and digital image making. There are currently two options available to the photographer wishing to explore *filmless photography*–electronic (motion or still) and digital. Electronic photography includes camcorders, which use videotape to record motion imagery, as well as electronic still video cameras, which use a 2-inch magnetic floppy disc to record up to 25 frames of video information. In both cases visual information is stored as analog video signals.

Frame capture cards are integrated circuit boards that can be attached to an expansion slot on the computer's main circuit board. These cards are designed to accept the electrical voltages that constitute a video signal and convert those voltages to digital information. These boards typically can process a number of video signal formats including NTSC, PAL, SECAM, S-Video, and component RGB. As a rule, video images that have been digitized using a frame capture card will be of lesser quality than images made with a digital camera system using an area array CCD. This is due to the lack of spatial and brightness resolution inherent in analog video.

Modem A *modem* (short for modulate/demodulate) is a device that allows two computers to communicate with each other over ordinary telephone lines. The digital information from the originating (sending) computer is modulated as a series of pulses (similar to the early telegraph using Morse code). The receiving computer uses its modem to demodulate the incoming pulses back into digital information.

Large mainframe computers can be set up as clearing houses of information that anyone with a microcomputer and a modem can access. Bulletin board services and information networks such as Compuserve, America On-Line, and Prodigy offer their subscribers far-reaching services that include such things as access to research libraries, electronic mail, public forums for the exchange of ideas, airline reservations, banking services, stock market quotes, and shopping. While a majority of this information is text-based, photographers, particularly photo-journalists, are also making use of this technology. Digital images can be sent all over the world instantly, without the photo-processing delays associated with traditional wire services.

The speed at which information can be sent is referred to as the *baud rate*. Baud rates associated with microcomputer modems start at 300 bits per second (bps) and go as high as 9600 bps. Baud rates of 1200 or 2400 bps are acceptable for communicating text-based information. Visual information, particularly digital colour photographs, contains significantly larger amounts of data and requires much higher baud rates in order to send this type of information in a reasonable amount of time. The current limits as to how fast computer data can be sent via modems is related to the bandwidth limits of present telephone systems.

PROCESSING Input devices provide the computer with raw material (data) that must be gathered, organized, and manipulated to create useful output. Computer processing is accomplished with software programs that provide a set of procedures and instructions that direct hardware components to gather raw data, structure it in ways that will allow the software to further manipulate and use the information, and finally save that information in formats that can be used later by a variety of output devices.

Central Processing Unit The central processing unit (CPU) is the heart of any computer. The term *CPU* is often used to describe the *black box* to which all input and output peripherals are connected. More accurately, the CPU is the microprocessor contained in a single integrated circuit chip. The vast majority of today's microcomputers use chips made by one of two manu-facturers. IBM PCs and compatibles use one of the following

Intel microprocessors: 8086, 80286, 80386, or 80486. The Apple Macintosh uses one of the following Motorola microprocessors: 68000, 68020, 68030, or 68040. These processors have been listed in order of technological advancement and performance with the 80486 and the 68040 representing the most advanced chip technology. The CPU is responsible for executing software instructions that manipulate computer data. The CPU's performance is given a rating based on the number of instructions it can execute in a given period of time. Ratings as high as 20 million instructions per second (mips) are possible on some systems using the "486" and "040" microprocessors.

Two factors that influence the CPUs mips rating are clock speed and data architecture. In order to coordinate all the discrete actions taken by the CPU, timing circuitry is used. Activities are timed and sequenced, creating a processing cycle. A computer's clock speed refers to the number of processing cycles per second that can be performed by the system. The frequency of CPU processing cycles (clock speed) can range anywhere from 8 to 50 megahertz *(MHz)*. The other factor affecting the CPU's performance is the data architecture used by the system. Digital information is a string of ones and zeros. Each digit in the string is referred to as a *data bit*. Large strings of bits are grouped into manageable bundles or units called *bytes*. Eight bits make up a data byte. A system's data architecture refers to how the computer organizes and processes these bytes for any one processing cycle. Microcomputers use either an 8-bit (1 byte), 16-bit (2 byte) or 32-bit (4 byte) architecture. Obviously, the number of bits involved in any one processing cycle, combined with the number of cycles that can be performed in a given time will determine the system's processing speed. Speed becomes an important consideration when a computer is used for image capture, manipulation, and output because of the huge amount of data needed to represent the image.

Data Bus A computer's data bus refers to the electrical connections and pathways between the CPU and all other system components. In most cases the data bus represents the primary bottleneck to data processing. The CPU can execute instructions much faster than the data can be moved between components and in most cases they must be programmed to wait for the data to catch up. The need for ever increasing processing speeds has led to the fact that future generations of computers will probably use light rather than electrical energy simply because electrons can't move fast enough to keep up with the anticipated capabilities of future CPUs.

Computer Memory Computer memory refers to those components that store data either temporarily, while being gathered, structured, and manipulated, or long term, once the data has been organized into its final form, ready for output. One of the specifications often cited is a computer's memory capacity and it is an important consideration for systems that will be used to manipulate visual information. Memory capacity is expressed in terms of the number of bytes of information it can store. Storage capacities are measured in kilobytes, megabytes, and gigabytes where 1 kilobyte equals a thousand bytes, 1 megabyte equals a million bytes, and 1 gigabyte equals a billion bytes.

Random-Access Memory *Random-access memory* (RAM) is used to temporarily store data while it is being processed by the system. It represents the computer's work area and the storage capacity set aside for this function is an important factor in how efficiently the system works. The act of placing data in memory is referred to as *writing to memory*. Obtaining information from memory is known as *reading from memory*. RAM memory is said to be volatile. Volatile memory will store data only as long as there is current applied to the circuitry. When the system is turned off, this temporary memory is lost. A computer must be configured with enough RAM memory to store operating system instructions and application software instructions, as well as the input data that will be manipulated by the software. For text-based applications such as word processing, spreadsheets, and databases, a megabyte of RAM is usually adequate. For applications designed to work with graphic design and visual information, it is not uncommon to need 8 to 12 megabytes of RAM storage to efficiently gather and manipulate data.

Read-Only Memory As its name suggests, *read-only memory* (ROM) cannot have data written to it as part of normal system operation. Data that are stored in ROM are installed when the chip is manufactured. ROM memory chips typically contain frequently used instructions and subroutines related to the operating system. ROM is an example of nonvolatile memory storage. Data in nonvolatile memory are stored permanently and it does not require electrical current to maintain the data.

Storage Memory Storage memory is often confused with the RAM and ROM memory used to process data. Storage memory involves using a variety of digital recording techniques and media to store and distribute software programs and the files those programs create. There are currently two methods being used to record data for later playback—magnetic and optical.

Magnetic systems mechanically position a write/read (record/playback) head to specific locations over a spinning disk of magnetic recording medium. Magnetic patterns of changing polarity are captured in much the same way as information is captured when making a recording to magnetic audio or video tape. In playback, magnetic polar patterns are read as the on/off patterns that represent the digital information presented during recording.

Optical systems use microscopic points of laser light to pit the surface of a reflective disk with burn marks that scatter rather than reflect light. To read back the information, the disk is spun in front of a laser light source. The pattern of burn marks breaks the beam of reflected light, causing it to pulse in a series of on-and-off patterns that the computer processes as binary data.

Important factors to consider in evaluating storage memory include total storage capacity, data access time, and data transfer rates. As a general rule, for photographers using a computer to manipulate visual information, the more storage capacity, the better. A single full-colour image can require 20-30 megabytes of storage. Data access time, measured in milliseconds, refers to how long it takes the storage device to locate all the specific pieces of data needed for a particular file. Data transfer rate refers to how fast data can be read from the storage device and presented to the CPU for processing. This rate, expressed in kilobytes per second, is related to the data architecture of the system.

Floppy Disks Floppy disks are computer storage media made from flexible disks of magnetic recording material very similar to material used in audio and video recording tape. The disk is mounted in a cardboard or plastic housing that protects it from dust and dirt. Floppy disks are available in 5-1/4 and 3-1/2-inch sizes. Floppy disk drives often use a serial data exchange method and have relatively slow access times, making them a fairly slow storage and retrieval method. Depending on how the disk is manufactured and the type of magnetic recording material used, a disk will use either a double-sided, double-density or high-density design. To be used, the disk must first be formatted. Formatting establishes specific regions on the disk where magnetic information can be recorded and later played back. Depending on the drive mechanism and how system software formats the disk, a floppy disk may be able to store 400 Kbytes, 720 Kbytes, 800 Kbytes, 1.2 Mbytes, 1.4 Mbytes, or 2.8 Mbytes of data.

Hard Disk Hard disk drives use a series of rigid platters that can be recorded to (write) and played back from (read) in much the same way as a floppy disk. The plates used in these drives have a much greater capacity to store information than do floppy disks. Hard disks' storage capacities can range anywhere from 20 megabytes to 4 gigabytes. Hard disks use parallel data exchange methods and use drive mechanisms that have data access times as fast as 15 milliseconds. This makes the hard disk drive one of fastest data storage and retrieval systems available.

Removable Hard Disk The removable hard disk is very similar in design to the fixed hard disk. The major difference is that the rigid magnetic platter is contained in a plastic housing that can be removed. This gives the user the ability to expand storage capacity by buying additional removable disks, using them the same way as floppy disks. Another difference is that the removable hard disk can store significantly more data. There are several removable disk designs that allow for storage capacities of 44, 88, or 90 megabytes. The access and read/write times for removable disks fall in the range of 50 to 100 milliseconds.

Compact Disk Read-Only Memory *Compact disk read only memory* (CD-ROM) storage offers an alternative to the magnetic recording process used with floppy and hard disks. The same technology used to distribute audio recordings in the form of compact discs, is used to record and distribute computer data. This method allows data to be written only once but read back as often as needed. Thus, the acronym WORM (Write Once, Read Many) is frequently used to describe this technology. CD-ROM offers large storage capacity in an easily distributed format; typically 650 megabytes of data, equivalent to 300,000 typewritten pages of text information, can be stored on a 4 1/2-inch compact disk. Data stored on a CD-ROM is much less likely to be damaged because the storage medium is not susceptible to extraneous magnetic energies that can destroy data nor the mechanical actions of a magnetic read/write head moving over the surface of the recording medium. The one drawback to CD-ROM is that the inherent access time and data transfer rate makes it one of the slowest forms of data storage available.

Magneto-optical Magneto-optical (MO) storage utilizes a combination of magnetic and optical technology to produce a system that can provide 125 megabytes of read/write storage on a disk the size of a 3 1/2-inch floppy. Some MO disks can store in excess of 1 gigabyte of data and, even though they have slower data exchange rates, they offer the same utility as a removable hard drive with ten times the capacity.

OUTPUT Computer output reverses the analog-to-digital processes of input to display to output devices, in an analog form, the results of computer processing.

Digital-to-Analog Conversion Digital-to-analog (D/A) conversion is the process by which the string of binary numbers resulting from data processing operations is converted into electrical voltages. There are a variety of output devices that can respond to these voltages to present information in the form of sight and sound.

Monitors/Video Cards Video display monitors provide immediate feedback as the user interacts with the system and, in some cases, also provide the final output. Depending on the application being used, video display requirements can be as simple as a monochromatic cathode ray tube. The vast majority of today's computer systems use colour video monitors to support programs designed to generate and display full-colour graphic information. Some systems may limit the number of colours that can be displayed at any one time–typically 256 colours. This is more than adequate for most applications. Photographers, however, will often require video systems that can display full-colour images containing millions of specific colours. The display capabilities of a computer monitor will be determined by special video interface circuitry, usually contained in an expansion card attached to the computer's main circuit board. Video display cards allow users to customize a system to their particular needs. The card will determine the number of colours that can be displayed, the type of video signal used (usually noninterlaced RGB), and the resolution characteristic of the display.

Printers The majority of tangible computer output will come from some form of printer. A variety of systems are used to apply ink, dye, and toner to paper including daisy wheel, dot matrix, inkjet, and thermal dye sublimation. Few systems, however, have had as much impact on the use of computers for visual communications as the laser printer. Using the principles of an electrostatic copier, the laser printer uses a beam of laser light to electrostatically charge areas on a piece of paper that correspond to the image being rendered. Magnetically charged toner is attracted to these areas and heat-fused to the paper, producing a high-resolution line image. Laser printers typically have resolutions of 300 dots per inch or greater and can replicate limited gray scales using halftone dot patterns. This output technology has spawned the desktop publishing industry and, with the advent of colour laser copiers, represents tremendous opportunity for photographers to become involved with using computers as a tool to create and display their work.

Halftone Output If photographers are going to have their work seen by the masses, they will, at some point, be involved with the halftone printing process. The computer is having a major impact on how images are published. Desktop publishing, electronic prepress, and proofing operations have now made it possible to take a digital file containing photographic images and go directly to the printing press, bypassing traditional photographic processes.

While this technology has been available in the printing industry for some time, it is now becoming available to personal computer users. As a result, photographers will have significantly greater control in getting their work into print.

Contone Output Continuous-tone colour output from a computer file is accomplished in one of two ways. The first uses a heat-transfer technology known as dye-sublimation printing. In this system, transparent yellow, magenta, and cyan dyes are transferred to special receiver paper creating 11 x 11-inch prints with a resolution of 300 dots per inch. In many cases these prints can rival the quality obtained using traditional photographic processes.The second method uses a film recorder to make a photograph of the image as it is formed on a high-resolution monochromatic cathode ray tube. Using additive colour principles, the image is formed by making three exposures through red, green, and blue filters. Film recorders are capable of very high resolutions, offering one of the best methods for producing colour negatives and transparences from digital files.

COMPUTER-TO-PLATE SYSTEMS
Photomechanical reproduction printing systems that use digital plates.

CONSTANT ANGULAR VELOCITY (CAV) A record/playback technique for the encoding and reading of data on a laser disc. CAV maintains constant disc rotational speed to enhance access time to randomly stored frames.

CONSTANT LINEAR VELOCITY (CLV) A record/playback technique for the encoding and reading of data on a laser disc. In CLV-type disc players the speed for the disc changes so that the track velocity is constant, thus increasing storage capacity. Such a design is appropriate for motion picture storage and display.

CONTOURING In electronic imaging, an unwanted effect whereby smooth gradations of tone in the original are imaged as a series of stepped tones (similar to posterization) due to an insufficient number of quantizing levels or faulty information processing.

CONTRAST The variation between two or more parts of an object or image with respect to any of various attributes such as luminance, density, colour, or size. Examples of subjective descriptions of contrast include low contrast (or flat), high contrast (or contrasty), and normal contrast, terms that are variously applied to photographic subjects, lighting, film, developer, printing paper, and prints. Examples of objective measurements of contrast include a 3:1 lighting ratio, a 160:1 scene luminance ratio, a 3.0 log exposure range, and a print density range of 2.0. Ratios with conventional numbers correspond to differences when the numbers are converted to logarithms, so that a luminous ratio of 100:1 corresponds to a log luminance range of 2.0 (2.0-0.0). Other measures of tonal contrast include gamma and contrast index, which are based on the slopes of straight lines on *D*-log *H* graphs, where a value of 1.0 represents the slope of a line at an angle of 45 degrees to a horizontal line.

We should make a distinction between local contrast and overall contrast in photographic images. In terms of the characteristic curve of a printing paper, the local contrast varies for subject tones represented on the straight line and on different parts of the toe and the shoulder, which correspond to the middle, highlight, and shadow subject tones, respectively. This difference is especially pronounced in prints that are commonly described as being too contrasty. In such a print the middle tones are contrasty but the lightest highlight and darkest shadow areas typically have no detail and therefore no local contrast.

The perceived contrast of a given photograph can change dramatically with changes in viewing conditions. It is well known that a print appears darker when it is viewed with a white surround than with a black surround, a perceptual effect known as *simultaneous contrast,* and also when it is viewed under a low level of illuminance, with corresponding changes in local or overall contrast. The contrast of a colour transparency appears to be much higher when it is viewed by transmitted light in an otherwise darkened room than when the room lights are on or the area around the transparency on the illuminator is not masked off, due to simultaneous contrast and the effects of flare with a light surround.

CONTRAST CONTROL There are a number of ways of altering tonal contrast when photographing a subject, including changing the lighting on the subject. In studio situations, a fill light is commonly used near the camera to lighten shadows created by a main light. A lighting ratio of 3:1 is considered appropriate for most formal portraits, for example, but higher and lower ratios are used for different effects. Outdoors there is less control, but electronic flash can be used to reduce the lighting ratio by filling in shadows created by direct sunlight for subjects that are relatively close. For more distant subjects, such as landscapes and buildings, it may be necessary to select a different time of the day, or a day on which the weather conditions are different to obtain a less contrasty lighting effect.

DISPLAY Viewing conditions can have a significant effect on the appearance of density and contrast of a photograph,

Increasing the illumination level on a normal print tends to make the print appear to be too light overall with a decrease in detail and contrast in the highlights. A low level of illumination tends to make the print appear to be too dark overall with a decrease in detail and contrast in the shadows. However, a print that has been printed slightly darker displayed under a higher-than-normal level of illumination appears to have a greater range of tones than a print having normal density displayed under normal room illumination.

Slides and motion pictures projected on a screen in a darkened room appear more contrasty than when there is ambient light in the room, because the ambient light lightens the dark areas proportionally more than the light areas and because the dark surround in the darkened room produces a simultaneous contrast perceptual effect.

COLOUR MATERIALS With colour materials the best way to control contrast is to control both the lighting ratio and the colour temperature. Little can be done during development without destroying the colour balance of the print or transparency. Care in how the prints are mounted and displayed will have an effect on contrast; colour temperature, light level, and surround are also important.

VIDEO INDOORS The first step in video contrast control is the same as that in photography: adjust the lighting of the scene to be videographed to match the recording system. In a studio situation, control is accomplished by adjusting the light level and adjusting the camera to a white level of 100% and a black level of 75%. A waveform monitor (a video lightmeter) that displays luminance values on an oscilloscope is used to make these adjustments. After adjustment is made for luminances, colour balance is established by adjusting the gain for rgb (red, green, blue) phosphors to a black level and then to a white level, and usually balancing for a flesh tone.

VIDEO OUTDOORS Adjusting overall contrast when videographing outdoors can be done by using fill-in lighting in the shadow areas to reduce contrast. Additional limited control can be done in-camera by reducing the white level to compress contrast or by *white clipping* to eliminate whites that are beyond the camera's recordable range. At one time these adjustments had to be performed manually, but now they are done automatically. In situations where the light level is too low and there is a danger of severely underexposing, it is possible to *push* the sensitivity of the video camera system by boosting the gain to maximum. As in photography, when you push film speed the result is weak, muddy shadows and graininess (noise).

The videographer can also control contrast by using the gamma correction circuit and the edge enhancement circuit, both of which are built into the camera. The edge enhancer is an electronic device that sharpens the video image by exaggerating the luminance transition between light and dark areas in the picture. This is analogous to the so-called adjacency or border effect in photography that produces an increase in sharpness by exaggerating the density differences at the edges of an image.

Video Display Contrast, brightness, and colour controls are also available on TV/video receivers and monitors. As with photographs, ambient light and lightness of the surround affect the appearance of contrast.

Electronic Still Photography The ultimate in contrast control of both tone and colour can be achieved by combining photographic and electronic systems. The photograph (print, transparency, or negative) can be scanned, digitized, manipulated with a computer software program, and then printed out using any of a variety of printing systems, including photographic. Image definition in the print, depending upon the system used, can approach that of an original photograph.

Books: Mathias, Harry, and Patterson, Richard, *Electronic cinematography* Belmont, Calif.: Wadsworth, 1985.

CONTRAST RESOLUTION In electronic imaging, the brightness range that the digitizer is capable of representing. This is also referred to as pixel depth, the number of bits that each pixel is capable of holding. The number of bits determines the number of gray levels that will represent the image.

COPROCESSOR In computers, the use for a special chip on the motherboard or other special board to speed up graphics and mathematics-intensive applications. The use of coprocessors is extremely important in rendering two- and three-dimensional design work.

COPY (1) A reproduction of a two-dimensional image. (2) The act of making a reproduction of a two-dimensional image. (3) In the graphic arts, any image (including photographs, drawings, paintings, and text) that is to be reproduced. (4) With an analog image such as a photograph or videograph, there is a loss of information when copies are made. Copies of digital images suffer essentially no loss (only 10^{-12}).

CRASH In computers, a slang term meaning to bring the computer to a nonfunctional state. Typically, the computer is unable to recognize any event and it cannot respond in any way. The usual way out of this stalemate situation is to reboot the computer.

CRISPENER In electronic imaging, a feature that sharpens unsharp image edges
See also: *Sharpness*.

CROPPING Altering the boundaries of an image. The trimming of a print or of an image to improve the composition. Usually applied to: (1) areas of a scene included by the camera; (2) area of a negative or transparency included on a print; (3) trimming or masking of a finished print or transparency; (4) the reproduction of a selected part of a photograph.

CRT See *Cathode-ray tube*.

CT MERGE In electronic imaging, the function of combining the files of two continuous-tone images to provide a smooth transition between the images.

CURSOR A symbol, such as a cross or blinking line or block, that locates on the monitor the insertion point where an action, such as cutting and pasting or the input, is to begin or conclude.

CUT-AND-PASTE A computer operation that is analogous to a scissors-and-glue operation with paper used on an image or text. More sophisticated programs are beginning to replace cut-and-paste with select-and-drag operations that perform the same function but more quickly and visibly.

CYCLE (l) An interval of space or time in which is completed one round of events or phenomena that recur regularly and in the same sequence. In photography, the term *cycle is* most commonly applied to processes, spatial frequencies, and temporal frequencies of electromagnetic radiation. For example, a processing machine may take 5 minutes to complete a specific sequence of processing steps; a camera may be able to resolve 50 cycles (light/dark line pairs) per millimeter; or a photon may have a frequency of 10^{15} cycles per second (see *Hertz)*. (2) In animation photography, a cycle is a series of drawings arranged so that the first drawing can be used after the last for a continuous repetition of the action as long as needed.

DATABASE In computers, the holding of information in an electronic form in a cross-referenced structured format that allows for rapid retrieval and cross-referring. Large databases are used for a variety of data-intensive fields. Some multimedia applications use databases as the referencing tools to rapidly access and display visual data.

DDL See *Digital delay line*.

DEBLURRING In computers, when an image is blurred from either linear motion in a specific direction or from a lack of depth of field, the image sharpness may be restored by deblurring techniques such as the use of a Wiener filter.

DECIBEL Abbreviated dB. Literally, one-tenth of a Bel. The use of the term decibel means that logarithmic scaling of the amplitude of a quantity divided by a reference amplitude has been employed. Such scaling is useful because the range of amplitudes encountered in sound is extremely large and because hearing judges relative loudness of two sounds by the ratio of their intensities, which is logarithmic behaviour. Differing factors are used when applying decibels to various quantities so that the number of decibels remains constant; 3dB is always 3dB, although it represents twice as much power, but only 1.414 times as much voltage.

For reference, 3dB is twice as much power, 6dB is twice as much voltage, and twice the perceived loudness is reached between 6 and 10dB depending on the experiment used. Thus, as much as nine times the sound power is required to make a sound twice as loud.

Because the use of the term *decibel* implies a ratio, the reference quantity must be stated. Some typical ones are:

dB SPL	referred to threshold of hearing at 1 kHz
dBm	reference 1 milliwatt, usually in 600 ohms
dBV	reference 1 volt
dBu	reference 0.7746 volts

DECODER A device that takes in composite video and decodes the signal information into separate signals for picture (RGB), sync, and timing. Decoders may be used to input video into a computer when sync signals are weak or when picture signals need boosting in a particular channel.

DEFECTIVE COLOUR VISION An abnormal physiological condition characterized by a chronic reduced ability to detect hue differences between certain colours.

DEFINITION A general term identifying the microcharacteristics of an image, as distinct from the characteristics of larger areas that are associated with tone reproduction—such as those presented in D-log H curves. Image definition of photographic images is a combination of the more specific subjective characteristics—sharpness, detail, and graininess—or the corresponding objective characteristics—accutance, resolving power, and granularity. These characteristics can be evaluated subjectively at different criteria levels by examining the image at a normal viewing distance, at close range through a magnifier, and through a microscope. Objectively, resolving power is measured by examining the image of a test target consisting of parallel black bars on a white background and identifying the smallest set where the bars are still discernible. The results are recorded as lines/mm, for example, 100 lines/mm. Acutance and granularity are measured by scanning suitable test images with a mathematical interpretation to the resulting data. The highest definition results with a combination of low granularity and solving power and acutance. The separate characteristics are not completely independent, however. An increase in granularity, tends to have an adverse effect on resolving power and acutance.

Definition. Two photographs of a single test pattern made with types of spread function giving low sharpness and high resolution (left), and high sharpness and low resolution (right). Source: Applied Optics, vol. 3, no. 1, 1964).

The concept of definition can be applied to other than photograph images, such as photomechanical and video images, although some of the terms and units of measurement are different. (Electronic enhancement to improve resolution in a hard copy can in some cases, reduce sharpness.)

DENSITY A measure of the light-absorbing characteristics of an area of a photographic image, filter, etc. Density is defined as the common logarithm of the ratio of the light received by the sample to that transmitted or reflected by the sample. $D = \log (I_0/I)$, where D is the density, I_0 is the illuminance (light level) on the sample, and I is the illuminance falling on the receptor after being affected by the sample.

There are very many types of photographic density, depending on the optical system used in the measuring instrument (the densitometer), the type of image (negative or positive, neutral or coloured) and the colour of light used in the measuring instrument (densitometer).

DENSITY-LOG EXPOSURE CURVE See *Characteristic curve*.

DENSITY RANGE The difference between the densities of the lightest and darkest areas in a photographic image. For a negative, the density range is a measure of the total contrast of the image and is related to the scale index (tolerable logH range) of the appropriate printing material. For a positive, the density range is a measure of the extent to which subject tones, from the darkest shadow to the lightest highlight, may be reasonably well recorded.

DENSITY SCALE The range of transmission densities (in negatives and transparencies) or reflection densities (in prints) from unexposed areas to the maximum density (nonreversal materials) or the minimum density (reversal materials) the material can produce. That portion of the density scale that is of practical use in printmaking is called the *useful density scale*.

DERIVATION Any of various special effects achieved by abstracting one or more attributes from an original photograph, thereby reducing realism. Example: making two reproductions from an original colour photograph, one abstracting contour lines and the other abstracting colour (but eliminating lightness differences), and then superimposing the two abstractions to form the final image.

DESKTOP PUBLISHING In graphic arts reproduction, a compact publishing system that includes a personal computer, word processor, plate makeup, illustration and other software, PostScript page description language, and imagesetter to produce halftone films.

DEVICE INDEPENDENT COLOUR A classification of PC-based electronic colour imaging systems.

DIASCOPE An overhead optical projector for showing enlarged screen images of transparencies or diapositives. Some overhead projectors have a scrollable plastic film roll onto which a lecturer can write notes, make diagrams and highlight information with special water-soluble markers. There are special video output cards in computers that send the computer screen image to a liquid-crystal display unit mounted on an overhead projector. This liquid-crystal display can then be projected onto a screen in order to show the computer screen image to an audience.

Syn.: *Overhead projector*.

DIGITAL In a measuring instrument (for example thermometer, densitometer), a display of the measured values as numbers, as distinct from the position of a pointer of a scale or a fluid level. The use of digital instruments reduces human error. Contrast with *analog*.

DIGITAL AUDIO A method of representing signals electronically and on various media that employs conversion from the analog domain into the digital one through the use of two processes: sampling and quantization. The forte of digital audio is replication—a copy is potentially not degraded in any way; rather, it can be considered to be a clone of the original source. Thus, mass production can be used to bring many users copies that are audibly indistinguishable from the original master. (Analog audio recording inevitably brings some degradation generation by generation because of imperfections in the analogy between the representation of the audio on a medium and the actual audio, but analog audio still predominates in many areas.)

Sampling is the process of capturing the amplitude of the signal at regular intervals quickly enough so that the desired audio signal is completely represented. The sampling theorem states that this process must occur at least somewhat more frequently than twice each cycle of the audio to be represented, so popular sampling frequencies have become 32 kHz (some broadcast links, especially in Europe), 44.1 kHz (consumer audio, including compact disc), and 48 kHz (professional audio).

The heart of digital audio is quantization. This is a process *of combining,* or measuring the amplitude of each sample in order to represent it as a set of numbers. Then, the numbers are combined with additional numbers used to provide protection against errors and to tailor the stream of resulting numbers for a specific purpose such as for a medium before recording or transmission. Some issues relevant to this process are the basic method, the number of bins, the regularity of the bins, and the deliberate addition of small amounts of noise called *dither* that acts to smooth the transitions across the bin boundaries.

See also: *Analog audio.*

DIGITAL DELAY LINE A method of producing a time delay of an audio or video signal, by converting from analog to digital representation at the input of the device, delaying by means of digital memory, and subsequent conversion from digital to analog representation at the output. Delay lines have many uses in both audio and video signal processing. In audio, the output of the delay is added together with the original signal to produce a range of effects from "thickening" of a voice to discrete echoes. In video, one-line delay lines are used for many purposes, including colour decoding of composite video signals.

DIGITAL EDITING See *Digital image.*

DIGITAL HALFTONE A halftone produced on a digital

device such as a laser printer. Typically the dot size is fixed by the resolution of the printer (300 dpi). The digital halftoning creates the effect of variable size by the process of dithering. The dithering process creates a cluster of two or more dots and varies the percentage of black dots in order to achieve a gray tone. A typical 300 dpi laser printer can produce a dithered cluster of 4 x 4 cells and achieve a halftone resolution of 75 dpi. However, the number of gray levels is a product of the cluster. In this example, the number of gray tones is 16 (4 x 4). If the number of required tones is increased, then the resolution (dpi) decreases.

DIGITAL IMAGE An image that is represented by discrete numerical values organized in a two-dimensional array. The conversion of images into a digital form is known as digital imaging. Hence, manipulation of the image in digital form is called digital editing, retouching, enhancement, and so on.

DIGITAL IMAGE BACK See *Camera, digital types imaging camera, electronic still camera.*

DIGITAL-IMAGING CAMERA See *Camera types.*

DIGITAL PHOTOGRAPHY For the past decade, the goal of digital photography has been to develop affordable capture, edit, and display systems that will compete with the quality of traditional silver halide processes. Some would argue that in the past several years that goal has been met. Others will note that with every advancement made on the digital side, advancements with silver halides keep raising the stakes. In either case, the accomplishments in digital technology must be recognized. In many areas, the image quality issue has been addressed to the point that digital photography not only competes with silver-based imaging, but it offers advantages that surpass traditional techniques. The photographer needs to be aware of these advantages and applications where digital imaging offers a better alternative for a given project.

There are three basic avenues available to the photographer wishing to explore digital photography's creative potential. The first involves using one of several electronic still-video camera systems to make photographs as with any other camera. In this system the image is stored as a video signal recorded to a 2-inch still video floppy disc. Once captured, the video signal is converted to a digital format through the use of a frame capture card. Another option is the use of a digital camera system that retrofits standard 35-mm and medium-format cameras to convert light energy directly to digital information at the instant the shutter is released. These data are stored to a portable hard disk for later manipulation by the computer. Existing silver-based images can also be converted to digital form with a flat bed or film scanner. These devices make digital copies of prints, slides, or negatives, resulting in some of the highest-quality digital images currently available.

The image quality produced by these methods can be classified as:

Scans of silver halide images—best
Digital camera systems—good
Electronic still video—fair to poor

In each method the analog-to-digital conversion process is accomplished through the use of a charge-coupled device (CCD). A CCD is an integrated circuit chip made up of thousands of pieces of light-sensitive semiconductor material. The spatial resolution of the image is directly related to the number of individual semiconductors that can be placed on the CCD chip. The CCD chip converts light energy falling on the chip to electrical voltage that is then converted to digital information using A/D circuitry. Current manufacturing techniques makes it very difficult to produce CCD chips in large quantities with enough pixel density to match the detail produced by silver halide films.

Resolution When evaluating digital-imaging capabilities, there are several areas of image resolution that must be addressed. Spatial resolution refers to the number of discrete points of picture information contained in a given area. The *pixel,* short for picture element, is the unit used to describe the smallest discrete point used in constructing a digital image. The number of pixels in a given area will be used to describe a system's spatial resolution; usually expressed as PPI (pixels per inch). Because digital images have a two dimensional aspect ratio of height and width, an image's spatial resolution will be expressed as a two-dimensional grid, for example, 2048 x 1365 PPI. In this case the image would consist of approximately 2.8 million points of picture information.

As a generalization, digital image files containing between 2.5 to 3.5 million pixels of visual information are thought to have a spatial resolution comparable to 35-mm negative film. It is difficult to make direct comparisons of equivalent resolutions between film and digital files. There are a number of variables that must be considered in measuring a system's resolving capability and in some instances, measurements can't be applied equally to both systems.

Brightness resolution refers to the number of gray levels that can be assigned to each pixel. Digital photography uses a binary numbering system to represent values (a string of digits made up of ones and zeros). Each digit in the binary string is referred to as a *bit.* The more digits contained in a binary string, the greater the number of specific values that can be assigned using that string. For example, a binary string containing only one digit would only be able to express two values (1 and 0). Two digits in the string could represent four values and so on. It is common when describing a system's brightness resolution to express it in terms of the number of binary bits used to assign brightness values. Therefore, a system that has an 8-bit brightness resolution has the ability to assign one of 256 shades of gray for any one pixel in the scene. This is more than adequate in dealing with the gray scales associated with black-and-white images. In the case of full-colour photographic images, a digital photography system will need a brightness resolution of 24 bits. This will allow any combination of 256 shades of red, green, and blue to be assigned to any one pixel in the scene, resulting in over 16 million possible colours.

Photometric accuracy is a way of describing how accurately a digitally assigned gray level represents the actual brightness level in the scene at a given pixel location. This characteristic is primarily a function of how well a CCD chip converts light energy into electrical voltage and how accurately the analog-to-digital circuitry converts that voltage into a binary number.

Memory Requirements A high-resolution digital image will require a significant amount of memory for data capture, image processing, and file storage. A high-resolution digital image is considered to be any image with a horizontal resolution of 2,000 PPI or more. To figure the memory requirements needed to work with such an image, multiply the number of pixels times the image's brightness resolution (expressed in bytes where 8 bits = 1 byte). In the case of a full-colour 35-mm image (24 bit brightness resolution) the file size would be calculated to be 2048 x 1365 pixels x 3 bytes of brightness resolution which equals 8.4 megabytes. This would represent the minimum memory capacity needed to store the image. In addition, many image-processing programs will require that additional storage space be maintained on the system's hard disk for the purposes of temporarily storing data for computation and to store backup copies of information to allow the user to undo certain procedures. Free workspace requirements on the hard drive can be as high as three times the file size, which in our example would be 25 megabytes.

Photo CD Photo CD has the potential to have a profound effect on a photographer's introduction to digital image making and may be instrumental in the transition from silver halide to the digital technologies of the future. Photo CD allows the photographer to use traditional photographic materials, scan the resulting images to create digital photographs, and store up to 100 of these images on a compact disc. Although the technology is being marketed for consumer use, its first impact will be felt in the areas of professional design, photography, and desktop publishing. The proliferation of photographic images in desktop publishing documents could represent new markets for photographers. The ability to conveniently distribute portfolios, to organize, catalogue, and market stock images, to organize and choreograph images to music, to create marketing and training material, and to allow viewers to interact with these images are just a few of the advantages this technology offers the photographer.

DIGITAL PLATES Printing plates made directly from digital data.

DIGITAL PRINTING Printing from digitally produced printing plates.

DIGITAL RECORDING Any method of recording, on tape, disc, or film, that uses digital audio.

DIGITAL RETOUCHING See *Digital image*.

DIGITAL (SOUND) A signal that has been converted to numerical representation by means of quantizing the amplitude domain of the signal (putting amplitudes into bins, each bin called by a number). This means that for each amplitude a number is derived for storage or transmission. The advantage of digital is that to the extent the numbers are incorruptible by way of error-protecting coding, the signal will be recovered within the limits of the original quantizing process, despite how many generations or transmission paths are encountered by the signal.

DIGITAL-TO-ANALOG CONVERTER (DAC) In computers, a component that converts digital data to analog information. Many cathode-ray tubes (CRTs) are analog driven devices. For the computer to display the image, the data must be changed from the digital domain to voltage in the analog world. Many A/D boards are also D/A boards. Targa boards, among other capture/display boards, contain both an A/D circuit and a D/A circuit.

DIGITAL VIDEO The images displayed by the monitor are digital representations held by and displayed through the computer. Such an approach to video gives opportunity to the manufacturing of *intelligent* television at high-definition levels.

DIGITIZER The device that converts analog data into digital data. The analog data are sampled and quantized. The number of bits that the digitizer is capable of quantizing determines the number of gray levels captured by the digitizer. An 8-bit digitizer can digitize 256 levels of brightness.

DIRECT CURRENT (DC, dc) Electrical current that flows in one direction only, as distinguished from alternating current, which periodically reverses direction. The abbreviation DC, or dc, is invariably used to describe a voltage whose polarity does not reverse, e.g., dc voltage.

DIRECT DIGITAL COLOUR PROOF Colour proofs made directly from digital data.

DIRECTORY A listing of the addresses of the files held on floppy and hard disks. The directory directs the computer to the file. Directories hold subdirectories and files. They are the basis for a hierarchical filing system for storing files.

DISC A thin, circular plate used to record information. Although disc and disk are sometimes treated as synonyms, disc is normally used for compact-disc (CD) audio recordings, electronic and film disc cameras, disc film, and the discs used in the Kodak Photo CD system, whereas disk is normally used in computer contexts such as floppy disk (or diskette), hard disk, and disk drive.

DISK Generically, the platter of magnetically coated material that stores data for the computer. These disks are interchangeable among computers of similar type. Software exists that allows for the reading of floppy disks across platforms. Data are recorded serially in concentric circles called tracks. Disks come in several sizes and density capacities. Originally, the flexible or floppy disk was 8 inches in diameter and held more than 360+ kilobytes of data on a single side. The current standard for most machines is 3 1/2 inches in diameter, double-sided, high-density with a capacity of 1.44 megabytes of data. Also available are 3 1/2-inch disks with capacities of 2.88 megabytes, but these are not widely used, and they require special drives. Specially manufactured 3 1/2-inch disks are entering the market that are capable of storing 21 Mb and more. These require special disk drives.

DISK OPERATING SYSTEM (DOS) Personal computing is diskette-based and requires that system software, i.e., the instructions to the computer on what to do and how to operate stored in a form accessible to the computer. Early computers usually lacked hard drives and so a floppy diskette called the operating system diskette was used to store data, programs, and the computer operating system. Current usage has made the term DOS limited to describing the operating system of IBM-type platforms using Microsoft's operating system.

DITHERING In electronic imaging, the variation in the number of ink dots to represent a tone of gray. Dithering requires that a physical area with a known matrix of dots called a cell be established. For example, a cell may contain an 8 x 8 matrix. If all 64 locations are filled with ink dots, then the area appears black; if all 64 locations contain nothing, then the area appears white. Varying the number of filled and unfilled cells can give the perception of a tone of gray. Electronically adjacent pixels are turned on or off or are assigned different colours, thus creating the appearance of a tone of gray or another shade or colour.

DOT The individual element of a halftone.

DOT MATRIX PRINTER A printing device that uses pins to strike an inked ribbon against the paper to imprint a character. The characters are composed of tiny dots created by small pins mounted in the print head. The greater the number of points the finer the characters printed. Twenty-four pin dot matrix printers offer the highest, smoothest looking quality characters. These are often referred to as NLQ (near letter quality) printers.

DOTS PER INCH (DPI) A unit of measure of the resolution capability of an input device such as a scanner or an output device such as a laser printer.

DRAW A computer function of many software art programs that allows one to literally draw in a freehand fashion using a mouse or other pointing device as one would use a pen. Draw programs will save its drawing in either vector or raster formats.

DROPOUT (l) In printing, the loss of highlight dots or the elimination of highlight dots in halftone negatives using a supplementary exposure that results in highlights printing white without dots. (2) A momentary loss of signal, usually applied to audio or video signals recovered from a medium or transmission path. The signal loss may not be complete but may result only in a change in level.

DROP SHADOW A graphic effect that attempts to suggest a three-dimensional quality to a image by placing a shadow (gray or subdued tone) under and offset to either the left or right of the object or characters displayed.

DRUM SCANNER (1) An input scanner that produces spiral scanning patterns by rotating the original on a drum as the light source and sensor assembly moves horizontally. (2) A specific type of scanner that converts photographic images, reflection or transparency, to electronic signals. Unlike flatbed scanners, drum scanning systems contain a second drum that takes the electronic output of the first drum and produces colour separations. Drum scanners are the nexus of prepress colour separation activities.

DYNAMIC RANDOM-ACCESS MEMORY (DRAM)
The memory component of the computer. These chips hold data and instructions supplied by the software program in a quickly accessible state, thus reducing the need for the computer's central processing unit (CPU) to continually access the program disk. These chips hold data as long as there is power. Once the power is turned off the DRAM loses its contents.

DYNAMIC RANGE (SCANNER) The density range or output of electronic scanners.

EDGE DETECTION In electronic imaging, a convolution technique designed to determine local contrast (gray level) differences across some measure of homogeneity. The zone of change between two different regions is processed by an operator so that the zone itself is obvious.

ELECTRICAL CONDUCTIVITY The ability of a material to conduct current. Metals have good conductivity, insulators have very poor conductivity, semiconductors are inbetween. The influence of light on the conductivity of certain materials is important to the operation of photoconductive cells and to electrostatic photographic processes. Conductivity is the reciprocal of resistivity.

ELECTRICAL CURRENT (I) The flow of electrons in a conductor. The direction of electron flow is from the negative terminal of a source through the external circuit and back to its positive terminal. In the eighteenth century, long before the nature of the electron was known, scientists thought electricity to be some kind of fluid and that it flowed downhill from the plus terminal of a source through the external circuit to the negative terminal. This is the direction of what is even now called *conventional current flow*. Current, however defined, is directly proportional to the applied voltage and inversely proportional to the resistance of the circuit (Ohm's law). The symbol of current is I. The basic unit of current is the ampere.

ELECTRICAL ENERGY The capacity to do work by means of electricity. Electrical energy is equal to power multiplied by time. Common units of electrical energy are the watt-second and the kilowatt-hour. One watt-second is equal to 1 joule. Electric power companies bill their customers for the number of kilowatt-hours of energy they use.

ELECTRICAL POWER (P) The time rate of the production or consumption electrical energy; 1 joule per second equals 1 watt. The symbol for power is P. In dc circuits

$$P \text{ (watts)} = V \text{ (volts)} \times I \text{ (amperes)}.$$

In single-phase ac circuits, however,

$$\text{True } P \text{ (watts)} = V \text{ (volts)} \times I \text{ (amperes)} \times PF$$

where PF is the power factor, the cosine of the phase angle.

ELECTRIC CELL A device that converts chemical energy into electrical energy. At minimum, a cell consists of an anode, a cathode, and an electrolyte. An assembly of two or more cells is a battery, although a single cell is commonly, but imprecisely called a battery.

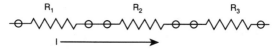

A series circuit has the same current (1) flowing through each element. Shown is a series circuit of three resistors: R_1, R_2, R_3.

ELECTRIC EYE (1) A photocell. (2) Identifying an automatic exposure-meter system that directly controls the aperture or shutter speed in response to light falling on a photocell.

ELECTRICITY A phenomenon occurring in nature based on the interaction of subatomic particles. In the Bohr model of the atom, electrons orbit around a nucleus consisting of protons and neutrons. The electrons carry a negative electrical charge, the protons carry an equal positive electrical charge, and the neutrons carry no charge. The number of protons in the nucleus is equal to the number of planetary electrons, rendering the atom itself neutral. The electrons are arranged in shells or energy levels; each level has a specific number of electrons it can accommodate. The outer, or valence, shell of an atom determines its electrical characteristics and how it will chemically react with other atoms. Electricity is generated when the electrons are separated from the protons by any of many means: chemical action (battery), moving magnetic field (generator), electromagnetic radiation (photovoltaic cell), heat (thermocouple), and, for static electricity, friction.

TYPES OF ELECTRICITY There are two types of electricity: static electricity and dynamic electricity. The effects of static electricity were studied in ancient times. A piece of amber rubbed with fur would acquire an electrical charge, but because amber is a good insulator, the charge remained stationary (static) on the surface of the amber. The charge could attract light objects and produce sparks. Little practical use was made of static electricity until the invention of the electrostatic printing process by Chester Carlson in 1938.

It is dynamic electricity that dominates the world of electricity and electronics today. In this form of electricity the electrical charges are in motion and called *electrical current*. It was only after 1800, with the invention of the voltaic pile, that scientists had a continuous source of current to work with.

For electrical current to flow there must be a complete path from one terminal of the source to the other terminal. This complete path is known as a *circuit*. The electromotive force, or voltage, of the source is the cause; the current that flows is the effect. Voltage sources are designated by the nature of the current they deliver: direct current or alternating current.

DIRECT CURRENT Direct current is the flow of electrical

charges in one direction only. The current need not be of constant amplitude to be considered direct current. A thorough knowledge of dc theory is necessary to understand how electronic circuits operate. There are many sources of direct current. Those having applications in photography include dry cells and batteries to power portable equipment, the photovoltaic (solar) cells to measure light levels in light meters and automatic exposure controllers, and, most importantly, the rectifier power supplies that convert the ac voltage from the mains to a constant (and frequently very precise) direct voltage for electronic circuits.

Ohm's Law Ohm's law states that the current that flows in a circuit is directly proportional to the applied voltage and is inversely proportional to the resistance of the circuit.

$$I \text{ (amperes)} = V \text{ (volts)} / R \text{ (ohms)}$$

When a circuit consists of more than one resistor, the effective resistance of a circuit depends on the configuration of the interconnections among the various resistors. The resistors can be connected in series or in parallel or in some combination of the two.

Series Circuit The resistors in a series circuit are connected end-to-end so the current through each resistor is the same and is equal to the applied voltage divided by the sum of the individual resistors.

$$I \text{ (amperes)} = V \text{ (volts)} / Rl + R2 + R3 \text{ (ohms)}$$

A series connection of resistors is frequently used as a voltage divider to obtain a voltage, or voltages, less than the voltage available from a power source. The voltage across each resistor is equal to the common current multiplied by the resistance of the resistor.

$$V_N \text{ (volts)} = I \text{ (amperes)} \times R_N \text{ (ohms)}$$

The sum of the voltages equals the applied voltage.

Parallel Circuit The resistors in a parallel circuit are connected across (or shunting) each other, thus providing as many paths for the current to flow through as there are resistors. The value of the voltage across each resistor is the same. The sum of the current through each of the resistors is equal to the current delivered by the *source*.

$$I_T + I_1 + I_2 + I_3 + \ldots$$

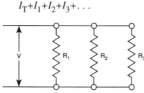

A parallel circuit has the same voltage (*V*) across each Shown is a parallel circuit of three resistors: *R1, R2, R3*.

Power The power consumed in any component in a dc circuit is equal to the voltage across the component multiplied by the current through it.

$$P \text{ (watts)} = V \text{ (volts)} \times I \text{ (amperes)}$$

Substituting $V = I \times R$, it may be calculated as:

$$P \text{ (watts)} = I^2 \text{ (amperes}^2) \times R \text{ (ohms)}$$

The power consumed by the circuit is equal to the sum of the power consumed by each component in the circuit.

$$P_T = P_1 + P_2 + P_3 + \ldots$$

ALTERNATING CURRENT Voltages and currents associated with audio systems and radio and television signals are examples of ac voltage and current. Most electrical power generated throughout the world is generated as ac power because it is more economical to transmit and distribute than dc power. The instantaneous amplitude of the voltage distributed by the power companies varies as a sine wave at a frequency of 60 hertz (cycles per second) in the United States, Canada, and a few other countries and 50 hertz in the rest of the world. Capacitors and inductors, as well as resistors, are widely used in ac circuits. Depending on the component, the current through it may be in phase or 90 degrees out of phase with the voltage across it.

Resistive Circuits The current through a resistor is always in phase with the voltage across it. Ohm's law applies just as it does for a dc circuit. The calculations for series and parallel circuits and for power are valid.

Capacitive Circuits When a capacitor is connected across an ac voltage, current will flow. The amplitude of the current is directly proportional to the applied voltage and inversely proportional to the capacitive reactance of the capacitor.

$$I \text{ (amperes)} = V \text{(volts)} / X_c \text{ (ohms)}$$

Capacitive reactance is a function of the frequency, f of the source and the value of capacitance, C.

$$X_c \text{(ohms)} = 1/2\pi f \text{(hertz)} \, C \text{(farads)}.$$

An important property of a capacitor is its ability to block a steady dc voltage while passing ac signals. The higher the frequency, the less the opposition to ac signals. This characteristic makes capacitors useful in the design of frequency selective filters, tuners, and dc isolators. The ac current that flows through a capacitor leads the voltage across it by 90 degrees.

Inductive Circuits In an ac circuit, the current that flows through an inductor (coil) is directly proportional to the applied voltage and inversely proportional to the inductive reactance of the inductor.

76

$$I \text{ (amperes)} = V\text{(volts)} / X_L \text{ (ohms)}$$

Inductive reactance is a function of the frequency, f of the source and the value of inductance, L.

$$X_L \text{ (ohms)} = 2 \; \pi f \text{ (hertz)} \times L \text{ (henries)}$$

The ac current that flows through an inductor lags the voltage across it by 90 degrees.

Impedance Impedance, Z, is the net opposition to the flow of current through a series ac circuit consisting of any combination of resistors, capacitors, and inductors. It is measured in ohms and is equal to

$$Z\text{(ohms)} = \sqrt{R^2 + (X_L - X_C)^2}$$

The current in such a series circuit is determined from Ohm's law for an ac circuit:

$$I \text{ (amperes)} = V \text{ (volts)} / Z \text{ (ohms)}$$

Power Power in a single-phase ac circuit is equal to the product of the voltage, the current, and the power factor, PF: The PF is equal to the cosine of the phase angle, θ

$$P \text{ (watts)} = V \text{ (volts)} \times I \text{ (amperes)} \times \cos \theta$$

If the circuit consists of only resistances, the voltage and current will be in phase and the phase angle is 0 degrees. Because the cosine of 0 degrees is 1.0, $P = V \times I$ (the same as for dc circuits). If the circuit includes inductors or capacitors the PF will be less than 1.0 and must be included in the calculation of power.

Three-phase circuits. An alternator with three windings equally spaced will produce three voltages that are 120 degrees out of phase with each other. These windings can be connected in wye or in delta configuration. When connected in wye, the line-to-line voltage is equal to 1.732 times the phase voltage v_ϕ

$$V_{LL} = 1.732 \; V\phi$$

Three-phase ac systems provide more efficient transmission and distribution of power and simpler starting of ac induction motors.

ELECTRODE
A terminal through which current enters or leaves an electrical or electronic device.

ELECTROLUMINESCENCE
The production of light by the flowing of an electric current through a medium, but not as a result of line emission or incandescence. Electroluminescence can only be produced using specific chemical compounds.

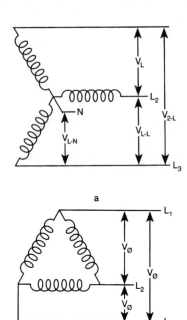

a

b

Three-phase circuits. (a) The wye connection generally has a fourth, neutral (N) wire connected to ground. The voltage from the neutral to any of the three lines, V_{N-L}, is equal to 0.577 x V_{L-L} (b) With the delta connection the line-to-line voltage is the same as the phase voltage v_ϕ.

ELECTROLUMINESCENT LAMP A light panel that sandwiches phosphors between conductive layers, one of which is translucent and has a transparent protective surface. Alternating voltage applied to the conductive sheets excites the phosphors, which emit light. The efficiency of the panels is low, but since they use no evacuated bulbs or filaments, they have a long life, and they are thin and can be made in a variety of shapes. If their light output can be increased closer to theoretical limits they may be widely used in photography in the future.

ELECTROMAGNETIC RADIATION The primary form of radiant energy. There are many categories of electromagnetic radiation: radio waves, microwaves, infrared radiation, light, ultraviolet radiation, rays, and gamma rays. All of these types of radiation are electromagnetic (EM) radiation, and they are all propagated in the same manner: electromagnetic radiation is made up of photons (or quanta). The photons have energy, but no mass, and travel at the speed of light in a vacuum, and at the speed of light divided by the index of refraction of the material in other materials.

A photon is a quantized packet of energy. These packets are designated as being quantized because only discrete energy levels are possible. The energy of any photon is equal to Planck's constant times the frequency of the photon ($E = hn$) Therefore, every group of photons, or burst of EM radiation, must have an energy level equivalent to an integral multiple of the energies of the photons present. In this sense photons are similar to particles. On the other hand, the energy of a photon is contained in an oscillating, self-limiting combination of electric and magnetic fields. These fields oscillate in a transverse manner, perpendicular to the direction of propagation and each other. In this sense photons are similar to waves. It is convenient to look at electromagnetic radiation as being made up of independent wavelike energy packets, sometimes called *waveicles*. EM radiation can be analyzed as it actually exists using quantum electrodynamics, or only the wave aspects of the radiation can be analyzed using wave theory. The advantage of using wave theory is that it is much simpler than quantum theory, allowing for practical analysis of more complicated systems. If the amount of radiation present is large, the quantum effects may not be noticeable in some applications.

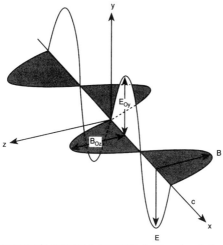

Electromagnetic radiation A schematic drawing of a photon. The photon is travelling in the x direction. The electric field (E_{oy}) is oscillating in the y direction, and the magnetic field (B_{oz}) is oscillating in the z direction.

As with mechanical oscillators, higher energy levels result from more rapid oscillations of the electric and magnetic fields in photons (this also follows from Planck's expression for the energy of a photon, given previously). This means that as the frequency of a photon increases, so does the energy. Both the frequency and the energy of a photon contribute to its characteristics, and result in the subdivision of the broad range of electromagnetic radiation into the well known categories listed here (in order of increasing frequency). Because of the law of conservation of energy, the frequency of a photon cannot change. Photons travel on until they are absorbed by a substance, increasing the energy level of the substance. A minor exception to this is when two gamma ray photons combine to produce an electron-positron pair. In this case the energy is converted to mass according to Einstein's relation $E = mc^2$. Only very high energy gamma rays have sufficient energy to form matter; the electronpositron pair being the smallest amount of matter that can be formed.

ELECTROMAGNETIC SPECTRUM The range of types of electromagnetic radiation presented according to category in order of decreasing wavelength, from long wavelength (and low frequency) radio waves to short wavelength (and high frequency) gamma rays. The visible part of the electromagnetic spectrum is generally considered to extend from 400 to 700 nanometers, although there is some variation in this range among individuals and also with the energy level and viewing conditions.

The Electromagnetic Spectrum

Frequency (Hz)	Wavelength (nm)	Type of Radiation
10^2	10^{16}	Long radio waves
10^3 (kHz)	10^{15}	"
10^4	10^{14}	"
10^5	10^{13}	AM radio
10^6 (MHz)	10^{12} (1 km)	"
10^7	10^{11}	FM radio & television
10^8	10^{10}	"
10^9	10^9 (1 m)	Short radio waves
10^{10}	10^8	"
10^{11}	10^7 (1 cm)	Microwaves
10^{12}	10^6 (1 mm)	"
10^{13}	10^5	Infrared radiation
10^{14}	10^4	"
10^{15}	10^3 (1 µm)	"
10^{16}	10^2	Light (~400–700 nm)
10^{17}	10	Ultraviolet radiation
10^{18}	1 nm	Soft x rays
10^{19}	0.1 (1 Å)	Hard x rays
10^{20}	10^{-2}	Gamma rays
10^{21}	10^{-3}	"
10^{22}	10^{-4}	"
10^{23}	10^{-5}	"

ELECTROMECHANICAL ENGRAVING Electromechanical engraving is a method of producing image carriers, or printing plates, by electromechanical means. Electromechanical engravers combine mechanical devices with electronic controls. These were first produced for making engravings for letterpress, but they are no longer used because of the decline in letterpress printing. Electromechanical engraving systems are used extensively for gravure. They consist of an input unit, an image recording and converting computer, and an output unit. The input unit consists of a rotating drum on which continuous tone or halftone positive or negative prints are mounted in position for reproduction with one or more reading heads that measure the scanned image densities and transmit them to the computer station. This station records the image densities and converts them to electrical impulses, which are transmitted to engraving heads equipped with diamond styli. These engrave gravure diamond-shaped image cells in the gravure printing cylinder corresponding in area and depth to the images measured on the input prints. The engraving heads are mounted in the output unit adjacent to the printing cylinder, which is engraved as it rotates. The ability to use halftone prints on these systems has made possible the use of the same halftone films for making gravure cylinders as are used for making lithographic printing plates. The films are called generic films and the process is called halftone gravure.

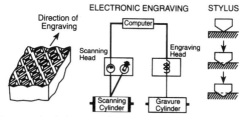

Electromechanical engraver for gravure.

ELECTROMOTIVE FORCE (EMF, E, V) The potential difference measured between two points in an electrical circuit. The term is often used interchangeably with voltage. When used, emf usually applies to the voltage generated by a source and has E for its symbol (instead of V). The unit of emf is the volt.

ELECTRON A subatomic particle of unit negative charge of electricity. One electron carries a charge of 1.602×10^{-19} coulomb.

ELECTRON BEAM RECORDING A direct method for recording the signals carried by a modulated electron beam on photographic material. The film is placed in an evacuated cathode ray tube and is exposed directly by the electron beam, producing a high-resolution image. By comparison, indirect methods record the phosphor image on the face plate of the tube.

ELECTRON GUN   See *Cathode-ray tube.*

ELECTRONIC   Identifying devices involving the flow of electrons in a vacuum in gaseous media, and in semiconductors.

ELECTRONIC DOT GENERATION Use of screening algorithms to produce halftones on scanners, output recorders, or imagesetters.

ELECTRONIC-IMAGE BACK See *Camera back; Electronic imaging*.

ELECTRONIC PHOTOGRAPHY Electronic photography is the electronic recording of optical images in analog or digital form. Image capture can be through the use of photo multiplier devices or linear or area charge-coupled devices (CCDs) with the recording on magnetic, optical, or solid-state media. Images may be made with a dedicated electronic still camera or video camera, or may be converted from silver halide originals into electronic form. The combining of silver halide and electronic technology is also known as hybrid technology.

ELECTRONIC PUBLISHING The production of printed material making use of a computer with an appropriate software program, which typically accommodates text and illustrations with layout control, and a peripheral printer.

ELECTRONIC RETOUCHING See *Digital image*.

ELECTRONICS That branch of electrical science that deals specifically with the flow of electrons in a vacuum, a gaseous medium, or a semiconductor. The rapid advances in the field of electronics in recent years are largely a result of research in semiconductor materials and the invention of the transistor. Since the invention of transistors in 1948 at Bell Telephone Laboratories, solid-state devices have replaced vacuum tubes for almost all electronic applications. Some of the reasons for the widespread use of transistors and other solid-state devices are (1) unlike tubes they have no filaments to consume power, especially important when used in battery-operated equipment; (2) they are much smaller and much lighter than vacuum tubes, permitting high density mounting on printed circuit boards; (3) they are rugged and reliable and have extraordinary long life. By the early 1960s, designers were incorporating many transistors, diodes, resistors, and all the interconnections on a single piece of semiconductor and calling it an integrated circuit (IC). Compared to similar circuit using discrete devices, an IC requires much less power, is much smaller, and is more reliable.

The development of solid-state electronics has had a significant impact on the design of all kinds of photographic equipment—cameras with automatic exposure control, autofocusing, and motorized film advance; processors with precision temperature control; high-volume computer-controlled colour printers; video colour negative analyzers; and most recently, cameras and recording media for electronic imaging.

See also: *Electricity*.

ELECTRONIC SCANNER An electronic scanner is a device used to convert black-and-white and colour originals into images ready for reproduction. The black-and-white scanner can enhance tone reproduction and produce halftone films. Colour scanners separate colour originals into red, green, and blue records and perform colour correction, retouching, and other modifications before outputting films for reproduction. There are two types of scanners: drum scanners using photomultiplier tubes (PMT) and red, green, and blue filters to produce the separations; and flat-bed scanners, which use charge-coupled devices (CCD) or linear arrays to record or separate the images.

ELECTRONIC STILL CAMERA See *Camera type.*

ELECTRONIC STILL PHOTOGRAPHY Electronic still photography is the electronic recording of individual optical images in analog or digital form. Image capture can be through the use of photomultiplier devices or linear or area charge-coupled devices (CCDs) with the recording on magnetic, optical, or solid-state media. Images may be made with a dedicated electronic still camera or a motion video camera, or they may be converted from silver halide originals into electronic form using a variety of available monochrome or colour scanners. The combining of silver halide and electronic technology is also called hybrid technology.

Electronic still photography began with the introduction of the Sony video still camera called MAVICA, an acronym for *magnetic video camera.* Announced on August 24, 1981, it was to be several years before Sony delivered a professional camera called the ProMavica.

ELECTRONIC ANALOG STILL VIDEO PHOTOGRAPHY Photography, either with a conventional or electronic still video camera, is an analog process. Whether the photographic image is captured in a still video camera, a video camcorder, or a scanner associated with a computer, the first step with each of these devices is the production of an analog image recorded in analog waveform using a CCD that, when exposed to light, creates a pattern of charges that are recorded as analog waves. A principle component of the electronic still video camera is an optical system, which is the same as that of a conventional silver halide still camera. The still video camera depends on either a charge-coupled device (CCD) or metal-oxide semiconductor (MOS) as the initial image-capturing device.

The CCD is the equivalent of a piece of film with the ability to record electronically what the lens of the camera has seen Only in the last few years have cost-effective imaging devices appeared. Patent literature is filled with new variations and modifications of basic sensors, using them for camera focusing, for white light balancing, and for all of the various functions needed by the complete electronic still video camera.

Initial standards for electronic still video photography were established in 1982. A greatly improved standard, Hi-band, was announced in mid-1988. These standards fit the standard NTSC (National Television Standard Committee)

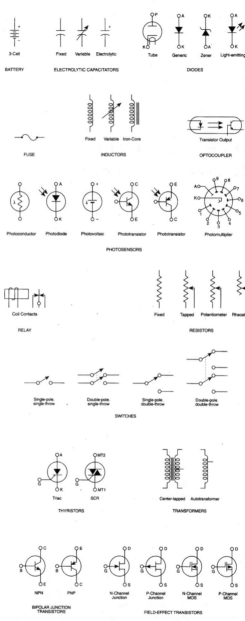

Electronics. Grapxic symbols commonly used in electronic circuit diagrams. (See entry for specific components for electrode identification.)

companies worldwide are part of the Electronic Still Standardization Committee in Japan.

With analog still video photography, the analog electronic signal that is recorded on the 2-inch magnetic floppy disk is similar to the signal recorded on conventional video tape. Because of the use of the floppy disk, many people think that the system is digital, but it is an analog system. The 2-inch floppy disk is one of the limitations still to be overcome for higher-resolution electronic still systems. The 2-inch disk contains 52 tracks—50 for field recording and 2 for control. Provisions are also contained in the standard to use alternative field tracks to record 9.6 seconds of audio associated with an adjacent image field.

If the still video floppy disk were a computer disk (a 2-inch disk with a slightly different plastic shell is being used in laptop computers), the disk capacity would be between 740 kilobytes (KB) and 1 megabytes (MB), depending on the manufacturer. Some manufacturers are thinking of using the 2-inch floppy as an electronic photography digital medium, but in a double-sided format with 1.5 MB on a disk.

A basic limitation for still video cameras and camcorders is the resolution capability of CCD sensors, the medium that records the picture scene in an analog form. There is an inherent optical difference between conventional film cameras and still video cameras. The sensors used to capture the electronic image are much smaller than the conventional 35mm film so that a lens used on a interchangeable lens still video camera has actually four times the magnification of a lens used with 35-mm film. As an example, a 50-mm lens used with an electronic sensor would be the equivalent of a 200-mm lens used with a 35-mm camera. This means that the development of wide-angle lenses is a greater challenge for the still video camera designer, while long focal length lenses for sports use or law enforcement surveillance are already available and at lower prices than equal focal length lenses for 35-mm cameras. Optical design is a much easier task at the long focal length end of the range since a 1000mm lens is equal to a 4000-mm lens in 35-mm photography, and the center portion of the lens is used that gives the greatest area of flat imaging and sharpness.

	Original	Hi-Band
1. Recording system		
Luminance	FM modulated recording system (NTSC/PAL System)	Same
White Peak	6.0MHz	9.7MHz
Synch. Peak	1.5MHz	7.7MHz
Frequency deviation	1.5MHz	2.0MHz
White Clipping	None	Less than 250%
Recording Current (Optimum)	7MHz	9MHz
Color Signal	R-Y, B-Y differential color lines. Subsequent FM-modulated recording in accordance with Still Video Floppy System.	Same
2. Disk Sheet	In accordance with Still Video Floppy System	Same
Thickness	40 μm	Same
Magnetic Sheet	Metal sheet or	Same

3. Disk Pack	In accordance with Still Video Floppy System	Same	
Dimensions	$60 \times 54 \times 3.6$ mm $(W \times H \times D)$	Same	
4. Track	In accordance with Still Video Floppy System	Same	
For picture/sound	From track 1 to 50 digital data	Same	
Cue Track	Track 52	Same	Analog still video photography stand
Track Pitch	100 Micron	Same	original and hi-band.

Analog still video photography standard, original and hi-band.

For the moment, all of the new still video cameras that have appeared are Hi-band cameras. Most manufacturers have chosen to go the route of field recording cameras that give 50 images per disk as opposed to frame-recording cameras that give only 25 images. There are some subjects that would be better reproduced if the frame option, with its greater information content, were available, but the field image is adequate for most amateur photography. Almost all of the new cameras have appeared with 380,000 or more pixel sensors that produce good-quality video images. Lenses for most prototype electronic still cameras are zoom lenses with macro focusing. This offers a great deal of creative opportunities for the person using the electronic still video camera.

There is still the problem of the video-look of still video pictures. The film-look that people have become used to through the proliferation of 35-mm film cameras has not been achieved by still video cameras. The inherent contrast of still video camera images combined with low exposure indexes limits the creative use of the still video camera. Some of the low light limitations have been overcome by providing $f/1.2$, $f/1.4$, or $f/1.8$ lenses on some prototype cameras. The real answer will be an improvement in the CCD sensors, but this may be a problem since most CCDs are used in the growing market of camcorders and the electronic manufacturers of camcorders are satisfied with current performance of CCDs for this use.

DIGITAL STILL VIDEO PHOTOGRAPHY An analog waveform continuously varies in value and time. To convert this to a digital signal, both the value and the time must be changed to noncontinuous values. The amplitude will be represented by a digital integer of a certain number of bits, and time will be represented as a series of those values taken at equal steps in time. The process of time determination is called sampling and the conversion of the amplitude is quantizing. Together these are called analog-to-digital conversion (A/D) or digitizing.

This conversion process is an approximation, but it has become much more refined with the improvement of A/D conversion devices and the use of higher rates. If the sampling rate is low, the result will be a very inaccurate representation of the signal. If the sampling rate is high, an almost exact copy of the original, both for colour and density, can be achieved. A/D chips developed in 1991 have a rate of 300 million samples per second, and we can expect that figure to increase substantially.

In the case of colour, the red, green, and blue information is handled as three complete, separate sets of data producing three complete sets of digital information. Three A/D circuits are used and the encoding is done simultaneously. As an image is digitized, a series of adjacent points in the image is created in the same pattern that the camera tube or solidstate imaging device originally scanned the image. These individual points are picture elements, or pixels. When reconstructing the image for display, each pixel is shown either as a small rectangle or square filled with colour calculated from the number of colour bits representing that pixel, or as a shade of gray if a black-and-white image is being recorded.

Asahi Optical Co., Ltd.	NEC Corporation
BASF Aktiegesellschaft	NEC Home Electronics, Ltd.
Canon, Inc.	Nihon Polaroid Corporation
Casio Computer Co., Ltd.	Nikon Corporation
Chinon Industrial, Inc.	Olympus Optical Co., Ud.
Citizen Watch Co., Ltd.	Philips International B.V.
Copal Co., Ltd.	Ricoh Company, Ltd.
Columbia Magnetic Products Co., Ltd.	Samsung Japan Electronics Co., Ltd.
Dai Nippon Printing Co., Ltd.	Sankyo Seiki Manufacturing
Eastman Kodak Company	Co., Ltd.
Elmo Co., Ltd.	Sanyo Electric Co., Ltd.
Fuji Photo Film Co., Ltd.	Seiko Co.
Hitachi, Ltd.	Seiko Epson Co.
Hitachi Maxell, Ltd.	Sharp Corporation
Kasei Verbatim Corporation	Sony Corporation
Keystone Camera of Japan, Ltd.	Space-Wide Enterprises Co.
	TDK Corporation
Konica Corporation	Thompson-Japan K K Co.
Kyocera Corporation	3M Company/Sumitomo 3M
Mamiya Camera Co., Ltd.	Ltd.
Matsushita Electric Industrial Co., Ltd.	Toshiba Corporation
Minolta Camera Co., Ltd.	Victor Company of Japan,
Mitsubishi Electric Corp	Ltd. (JVC)

Electronic still standardization committee members.

If the resolution of a system is low, it will result in a fuzzy picture showing the individual pixels, this is called pixelation. The degree of pixelation depends on how far you are away from the image and the corner-to-corner diagonal of the screen. A large viewing screen can appear sharp with a fewer number of total pixels, whereas a small viewing screen requires a large number of pixels to appear sharp.

Digital still video camera systems are beginning to appear. These systems begin with the same analog CCD, but the picture information is converted to a digital signal in the camera and stored in either a static random-access memory (SRAM) or electronically erasable programmable read-only memory (EEPROM). Digital still video camera systems have already been shown in prototype form by several different manufacturers

Canon RC-570 still video camera. (Courtesy of Canon U.S.A., Inc.)

with the first systems already available for sale. However, there are significant variations in the various systems. One prototype system was equipped with a 2 megabyte card—the camera produced 52 images through the use of a in-camera discrete cosine transform (DCT) compression algorithm. Another stored 10 images on a 16 megabit (Mbit) card, while a different system stored 20 pictures on an 8 Mbit memory card. Another system, jointly developed and marketed by Fuji Photo Film Co. Ltd. and Toshiba Corp., offers two different memory cards—a six- or twelve-image version in high-quality mode. This system will be one of the proposed standards. Sixteen Japanese manufacturers have begun to study a standard for digital still video photography imaging.

A digital camera has been developed that does not depend on the NTSC video standard, the current video standard for the United States and some other parts of the world. The Kodak Professional Digital Camera System (DCS) blends a conventional Nikon camera and digital imaging technologies. This system consists of two camera backs—one colour and one monochrome—that replace the camera's standard back, a camera winder, and a Kodak digital storage unit (DSU) that stores up to 158 uncompressed, or 400 to 600 compressed images. The digital storage unit incorporates a 200-megabyte Winchester disk and Joint Photo Experts Group (JPEG) compatible image compression capability. The imaging area of the DCS electronic digital camera back is only half that of a 35-mm film frame. So, the focal lengths of the Nikon-mount lenses used are effectively doubled. For example, a conventional 200-mm lens becomes a 400mm lens with the system. Both backs use a 1280 x 1024 pixel imager. The DCS produces colour images equivalent to exposure indexes (EI) of 200, 400 (system nominal speed), 800, and 1600. Monochrome images are equivalent to EI 400, 800 (system nominal speed), 1600, and 3200.

In the United States it appears that the coming High Definition Television (HDTV) standard will be digital. The results of this digital approach will further enhance the field of

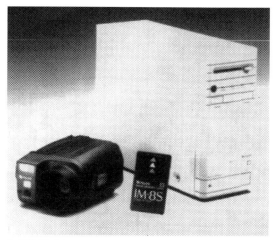

Fuji FUJIX digital still camera system. (Courtesy of Fuji Photo Film U.S.A., Inc.)

electronic photo imaging in digital form at resolutions that begin to approach those of film, as perceived in the eyes of the viewer. The ultimate impact of these improvements will be the ability to greatly enhance the quality of the video pictures. Video images will rapidly approach the quality expected from conventional photographic material.

THE FUTURE At the same time that all of these changes are occurring, we should not forget the introduction of multimedia for the computer. While some see this only as an educational tool, it may ultimately be much more widespread. Multimedia brings interactive technology into the computer, combining video, sound, text, and photographs.

Standards are beginning to emerge for multimedia, and this may be a significant area of growth with the continued need for digital photographic images. This leads to the simple conclusion that the need for digital photographic images will continue to grow at a logarithmic rate far exceeding the recent significant advances in the development of conventional silver halide technology. A Fuji researcher, a number of years ago, said that the limits had been reached for silver halide technology. This may now be closer to reality since the cost of admission for companies entering the electronic digital photography area is much lower than the cost of entry into the silver halide area and therefore easier. The companies developing electronic photography products, in many cases, will be companies that in the past had not been in the photo-imaging marketplace.

Much work is being done on better and higher-resolution CCDs, particularly for use in HDTV systems. The result will be CCDs with an increase of five to ten times the resolution of the 1991 camcorder and still video sensors. These coupled with improved memory chips will bring in a new era of electronic image capture both in the still and video areas.

OTHER MEANS OF ELECTRONIC DIGITAL CAPTURE Motion video camera or camcorders offer another means of capturing electronic photographs. Cameras using vacuum-tube technology have been mostly replaced by CCD-chip cameras. Chips are more stable and resist mechanical problems such as damage from being dropped. Video cameras usually operate at a total level of 8 bits of total red, green, blue (RGB) colour because of the basic limitation of the colour component of the NTSC colour signal. Luminance or brightness has been enhanced, but the signal is limited by the NTSC bandwidth. Since video images are analog, they require the use of A/D conversion, usually done in a computer by using a plug-in board.

Another way of capturing photographs digitally is scanning. Scanners can range from large, high-resolution rotary scanners, which were first developed for image separation in printing, to flatbed or hand-held scanners that can have resolutions up to 1200 dots per inch (DPI). The flatbed or handheld scanners use linear arrays that are like the CCDs found in camcorders or still video cameras but with the sensor elements located in a single line requiring three separate passes of the scanning head, one for each colour. In 1990, tricolour arrays using three rows of elements became popular allowing full-colour scanning in a single pass of the scanning head. Area arrays, much like those found in cameras but with higher resolution, have been used for new, faster scanners. For 35-mm film scanning, resolutions close to that of the Kodak Digital Camera System have been available.

The major limitation of scanners has been resolution. Normal desktop scanners operate in the 300 dpi range. Some high-resolution scanners offer resolutions from 1000 to 3000 dpi, but the cost jumps sharply for the higher resolutions, as do the scan time and the file size. Some of these higher-resolution scanners can take 10 minutes or more to scan and can reach file sizes of over 200 MB, not an easily handled data file. Another consideration in colour scanning is the colour depth of each scanned RGB pixel. Six bits or more per colour are necessary to assure a natural-looking colour without *banding,* a striping of colour steps. This adds to the storage demands of a system as well as to the capabilities of the scanner.

Added together, the various forms of image capture provide the opportunity of increasing the use of electronic photography. Whether a still video camera, a scanner, or a motion video camera adapted to still work, these all open new ways of using electronically or digitally captured images.

IMAGE STORAGE Magnetic storage has been the most cost-effective way of image storage up to this time. The capacity of floppy disks has been increased as has the capacity of the Winchester hard disks. WORM (write once read many) optical disks have provided large-capacity storage media in a nonerasable form. In the late 1980s, the introduction of magneto-optical erasable disks have added additional capability for image storage. The high capacity of this medium has made it ideal for image storage of any size image, and newer technology has brought the record and playback speeds on a par with magnetic material.

Kodak's Photo CD provides an additional hybrid nonerasable digital storage product for industrial, commercial, and consumer use. The Photo CD is the same size as the popular audio CD or CD-ROM but its resemblance stops there. The Photo CD stores 100 colour digital electronic images scanned from 35-mm film at about the same resolution as a 35-mm negative — 18 million pixels. The Photo CD can be used on the CD-ROM HA and CD-I players. The transfer process includes a Kodak-developed scanner with a 2K RGB linear array sensor, a Sun SPARC workstation at the data manager, a Kodak XL-7700 to produce 42-image proof cards for the Photo CD boxes, and a CD optical disc writer from Philips. Kodak will make the optical media and materials for the printer. The Photo CD discs can be used for NTSC, European PAL, and SECAM standard video playback and current Japanese Muse HDTV through internal electronic functions.

IMAGE TRANSMISSION Computers have been talking to each other via modems for a number of years. The digital transmission of data — be it information from stores corporations, medical facilities, or even home computers and the vast computer network — is a service being offered. While initial modems in 1980 were slow, with ranges of 80 to 300 bits per second (bps), in 1991, through the use of special lines and equipment, it is actually possible to send almost 10,000 bps of information. This will continue to increase substantially as fibre optic transmission lines become available in the future. For data, the 1991 speed might be acceptable; for images, the cost of telephone time combined with the actual wait for images is, for the most part, unacceptable.

To overcome this, special transmitters have been designed by a number of companies for both transmission of still video electronic photographs and conventional film images in electronic form in 1 to 4 minutes. These images can be received, generally, as digital images suitable for digital processing or direct separation in systems used by many newspapers and magazines.

IMAGE PROCESSING High-resolution colour imaging on personal computers was pioneered by an AT&T *intrapreneurial* venture, the Electronic and Photographic Imaging Center (EPlCenter), Indianapolis, Indiana, founded in mid-1984, later becoming TrueVision, Inc. The company produces one of the most widely recognized of the high-end graphic boards available for the IBM PC/XT, AT, and compatibles. Several hundred third-party companies offer imaging software that utilizes Targa, and a number of video conversion boards (some with bundled software) are available. Competition has brought dramatic changes in the workstation market. These new platforms from more than a half dozen companies have brought greater performance and capability, all at reduced cost. The future will depend on digital technology. It has never been truer that digital technology is getting better and lower in price than ever, particularly with respect to electronic imaging.

A digital photographic image is a redundant image where the same information may appear more than once. Where the same colour is at different pixels within the image, this may be one redundancy, either horizontal or vertical. If the image is moving, there may be a redundancy between succeeding images. If there are straight lines of information, this may create another redundancy. Compression of images depends on this redundancy of information in the image. Images may be compressed because of the dependence of each pixel value on the value of its neighbors. The larger this dependence, the more compression is achievable. The information content of images depends on the resolution, noise travel level, bit depth, and many other factors and is difficult to quantify, but three types of redundancies can be identified:

Spatial redundancy due to the correlation (dependence) among neighboring pixel values.

Spectral redundancy—due to the correlation of colour planes (RGB) or spectral bands.

Temporal redundancy—due to the correlation between different frames in a sequence of images.

Images are referred to as lossless when the reconstructed pixel values (compressed/decompressed) are identical to the original values. For lossless compression, the bit rates equal to the information content of an image can be obtained. Lossy compression has some discrepancies between the original and reconstructed pixel values. With lossy compression, lower bit rates can be achieved depending on how much distortion can be tolerated.

There are a number of different techniques for compressing images. One of the simplest techniques for image compression is truncation. With truncation, data are reduced by throwing away some parts of the bits for each pixel. These are usually the least significant bits for every pixel. Another simple preparation scheme is the use of a colour look-up table (CLUT). This is usually not a satisfactory approach for photographs that usually will use a colour look-up table of 30,000 or more colours. The CLUT approach is done at no more than 8 bits per pixel. For this application, colour look-up tables have 256 colours or less. The third simple method is runlength (RL) coding where the same pixel is repeated, such as a solid colour, and a single value is substituted—a count of how many times to repeat the value. This again is only possible when simple colours exits.

After some four years of work, JPEG has produced a colour image data compression standard. Image compression has become easier with the advent of new discrete cosine transform (DCT) chips from several developers of microchips. These chips provide a dedicated means DCT computation. This means that image compression and decompression can be improved and the process made faster.

The evolution of compression technology for images is still continuing. The introduction of new still image and video fractal compression technology from Integrated Systems provides another approach to image compression. The P.OEM (pictures for original equipment manufacturers) software, a compression technology, has been demonstrated with software-based video, both colour and gray scale, at frame rates of up to 30 frames per second using a 386-33 mHz machine with sight and sound from a floppy disk.

PROCESSING PLATFORMS Most common among the platforms used for retouching electronic still photographic images are the Apple Macintosh, IBM-PC and a variety of clones, and Sun SPARC platforms. Systems available range from sophisticated dedicated retouching systems using specially formatted platforms to a wide variety of PC- or Macintosh-based systems. A typical dedicated system might include a rotary scanner for image input, a Sun, Macintosh, or PC-based processing platform, with output to a film recorder or a rotary film writer. Images may be input and output on tape also.

SOFTWARE Image software development has concentrated primarily on software for the Apple Macintosh computer. There are several different categories of photoimaging software that are now available. Retouching software, such as Adobe PhotoShop, allows an image to be scanned on a variety of plat-forms. The images can then be enhanced with contrast and colour changes or a variety of pictorial effects that can improve or enhance the image. Page makeup software allows the combining of type and photographs into a final form for output to a film recorder or to an imagesetter for preparation of separa-tions, or to magnetic tape or other digital form for printing. Picture filing software allows the filing and retrieval of digital photographs through assigned work descriptors used as search criteria.

IMAGE DISPLAY AND OUTPUT Viewing electronic still photographic images on a screen is referred to as a soft viewing. This is because no permanent copy is made of the screen image unless a film image or film capture device is used. The word hardcopy comes from the photocopy machine industry and the various aspects of creating a rigid or permanent copy of an image.

DISPLAY MONITORS The most common display monitor, whether it is contained in a home television set or a dedicated colour display monitoring device for a video system or computer, is a cathode ray tube (CRT). The CRT uses a viewing screen that is coated, in the case of a colour tube, with either bands of phosphors that produce red, green, and blue or indi-vidual dots of phosphor. Electrons are emitted from a cathode in the narrow end of the tube and these are focused either magnet-ically or electrostatically into a small spot on the screen and positioned by either magnetic or electrostatic deflection. The cathode and electronic focusing lenses are part of the tube called the gun with the beam being accelerated towards the phosphor by high voltage at an anode.

The first CRTs appeared just before the turn of the century and remain a major display medium for both video and computer imaging. The CRT is an inexpensive device with many desir-able features including the ability to produce tubes of 35- and even 45-inch diagonal proportions. The one problem of CRTs is the bulk that they represent. Even some of the newer designed tubes with their much shorter form still make it difficult to create wall displays or briefcase-sized devices. The CRT needs a considerable distance from the gun to the screen to focus and scan the image.

Because of some of the shortcomings of the CRT, much effort has been expended to develop a form of flat display device. Work on flat-panel displays has continued for some 20 years, and the best results have been shown by liquid crystal displays (LCDs). Liquid crystal compounds are assembled in a thin film (approximately 0.5 mil in thickness) between parallel transparent conductors. When the electronic field is applied, a scattering effect allows light to reflect or pass through the conductors. The most recent development of the active screen places a transistor at each pixel location to produce extremely high resolution results.

Liquid crystals range from unique 2000 X 2000-line liquid crystals produced by Hitachi and written with a laser to control a tungsten light source to colour 14-inch LCD screens already suitable for computer graphic display. Colour is obtained by using a dichroic dye in the crystal colour materials that the light passes through.

Those who work with colour imaging systems are concerned that the colour you see is the colour you get (CYSI/CYG). With increased use of colour monitors as the viewing choice for electronic images, particularly in the graphics area, more efforts are being made to assure a match in colour between the soft screen and the hardcopy images. While this concern was a key part of the printing industry's move to digital imaging, it is now reaching into the world of electronic photography also. The solutions offered include computer-controlled monitors and testing programs for monitor standardization. The important fact is that awareness of this problem should result in better viewing conditions much like the standardization that occurred in the colour transparency and print viewing standards work of several decades ago.

HARDCOPY PRINTERS It is important to have the ability to create a hardcopy of an electronic still photograph in a photorealistic form. Colour printers are not new, but the most recent series of thermal dye-transfer printers have begun to approach the level of photorealism expected of good electronic still photographs.

For both the professional and general user, hardcopy prints are still a significant need. There are many approaches to creating prints from electronic images — some work very well, others adequately, and some leave much to be desired. Much is related to what the application for the prints will be. If prints are desired for publication, the resolution must match the resolution of silver halide prints, or otherwise moire or wavelike patterns develop because of the inconsistencies between the graphic arts screening process and the pattern that already exists on the electronic prints.

There are some criteria that must be met to achieve good quality hardcopy. (1) The resolution must be high enough to reproduce all the information contained in the electronic version of the picture. The increased resolution of the images with the continued development of true digital electronic still cameras and HDTV-based systems will become a major obstacle to some available systems. The minimum resolution acceptable to the eye must be at least 200 dpi. (2) Colour reproduction must be accurate with good separation of tones. (3) The gray scale reproduction for each colour must be a minimum of 6 bits per colour with a scale approaching that of conventional silver halide photography. (4) The print time must be 1 to 2 minutes for a completed print. A short time would be even more advantageous. (5) The system must be easily coupled to existing computer or video systems. (6) The finished print must give the appearance of a conventional silver halide colour photograph. In these criteria, some judgmental factors are certainly based on individual preferences, and other conditions could be added like storage life and unexposed storage life, as well as environmental impact.

In discussing the various approaches to hard copies, two distinct forms of control over the scale of the images produced become apparent. In systems such as conventional silver halide photography or thermal dye-transfer printing, either light or heat will create a proportional value equal to the density of the pixel desired. In other systems such as inkjet, ion deposition, or thermal wax transfer, this variation is created by the size of the ink drop or by breaking the single pixel down to the micropixels and increasing or decreasing their size. This variation of the two basic systems is one of the reasons why the thermal dye transfer process has won popular support.

As a colour print output system, the thermal dye transfer print system, also referred to as dye sublimation or D2T2 (Dye Diffusion Thermal Transfer), uses a colour ribbon that is the same size as the finished print with gravure-printed layers of cyan, magenta, and yellow dye, each the size of the finished print. Dyes are applied one at a time to high-gloss finish receiver paper, similar in characteristics to conventional photographic paper. Thermal dye transfer printers range in size up to 11 x 17 inches.

Inkjet printers have also begun to serve the needs of quality photographic imaging. Inkjet printers produce photorealistic results through the use of electrically charged particles that can be deposited in a series of micropixel portions to create shadings. While early inkjet printers suffered from problems of clogged jets and lack of speed, contemporary inkjets self-clear each time, use piezo or other electrical charge techniques to increase colour fidelity, and are available with improved inks.

There are now several new approaches to colour silver halide image printing. Ilford premiered a new liquid crystal light valve (LCLV) printer that produces continuous-tone colour prints, transparencies, and 35-mm slides directly from computer-based digital input with true photo quality. Digital images are written by a laser onto three LCLV cells and then the image is projected by tungsten light on the photo medium and processed. The whole operation is done in white light. Both print and transparency materials are provided in daylight-load roll cassettes. The images have 256 levels of gray for each colour. This is a palette of 16.7 million different colours. The resolution of each LCLV is 3500 x 2550 pixels. For 8 1/2 x 11-inch prints, that is 300 pixels per inch or 3500 lines for 35-mm slides. Writing to the cell takes less than 2 minutes with processing and drying takes 3 1/2 minutes. Once the image is written, multiple images may be made without rewriting. Images are written with a laser on the 3M Colour Laser Imager. The system uses infrared-sensitive colour print material. The resolution of the system is 300 dpi.

Fuji Pictrography 2000 is an LED-written product. The silver halide print materials (reflective and transmission) require no chemical processing, only water and heat. Each component colour of the image is graded in 256 steps for 16.7 million shades of colour at a resolution of 11.2 dots/mm (284 dpi).

FILM RECORDERS Film recorders use high resolution CRTs to produce an individual record of red, green, and blue images for transfer to colour silver halide film. Film recorder outputs can range from 35 mm to 8 x 10 inches at resolutions of 1000 x 1000 to 16,000 x 16,000 pixels. The cost of higher-quality film recorders is much lower than the cost of graphic art image setters but they require long exposure times because of the amount of information written to the CRT.

Books: Larish, John J., *Understanding Electronic Photography*. Blue Ridge Summit, Penn. Tab Books, 1990. Larish, John J., *Digital Photography, Pictures for Tomorrow*. Torrance, Calif. Micro Publishing Press, 1991. Larish, John J. *Photo CD: Quality Photos At Your Fingertips*. Torrance Calif. Micro Publishing Press, 1993.

ELECTRON IMAGING
The use of electron energy to produce images. A scanning electron beam excites phosphors, which in turn emit light, on the screen of a cathode ray tube. The image can be viewed directly as on a television screen, radar screen, or oscilloscope, or it can be photographed. If high resolution is required, then special electron-recording film and equipment are used to record the electron beam image directly.

ELECTRO-OPTICS (EO)
A rapidly growing branch of electronics related to such devices as lasers, fibre optic transmitters and receivers, bar code readers, optical character readers (OCR), optocouplers, and light emitting diode displays.

ELECTROPHOTOGRAPHY
Schaffert (1975) defines electrophotography as image-forming processes that involve the interaction of light and electricity. Within the framework of Schaffert's definition, many different processes exist. Of these, processes that involve the development of electrostatic charge patterns on insulator surfaces, as originally described by Carlson (1942), are the most highly developed. Schaffert and Oughton (1948) described these as "xerography," derived from the Greek words *xeros* for dry and *graphein* for writing. The literal meaning of the word is thus "dry writing."

In the 50 years since the first xerographic copy was created, xerography has established itself as one of the leading technological innovations of this century. Today, more than 1 trillion documents are generated annually by this technology. Xerography is currently used in all commercial copiers. With the advent of semiconductor lasers and lightemitting diodes in the late 1970s, it has also been widely used for printing. This entry includes a review of the early development of electrophotography and then describes the xerographic process, followed by a review of alternative electrophotographic processes.

EARLY HISTORY Processes by which electrostatic charges are used for image reproduction can be traced to the formation of charge patterns by Lichtenberg (1777), which still bear his name. Lichtenberg images were prepared by scattering dust on the surface of resin insulators that had previously been sparked. A decade later, Villarsy (1788) was able to determine the polarity of Lichtenberg figures by using a mixture of red lead and sulphur powders. The first practical demonstration of electrostatic recording was by Ronalds in the early 1840s. The instrument produced by Ronalds was called an electrograph and involved the movement of a stylus contact, which was connected to a lightning rod, across an insulating resin surface. The charge pattern; induced by atmospheric electricity, was made visible by dusting the surface with charged powder particles.

During the latter part of the nineteenth and early part of the twentieth centuries, there were a number of observations in which electrostatic images were made visable. All had in common the displacement of powder, dust, or smoke to charged surfaces. The first sustained efforts for the reproduction of electrostatic images were in the 1920s and 1930s by Selenyi. The technique used by Selenyi involved the writing of electrostatic images on insulating surfaces by electrons or ion beams. The images were subsequently made visible by dusting the images with positively charged lycopodium powders. An important aspect of Selenyi's process involved the use of electrons or ions, rather than light, for writing the images. As such, Selenyi's processes are more properly described as electrographic, rather than electrophotographic. Reviews of early work on electrostatic recording have been given by Carlson (1965) and more recently by Mort (1989).

Many of the early attempts to create electrostatic charge patterns were based on the photoelectric effect, the process by which electrons are ejected from a solid by the absorption of radiation. A fundamental limitation of processes based on the photoelectric effect is that they require very high exposures. In the 1920s and 1930s, several attempts were made to use photocurrents to control chemical changes in specially treated papers. From the results of these studies, Carlson concluded that chemically based phenomena of this nature were not feasible with the magnitude of photocurrents that could be produced under conditions of practical interest. As a result, Carlson and Kornei began to experiment with the creation of electrostatic latent images on the surface of photoconducting insulators. The results of these experiments led to the discovery of an image-forming process that Carlson later described as "electrophotography."

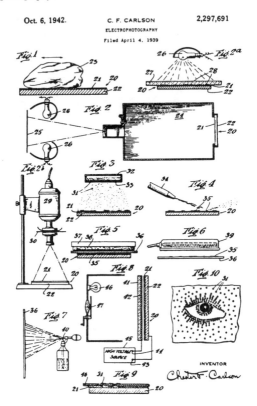

Oct. 6, 1942. C. F. CARLSON 2,297,691
ELECTROPHOTOGRAPHY
Filed April 4, 1939

INVENTOR
Chester F. Carlson

The date of reduction-to-practice of Carlson's discovery is October 22, 1938, and described by Dinsdale (1963). The discovery is best described in Carlson's own words: "October 22, 1938, was an historic occasion. I went to the lab that day and Otto had a freshly-prepared S coating on a Zn plate. We tried to see what we could do toward making a visible image. Otto took a glass microscope slide and printed on it in India ink the notation '10-22-38 ASTORIA.' We pulled down the shade to make the room as dark as possible, then he rubbed the S surface vigorously with a handkerchief to apply an electrostatic charge, laid the slide on the surface and placed the combination under a bright incandescent lamp for a few seconds. The slide was then removed and lycopodium powder was sprinkled on the sulphur surface. By gently blowing on the surface, all the loose powder was removed and there was left on the surface a near-perfect duplicate in powder of the notation which had been printed on the glass slide. Both of us repeated the experiment several times to convince ourselves that it was true, then we made some permanent copies by transferring the powder images to wax paper and heating the sheets to melt the wax. Then we went out to lunch to celebrate."

The first seminal patent on electrophotography was awarded to Carlson in 1942. In 1944, Carlson was awarded a patent on an automatic copying machine. In that same year, Carlson undertook an agreement with the Battelle Development Corporation, a subsidiary formed by the Battelle Memorial Institute for the purpose of sponsoring new inventions. Under the agreement, Battelle agreed to conduct further research in support of Carlson's invention. In 1947, the Haloid Corporation acquired a license to the process and began support of research at Battelle. At that time, the Haloid Corporation had a product line of photocopying machines based on wet chemical processes. During the late 1940's and 1950's, many significant improvements in the electrophotographic process were made. A major innovation was that amorphous Se, α-Se, layers were insulators with much higher photoconductivity than S or anthracene used in Carlson's original research. Other significant discoveries were screen-controlled corona charging devices, the development of two-component developer particles, and electrostatic transfer methods. The first public announcement of the process was at the annual meeting of the Optical Society of America on October 22, 1948, the tenth anniversary of Carlson's discovery, by Schaffert and Oughton. At that time, the process was given the name of xerography. The first sale of commercial xerographic equipment was of Haloid's Xerox Copier Model A in 1949 and the Copyflow printer in 1955. Due to the commercial significance of xerography, the Haloid Corporation was renamed Haloid-Xerox in 1955 and the Xerox Corporation in 1961.

For reviews of early work, see Wilson (1948), Carlson (1948, 1949), Schaffert (1950), Oliphant (1953), and Dessauer, Mott, and Bogdonoff(1955).

XEROGRAPHY In xerography, the primary image-forming step involves the formation of an electrostatic latent image on the surface of a photoconducting insulator. The latent image is made visible by toner particles, transferred to a receiver, then made permanent by a fusing or fixing process. In a variant of this process, the photoconductor is coated on the receiver, thus eliminating the transfer process. This process is separately discussed in the following section.

In conventional xerography, the overall process can involve as many as seven steps. In step 1, a uniform electrostatic charge is deposited on the photoreceptor surface. This is accomplished by a corona discharge. In the second step, the photoreceptor is exposed with an optical image of the object to be reproduced.

This selectively dissipates the surface charge in the exposed regions and creates a latent image in the form of an electrostatic charge pattern. In step 3, electrostatically charged toner particles are brought into contact with the latent image. The toner particles are transferred to a receiver in step 4, then fused in step 5. In step 6, the remaining toner particles are removed from the

This special commemorative stamp was issued in honor of Chester Carlson.

photoreceptor surface. Finally, in step 7, the photoreceptor is uniformly exposed to remove any remaining surface charge. Following step 7, the process can be repeated. The various steps are carried out around the periphery of a photoreceptor drum or belt. Drums are commonly used for low-volume copiers and printers while belts are more common in high-volume copiers. Each of the various process steps is separately discussed in the following sections. For reviews of the xerographic process, see Schaffert (1975), Scharfe (1984). Williams (1984), and Schein (1988).

Corona Charging The initial step in the xerographic process is the deposition of a uniform charge on the photoreceptor surface. Xerographic photoreceptors are between 20 and 60 mm in thickness and prepared on electrically conducting substrates. The substrate electrode is maintained at ground potential. The photoreceptor is charged to potentials of several hundred volts in the dark by a corona discharge. Potentials in this range correspond to surface charge densities between 10^{11} and 10^{12} charges/cm^2. To prevent the dissipation of the surface charge in the time between the charge and development steps, it is necessary that the dark conductivity be extremely low. Further, the free surface and substrate electrode must form blocking junctions to the photoreceptor. The corona charging apparatus is usually comprised of a series of stainless steel or W wires, typically 100 mm in diameter, strung between insulators in a stainless channel. The corona wires are maintained at very high (5-15 kV) potentials. The fields in the vicinity of the corona wires are sufficiently high that any free electrons in the region of the wires will be accelerated to velocities such that ionization of the gas molecules will occur. The concentrations of the ionized gas molecules are primarily determined by the corona polarity and the atmosphere (Shahin, 1969). For positive coronas, the dominant species are hydrated protons of the generalized formula $(H_2O)_nH^+$, where n = 4-8. For negative coronas, CO_3^- is the principal specie. Corona discharges from bare wires usually show significant nonuniformities in intensity. The corotron was invented to avoid problems associated with nonuniform

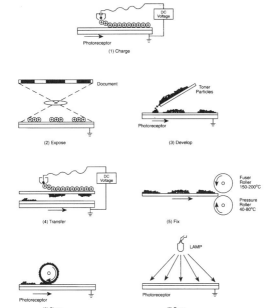

A schematic of the various steps in the xerographic process.

charging. Corotrons are corona devices that contain an auxiliary electrode in close proximity to the corona wire. The purpose of the auxiliary electrode is to control the field geometry such that the corona potentials are more uniform. Corotrons can have many different electrode arrangements. Usually the auxiliary electrode is at a very low, or ground, potential. The emission uniformity along a corona wire is strongly influenced by the polarity. Uniformity is good for positive coronas and poor for negative coronas. The scorotron was developed to resolve the problem of nonuniform charging with negative potentials. The scorotron contains a metal screen, or grid, between the corona wires and the photoreceptor and set to a potential that closely approximates the potential to which the photoreceptor is to be charged. The purpose of the scorotron screen is analogous to the control grid of a vacuum triode.

Latent-Image Formation In the second step, the photoreceptor is exposed with an imagewise pattern of radiation that corresponds to the image that is to be reproduced.

Absorption of the image exposure creates bound electronhole pairs. Under the influence of the corona-induced field, the pairs separate and are displaced to the free surface and the substrate electrode. As a result, the surface charge is dissipated in the exposed regions and an electrostatic latent image is created. For copiers, the image exposure is reflected from a document, then

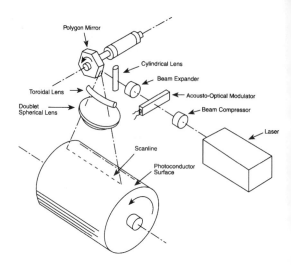

A schematic of a printer in which the photoreceptor is in a drum configuration (after Fleischer, Latta, and Rabedeau). Reprinted with permission from IBMJ. Res. Dev., 1977, 479. Copyright 1977, the IBM Corporation.

imaged onto the photoreceptor through a lens. The source of radiation is usually a xenon-filled lamp for flash exposures or a quartz-halogen or fluorescent lamp for scan or continuous exposures. To reproduce colour originals, it is necessary that the photoreceptor have sensitivity throughout the visible region of the spectrum. For printers, exposures are derived from either a laser or an array of light-emitting diodes. In this case, the photoreceptor need be sensitive only at the emission wavelength of the laster or light-emitting diode. Laser exposures are usually scanned across the photoreceptor surface by a spinning polygon mirror. Most printers use either HeCd, Ar, HeNe, or GaAlAs lasers. For most applications, latent image formation requires exposures of approximately 10 ergs/cm^2. These correspond to an ASA rating of approximately unity.

In Carlson's original patent, anthracene, sulphur, and mixtures of sulphur and selenium were described as photoconducting insulators suitable for the creation of latent images. From the patent, it is clear that Carlson understood that latent image formation involved the selective dissipation of the corona-induced potential by the creation of free charges. The materials described by Carlson had very limited photoconductivity, however, particularly in the visible region of the spectrum. Further, these materials had very poor mechanical properties and could not be readily prepared in large areas. One of the initial responsibilities of the Battelle group was the development of materials with improved photoconductivity and mechanical properties that could be readily prepared in a large-area configuration. A major accomplishment of the Battelle group was the development of α–Se as a xerographic photoreceptor. Photoconductivity in α–Se was discovered independently in the late 1940s by two laboratories searching for large-area photoconductors suitable for imaging application. One of these was the RCA Laboratories, which was investigating the use of photosensors in vidicon technology. The other was at Battelle where photoreceptors for xerography were pursued. Both applications require materials with very low dark conductivity and high photosensitivity. During the 1960s and 1970s, α–Se and alloys of α–Se with arsenic and tellurium were widely used as photoreceptors. Other materials that were used were dispersions of inorganic particles, mainly ZnO, CdS, and CdSe, in a polymer host. In the past decade, organic materials and α–Se have been increasingly employed. The use of ZnO, CdS, and CdSe has been largely discontinued.

While α–Se was widely used in the early development of xerography, it has several limitations. The first is that it is susceptible to crystallization to the more stable trigonal form. The dark conductivity of trigonal selenium is such that it is not usable for xerography. This was eventually solved by the addition of small amounts of As. Another limitation is that α–Se shows very little photoconductivity in the longwavelength region of the visible spectrum. A solution to this problem involved the incorporation of either tellurium or arsenic, in relatively high concentrations. Films containing 40% arsenic (As_2Se_3) show comparable levels of photoconductivity in the blue, green, and red regions of the spectrum. The most significant limitation of α–Se and related alloys is that these materials cannot be prepared in a flexible belt configuration. This poses significant process limitations for colour or high-volume applications. For a general review of α–Se and related alloys. for xerography, see Pfister (1979a, 1979b) and Kasap (1991).The use of organic photoreceptors for xerography was first described in the late 1950s. Organic photoreceptors contain a strong electron donor or acceptor in a host polymer. Usually a pigment is added to impart the desired spectral sensitivity. Organic photoreceptors can be prepared in a belt or drum configuration. These are usually fabricated in a multilayer configuration by solvent coating methods. These materials are well-suited for xerography, particularly for highvolume applications, colour applications, or applications that involve near-infrared exposures. Further, the fact that they can be readily prepared in large areas by solvent-coating processes introduces significant cost advantages. The basic limitations are that they are relatively soft and have low abrasion resistance. For these reasons, the process lifetime is substantially less than α–Se or α–Si. For reviews of organic photoreceptors for xerography, see Nguyen and Weiss (1988, 1989), Melnyk and Pai (1990), and Borsenberger and Weiss (1991).

Amorphous silicon is usually prepared by plasma-induced chemical vapour deposition. The preparation of α–Si by this technique was first reported in the 1960s. During the 1970s and 1980s, α–Si was widely studied for both photovoltaic and xerographic applications. For xerography, the basic advantage of α–Si is high hardness, which leads to a very long process lifetime. Other advantages include high mobilities and bipolar transport. The advantage of high mobilities is that they permit a reduction in the process time between exposure and development. Bipolar transport permits the use of either polarity of the corona-induced surface potential. This, in turn, permits the reproduction of positive or negative images and the same developer. The major limitations of α–Si are high dark conductivities, high capacitance, cost, and factors related to health and environmental considerations. For a general review of the use of α–Si for xerography, see Mort (1991).

Image Development In the development step, toner particles are transferred to the surface of the photoreceptor. If the toner particles have the opposite polarity of the charged regions, they are attracted to the charged, or unexposed, regions, which correspond to the dark areas of the original image. This form of development is described as charged-area development and widely used in copiers. If the toner particles are of the same polarity, they are attracted to the discharged areas. This method, which is described as discharged-area development, is frequently used in printers. Variations of the amount of toner deposited in the image areas are due to differences in the charge density of the latent image. Most organic photoreceptors are charged negatively, while α–Se and α–Si are usually charged positively. Toners contain a small concentration, 5-10%, of a colourant in a resin binder. The role of the resin is to bind the colourant to the receiver, thus creating a permanent image. For black-and white reproduction, the most common colourant is carbon black. For colour applications, phthalocyanines are usually used for cyans, azo compounds for yellows, and quinacridones for magentas. Toner particles are in the range of 5-20 µm, and usually charged by contact electrification with carrier particles. Carrier particles, or beads, are typically 100 µm in diameter. The beads may contain a thin polymer surface layer to control the toner charge. In magnetic development, a further requirement is that the beads be magnetic. Carrier particles serve several functions: (1) they provide a means for charging the toner, (2) they scavenger the toner from background areas of the photoreceptor, and (3) in the case of magnetic carriers, they provide a means for transport of the toner particles to the latent image. For a review of carrier materials, see Jones (1991).

While most copiers and printers use dry development processes, liquid development is used in some applications. Liquid toners are comprised of a colloidal dispersion of pigmented particles in an insulating liquid. A charge-control agent is added to impart the desired charge on the pigment particles. Ionic surfactants or metal soaps are usually used as charge-control agents. Liquid toner particles can be charged positively or negatively. The particles are significantly smaller than dry toner particles. Due to their small size, liquid toners have much higher resolution capability. For this reason, liquid toners have been used in a wide range of highquality colour printing applications.

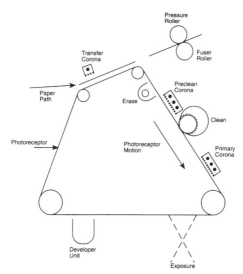

A schematic of a copier in which the photoreceptor is in a belt configuration.

Early xerographic processes used gravity to cascade carrier and toner particles over the electrostatic image. Carriers for cascade development were usually glass or metal beads. Cascade development was used in all early Xerox copiers. The major limitations of cascade development are that the process is not amendable to high process speeds, the inability to reproduce solid areas, and the physical size of the development system. For these reasons, cascade development was replaced by magnetic brush development in the mid-1970s. Magnetic brush development was invented in the 1950s. It is used today in almost all high-volume copiers and printers. In magnetic development, the carriers are usually iron, cobalt, or strontium ferrites. In this the magnets are stationary while the brush roll rotates, bringing the magnetic carrier beads and attached toner particles into contact with the electrostatic latent image. Key requirements of magnetic brush development are the need to monitor the toner concentration and the addition and mixing of fresh toner. In the final step in the development process, toner particles are separated from the carrier beads and transferred to the photoreceptor. Toner detachment from the carrier will occur when the detachment forces due to the electrostatic latent image overcome the adhesion forces due to the carrier.

Single-component developers do not contain a carrier. Usually these are transferred to the photoreceptor by a donor roller. Since it is not necessary to control the toner-to-carrier ratio of single-component developers, there are advantages of mechanical simplicity of the development apparatus. A further advantage is that abrasive wear of the photoreceptor is usually reduced. There are, however, several limitations.

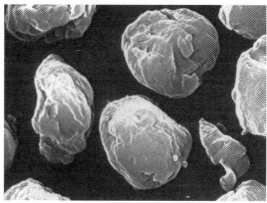

An example of typical toner particles used in a copier. The magnification is 2000X.

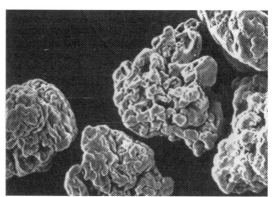

An example of a typical carrier bead. The magnification is 200X.

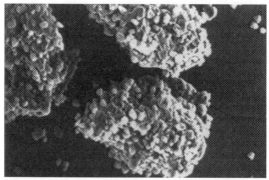

Attachment of the toner particles to the carrier bead. The magnification is 200X.

For process colour applications, the developers must be nonmagnetic. Depending on the charging method, another disadvantage may be low charging rates. A further problem is filming of the photoreceptor and the developer roller. Single component developers can be charged by induction, injection, contact, or by corona charging. In single-component developers, the detachment forces due to the latent image must overcome the forces between the developer particles and the donor roller to transfer the particles to the photoreceptor. While two component developers still dominate the industry, single-component developers have received increasing emphasis in recent years.

For reviews of image development, see Williams (1984), Schein (1988), and Hays (1991). For a discussion of dry toner technologies, see Gruber and Julien (1991). For liquid development, see Schaffert (1975), and Schmidt, Larson, and Bhattacharya (1991).

Toner Transfer In the transfer step, toner particles are transferred from the photoreceptor to the receiver. This is normally accomplished by electrostatic transfer. In electrostatic transfer, a receiver is placed in contact with the toned image, either a corona discharge or a roller with a polarity opposite to the toner particles is passed over the receiver; then the receiver is separated from the photoconductor. For efficient transfer, there must be intimate contact between the photoreceptor and the receiver. The density of the transferred image is usually slightly less than the original. Maximum toner transfer efficiencies are between 80 and 95%. Toner transfer occurs when the forces on the toner due to the fields from the charge on the receiver exceed the adhesion forces between the toner and the photoreceptor. For conventional sized toners, adhesion is primarily due to image forces. Other techniques include roller transfer and techniques based on adhesive transfer. Adhesive processes have the advantage that they are more uniform than electrostatic process and much more efficient for small-sized particles. A limitation is the difficulty in transferring thick layers.

Image Fusing After the toner particles are transferred to the receiver, some form of fixing or fusing is required to render the image permanent. This can be accomplished by pressure, heat, radiation, or solvent fixing. Solvent fusing generally does not work well with a wide range of receivers and requires complex solvent entrapment equipment. Cold pressure fusing processes are limited to low-volume applications and generally give lower image quality than hot pressure processes. Further, cold-pressure fusing requires special toners. The advantage is the absence of standby power requirements. Radiant fusing is generally not amendable to high process speeds. For these reasons, processes that involve combinations of heat and pressure are the most widely used. This is normally accomplished by hot-roll pressure devices in which at least one roll is heated. Offset can be avoided by the use of special oils wicked onto the surface of the roll. Most rolls use either silicone rubber or poly(tetrafluoroethylene). For reasons of stability and durability, the latter is more common.

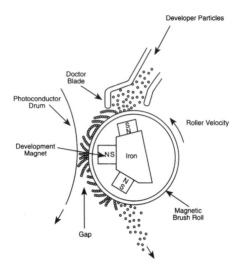

A schematic of a typical magnetic brush development system (after Schein). Reprinted with permission from Electophotography and Development Physics, 1988, Springer-Verlag, Berlin, p. 27. Copyright 1988, Springer-Verlag.

Photoreceptor Cleaning When toner particles are transferred from the photoreceptor to the receiver, some particles remain and must be removed before the subsequent image-forming process. Toner to photoreceptor adhesion results largely from electrostatic and dispersion forces, which must be broken to separate the toner particles from the photoreceptor. Schaffert (1975) mentions a number of techniques that can be used: rotating brushes, solvents, wiping the photoreceptor surface with disposable fibre webs, air blasts, skive blades, and abrading the surface with particles having a polarity opposite to the toner particles.

In most applications, toner removal is accomplished by either skive blades, magnetic brushes, or fibre brushes. Low volume machines usually use metal or polymeric blades. For mid- and high-volume machines, mechanical magnetic or fibre brushes are widely used. Blade cleaning has advantages of mechanical simplicity and process compactness. The use of this technique on seamed photoreceptors requires provision such that the blade can be intermittently deactivated. In magnetic brush cleaning, the photoreceptor surface is abraded by carrier particles that are transported to the surface by rotating magnetic fields. Fibre brush cleaning is usually accomplished by a vacuum-assisted rotating brush. After the toner is separated from the photoreceptor surface, it is usually removed by air flow.

Cleaning is a major factor in determining the photoreceptor process lifetime. For conventional cleaning processes, lifetimes of chalcogenide glass and α-Si photoreceptors are in the range of 10^6 (1 million) impressions. For the same conditions, lifetimes of organic photoreceptors are typically 10^4 to 10^5 (10,000 to 100,000) impressions.

Photoreceptor Erase The purpose of the erase exposure is to remove any residual electrostatic charges so that prior to the subsequent process cycle the surface charge density is spatially uniform. If a residual electrostatic image is present prior to the subsequent corona charging step, the surface potential and photosensitivity will be different in areas corresponding to the preceding image and background. Erase exposures are frequently used in conjunction with a corona. Erase exposures are considerably more intense than image exposures and usually continuous. Flash exposures are seldom used for erase purposes.

Summary The fundamental image-forming process in xerography is the creation of an electrostatic latent image on the surface of a photoconducting insulator. To create the latent image, the photoreceptor is charged by a corona discharge and then exposed to an imagewise pattern of radiation. The exposure creates free electron-hole pairs. Under the influence of the corona-induced field, the pairs are displaced to the free and substrate surfaces. Thus, the corona-deposited surface charge is dissipated in the exposed regions and a latent image is created that corresponds to the image that is to be reproduced. To develop the latent image, electrostatically charged toner particles are brought into the vicinity of the latent image. Due to the fields created by the charges on the photoreceptor surface, the toner adheres to the latent image, converting it to a visible image. The developed image is transferred to a receiver and rendered permanent by a fusing or fixing process. Finally, the photoreceptor is cleaned of any remaining toner particles and then erased to eliminate any residual surface charges. Following the erase step, the process can be repeated.

OTHER PROCESSES Within the framework of Schaffert's original definition of electrophotography, many different processes exist. Due to the very considerable process complexity of conventional xerography, there have been many attempts to develop alternative technologies. A discussion of early work has been given by Carlson (1965), Claus and Corrsin (1965), and Schaffert (1975). Recent work has been reviewed by Schein (1988). Prominent among the alternative technologies are the following:

Electrofax In Electrofax, a photoconductive layer is bonded to paper. The coated paper then serves as the medium for both the formation of the latent image and the final image, thus eliminating the transfer and cleaning processes. As such, the process offers significant cost advantages. As with conventional xerography, the process involves the creation of an electrostatic latent image that is subsequently developed by charged toner particles. Such a process was commercialized by RCA in the early 1950s. In the Electrofax process, the photoconductor contains a dispersion of ZnO particles in a low-molecular-weight silicone binder. The process was widely used for low-volume black-and-white applications during the 1950s and 1960s. For economic and aesthetic reasons largely related to the need for specially prepared paper, this process has declined steadily in recent years. For a description of the Electrofax process, see Young and Greig (1954) and Amick (1959a, 1959b).

Persistent Internal Polarization Certain photoconducting materials can be polarized by the simultaneous presence of radiation and a field. The resulting polarization persists after the field and radiation are removed. Persistent internal polarization is based on trapping. The polarization requires a very high concentration of trapping centres. This phenomenon was discovered independently in the United States and the Soviet Union in the late 1950s. In the United States, the phenomenon is described as persistent internal polarization. In the Soviet Union, such materials are described as photoelectrets. Latent images can be created by either the selective polarization in exposed regions or by first producing a uniform polarization of the photoconductor surface followed by a depolarizing image exposure. In principle, multiple copies can be made from a single exposure. The limitations of the process are very high exposures and latent image stability.

Photoconductive Pigment Electrophotography In photoconductive pigment electrophotography, the photosensitive material is incorporated in the toner particles. The particles are then dispersed in either an insulating liquid or softenable resin. Absorption of the image exposure creates a variable charge on the particles which are then displaced in a constant field. In conventional xerography, the photoinduced discharge modulates the field at the photoreceptor surface while the charge on the toner remains constant.

There are several variations of this process. Photoelectrophoresis uses toner particles dispersed in a liquid and is primarily used for colour reproduction. Manifold imaging uses a receiver precoated with a thin toner layer. Migration imaging uses a thin layer of toner particles dispersed in a thermoplastic host. Migration imaging has potential for microimaging applications. For colour reproduction, the fundamental limitations of photoconductive pigment electrophotography are that it is difficult to achieve high colour densities. problems related to efficient colour separation, and problems of liquid management. For black-and-white applications, the principal limitations are cost and problems related to output rates.

Other Processes of Interest In ion-flow electrophotography, a photoreceptor is coated onto a metal screen that is then placed between the corona and a dielectric receiver. Exposed regions of the screen then permit ions to pass to the receiver while nonexposed regions become charged and block the ion flow to the receiver. Processes that involve transfer of the electrostatic latent image, rather than the toner, have also been proposed. By this method, the electrostatic latent image is transferred to a dielectric-coated paper prior to development. Transfer is accomplished by placing the paper in contact with the photoreceptor in the presence of a field. As with Electrofax, the principal limitation of the process is the need for a special paper. Numerous other processes have been proposed. These include processes based on electrophotolysis, electrothermography, photoadhesion, and photoemission.

At present, none of these processes is competitive with the quality, cost, and output rates of xerography for copier applications. For printers, the principal alternatives to xerography are ink jet and thermography. For a more detailed discussion of alternative technologies, see Schaffert (1975), Jaffe and Mills (1983), and Schein (1988).

SUMMARY *Electrophotography* is defined as image-forming processes that involve a combination of light and electricity. *Xerography is* a branch of electrophotography that involves the development of electrostatic charge patterns formed on insulating surfaces. Xerography is the most highly developed form of electrophotography at present.

Relative to other forms of electrophotography, xerography has many advantages. Of these, cost, image quality, and process speed are the most significant. Xerography is currently used in all commercial copiers. With the advent of semiconductor lasers and light-emitting diodes, xerography has also been widely used for printing. For office and desktop applications, xerography has become the dominant nonimpact printing technology.

References:

Amick, J. A. (1959a). *RCA Reu* 20:753.

Amick, J. A. (1959b). *RCA Reu* 20:770.

Borsenberger, P. M., and Weiss, D. S. (1991). In *Handbook of Imaging Materials,* A. S. Diamond (Ed.). New York; Marcel Dekker, p. 379.

Carlson C. F. (1942). U.S. Patent 2,297,691

Carlson C. F. (1944). U.S. Patent 2,357,809

Carlson C. F. (1948). *Engr Sci.* 12:11.

Carlson C. F. (1949). *Photogr. Age,* Mar., p. 10.

Carlson C. F. (1965). In *Xerography and Related Processes,* J. H. Dessauer and H. E. Clark (Eds.). London: Focal Press, p.15

Claus, C. J., and Corrsin, L. (1965). In *Xerography and Related Processes,* J. H. Dessauer and H. E. Clark (Eds.). London: Focal Press, p. 451.

Dessauer, J. H., Mott, G. R., and Bogdonoff, H. (1955). *Photogr Eng. 6:* 250.

Dinsdale, A. (1963). *Photogr Sci. Eng.* 7:1.

Fleischer, J. M., Latta, M. R., and Rabedeau, M. E. (1977). *IBM J Res. Deu* 479.

Gruber, R. J., and Julien, P. C. (1991). In *Handbook of Imaging materials,* A. S. Diamond (Ed.). New York: Marcel Dekker, p. 159.

Hays, D. A. (1991). *J. Imag. Technol.* 17:252.

Jaffe, A. B., and Mills, R. N. (1983). *S/D* 24:219.

Jones, L. O. (1991). In *Handbook of Imaging Materials,* A. S. Diamond (Ed.). New York: Marcel Dekker, p. 201.

Kasap, S . O, (1991). In *Handbook of Imaging Materials,* A. S. Diamond (Ed.). New York: Marcel Dekker, p. 329.Lichtenberg, G. C. (1777). *Novi Comment, Gottingen* 8:168.

Melnyk, A. R., and Pai, D. M. (1990). *SPIE* 1253:141.

Mort, J. (1989). *The Anatomy of Xerography.* Jefferson, NC: McFarland and Company.

Mort, J. (1991). In *Handbook of Imaging Materials,* A. S . Diamond (Ed.). New York: Marcel Dekker, p. 447.

Nguyen, K. C., and Weiss, D. S. (1988). *Denshi Shashin Gakkai-shi (Electrophotography)* 27: 1.

Nguyen, K. C., and Weiss, D. S. (1989). *J. Imag. Technol.* 15: 158.

Oliphant, W. D. (1953). *Discovery* 14:175.

Pfister, G. (1979a). *Contemp. Phys.* 20:449.

Pfister, G. (1979b). *J. Elect. Mater* 8:789.

Ronalds. (1842). In *Encyclopedia Britannica.* Edinburgh, Vol. 8, p. 661.

Schaffert, R. M. (1950). *The Penrose Annual* 44:96.

Schaffert, R. M. (1975). *Electrophotography.* London: Focal Press .

Schaffert, R. M., and Oughton, C. D. (1948). *J. Opt. Soc. Am.* 38:991.

Scharfe, M. E. (1984). *Electrophotography: Principles and Optimization.* Letchworth, England: Research Studies Press.

Schein, L. B. (1988). *Electrophotography and Development Physics.* Berlin: Springer-Verlag.

Schmidt, S. P., Larson, J. R., and Bhattacharya, R. (1991). In *Handbook of Imaging Materials, A. S.* Diamond (Ed.). New York: Marcel Dekker, p. 227.

Shahin, M. M. (1969). *Appl. Opt. Suppl. Electrophotogr* 3:106.

Villarsy. (1788). *Voight's Mag.* 5:176.

Williams, E. M. (1984). *The Physics and Technology of the Xerographic Process.* New York: John Wiley and Sons.

Wilson, J. C. (1948). U.S. *Camera* 11:46.

Young, C. J., and Greig, H. G. (1954). *RCA Rev* 15:469.

ELECTROSTATIC Pertains to static electricity; that is, electrical charges at rest as distinguished from current or dynamic electricity, which is electric charges in motion.

ELECTROSTATIC LATENT IMAGE Imagewise charge patterns used in xerography. The patterns are subsequently made visible by toner particles, transferred to a receiver, then made permanent by a fixing process. The latent image is created by uniformly charging a photoconducting insulator by a corona discharge, then exposing the photoreceptor to a light image. Absorption of the image exposure creates free electron hole pairs that dissipate the surface charge in the exposed regions, thus creating a latent electrostatic image that corresponds to the image to be reproduced.

ENCODER A device that takes a RGB picture signal and timing signals and composites these data into composite video.

ENHANCED GRAPHIC ADAPTERS (EGA) In computers, this cathode-ray tube (CRT) superseded colour graphics adapter (CGA) and provided higher resolution and more colour. Typically EGA could provide resolution of 640 x 350 and 16 colours from a palette of 64 colours. In text mode, one of twelve modes, characters are formed from an 8 x 14 matrix, thus giving higher text resolution.

ENHANCEMENT Any method by which an image may be improved, such as airbrushing or retouching with photo oils, but commonly understood to be a computer related process whereby an original is scanned and digitized, then manipulated with image management software. The image may be sharpened, its colours may be corrected, and inappropriate elements may be removed. Certain elements may be emphasized by changing their tonal value or the value of the surrounding areas. Rotation or combination with elements of other images are other possibilities. Output can be to a digital storage medium, a film recorder, or a prepress device. EVGA In electronic imaging, an abbreviation for extended video graphics array (VGA), meaning a display that can achieve a resolution of 1024 x 768. This high resolution is usually noninterlaced, although it may be found interlaced.

EVOLUTIONARY OPERATIONS (EVOP) A statistical method of improving a process (such as photographic development) by making a systematic series of changes about the usual levels. Only small changes are made, too small to produce defects in the output, and the results tested. Only if a favourable outcome is assured is the process changed in the appropriate way.

EXTENDED MEMORY A de facto requirement in the processing of images or the using of multimedia on DOS based platforms. Extended memory occurs above 1 megabyte. Four to eight megabytes has become standard RAM in multimedia machines.

Fax Facsimile

FACSIMILE (1) An exact copy or a copy that closely resembles the original. (2) A scanning copying system that forms electrical signals that can be transmitted to another location where the scanning process is reversed to recreate the image on photographic paper.

FAKE COLOUR A multicolour image made from a monochromatic original. Many methods exist for achieving this end, including hand colouring and computer enhancement.

FAX Slang for facsimile.

FEATURE In electronic imaging, an area defined by a mark, or the name given to any shape or to an entire page.

FEEDBACK A component of the output of a system that is *fed back* into the input of the system. Feedback can be intentionally introduced into a system for a desired effect or signal processing purpose, or can be an unwanted effect (such as the squeal in public address systems). Feed-back is most commonly associated with audio systems, but is gaining importance in electronic imaging systems.

FIELD (1) The entire subject area imaged within a specific format of a camera, viewfinder, or other optical device, also known as the *field of view*. (2) The entire subject area that is imaged within the circle of good definition of a lens. (3) The imaginary surface that represents the best focus for each point of a flat object perpendicular to the lens axis. (4) In television, one of the two scans of the scene that are interlaced on the viewing screen. (5) In video, the scanning of an image in interlaced mode is done in two passes. Each pass contains one-half the data or resolution. Each one of these passes is known as a field. The field is scanned every 50th (60th) of a second PAL (NTSC).

FIELD-EFFECT TRANSISTOR (FET) A three-terminal semiconductor device in which a voltage applied to the input terminal controls the current through the device. It differs from a bipolar junction transistor (BJT), which uses input current to control the current through it. The input terminal of an FET is known as the *gate* and corresponds to the base of a BJT. Voltage applied to the high-impedance gate controls the flow of current through a thin bar of semiconductor material called a *channel*. Connections made to the ends of the channel are called the source and the drain and correspond to the emitter and collector of a BJT, respectively. There are two types of FETs: the junction FET (JFET) and the metal-oxide semiconductor FET (MOSFET). Large-scale integrated circuits are built primarily using MOSFET devices because they consume little power to operate. Both types are available as *P*-channel and *N*-channel FETs, according to the type of semiconductor used in their fabrication.

FILE (1) In computers, the file is the basic structure for saving or storing data. Images, spreadsheets, and text documents are stored as files to be retrieved later by the programs (applications) that created or can operate on the file. (2) In electronic imaging, the digital database that represents a picture or a line image, or a set of instructions.

FILM RECORDER A device to reproduce an electronic analog or digital image on conventional colour or monochrome silver halide film using a monochrome high-resolution cathode-ray tube (CRT). For colour imaging, individual exposures are made through red, green, and blue filters to provide records of the analog or digital colour image information in raster or bitmap form. Monochrome exposures can be made without a filter or through the same filter set with individual exposures.

FIRMWARE In computers, an instruction set or program that is stored and retrieved from programmable ROM or plug-in modules that are self-initiating and do not typically require software. Firmware differs from software in that the application exist as a program on a floppy disk or in a hard drive, while firmware is built into a chip or PROM.

FLATBED SCANNER A type of scanner that scans flat art that is placed on a flat surface similar to the image capture area of a photocopier and renders an image of the scanned object via a charge-coupled device (CCD) array that converts the optical density differences into electronic signals that are quantized into whatever gray levels are supported by the scanner.

FLICKER The perception of a rapid variation in brightness when viewing a rapidly flashing light or series of intermittent images that alternate with darkness as with motion picture and video images. Persistence of vision prevents flicker with appropriate values of image frequency and luminance.

FLIP In electronic imaging, a computer function for rotating an image 180° about a horizontal axis, thus reversing the image from top to bottom.

FLOP In electronic imaging, a computer function for rotating an image 180° about a vertical axis, thus reversing the image from left to right.

FLOPPY DISK See *Disk.*

FLYING-SPOTSCANNER An image-forming device employing a beam of electrons (cathode-ray tube) or light (electronic printer) that moves systematically over an area and varies in intensity to form an image. In cathode-ray tubes the beam of electrons produces fluorescence on the screen. In electronic printers, the light beam exposes a photosensitive material.

FOURIER TRANSFORM A mathematical operation whereby a function (such as a two-dimensional image) is broken up into sine and cosine wave components. The image is then completely represented by coefficients indicating the magnitude and phase of each of these components. Such a representation is called a *frequency domain* representation. A wide variety of mathematical techniques are based on the Fourier transform—it is the foundation for most modern image evaluation techniques and a significant percentage of the more powerful digital image processing techniques. A common example of a Fourier transform is the modulation transfer function, which is the Fourier transform of the point spread function for an image.

FRAME (1) A single photograph in a motion picture, film-strip, microfilm, computer animation field, or similar sequence of photographs. (2) The area within the film aperture in a camera or projector. (3) An enclosed border made of wood, metal, plastic, or other material used to enhance and protect a photograph. (4) The limiting border in a viewfinder. (5) In television, two interlaced fields. (6) To set up a camera to include only the desired subject area of the photograph. (7) To adjust the motion-picture projector so that the frame line does not show on the screen. (8) A box, drawn with a computer, around a text or picture block. (9) An area of a computer image page activated or set aside to create or import a graphic image. (10) A set of 625 individual scan lines on a television screen. The screen generates (draws) 25 separate frames each second. (11) A collapsible or permanently constructed rectangle, usually of plastic or aluminum, to support a stretched-out projection screen, reflector, diffuser, etc. for photographic presentation or lighting control.

FRAME CAPTURE In video, the act of freezing one frame's worth of data (1/25 of a second, NTSC) and flash converting that analog data into digital form.

Syn.: *Frame grab.*

FRAMEGRAB See frame capture.

FRAME RATE In video, the speed at which a frame is displayed 1/25 of a second, PAL (1/30 of a second, NTSC); also known as *real time.*

FRAMES PER SECOND (FPS) The number of individual images, filmed or projected, per second. The normal frame rate for motion pictures is 24 frames per second.

FRAME STORE A device for the storage of still video frames for subsequent insertion into future video.

FREEZE (1) To obtain a sharp image of a rapidly moving object, typically by the use of a high shutter speed or electronic flash of short duration. (2) To stop the motion during the viewing of a motion picture or video by using a single frame for prolonged viewing.

FREEZEFRAME (1) See *Frame capture.* (2) A motion-picture optical effect in which a single image is repeated in order to appear frozen in place, that is, stationary, when projected.

FREQUENCY (υ) The number of complete events of a regular cyclic sequence, usually counted out over 1 second. The term is especially applied to the wave propagations of various forms of energy such as electromagnetic radiation and acoustic energy, as well as regular mechanical movement. The frequency of an oscillation is inversely proportional to the wavelength and directly proportional to the velocity of a wave, as given by the equation $υ = v/λ$. The velocity v and the wavelength λ must both be measured using appropriate units, i.e., meters per second and meters.

As described, frequency is another means (along with wavelength and energy) for specifying the exact nature of a photon of electromagnetic radiation. The frequency of a photon is equal to the speed of light in a vacuum divided by its wavelength. For example, a photon with a wavelength of 600 nm has a frequency of 5×10^{14} hertz. Since frequency is related to energy, by the law of conservation of energy the frequency of a photon cannot change. Changes in the speed of a photon as it passes through materials with different indexes of refraction result in changes in its wavelength. Most commonly, longer wavelength electromagnetic radiation (such as radio frequency radiation) is expressed in terms of frequency and shorter wavelength radiation is expressed in terms of wavelength (when propagating through a vacuum).

Electrical energy is also generally distributed as alternating current (sinusoidal voltage) and therefore has a frequency. This frequency varies around the world, usually being either 50 or 60 hertz. Purely resistive loads, such as light bulbs or heaters, function equally well at either frequency (providing the voltage, which also differs, is correct), but other devices may function incorrectly, or even be harmed, by operating them at the wrong frequency.

FREQUENCY DISTRIBUTION A display, usually in the form of a graph, of the results obtained from the repeated examination of a process, showing the number of occurrences of different outcomes. Such a graph permits the identification of the process as caused by chance, if a near Gaussian (bell-shaped) pattern appears. Otherwise, one can detect the influence of nonchance effects if, for example, the pattern is skewed.

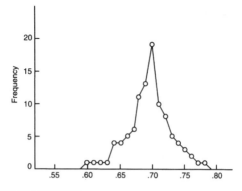

Frequency distribution.

FREQUENCY MODULATION (FM) A means of transmitting a signal by combining the signal with a constant frequency *carrier wave* so that the frequency of the carrier wave is changed by the signal. The receiver then decodes the fluctuations in the frequency of the carrier wave to reconstruct the original signal. Frequency modulation is a common means for radio and television transmission.

FREQUENCY RESPONSE (1) See *Modulation transfer function*. (2) The amplitude output with respect to frequency characteristic of a system under test. One method of measurement is to drive the system with a sine wave that sweeps from one end of the desired frequency range to the other while measuring the amplitude of the output. The resulting curve of amplitude versus frequency, usually plotted in decibels of amplitude versus logarithmic frequency, is a frequency response curve.

FRONT PORCH That part of the image in composite video broadcasting between the front edge of the horizontal blanking and front of the horizontal sync signal.

FUSE A protective device consisting of a wire or thin strip of a metal that has a low melting point. When current passing through the wire exceeds a prescribed level, the wire melts and opens the circuit. Fuses are used primarily to reduce the danger of fire or damage to wiring or to equipment. They are rated in voltage as well as current. Fuses are also available in different physical sizes and shapes and with different speeds of response: quick-blow, slow-blow, etc. It is important to always replace a fuse with the same rating and type as was originally used in the device. Never replace with a coin or a piece of wire.

GUI Graphical users interface

GAUSSIAN DISTRIBUTION For a set of numbers, a pattern of variation about a central value caused by change. The plot of such a pattern, often called, from its shape, the *bell* curve, is completely defined by the arithmetic average and the standard deviation.

GENERATION One of a sequence of images of the same subject in which each image is made from the next lower generation image except for the first, which is made directly from the subject. Each generation normally consists of a negative image and a positive image, or a reversal image. It should be noted that if a first-generation copy is a reproduction of an original photograph, it is a second-generation image. Second- and higher-generation images are made for any of various reasons, including to alter the size or tone reproduction characteristics of an image and to obtain multiple copies.

GIGABYTE One billion bytes or 1024 megabytes.

GLITCH In the vernacular of electronic imaging, an error, bug, or problem that unexpectedly occurs.

GLOBAL CHANGE An overall colour change in electronic image correction or processing.

GRADATION A more or less gradual change of tone, colour, texture, etc. between adjacent areas of an object or the corresponding image. Gradation provides the viewer with information concerning the three-dimensional attributes of the subject, such as the facial features of a portrait subject as revealed by the variation of tones produced by the lighting.

GRAPHIC ARTS Another name for graphic communications and printing. It encompasses all the operations of image processing in the reproduction of text and illustration copy in quantity.

GRAPHIC ARTS IMAGING For over 400 years after the invention of printing by Gutenberg, illustrations were produced manually by hand retouching, copperplate intaglio engraving, woodcuts, steel engraving, and hand-drawn lithographic stones. The invention of photography in 1839 revolutionized imaging and created new printing processes for graphic arts. Lithography became photolithography, engraving became photoengraving, intaglio engraving became photogravure, collotype was called photogelatin, and platemaking for printing was called photomechanics. Graphic arts photography was the means for imaging and producing illustrations for all graphic arts processes for more than 100 years until electronics and computers revolutionized graphic arts imaging in the 1980s.

GRAPHIC ARTS PHOTOGRAPHY The processes, equipment, and materials used in graphic arts photography are described in this encyclopedia under the entry *Photomechanical and Electronic Reproduction.* Most images for reproductions originate as photographic prints or colour transparencies. All printing processes with the exception of some conventional gravure, collotype, and screenless lithography are binary processes that cannot print gradient tones of ink. All intermediate tones for these processes must be converted to halftones. Also, because colour reproduction is based on the three-colour theory of light, all colour originals must be divided into four separate photographic records, or separations, that represent the cyan (C), magenta (M), and yellow (Y) components of the colour images plus black (K). Because printing inks do not have correct colour absorptions, colour separation films must be corrected to compensate for these absorption errors. This is usually done manually by dot etching using silver solvents or photographically by controlled exposures to adjust dot sizes to correct the colours.

The purpose of graphic arts photography is to convert line images such as text and line illustrations into high contrast images on photographic films and continuous-tone photographs into halftone images; to photograph colour images through red, green, and blue filters, and a contact screen to produce halftone separations of the three printing colours, CMY and black (K); and to correct the images for reproduction. After photography and correction, the films are used to make colour proofs of the images for approval by the customer. After approval, the films are assembled into page layouts that are combined by contact exposures onto single films for each colour separation. The single films for the individual pages are proofed again and composed into signature layouts for the press by mounting them in imposition order on orange or red plastic layout sheets that are used for making the printing plates. These are all labour-, skill- and cost-intensive operations.

Electronic Imaging The trend to electronic imaging was generated by the need to shorten deadlines for printing by time-sensitive publications like weekly newsmagazines This was accomplished by electronic imaging that reduced and/or eliminated the labour- and skill-intensive operations of graphic arts photography and conventional prepress functions. The systems of electronic imaging used for these purposes are described in the section entitled "Electronic Prepress" in the article *Photomechanical and Electronic Reproduction.*

Electronic scanners are used to make colour-corrected halftone colour separations for reproduction. Special scanners are used to convert black-and-white or colour images to single or duotone (two-colour) halftone images. Even original photography is being replaced by electronic cameras using sensors like CCDs (charge coupled devices) for recording the images that are converted to digital data for image processing. Colour electronic prepress systems are used to enhance colour correction, perform airbrushing, retouching, pixel editing, cloning, and other image manipulation, compose type and pages, and output high quality halftone images. Electronic layout and stripping systems assemble images into page layouts and pages into plate impositions.

These high-end electronic systems are expensive and device dependent as they use dedicated hardware with proprietary formats that make interfacing between systems by different manufacturers difficult. New device-independent systems using off-the-shelf components and universal standard page description languages are completely interfaceable, have most of the features of the high-end systems, are much less expensive, have various levels of sophistication, and provide links with existing high-end proprietary systems.

GRAPHICS TABLET An interactive device for inputting data into a computer graphics program. These devices locate positions on a tablet (grid) that correspond to locations on the monitor. A stylus or pointing device can cause a voltage difference at any position on the tablet. These voltages are converted to coordinates and stored. Sonic graphics tablets use sound to locate position. The time it takes to note the sound by sensors at the edge of the tablet is employed to determine location. The stylus is used as a pen would be used on a sheet of paper (tablet).

GRAPHIC USER INTERFACE (GUI) The GUI is intended to utilize graphic elements such as symbols, menus, and icons to assist the computer operator interacting with the computer's operating system: The graphic objects are accessed via a mouse or other pointing device.

GRAY Name given to colours that do not exhibit a hue and that are intermediate in lightness between white and black.

GRAY SCALE (1) In electronic imaging, the range of brightness available to a digital system based on the power of 2. Each bit can represent a brightness. In a 2-bit gray scale (2^1) there are two gray tones available. In a 4-bit gray scale (2^2) there are four gray tones available. In a 7-bit scale (2^7) there are 128 grey tones available. (2) A set of neutral patches arranged in order from light to dark used for producing on a test sample a set of different exposures. The patches are identified with numbers related to the resulting relative log exposure values. Reflection gray scales may be placed in the scene; ignoring the effects of surface reflections and camera flare, the log exposure change from one patch to the next is equal to the density change, typically 0.10. Transmission gray scales are used in some types of sensitometers and for checking the performance of a printer, as well as for other uses in testing.

GROUND (ELECTRICAL) A connection to earth for ac power lines. For safety reasons, ground must be connected to the metal enclosure of equipment supplied by mains of 120 (nominal) volts or higher. In electronic equipment, ground is usually connected to the metal chassis and to one side of the internal dc power supply and becomes the reference for all voltage measurements.

GROUND FAULT CIRCUIT INTERRUPTER (GFCI)
A device used to protect people from electric shock. A GFCI opens a circuit when the current in the neutral wire is not equal to the current in the hot, or live, wire. Such inequality would occur when current flows through the body of a person directly to ground rather than returning to the power source via the neutral wire. Local electrical codes usually require a GFCI to be installed in wiring going to electrical outlets located in kitchens, bathrooms, near swimming pools, or any place near water. Even if not required, GFCI should be installed in all circuits in darkrooms, near photo processing machines, and other wet locations.

GROUP OPERATORS
In electronic imaging, an image-processing operation that takes into account the gray level of neighbouring pixels surrounding the pixel of interest. A scalable odd number array (3 x 3, 5 x 5, 9 x 9) or mask is often used to do the filtering.

HALFTONE GRAVURE The process of using halftone prints on electromechanical engraving machines to produce gravure printing cylinders.

HALFTONE PROCESS The halftone process is used to represent continuous tone images, such as photographs, with binary printing processes; that is, processes that can print either solids of the ink on the press or no ink. (This use of the word *halftone* should not be confused with *halbton* which is the German word for continuous tone.) The halftone principle is based on an optical illusion in which tones are represented by a large number of small dots of different sizes with equal optical density and equal spacing between their centres.

The halftone principle is possible because of the limited visual acuity of the human eye. The eye cannot distinguish two points separated by less than one minute of arc. At a normal reading distance of 10-12 inches, this corresponds to two dots separated by about 1/250th of an inch. This is equivalent to a screen ruling of 125 lines per inch (lpi). Halftones with screen rulings higher than 125 lpi have dots indistinguishable to the normal eye. Newspapers have pictures with screen rulings from 60 to 100 lpi; low-budget magazines, newsletters, and other publications use illustrations with screen rulings from 100 to 120 lpi; magazines, catalogs, and other medium-quality publications use screen rulings from 133 to 150 lpi; high-quality printing uses screen rulings of 175 to 250 lpi.

Screen rulings are oriented at different screen angles. Since most screen rulings use a square matrix, screen angles repeat every 90 degrees. Dots oriented at 0 degrees or 90 degrees form rows that the eye can see as disturbing patterns with a screen ruling of 133 lpi and higher, even though the eye cannot resolve the individual dots. Therefore, single-colour (black-and-white) halftones are almost always placed with the screen angle at 45 degrees. In colour printing it has been found that dot images separated by exactly 30 degrees produce minimum moire effects, or interference patterns. Since there are only three 30-degrees in 90 degrees, there are problems in four-colour printing with regard to the placement of the fourth colour. Conventional angles are usually black 45 degrees, magenta 75 degrees, yellow 0 degrees or 90 degrees, and cyan 15 degrees or 105 degrees. To eliminate the moire pattern caused by the spacing of yellow between magenta and cyan, the yellow is sometimes printed in a coarser or finer screen ruling.

The original halftone screen consisted of a grid of straight lines ruled and inked on two sheets of optically flat glass cemented together at right angles. The lines were the same width as the spaces between them. Glass screen photography requires (1) precision equipment in the camera back to mount the screen and maintain accurate screen distance, and (2) experienced craftsmen with expert skills to produce satisfactory halftones. Because of these constraints, glass screens are now practically obsolete, having been replaced by either contact screens or electronic dot generation. Contact screens are made on film and are used on camera backs, enlarger platforms, or vacuum frames. They are usually made from glass screens. The dots are vignetted with variable density across each dot. There are gray screens with dots consisting of deposits of silver in the film and dyed screens—usually magenta—with dots in which the silver has been replaced by a dye. There are square, round, and elliptical dot screens for special effects, especially in the middletones, double-dot (Respi), and triple-dot screens for special effects in the highlights.

Electronic dot generation (EDG) is performed by special computer programs on electronic scanners, and on prepress and desktop publishing systems. They combine the picture elements, or pixels, of digitized images into data that simulate dot sizes, shapes, screen rulings, and angles of conventional halftone screened images. Special films and processing are used to produce high-contrast images for reproduction.

Halftone process. Moire patterns in printing due to improper screen angles.

HARDCOPY (1) A computer-screen image printed out on paper or film. (2) A photographic print from a microfilm or other image projection, as distinct from an image projected only for visual inspection.

HARD DISK A magnetic storage device that is capable of holding thousands of megabytes, in contrast to floppy disks that hold approximately 3 MB. Hard disks are also referred to as fixed disks. These disks contain a platter that is spun at a high speed and a read/write head that accesses data. The hard disk maintains its integrity (data) when the power is off. Density of these disks is measured in hundreds of millions of bytes.

HARDPROOF A proof (test image) on paper as opposed to a soft proof, which is a corresponding image on a video display terminal.

HARDWARE All the components of a computer system except the programmed instructions, that is, except the software.

HEAD (1) An electromagnetic subdevice in a floppy disk drive

124

or hard disk drive that reads and writes data to the disk. The head provides directed current that affects the magnetic property of the media, causing data to be written to, read, or erased from the magnetic disk or tape. (2) The top or the principal functioning part of certain devices such as a tripod head, the part of a tripod that holds the camera and commonly provides for controlled tilting and panning of the camera.

HEAD ALIGNMENT A term applied to film and tape recording of analog or digital, and to audio, video, or other signals, meaning the correct positioning of the head with respect to the tape or film. Important considerations include the need for continuous intimate contact between the tape or film and the head or else severe spacing loss will occur.

HERTZ The unit of frequency; 1 hertz being 1 cycle per second. Used for sound, electromagnetic radiation, and other wave motions.

HIDDEN LINES / SIDES In computer graphics, the modelling of a three-dimensional object in wire frame mode will display all the necessary lines to fully visualize the object. When the object is displayed as a solid, not all of the lines are visible. Those lines that are hidden by a surface are not visible, hence they are called hidden lines. These lines remain a mathematical formula and are only displayed if the object is viewed from another vantage point.

HIGH COLOUR A general-purpose PC graphics board that is capable of surpassing VGA specifications. High colour graphics boards can display 32,768 (15-bits) colours at a spatial resolution of 800 x 600 pixels. Fifteen-bit displays allow for the representation of 32 shades of red, x 32 shades of green x 32 shades of blue. High colour display is not photographic quality, but it does render colour at PAL and NTSC levels.

HIGH-CONTRAST Identifying a lighting, film, developer, printing material, etc. used to increase tonal separation, either to achieve a high-contrast effect or to compensate for a low-contrast effect elsewhere in the system.

HIGH DENSITY (HD) HD floppy disks can hold between 1.2 Mbytes and 2.88 Mbytes. Floppy disks are marked HD (high-density), DD (double-density, = 720 Kbytes) or SD (single-density, = 360 Kbytes).

HIGHLIGHT A light area in a scene, photograph, or other image, especially one where the lighting has contributed to the effect, such as a highlight produced by the main light on the cheek, nose, or forehead of a person in a portrait. Highlights may be identified more specifically as specular (a mirror-like reflection on a polished surface) or diffuse (a reflection on a dull surface).

HIGHLIGHT MASKING To facilitate the reproduction of colour positives, it is sometimes necessary to reduce the difference in density between highlight and shadow areas. An unsharp mask of low density is made and sandwiched in registration with the original positive. Substantial increases in highlight detail may be obtained. This technique can be applied to the printing of negatives as well.

HIGH-PASS FILTER (1) An electrical filter that passes frequencies above a defined and usually adjustable one, while rejecting frequencies below the cutoff frequency. High-pass filters are most often used to reduce the effects of background noise, which often has predominant low frequency content, while minimally disturbing the desired signal, such as voice. (2) The attenuation of low frequency data in an image. This operation enhances high-frequency data such as the transition from low-contrast data to highcontrast data (edge). Detail is generally enhanced.

HIGH-SPEED PHOTOGRAPHY The realm of high-speed still photography is generally determined by the exposure times used or the picture repetition rate. Exposure times of leaf or diaphragm mechanical shutters in still cameras generally have a minimum time limit of around 1/500 second, while modern focal plane shutters have achieved exposure times as short as 1/8,000 second. Generally, when photography with exposure times shorter than about 1/1000 second is contemplated, it is classed as high-speed work and nearly always requires special techniques.

To arrest motion in a picture, either the shortest exposure possible is used or the camera is moved in synchronism with the subject (permitting the background to blur).

A formula for the maximum permissible exposure time is

$$T = L/500 \times V \text{ seconds}$$

where L is the largest subject dimension to be recorded and V is the subject speed in the same units as L per second. For example, for a car moving at 68 mph, 100 feet per second (fps), the longest frame dimension, L, might be 50 feet. Thus,

$$T = 50/ (500 \times 100) \text{ or } T = 1/1000 \text{ second}$$

This is just on the limit for a normal shutter and no camera motion.

It should be noted that both V and L determine the exposure time—increasing V or decreasing L both demand shorter exposures. Many research subjects are both faster and smaller than a car.

Another method for determining exposure time is based on the concept of maximum allowable blur based on subject dimensions. A decision on what this dimension is at the subject may be influenced by several factors, each depending on user-defined criteria. These may include such items as total absence of blur at a given degree of magnification of the reproduction, size of smallest object within the subject of which useful detail needs to be recorded, etc.The formula,which also takes into account the direction of subject motion, is

$$T = \text{size of smallest detail within subject} / (K \times \text{velocity of subject} \times \cos A)$$

where K is a quality constant, generally a number from 2-4, and A is the angle between film plane and subject direction.

Even an air rifle dart with a relative slow speed (100 fps) but only an inch or so long, within which it is desired to perceive detail as small as 1/200 inch, according to formula and practice, requires an exposure as short as 4 microseconds (μsec) (1/250,000 second).

The two main methods of taking high-speed still photographs are the use of a suitable high-speed shutter system and the use of a short-duration flash while the shutter is open.

High-speed shutter systems may be magneto-optical, electro-optical, or electronic units using image-converter tubes. High-speed flash systems may use electronic flash discharges or sparks, or special discharges such as x-ray flashes for high-speed radiography.

MAGNETO-OPTICAL SHUTTER A magneto-optical shutter uses the Faraday effect, that is, the rotation of the plane of polarization of light passing through a transparent medium in a magnetic field. To use the Faraday effect, a suitable medium in a magnetic coil is placed between crossed polarizers. Dense flint glass is generally used, since it shows considerable rotation of the plane of polarization for a given magnetic field and is convenient to handle. With no current in the coil, there is no magnetic field, no rotation of the plane of polarization occurs, and therefore no light is transmitted. When a suitable current is applied (often 1,000 amperes needing 10,000 volts) the plane of polarization is rotated until it agrees with the second polarizer, and the maximum light is transmitted. This current can be supplied by discharging a capacitor through the coil using a spark gap as a switch. The time of the discharge depends on the

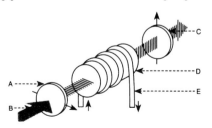

Magneto-optical (Faraday) shutter. A, first polarizer; B, light ray from subject; C, second polarizer; D, glass cylinder; E, coil. The second polarizer passes light only when the glass cylinder rotates the plane of polarization under the influence of the magnetic field. This is created by a high-voltage pulse passed through the coil.

capacitor size, the voltage, and the number of turns in the coil. Exposure times down to 1 μsec have been achieved.

In practice, a cylinder of the glass is placed in front of the lens and coaxially with it, together with the crossed polarizers, while the coil surrounds the cylinder. The capacitor discharge may be controlled by a spark gap, the spark in turn is actuated by the subject itself (i.e., the shock wave or the flash from an explosion under examination).

ELECTRO-OPTICAL SHUTTER (KERR CELL SHUTTER) Kerr discovered that certain media in the presence of an electric field become birefringent, that is, light polarized in one plane has a different velocity in the medium to light polarized in a plane at right angles. The usual Kerr cell shutter consists of a glass cell fitted with electrodes and filled with nitrobenzene and placed between two polarizers. The whole assembly may be mounted in front of the camera lens or within the optical system. The first polarizer is set such that its polarizing plane is at 45 degrees to the cell plates and the electric field. Plane-polarized light entering the cell becomes circularly polarized, that is, it has two equal components, each at 45 degrees to the original plane of polarization, 90 degrees to each other.

If a suitable voltage is applied to the plates (commonly near 20,000 volts), the phase difference produced by the differing velocities is such that on recombining at the second polarizer, the resultant plane-polarized beam is in agreement with this polarizer. With no voltage applied, no phase change occurs and the resultant beam is polarized such that no light is transmitted. Thus, by switching the voltage on and off, a shutter is produced, and exposure times down to a few thousandths of a microsecond (1/200,000,000 second) are possible.

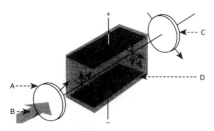

Electro-optical shutter (Kerr cell). A, first polarizer; B, light beam from subject; C, second polarizer; D, electrodes in liquid cell. The liquid becomes birefringent on application of a high-voltage pulse to the electrodes.

IMAGE TUBES A variety of image tubes exist, including image converters, orthicons, image-orthicons, and image-intensifiers. Some of these image tubes can act as highspeed shutters. Metals, particularly cesium, have the property that, in a suitable electric field, they emit electrons when irradiated with light. Also, certain materials exist that emit light when bombarded by electrons (e.g., a television screen).

A combination of such materials in one evacuated tube can produce an image converter. The light receiver is called a photocathode, and the light emitter is the screen. An image is focused on the photocathode by a lens. By applying suitable electric and magnetic fields the image can be faithfully reproduced on the screen, which in turn can be photographed by a recording camera. With no voltage applied to the tube, no picture is produced. Thus, by turning the electric field on and off, the tube acts as a shutter. The voltages used are usually between 6,000 and 25,000 volts. In some tubes, other electrodes (grid electrodes) are inserted that can control the tube with lower voltages (e.g., about 300 volts). Additionally, by suitable electrodes or magnetic coils, the image on the screen can be deflected, permitting other techniques.

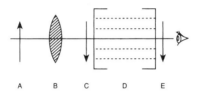

A   B   C   D   E

Image tubes. Holst image converter. A, subject; B, lens; C, semi-transparent photocathode; D, electron stream; E, viewing screen observed by eye. As the image of the subject is formed on the photocathode, the photocathode emits electrons, which travel through the evacuated tube and excite the fluorescent screen to produce an image.

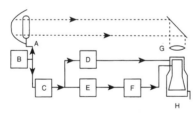

Image converter setup. This system is used for single photographs of nonluminous objects that are illuminated by a flashtube. The image converter shutter is synchronized with the peak of the flash. A, electronic flashtube powered in the usual way; B, trigger circuit; C and E, variable delay circuits; D and F, thyratron switches; G, lens: H, image converter.

The orthicon or iconoscope uses as the light receiving element a mosaic of photoemissive elements. These store an image that is later scanned off by an electron beam. The image-orthicon has a photocathode, similar to the image converter. The electrons from the cathode strike a storage plate, which is again scanned later. An image-intensifier has a photocathode and a number of secondary emissive surfaces, the electron beam passing from one to another in turn and being amplified before reaching either a screen or a storage plate. The gains possible to intensifiers, to date, are several thousand fold. An image converter can give some light intensification, e.g., at 25,000 volts, the light gain in a simple tube can be ten times.

Using image converters, exposure as short as fractions of 1 nanosecond (nsec) have been achieved, and it is in these devices, particularly, that further advances will be made.

HISTOGRAM In computers, a description of a continuous-tone image through the tabulation of the number of pixels for each gray level extant. The tabulation is displayed as a bar graph or histogram with the vertical axis as the number of pixels and the horizontal axis being the number of gray levels.

HOME In some computer applications, *home is* used as a synonym for the main menu. Home is the starting place from which to launch subapplications from the main program. In HyperCard, a relational database, home is the launching pad for stacks.

HORIZONTAL SYNC When a line of video scan is complete, a signal is issued indicating the end of the line and the need to shut off the electron beam so that a new line of scan may begin. The horizontal sync signal lasts for ≈10.9 microseconds and separates each horizontal line of scan.

HUE Attribute of a visual sensation according to which an area appears to be similar to one, or to proportions of two, of the perceived colours, red, yellow, green, and blue. Hue varies with the wavelength composition of the light. The other two attributes of light are lightness (or brightness) and saturation (or chroma).

HYBRID IMAGING The use of two or more imaging technologies to produce an image. For example, Photo CD is a hybrid imaging system. An image is captured on 35-mm film, scanned, digitized, and recorded on a special compact disc (CD). Up to 100 colour and black-and-white images can be recorded on the disc. The disc can then be used to display soft copy on a video or computer screen, or, a thermal printer can be used to make hard-copy quality prints or slides.

ICON A primary graphical object in a graphical user interface. The icon may represent a device such as a drive or scanner. It may also represent a file, message, or application. Icons may change their appearance when an event occurs. An open file may be represented by a differently appearing icon than when the same file is unopened.

IDEAL TONE-REPRODUCTION CURVE A 45 degree straight-line relationship in a graph of the tonal relationship between an original subject and a photographic reproduction where the line represents facsimile tone reproduction, an effect that cannot be achieved with conventional photographic materials and procedures.

IMAGE A representation of an object or other stimulus. With respect to photography and other light-sensitive systems, the word *image* is applied to the optical images formed by a camera, enlarger, and projector lenses, the latent images resulting from exposure of light-sensitive materials, the negative and positive black-and-white and colour images resulting from processing exposed sensitized materials, the ink images produced by photomechanical reproduction of photographs, the light images displayed on video and other cathode-ray tubes, and the visual images perceived when viewing original subjects or reproduction images.

A great amount of research effort has been expanded on the analysis of images both at the macro level (for example, tone reproduction and colour quality) and at the micro level (for example, image definition). With respect to the images formed by lenses, all optical systems introduce some image degradation, but research has resulted in dramatic improvements in lenses. Modulation transfer function (MTF) curves provide valuable information concerning image definition while other optical procedures provide more detailed information about such factors as specific aberrations, flare, transmittance, and the effect the lens has on image colour quality. Lens speed, as calibrated in f-numbers and t-numbers, is an important factor for some photographic purposes because faster lenses produce higher-illuminance images and shorter exposure time, but with the disadvantages of a shallower depth of field and the need for more elements to control aberrations.

Even more dramatic improvements have been made in image recording and reproduction with silver halide materials and with alternative imaging systems. The microimage definition of silver halide images has traditionally been measured in terms of resolving power (detail), granularity (graininess), and acutance (sharpness), or, more recently, modulation transfer function. Macroimage characteristics such as tone and colour reproduction have commonly been presented in the form of D-log H or characteristic curves for specific sensitized materials and four-quadrant tone-reproduction curves for entire systems. The same or analogous methods are used to evaluate images produced by alternative systems to silver halide photography, including nonsilver chemical processes, photomechanical reproduction, video, and electronic still photography. Limitations on recording detail with photomechanical-reproduction processes are commonly specified in terms of lines or dots per inch, and in terms of pixels with electronic imaging. Many factors in addition to image quality need to be taken into consideration when comparing imaging systems, including sensitivity, cost, permanence, convenience, and ease of manipulation.

The human visual system is an important factor in any study of imaging. Variations in individual eyesight are taken into consideration by identifying an average or normal specification for various measurements, such as 20-20 for resolution with a Snellen eye chart, normal colour vision for the absence of identifiable defective colour vision, and 10 inches as the average minimum distance for comfortable accommodation. Examples of applications of this type of information include determining the maximum acceptable circle of confusion for camera depth of field scales, determining the minimum resolving power needed for a specified imaging system or application such as microfilming, and establishing standards for the spectral quality and light level to be used for transparency and print viewers.

IMAGING TECHNOLOGIES The following table lists the imaging systems and applications for five major imaging technologies:

1 . silver halide photography
2. nonsilver chemical photography
3. graphic arts and mechanical imaging
4. electrophotographic imaging
5. electronic imaging

COMPARISON OF IMAGING MODALITIES In the past several decades there has been an astonishing emergence of various imaging modalities that have offered the user alternative choices to traditional silver halide technology, including video, direct thermal printing, and electrophotography, which have often competed directly with conventional photography. The following table lists a number of imaging systems and selected characteristics of each technology, with a qualitative description and comparison of characteristics, strengths, and weaknesses of selected imaging systems.

ELECTROPHOTOGRAPHIC IMAGING Electro-photography has undergone dramatic evolution and development since it was invented by Chester F. Carlson in 1938. Today electrophotography is a multibillion dollar industry that has provided monochrome and full-colour hardcopy output not only for business but for the individual end user. Advantages of electrophotography include plain-paper copying and printing, high-speed output, dry processing that eliminates wet solutions and chemicals, low cost per copy for black/white output, and near-photographic quality for full-process colour output.

Electrophotography enjoys a large amplification factor of 10^6-10^7 modest exposure energy requirements, or high speed, which enable high throughput rates of up to 120 copies per minute. The spectral response range for electrophotography is from about 280-400 nm for amorphous selenium photoconductors, and up to 830 nm for bilayer organic photoconductors. This enables the use of solid state gallium, aluminum, arsenic (GaAlAs) semiconducting lasers as exposure sources, and today's desktop printers use these light sources together with organic photoconductors (OPCs). The resolution capability of conventional electrophotographic copiers and printers is about 12-20 lines/mm. This is enabled by the use of conventional optics for analog copying, or by the use of laser spot rasterized scanning or light-emitting diode (LED) array light sources for digital copying. Printing is achieved by the use of LED arrays, laser raster output scanners, or liquid crystal shutter arrays. Higher resolution is possible using nonconventional electro-photographic technology. Stork Bedford B. V. Corporation has developed a colourproofing system using a crystalline cadmium sulphide photoconductor and liquid toning that is capable of resolutions exceeding 1000 lines/mm. This yields full-process colour hard-copy output that approaches silver halide photo-graphic quality. A recent trend in increasing imaging resolution involves software algorithms that improve the apparent resolu-tion possible with hardware implementations. For example, an electrophotographic engine with mechanical hardware design capable of a resolution of 300 lines per inch ($\approx$12 lines/mm) may be enhanced to 1200 lines per inch ($\approx$48 lines/mm) by use of software to modulate laser intensity.

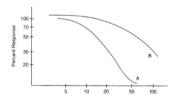

Image Modulation transfer function (MTF) for a television (CRT) (A), and for a moderate-speed black-and-white film (B). (Adjacency effects during chemical development account for the over 100% response of the fiim at low frequencies.)

ELECTRONIC IMAGING SYSTEMS

Television and HDTV There are today three worldwide tele-vision standards: the National Television System Committee (NTSC) standard used in the United States and Japan; the phase alternating line (PAL) used in the United Kingdom, South America, Africa, and parts of Europe; and Sequential couleur a Memoire (SECAM) used in France, the former Soviet Union, and Eastern Europe.

In the last decade, television has undergone significant advances in technology, driven principally by work in Japan.

Imaging Technologies, Systems, and Applications

Technologies	Systems	Applications
1. Silver halide photography	A. Monochrome (black and white)	• Black-and-white negatives, prints, transparencies • Instant black-and-white prints, negatives, slides • Instant additive color slides • Dry silver—hard copy, overheads
	B. Color chromogenic systems	• Photofinished color prints, slides, transparencies • Color output from electronic imagery
	C. Color nonchromogenic systems	• Instant color prints, transparencies • Dye bleach color prints, transparencies
2. Nonsilver chemical photography	A. Photopolymer and resist systems	• Plates, proofs, resists—circuit boards and chips
	B. Diazo and vesicular systems	• Plates, proofs, resists—circuit boards and chips, overheads, microfilms
	C. Dye imaging—photochromics, leucodye systems	• Proofs, duplications
	D. Thermal systems	• Nonimpact printing, overheads
3. Graphic arts and mechanical imaging	A. Press printing systems • Lithography • Gravure • Letterpress—flexography • Screens	• Press printing • Circuit board printing
	B. Automated typing systems	• Impact printing
	C. Ink-jet systems	• Nonimpact printing
4. Electrophotographic imaging	A. Xerographic systems	• Plain paper offset
	B. Electrofaxic systems	• Office copy, proofing systems, litho plates for G/A, slide copiers
	C. Laser scanning xerography	• Nonimpact printing
	D. Electrostatic, dielectric, and magnetostatic systems	• Nonimpact printing
5. Electronic imaging	A. Television	• Television, home video • Taped playbacks—broadcast and VCR
	B. Electronic taking imagery	• Graphic arts prepress systems • Medical CRT applications • Remote sensing, infrared, radar • Airport x-radiograph devices
	C. Computer generated imagery	• Word processors, phototypesetters • CAD/CAM • Facsimile • Computer output microfilm

Source: Allan Shepp, "Introduction to Images and Imaging," John Sturge et al. *Image Processing and Materials*. New York: Van Nostrand Reinhold, 1989, p Courtesy Van Nostrand Reinhold.

Comparison of Imaging Modalities

Imaging System	Amplification Factor	Exposure Energy Power (μJ-cm^{-2})	Resolving Power (l-mm^{-1})	Unsensitized Sensitivity Range (nm)	Sensitized Sensitivity Range (nm)
Silver halide—fast	10^9	5×10^{-4}	50	<200–500	Up to 1300
Silver halide—medium	0.2×10^9	10^{-2}	150	<200–500	Up to 1300
Dry silver (3M)	10^6	10^{-1}–20	100–400	<200–500	
Vidicon tube	10^{10}	10^{-5}	5	<400–800	
Charge-coupled device		10^{-3}	600	400–1000	Up to 9 μm
Electrophotography	10^6–10^7	10^{-1}	20–>30	280–400	Up to 830
Photopolymerization	>10^6	10^2–10^5	500	280–400	Up to 600
Photoresist	>10^3	4×10^3–10^5	>1000	<200–500	ion beam, x-ray electron bea
Diazo	1	3×10^4–10^7	>1000	350–450	
Photochromism	1	10^4–10^5	1000	uv–vis, narrow bands	
Thermal transfer dye diffusion trans.	—	—	20	—	—
Ink Jet	—	—	4–12	—	—

Television recording utilizes a television camera tube in an electronic device that converts an optical image into an electrical signal. The vidicon is the most widely used camera tube today, and its small size and simplicity permit its use by inexperienced users. Charge-coupled device (CCD) technology has begun to replace the use of camera tubes; however, recent technological developments in Japan have resulted in the *high gain avalanche rushing amorphous photoconductor (HARP)*, and *amplified MOS intelligent imager* (AMI) camera tubes that are from 10 to 100 times as sensitive as CCD camera tubes. CCD technology will be discussed later.

Japan embarked on HDTV (high definition television) research more than 20 years ago and has invested an estimated $1 billion. HDTV offers improved resolution capability with 1125 scanning lines (versus 525 for NTSC), and an aspect ratio of 16:9 which is 25% wider than conventional television. The picture spans a horizontal visual angle of 30° at the specified viewing distance, which has been verified in experiments to be large enough to induce a sensation of reality. Proposed technical standards for HDTV are:

Number of scanning lines	1125
Aspect ratio	16:9
Interlace ratio	2:1
Field frequency	60 Hz
Bandwidth of video signal	
Luminance (Y)	20 MHz
Chrominance (Cw)	7.0 MHz
Chrominance (Cn)	5.5 MHz
Viewing distance	3 x H (screen height)
Angular width of screen	30 degree

Japan has introduced satellite broadcasting of HDTV programming on selected channels in Japan. It is uncertain when HDTV or some subset of HDTV will be introduced in the United States.

CHARGE-COUPLED DEVICES CCD technology has largely replaced the use of vidicon and saticon camera tubes in television today. Present requirements to support aerospace as well as HDTV specifications call for high overall resolution of 1000 TV lines or more, a large field of view, and large dynamic range. The CCD detector used in cameras is typically 18-mm format, but the future will require 25-mm format, with associated higher costs for the devices. CCD arrays are monolithic devices composed of photosites (sensors), analog shift registers, and a charge-sensing output amplifier. CCDs do not employ *scanning* techniques as do traditional camera tubes, and although they are slower (less sensitive) than vidicon devices, they offer higher resolution. Modern device arrays of 2K x 2K photosites are capable of ≈600-700 lines/mm after proper consideration is given to Nyquist sampling to eliminate aliasing. The spectral response depends upon the materials and sensor structures employed. For conventional silicon, the range of sensitivity is 400-1000 nm. The spectral sensitivity may be extended into the infrared, for example, platinum silicide sensors are responsive to 4-5 μm, indium antinomide to 5 μm, and iridium silicide to 9 μm. CCD camera tubes have replaced conventional photographic media in all of the modern astronomical observatories in the world due to their far infrared sensitivity and digitized imagery capabilities. Improved solid-state sensor designs including large-area CCD sensors, higher-resolution arrays, together with improved optics and electronics will accelerate the replacement of tube camera with CCDs.

IMAGE AMPLIFICATION Electronic system for intensifying an optical image as much as 15,000 times by conversion into electron streams, amplification, and reconversion into light. The optical lens of an image-amplification device focuses the low-intensity source image on a collector screen consisting of multiple CCDs (charge-coupled devices) or an electron-emissive photocathode. The electron stream produced by the CCDs is amplified by a multiplier circuit; the stream from the photocathode is amplified by an accelerating voltage. The output from the amplification stage is focused on a luminescent screen, at which point the image may be viewed or recorded by traditional photographic techniques.

Image amplification may be applied profitably to infrared recording where direct imaging with low sensitivity emulsions would require long exposures. Amplification can reduce the exposure time by 1000 x or more. The process may be used to photograph starlit subjects at night with exposures of less than one second, study high-speed phenomena, perform astronomical observations, and conduct surveillance.

The term image amplification is also applied in silver halide imaging to the amplification of the latent image by several orders of magnitude during development.

IMAGE DISSECTION   In a conventional high-speed camera, film must move across the image field very rapidly. Practical limitations are imposed by the distance the film must travel and the length of film required to make a substantial number of images. Image-dissection cameras solve these problems by limiting the movement of the film or keeping it stationary, and by making many images on one plate.

In image dissection cameras, the incoming light passes through an objective lens and is divided into as many as 80,000 elements. If a multiple-lens screen is used for dissection, the division is made by a lenticular plate, a crossed pair of lenticular plates, or a fly's-eye array of spherical lenses. A Nipkow disc with a spiral pattern of scanning holes rotating behind the objective lens can be used to achieve image deflection. In place of a screen, a fibre optical bundle can be shaped so that the bundle is tightly grouped on the input end to accept as much of the image as possible, and spread out on the film end to form advantageous array configurations.

The many image points of the dissected image are evenly separated from each other by spaces that can be measured in point widths. The image needs to be moved only one image point to record the next image in the sequence. If the separation between points is ten times the point width and the tracking motion is parallel to the array, then at least ten frames in sequence are possible; if points have this separation in both directions, there can be up to 100 frames in a sequence. If the tracking motion is at a slight angle to the array, 50 frames may be recorded without overlap. This procedure can be repeated until the entire sheet of film is covered with scrambled images. The film is then processed, placed back in the camera, and the original images are reconstituted from the separated elements.

In high-speed applications, image-dissection cameras give relatively long recording times and miss very little action because imaging is virtually continuous. Processing is simplified because each sheet of film contains many images, an advantage that makes image dissection attractive for document recording as well. The process has been used for studying projectiles and explosions. In cine-microscopy, it has been employed to examine liquids and particles such as coal dust.

Image dissection may be accomplished by scanners or charge-coupled devices (CCDs) whose digital or electronic outputs may be stored, transmitted, or processed by computers. These systems are inherently faster than photochemical systems.

IMAGE ENHANCEMENT Generally, the term image enhancement refers to any method by which an image may be improved, but it has come to be understood specifically as denoting the digitization and manipulation of an image to produce an extensive array of effects. Images on film or paper are translated from analog dye or silver to digital data by a scanner.

Sharpness may be enhanced by digitally examining transfer edges. The rate of change of tone at these boundaries indicates the degree of sharpness. Sharpening is achieved by comparing maximum and minimum values on either side of the edge and accelerating the rate of transition between them.

The slope of the dye density curve of the red, green, blue, and black components, or of the yellow, magenta, cyan, and black components, may each be controlled separately. This procedure effects an overall change in colour or tonal contrast, a change of the contrast of one colour relative to the others.

IMAGE PROCESSING The alteration, enhancement, and analysis of images for the purpose of improving the pictorial representation or extracting data from the image. Image processing relies on a number of well-tried algorithms that simplify and speed the process. While image processing is applicable to optical and analog approaches, the term's use is mostly limited to digital imagery.

IMAGE RECONSTRUCTION The assembly of an easily interpreted image from a set of fragmentary or dissected records. These components may be matrices from an assembly process, such as dye transfer, or streak camera records, or the products of wavelength interference, as in the Lippmann or holographic processes.

IMAGESETTER A device that outputs text, line art, and tonal pictures in position.

IMAGING SCIENCE Imaging science is a new scientific specialty that brings together a broad variety of disciplines to study how images of all types are formed, recorded, transmitted, analyzed, and perceived. An *image* until recently has generally referred to a two-dimensional, silver-halide-based photograph. In the context of imaging science, an image may refer to any multidimensional representation, and is often based on a variety of new technologies, such as ultrasound systems using acoustic energy, satellites transmitting digital images, and electron microscopy.

While moving beyond silver halide technology, imaging science grew out of the science of photography, and includes optics, the science of light. It also brings together the divergent disciplines of chemistry, physics, computer science, mathematics, statistics, digital image processing, and colour science, among others.

Because it is a new science, only a few academic programs offering imaging science as an integrated discipline are available at the undergraduate and graduate level. Areas of research within the broad umbrella of imaging science include the following:

- remote sensing, involving the capture and analysis of aerial and satellite photography
- medical diagnostic imaging, including ultrasound and magnetic resonance imaging
- graphic arts, including electronic prepress systems
- robotic and machine vision and artificial intelligence
- digital image processing, in which images are captured in digitized form for ease in analysis, compression, and transmission
- morphological image processing, concerned with computer algorithms designed to recognize shapes and textures
- colour science, including standardization, nomenclature, and specification of colour
- optical and electron microscope imaging, including fault detection and metrology, beam propagation phenomena, atomic force microscopy, and scanning tunnel microscopy
- silver halide technology, including chemical and spectral sensitization, and latent image stability and processing
- human visual perception, studying the links between a physical image and how is it perceived, including the use of psychophysics
- optics; design, astronomical systems

Applications of these emerging technologies in business, industry, government, and the military have been growing rapidly. They include medicine (medical diagnostic imaging), agriculture and environmental studies (remote sensing), military reconnaissance, printing and publishing (colour measurement, digital graphics, electronic imaging and printing), and computer science industries (digital image processing, artificial intelligence, and robotic vision).

While imaging science is relatively young as a distinct discipline, it is in fact the combination of its separate components under a single umbrella that is new. In the past, scientists and engineers could only specialize in individual disciplines. As the relationship among these disciplines grew along with their application to emerging imaging technologies, the need for individuals trained across these areas has become clear. Today, imaging scientists are able to bring this interdisciplinary approach to the design and analysis of complex imaging systems.

INDEXED COLOUR In electronic imaging, a look-up table containing colour information that facilitates displaying 24-bit colour on an 8-bit driven monitor.

INFORMATION (IMAGE) The actual or potential maximum data contained in an image, commonly specified in terms of the binary digit or bit, the amount of information that is conveyed by a *yes* or *no* answer when both are equally probable. The information storage capacity of different sensitized materials or imaging systems can be expressed as bits per unit area, such as 1 million bits per square cm.

INFORMATION THEORY General name given to theorems relating to the transmission and recording of information and which permit the evaluation of the efficiency of recording and reproducing systems, and the choice of systems for particular purposes. The basis of these theorems is that quantity of information can be given a precise scientific definition that is in keeping with intuitive ideas. The natural units of information fall on a binary scale, and the ability of a system to transmit or store information is sometimes termed the information capacity.

INFRARED (IR) RADIATION Electromagnetic radiation with wavelengths between 700 and 15,000 nm. Infrared radiation is made up of photons with wavelengths longer than those of light, but shorter than those of microwaves. Infrared radiation is perceived as heat, and is of particular interest to photographers because photographic emulsions can be sensitized to radiation with wavelengths as long as 1200 nm (although normal IR film is only sensitive to about 900 nm). Electronic detectors can be constructed that are sensitive to the entire IR range. Infrared radiation has the ability to penetrate fog and haze to some extent, and is not scattered by the atmosphere as much as light. Healthy plants also reflect infrared radiation strongly. These characteristics combine to give dramatic effects in monochrome infrared photography—black skies and white foliage. Infrared photography can also be used to determine the health of plants in aerial photography, for biomedical, scientific, and industrial photography, for photography in the dark (only under infrared illumination), and for the examination of documents and artwork.

INITIALIZE In computers, the starting for the first time of a component, such as initializing a video board. In order to write to a disk, it must be initialized (formatted) so that it is prepared to receive data. This initialization organizes the sectors and tracks appropriately

INK-JET PRINTER A computer-controlled output device that sprays ink through very fine nozzles. The fineness of the nozzle determines the dot size of the ink spray. Usually, the water-based ink will be sprayed in liquid form or it may be heated and sprayed as a bubble. Inkjet printers can resolve between 150 dpi to 360 dpi. Colour output is possible.

INK-JET PRINTING See *Photomechanical and electronic reproduction, digital printing systems.*

INPUT Something that is put into a device, process, etc., such as the light that falls on the photoelectric cell of an exposure meter as it is being used to make a measurement, the electric current that powers an electronic flash unit, two known values entered in the equation 1/focal length = 1/object distance + 1/image distance to determine the unknown third value, and information entered into a computer program that is being used for film processing quality control.

    INPUT/OUTPUT The terms *input* and *output* are interdependent, and they are commonly combined in the form of input/output to represent the beginning and end of a process. In the process of making a photograph, for example, the subject is generally considered to be the input and the photographic image the output. The photographic process, however, can be broken down into a series of steps that can be considered as microprocesses. The light falling on the subject, for example, represents the input for the smaller process whereby the subject modulates the light by means of variations of absorption and the output is represented by the resulting luminances. These output luminances for the various subject areas in turn represent the input for the formation of the optical image by the camera lens, which in turn serves as the input for the formation of the latent image in the film emulsion, which then serves as the input for the development of a negative image, and so on through the printing process. Thus, certain items can be classified as input or output only in the context of a specific process.

    Whereas the photographic image was considered above to be the final output, photographs are normally made to be viewed, so that the photographic image can be considered to be the input for the process of visual perception, but of course the visual process can be subdivided into a series of microprocesses also. In the literature on visual perception, input is commonly referred to as stimulus and output as response. Stimulus-response psychology represents the point of view that the task of the psychologist is to discover the functional relationships that exist between stimuli and responses.

    Evaluation of photographic materials or a photographic process commonly involves comparing the output (the image) with the input (the subject). In practice, this is not always convenient or even possible, so we often compare the photographic image with a memory of the appearance of an object or scene at the time the film was exposed, a subjective and undependable method of evaluation.

    TEST TARGETS One way to avoid the errors introduced by

the vagaries of memory concerning the appearance of the original scene is to use an appropriate test object that can be saved and compared with the photographic image, or that can provide an objective measurement of some aspect of the imaging process. Some of the items that are commonly used as artificial subjects for testing purposes are listed below. The choice of test target depends on which attributes of the subject or the imaging process are to be compared or measured.

Neutral Test Card A gray card having a reflectance of approximately 18% is referred to as a neutral test card, a gray card, or an artificial midtone since it has been determined that this tone appears to be midway in lightness between white and black. This tone corresponds to a middle value of 5 in the Munsell system of colour notation and to Zone V in the Zone System. It is an appropriate tone to use for reflected-light exposure meter readings and should produce approximately the same results as an incident-light exposure meter reading. As an artificial subject, it can be used in the darkroom when making prints to assist in determining the proper density of a print. Actually, however, it has been found in tone-reproduction studies that viewers tend to prefer prints in which the midtones are a little lighter than the corresponding tones in the original scene.

Gray cards are also useful when making colour photographs. Including a gray card in the original scene can assist the colour printer in determining the proper colour filtration by means of red, green, and blue density readings of the colour negative, or similar readings made with a darkroom colour analyzer light meter. Neutral subject areas are also useful in colour photographs for judging the colour balance of the photographic image subjectively since variations of colour balance are easier to detect in neutral areas than in areas having highly saturated hues such as a red apple or a blue sky.

Gray Scale A series of neutral tones, usually in the form of discrete calibrated steps that are arranged in sequence from light to dark with a typical density range of approximately 0.0 to 2.0. Gray scales having uniform density increments between steps tend to be more useful, but some gray scales have modified increments that provide the appearance of more nearly equal increments in lightness, which requires larger density increments on the dark end. Although gray scales can be used alone as an artificial subject they are often included with other subjects but in a position where the image appears near the edge of the photograph where it can be eliminated by cropping or trimming.

Gray scales offer the advantage over gray cards of providing information about the local and overall contrast of the image in addition to the density of any tone of interest. Evaluation of image density and contrast can be done subjectively by visually comparing the image of the gray scale with the original gray scale, or objectively by comparing measured densities of the image steps with the corresponding marked densities on the original gray scale.

Step Tablet Transmission gray scales are commonly referred to as step tablets. Typical step tablets have a density range of approximately 0.0 to 3.0 with either 20 increments of 0.15 or 10 increments of 0.30. A step tablet can be used, for example, on an illuminator along the edge of a transparency that is being copied or along the edge of a negative or transparency in an enlarger. Step tablets are also used in sensitometers to provide a series of known exposures to sensitized materials for the purpose of determining the tone reproduction characteristics of the material or of determining the effects of changes made in processing conditions. The input and output data of such tests are commonly presented in the form of density versus log exposure graphs where the relationship between input and output is revealed in the form of a characteristic curve.

Transmission tablets that have a continuous change in density from light to dark rather than discrete steps are referred to as continuous-tone tablets or wedges. Such tablets are used with automatic equipment that measures the densities by scanning the image from one end to the other and simultaneously plots a characteristic curve.

Colour Chart A panel containing patches of selected colours that is designed to be photographed, with or without other objects, for the purpose of evaluating colour reproduction quality. Such charts are sometimes identified as colour rendition charts or colour control charts. The colours selected typically include the additive primary colours (red, green, and blue), the subtractive primary colours (cyan, magenta, and yellow), white, and black. The Macbeth ColorChecker has 24 patches that include typical subject colours such as light skin, dark skin, blue sky, and foliage, and a six-step gray scale in addition to the additive and subtractive primary colours, and it was designed to be used with photomechanical and television reproduction systems in addition to photographic systems. The colours are also identified with ISCC/NBS names, and specifications are provided for both the CIE system of colour measurement and the Munsell system of colour notation.

RESOLVING POWER TEST TARGET

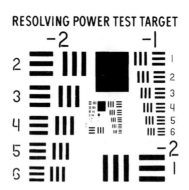

A bar type resolving power test target. The resolving power is based on the smallest set of bars that can be resolved when the image of the test target is examined with a microscope.

Resolving Power Target A pattern of alternating dark and light bars that decrease systematically in width, that is used to measure the resolving power of a photographic system or component. The resolving power is determined by the narrowest set of target bars that can be distinguished as being separate in the image and is expressed in terms of lines per millimeter, where a line is a dark-light pair of bars. To determine the resolving power of a lens, the aerial image formed by the lens is examined with a microscope. When a photograph is made of the target, the resolving power determined from the image is that of the system, which includes all of the components such as camera lens and film for a negative or transparency, and camera lens, film, enlarger lens, and paper for a print. Targets having bars with sharp edges are sometimes referred to as square-wave targets, as distinct from sine-wave targets. Reflection-resolving power targets are provided in both high-contrast and low-contrast versions, and transmission targets, which are capable of providing higher density ranges than reflection targets, are also available.

Alphanumeric Target With conventional resolving power targets, the observer selects the smallest set of bars where the correct number of bars, commonly three dark bars on a light background, can be identified, a process that results in variability, especially with inexperienced observers. Alphanumeric resolving power targets contain block letters and numbers, each of which contains three parallel bars that are similar to the bars on the conventionally resolving power targets. With alphanumeric targets the observer selects the smallest set of characters on the basis of recognition of the letters and numbers. Since the accuracy of the identifications can be checked, and incorrect selections are rejected, variability with repeated observations made by one person and observations made by different people is low.

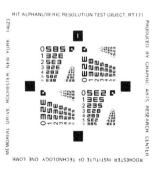

Alphanumeric resolving power test target. Since the accuracy of the tester's choice of the smallest resolved set of characters can be checked, variability is lower than with conventional resolving power test targets.

Sine-Wave Target Sine-wave targets, like conventional resolving power targets, have alternating light and dark bands of varying widths, but the transition between adjacent bands is gradual rather than abrupt. Even though resolving power data are valuable in evaluating optical systems and photographic materials and processes, it has long been known that the observed sharpnesses of two images sometimes vary *inversely* with their resolving powers. Modulation transfer function curves based on the relative contrast of the light and dark bands in the image of a sine-wave target reveal how an imaging system that produces high contrast in large image areas and low contrast in small image areas can appear sharper and yet reveal less fine detail and therefore have a lower resolving power than another imaging system having the reverse contrast relationships.

Lens Aberration Test Targets The simplest of all the different test targets is undoubtedly the artificial star target produced by making a pinpoint opening in a thin piece of opaque material and placing a light source behind the opening. Examination through a microscope of the image formed by a lens with the point source of light in various positions on and off axis and with modifications of the spectral quality light can reveal considerable information about the shortcomings of the lens.

There are other specialized test targets designed to reveal specific lens aberrations such as distortion and chromatic aberrations. Although sophisticated lens testing is done by specialists in an optics lab equipped with a precision lens bench, simple charts containing a variety of targets are available for photographers who want to test their own lenses.

Vision Test Targets Two widely used targets for testing visual acuity are the Snellen chart containing letters of progressively decreasing size, and a geometrical design used to detect astigmatism. Pseudoisochromatic test targets for detecting defective colour vision consist of patterns of neutral and coloured dots such that figures that are visible to persons with normal colour vision cannot be seen by those with defective colour vision.

Numerical Input Whereas subjective evaluation of input factors or input/output relationships are commonly expressed in general terms such as light, dark, flat, and contrasty, objective measurements normally involve numbers. Examples of useful measurement data at the input stage of picture making include the colour temperature of the light source for colour photography, incident-light measurements at the subject to determine the lighting ratio, reflected-light measurements of a scene to determine camera exposure settings and scene contrast, and the measurement of a dimension of an object or scene when information about size or distance is required.

Quantitative input information is commonly required in order to determine precise input-output relationships. These relationships can be presented in a variety of terms including as a ratio (such as a scale of reproduction of 1:1), a table (such as a depth-of-field table that lists f-numbers and corresponding depth-of-field distances), a graph (such as a film characteristic curve), and miscellaneous forms (such as dial and slide-rule devices and nomographs).

Graphs are an especially efficient method of presenting input-output relationships, since by plotting a limited number of points and connecting them with a smooth line, it is possible to interpolate to determine the output for any input value that falls between the limits. A time-contrast index graph for the development of black-and-white film can be prepared with data for only three different developing times, for example, and a film characteristic curve, which has a more complex shape, can be prepared by using a step tablet that produces only 11 different exposures on the film.

The input for graphs, or for any input-output relationship. is referred to as the independent variable and the output as the dependent variable.

INPUT/OUTPUT (I/O) A device that allows data to be entered into the computer (mouse, graphics tablet) or a device that accepts data for review (monitor, printer). I/O may also refer to the controller of these devices. I/O compatibility is a major consideration in the fabrication of an imaging or graphics computer workstation.

INPUT SCANNER Any advice that can capture an electronic representation of reflection or transmission of original material and convert it into a digital representation of the original.

INTEGRATED CIRCUIT (IC) Microminiature circuit containing many transistors, diodes, resistors, capacitors, and connecting wiring on a single semiconductor chip. Integrated circuits are the building blocks of modern electronic circuits. Thousands of different IC circuits are commercially available. They can be divided according to their use: linear, digital, and hybrid. Linear ICs are used to amplify audio, video, radio frequency, and other analog signals. An operational amplifier used extensively in analog computers is a linear IC. Digital ICs are used to perform a variety of functions in digital computers, such as logic gates, flipflops, registers, accumulators, and the central processing unit (CPU). Digital ICs are also used in the long-distance transmission of intelligence by telephone lines and radio and in the storage of data, including photographic images, on floppy and hard discs, on magnetic tape, and on compact discs. Hybrid ICs contain on a single chip both linear and digital circuits, for example, the digital-to-analog converter and the analog switch. ICs are fabricated using bipolar or metal-oxide semiconductor (MOS) technology. They are available in dual in-line packages (DIP) or as surface mounting devices to facilitate automatic assembly on printed circuit boards.

INTERACTIVE Communication between the computer and the user. There are several levels of interactivity. The highest level occurs in a time span that is real or near real time.

INTERFACE A means of connection between two independent devices with different connectors, formats, data storing or protocols. Sometimes called a black box.

INTERLACE The scanning method of displaying images on the cathode-ray tube (CRT) whereby each of two fields is displayed every 50th of a second. The "a" field is composed of every odd line and the "b" field is composed of every even line. The two are interlaced together to represent one frame.

INTERMODULATION DISTORTION The generation of waveforms (by an amplifier or photographic system) other than those that are fed into the system. These extraneous waveforms distort the reproduction of the original waveform. Intermodulation distortion is a problem in audio and image reproduction systems.

INTERNATIONAL ELECTROTECHNICAL COMMISSION (IEC) An international standards-making body located in Geneva, Switzerland, with activity in audio, electroacoustics, video, television, and photography, among many other fields. It is probably best known to the lay public as the organization that standardized the categorization of Compact Cassette tape types in four types numbered I, II, III, and IV and film speeds. Its standards are generally available within each country from the local standards-making body, such as ANSI in the United States and B.S. in England.

INTERPOLATION A method of image processing whereby one pixel, block, or frame is displayed or stored based on the differences between the previous and subsequent pixel, block, or frame of information. Using such a technique allows for the magnification of a section of the image without blocking.

JPEG Joint Photo Experts Group

JAPANESE INDUSTRIAL STANDARDS COMMITTEE (JISC) The national standardizing organization of Japan.

KERNEL A targeted group of pixels in a closely defined array that can be convolved, i.e., evaluated with weighted coefficients. The value of each pixel in the kernel is dependent upon its neighbors. The array of weighted coefficients is called a mask. The size of the mask is the same as the kernel. In many texts the terms *kernel* and *mask* have become interchangeable.

KERNING The adjustment of the space between type characters to improve their visual appeal. Certain page layout programs, including QuarkXPress, and languages such as PostScript allow desk-top publishing to adjust spacing.

KEYING Keying is the act of combining pictures from one signal source into a picture sourced from a different signal. Keying can be controlled by frames or by colour, such as chromakeying.

KEYSTONE EFFECT A convergence of parallel subject lines in the image when a camera or projector is tilted up or down. Elimination of convergence in a camera requires the film plane to be parallel to the subject, and elimination in a projected image requires the transparency to be parallel to the projection screen.

LANDSCAPE ORIENTATION In computers, a page format with the horizontal axis being the longer dimension, in contrast to portrait orientation.

LASER (light amplification by stimulated emission of radiation) A device that emits a beam of coherent, monochromatic, electromagnetic radiation in the visible or near-visible region of the spectrum. Lasers work because of the phenomenon of stimulated emission, whereby an atom in an excited state is triggered into emitting a photon by the incidence of a similar photon. With stimulated emission, the emitted photon has the same phase as the incident photon, i.e., the two photons are coherent. The laser concept is based on a large number of stimulated emissions occurring simultaneously.

The first operating laser was constructed by Theodore Maiman in 1960. It is interesting to note that the announcement of this invention was at a news conference; the paper that was to have announced the invention in a more conventional form having been rejected by the journal *Physical Review Letters*. Maiman's device consisted of a small, cylindrical, synthetic, pale pink ruby rod containing a small amount of chromium oxide. The rod's end faces were polished flat, parallel, and normal to the axis. Then both were silvered (one only partially) to form a resonant cavity. The rod was then surrounded by a helical electronic flashtube. When the flashtube is flashed, a large number of the ruby molecules are forced into an excited state. Under normal conditions these spontaneously and randomly decay, producing monochromatic (694.3 nm) but incoherent light. In the laser, however, such large numbers of molecules are in an excited state that the first to decay stimulate emission of coherent light in the rest. The continuous beam of the laser is produced by repeatedly flashing the flashtube to pump the molecules back to the excited state as soon as they decay thereby allowing for continuous stimulated emission.

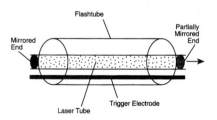

Laser. The flashtube keeps all the atoms or molecules in the laser tube at an excited state. The laser beam emerges from the partially mirrored end.

LASER POINTER A device, usually about the size of a large fountain pen, that is used to project a highly visible red dot onto an image or an object. The laser diode emits a beam of highly coherent and intense red light that is easily visible in either a daylight environment or in a darkened theater or lecture hall. This laser light beam can travel more than 200 feet with little dispersion or softening of the dot. The beam is so intense that the dot shows up easily on any surface, whether it is a flat two-dimensional object, a three-dimensional object, or an image that is projected onto a projection screen or wall. The laser pointer is battery powered, light in weight, and easily handled by a lecturer giving a presentation.

LASER PRINTER An output device that prints text and dithers images through the use of a laser light source and electrostatic imaging techniques. The RAMs in these printers process font data, the text itself, and direct the laser activity. The spot size of the laser will determine the resolution of the printer. Current printer standards are between 300 and 400 dpi.

LAYOUT (1) An arrangement of photographs, prints, or typographic material used as a guide for those engaged in preparing copy to be readied for printing, for example, advertisements, or for other types of display such as books and magazines. (2) In animation, a careful plan of the action as a guide for the animator

LIBRARY In computer parlance the library is a repository of a file from which the software may make calls. The calling of subroutines or procedures from the library can speed software development and provide for standardized approaches to the writing of code.

LIGHT-EMITTING DIODE (LED) A semiconductor diode that emits light or infrared radiation when current passes through it. The colour emitted is red, green, or orange depending on the type of semiconductor used and the colour of the plastic housing or lens. LEDs are used extensively in alphanumeric display panels and as a pilot light or a warning indicator. For example, some cameras use an LED to alert the photographer that the scene is not bright enough and that a flash exposure is required.

LIGHTFAST Permanence of a photograph, or any coloured material, under the influence of light.

LIGHTING CONTRAST The relative amounts of light received by the highlight and shadow areas of a subject or scene. When evaluated subjectively, lighting contrast is identified in general terms such as high, normal, and low. When measurements are made, lighting contrast is typically expressed as a ratio, such as 4:1, although it can also be expressed as a difference in light-value numbers (in the APEX system) or equivalent exposure stops—where the difference would be 2 in both units for a 4:1 lighting ratio.

LIGHTING RATIO The ratio of the incident light received by the highlight and shadow areas of a scene. Thus, lighting by a main light and a fill light of equal intensity is expressed as a 2:1 ratio, assuming both sources illuminate the highlight area, but only the fill illuminates the shadow area. Lighting ratio depends on the relative distances of the lights to the subject, as well as on their intensities. Therefore, a photographer can achieve a high lighting ratio using two lights of equal intensity

The ideal ratio depends on both subject and aesthetic judgment. Ratios lower than 2:1 and higher than 6:1 are seldom used in controlled lighting situations.

LIGHTNESS The aspect of colour that applies to reflecting surfaces and that relates the appearance of such surfaces to a scale of grays. Whites are grays of high lightness and blacks are grays of low lightness. In a print, highlights are tones of high lightness and shadows are tones of low lightness. Brightness is similar to lightness but differs in that brightness is applied to surfaces seen as sources of light, rather than as reflecting surfaces.

LIGHT PEN An input device that detects light emitted from the cathode-ray tube (CRT) and locks onto the cursor of a computer screen. The movement of the pen across the screen is automatically tracked, allowing the user to modify images directly, as a pen does on paper.

LIGHT VALVE An optical or mechanical device used to control the transmission of light. Various forms are in use, such as a pair of contrarotating linear polarizing filters whose transmission varies nonlinearly with their relative angle. A pair of louvre shutters opened and closed very rapidly modulate light in cine film printers.

LINEAR (1) Specifying a scale of numbers in which arithmetic values are equally spaced. A thermometer scale is linear. Contrast with *ratio scale*. (2) As applied to a function, one that plots as a straight-line graph. The general formula is $y = a + bx$, where *a is* the intercept and *b is* the slope (steepness) of the line. (3) As applied to a system, one in which the output is directly proportional to the input. Most photographic systems are not linear. (4) As applied to perspective in a photograph, depth perception for the viewer arising from the convergence of parallel lines or the reduction in image size with increased object distance. (5) Identifying a magnification value that is the ratio of length of the image to the length of the object, as distinct from a ratio of areas. A linear magnification of 5x is equivalent to an area magnification of 25x.

LINEARIZATION A form of electronic imaging system calibration to control image quality by adjusting all the output optical, physical, and electrical elements of an imaging system.

LINEAR OUTPUT Output that varies proportionally to the input. Video displays are linear with respect to the accuracy of the tone reproduction.

LINE IMAGE A drawing, type, or other image consisting of a single tone on a background of a contrasting tone, such as a black ink drawing on a white background. When a line original is to be reproduced, photographically or photomechanically, for example, it is identified as a line copy.

LINE PAIR In a resolving power test target consisting of alternating light and dark bars of equal width, a line pair consists of one light bar and one dark bar. When resolving power is specified in terms of lines per millimeter, the numbers are based on line pairs. To avoid confusion, the term *line pairs is* sometimes used.

LINES PER INCH (LPI) A measure used by printers to determine the resolution of the line screen for the image. Newspaper images are typically 65 lpi while magazines are commonly 133 lpi. These resolutions also depend upon the type of imager being used and the quality of the substrate upon which the image is being printed.

LINE WORK FILE An electronic image file, typically for a light image against a dark background without intermediate gray tones, formed either by scanning a line image into the system or by forming the image in the system.

LINKING In computers, the connecting of code to a library that supports the calls made by the code. Linking will allow the code when compiled to become executable, i.e., stand by itself for running.

LIQUID CRYSTAL DISPLAY (LCD) A readout device commonly used on digital meters, digital clocks, and calculators. Two types of units are available: field-effect and dynamic-scattering. Both types use an organic material that will flow like a liquid but has a molecular structure similar to that of a crystal. The liquid crystal is sealed in a thin glass enclosure with transparent electrodes on the front and back surfaces. Typically, on each side of the liquid crystal there are seven electrodes in the form of a figure eight. An electrostatic field resulting from a voltage applied across opposite electrodes will cause the crystal between the electrodes to reflect or transmit light, depending on the type. By applying voltage to two or more pairs of electrodes any digit from 0 to 9 can be displayed. LCDs require much less power to operate than light-emitting diode displays but do require an external source of light, usually ambient light, for display.

LIQUID CRYSTAL DISPLAY PROJECTOR Liquid crystal display (LCD) technology was developed in 1973 and was most commonly used in digital watches and handheld calculators, where light weight, low power, and high resolution made it the ideal presentation medium. Liquid display material is activated electrically and is now also used to form images for laptop computers and word processors. These items use a *duty-type* LCD, where the individual pixels are controlled by a liquid crystal matrix. These *duty type* LCDs can be used to display colour and video images, but they have slow response times that make them impractical for rapidly changing images. On the other hand, *active matrix* LCDs have a transistor at each pixel point that controls only that pixel and can respond much more rapidly to image changes. This new generation of *active matrix* LCDs is competitive with conventional CRT displays (TV monitors). Because these new LCDs provide a quick change response time, high resolution, impressive picture quality, and excellent colour reproduction, they are being used for the video market and high-speed computer-aided design displays. LCDs consume very little power and are extremely light weight compared with conventional CRT displays, which make them ideal for use as very large, flat-screen, wall-mounted video image displays. This technology also provides for convergence-free colour video projection systems.

LITHOGRAPHY Lithography (a generic term that includes offset, lithography and planography) is a planographic printing process in which the image and nonimage areas are essentially on the same plane of a thin metal-, plastic-, or paper-based plate, and the difference between them is maintained by the physico-chemical principle that grease and water don't mix. Offset lithography differs from the other printing processes in that an intermediate blanket (offset) cylinder is interposed between the plate and the impression cylinder. The inked image is offset from the plate cylinder to the blanket-covered cylinder from which it is transferred to the paper as it feeds over the impression cylinder. Practically all lithography is done by the offset principle. As a result the term *offset* has become synonymous with lithography.

The light-sensitive coatings on lithographic plates are selected so that the image area after exposure and processing is ink-(grease) receptive and water-repellent, and the nonimage areas are treated to render them water-receptive and ink-repellent. When the plates are run on the press, in every revolution water is transferred from the dampening system rollers to the nonprinting areas of the plate and ink is transferred from the inking rollers to the image areas. A delicate balance, known as the ink-water balance, must be maintained between the ink receptivity of the images, the water receptivity of the nonimage areas, and the ink and dampening solution amounts and properties.

The ink-water balance is not a constant property. It varies according to many conditions of the inks, dampening solutions, paper, temperatures, etc. Establishing a proper balance is a big part of the make ready operations to produce an OK sheet and is the hallmark of experienced pressmen. Once established, it remains reasonably constant as long as the press is running. As soon as the press is stopped, the ink-water balance is destroyed and must be re-established when the press is restarted. This takes time and causes paper waste until the new balance is established, and often it is not the same as it was before the press stopped, which causes variations in the colour balance and consistency of the printing.

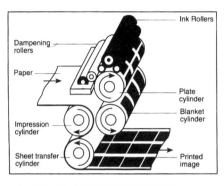

Lithography. Diagram of offset lithographic press.

LOAD The transfer of data or the application from storage (hard or floppy disk) to the memory (RAM) of the computer.

LOCAL CONTROL Any method by which the tones in limited areas of a photographic image are managed or manipulated. These may include dodging, burning, spotting, etching, or masking. Such techniques may be applied manually with conventional darkroom tools, or digitally, by scanning the original image and manipulating with a computer and image processing software.

LOCK-UP A glitch that prevents a computer from accepting instructions from an input device. In effect, the user is locked out and the keyboard is locked up. In MS-DOS systems, holding down the control, alternate, and delete keys at the same time will undo a lock-up by warm booting the system. Other computers require a different sequence of keys to escape from a lock-up.

LOG See *Logarithm.*

LOGARITHM If the series of numbers 100, 1000, 10,000 is rewritten as 10^2, 10^3, 10^4, the values 2, 3, and 4 are logarithms of the original numbers to the base 10. Thus, a logarithm, often shortened to *log,* is an exponent, or power, that generates a plain number when used with the base.

An increase of 1 in the log implies a multiplication by 10 of the corresponding arithmetic value, which is called the *antilog.* Also, a division of the antilog by 10 is equivalent to a decrease of 1 in the log. Therefore, the log of 10 is 1, and the log of 1 is 0.

The series can be expanded indefinitely, as in the following table:

Number	0.0001	0.001	0.01	0.1	1	10	100	1000	10,000
Logarithm	-4	-3	-2	-1	0	1	2	3	4

An interval scale (equal increments) of logs corresponds to a ratio scale (change by a constant factor) of numbers. Because zero is never reached in a ratio scale, there is no log for the number zero or for a negative number.

Numbers between 1 and 10 necessarily have logs between 0 and 1, i.e., decimal values. The log of 2, for example, is 0.30. Multiplying a number by 2 increases the log by 0.30. Thus the log of 4 is 0.30 + 0.30, or 0.60, and the log of 8 is 0.90. By the same process, the log of 200 is the sum of the logs of 100 and 2, i.e., 2.30. The whole number part of the log is called the *characteristic,* and the decimal part is called the *mantissa.* The log of 4000 is 3.60; the characteristic is 4, and the mantissa is 0.60.

The logs of numbers less than 1 have negative characteristics. For example, the log of 0.02 is the log of 0.01 plus the log of 2, or -2 + 0.30. This log can be written in several ways: 0.30 -2, or more often [2].30, where the characteristic (-2) is transferred to the front of the log, and the minus sign placed over it, to indicate that only the characteristic is negative. An obsolescent way of writing such a log is 8.30 -10, where the 8 and the -10 are equivalent to the -2.

The log of 0.02 can also be expressed as -1.70, where the entire log is negative, as distinct from the bar-notation [2].30 expression, where only the characteristic is negative. Electronic calculators are based on the negative log system, whereas the bar-notation system is used more commonly in photography.

Logarithms have many applications in photography. There are two major reasons for this fact:

1. The human visual system responds nearly uniformly to uniform logarithmic changes in the light stimulus, if the range of light levels is not excessive. Equal multiplications of the light level produce nearly equal changes in the response. If, for example, a person is asked to choose, from a large number of patches ranging from white to black, a set of those patches that are equally spaced, that person's choices, when measured with a meter, are separated by approximately equal logarithmic intervals.
2. Photographic films and papers also respond more evenly to logarithmic changes in the energy they receive than to arithmetic changes. For example, an increase of 1 second in exposure time is a large change if the original time is also 1 second but has little significance if the first time is 10 seconds. Therefore, it is the factor by which the time changes (2 x in the first case but only 1.1 x in the second) that is meaningful. When it is the factor that counts, logs are appropriately used.

A few of the numerous examples of the use of logarithms in photography are as follows:

1. Density, the measure of the photographic response of films and papers, is a logarithm. It is approximately proportional to the silver (or dye) content of the finished image, if properly measured.
2. The *characteristic curve* showing the response of photographic materials to received exposure is plotted with log scales on both axes.
3. A one-stop exposure change implies a change by a factor of 2 and thus a logarithmic change of 0.30. Thus, camera settings are spaced logarithmically.
4. Speed values for films and papers are similarly spaced, although this fact may be obscured by the actual numbers used.
5. The APEX system for computing camera settings from light values and speed values is based on logs.

LOGIC BOARD The primary circuit board in a computer that holds the CPU, ALU, RAM, ROM, and the bus network for the various peripherals.

LOOK-UP TABLE (LUT) An image-processing operation that accepts input and maps it via a table based on some point processing algorithm to specific output. The conversion of RGB to CMYK (input to output) relies heavily on a colour look-up table (CLUT).

LOOP In computer programming, a loop is a structured set of instructions that are repeatedly executed until some condition is satisfied.

LOW-CONTRAST Identifying a lighting, film, developer, printing material, etc. used to decrease tonal separation, either to achieve a low-contrast effect or to compensate for a high-contrast effect elsewhere in the system. Also, identifying an image having less than normal contrast. Film resolving powers, for example, are determined using both high-contrast and low-contrast test targets.

LOW FILTER See *High-pass filter*.

LOW-PASS FILTER (1) An electrical filter that passes signals at frequencies below a cutoff frequency, while attenuating frequencies above cutoff. The term is used by electrical engineers and by professional audio personnel, but note that the term used for the same thing in the consumer marketplace is a high filter. (2) In electronic imaging, the attenuation of high-frequency data in an image. This operation enhances low-frequency data. The low-pass filter will smooth the appearance of the image, and it is useful for eliminating noise in the image.

LUMINANCE GAIN A measure of the directional

reflectance characteristics of a projection screen. It is defined as the ratio of screen luminance in a given direction to that of a lambertian reflector receiving the same illumination. While an ideal lambertian reflector would provide a wide viewing angle, screens can be designed to increase the luminance across expected viewing angles by redirecting the power that would otherwise be directed above, below, or to the sides of viewers.

MACBETH COLORCHECKER A checkerboard array of 24 colour squares, including the additive primary colours (red, green, and blue), subtractive primary colours (cyan, magenta, and yellow), colours of objects of special interest such as human skin, foliage, and blue sky, and six neutral colours that range from white to black.

MACH BAND Originally, an optical illusion produced when a subject area having a lighter uniform tone gradually blends into an area having a darker uniform tone whereby a dark band is seen near the edge of the darker area and a light band is seen near the edge of the lighter area. The term now is also applied to the effect seen when viewing adjacent areas that have abrupt rather than gradual changes in tone, such as the steps in a gray scale.

MACHINE CODE The binary language that the computer understands and into which higher-level languages are translated.

MAGENTA Colour name given to colourants that absorb the greenish third of the spectrum. They usually look a bluish red, but if they have high unwanted blue absorptions they can look predominantly red. In the graphic reproduction industries the green-absorbing ink was formerly called red.

MAGNETIC FILM A magnetic recording medium consisting of a base film coated with an oxide and binder, and optionally coated on the opposite side with a conductive backing. The base is perforated according to the standard in use and made of tricellulose acetate or polyester. The oxide is a magnetically "hard" material, designed to be relatively difficult to magnetize and then to hold the magnetic field for a very long time for future reproduction.

MAGNETIC FLUX The strength of the magnetic field in an area, as determined by the field intensity and the magnetic permeability of the medium. Magnetic flux is expressed as a concentration of field lines in diagrams of magnetic fields (such as a diagram of a bar magnet), and is measured in webers. Magnetic flux density is a significant consideration in the recording and storage of magnetic recording media.

MAGNETIC HEAD An electromagnetic device designed to erase, record, or reproduce magnetic film or tape. It is i made of a magnetically "soft" core material on which is wound a coil of wire. (Magnetically soft material inherently does not retain a magnetic field; one of the greatest difficulties in head design is finding magnetically soft materials that are also mechanically hard for long wear.) The core is gapped so that magnetic flux may leak out in the case of erasure and recording, and be received by the core material in the case of playback. A current through the coil of wire sets up a magnetic field in the core, which then leaks out to the tape or film by way of the tap in order to record; for reproduction the process is reversed.

MAGNETIC IMAGE RECORDING Images may be recorded on magnetically sensitive material in a process similar to the way audio is recorded, whereby sound pressure is converted into a series of electrical impulses by a diaphragm connected to a magnet. When the diaphragm moves, a current is produced. A charge-coupled device (CCD) can convert a still image into a pattern of electrical impulses as well. In either case, the signal is amplified and recorded on a metallic oxide-coated tape by applying the signal to an electromagnetic head that magnetizes the particles on the tape, storing the information. The signal may also be digitized by an analog-digital converter before storage on the magnetic medium. Playback induces magnetic impulses in the head that are converted to an electrical signal and amplified. Digitized signals are reconverted by a digitalanalog converter before amplification. Digitized images can also be stored on a fixed magnetic card.

Other magnetic imaging systems exist. Messages, computer output, and cathode-ray tube (CRT) hard copy can be recorded as a latent image on an endless magnetic belt that is then dusted with toner. The image is transferred by contact to plain paper and fused; the belt is cleaned and degaussed. In another system, a magnetic field may cause chemical reactions in liquid droplets containing colour-forming chemicals, creating an additive three-colour display.

MAGNETIC STORAGE Any disk, film, tape, drum, or core that is used to store electronic information.

MAGNETIC TAPE A strand of material intended for magnetic recording that contains two essential ingredients—a base and a magnetically responsive coating. Tape is distinguished from film by the lack of perforations on tape; the base material is also generally less thick. The base consists of acetate (historically) or of polyester, usually between 0.5 and 1.5 mils thick. The coating consists of a magnetic oxide, along with binders, lubricants, and antistatic agents. Optionally, the tape may be back coated with an antistatic backing intended to also improve winding characteristics. Note that with back-coated tapes, the oxide side may not be immediately obvious because both sides contain coatings.

MAIN-FRAME COMPUTER A large multitasking computer that may support a number of dumb terminals through sophisticated time-sharing software. This host processor operates at high speed and serves a large group of users via a local area network (LAN).

MANTISSA The decimal part of a logarithm, which specifies the digits in the corresponding number. For example, in the logarithm 1.301, the mantissa is 0.301, implying the digit 2 in the plain number which is *20*.

MAPPING In electronic imaging, the process of transforming input brightness to output brightness.

MASK/MASKING Masks are supplementary neutral density images used in register with an original image to modify or adjust the characteristics of the original. The purpose may be the reduction of overall or local contrast to enhance highlight or shadow detail, correction of tone reproduction, correction of colour separations to allow for variations in the performance of dyes or inks, or the removal of yellow, magenta, or cyan ink, and the proportional substitution of black ink to get clean dark tones in photomechanical reproduction.

Masks may consist of silver or dye images, and may be gray or coloured. They may be purely electronic. They may be made on a single emulsion film, or on a film having three or more layers, producing the equivalent of five or more masks. They may be on wet process or vesicular film, sharp or unsharp, of limited or full tonal range, positive or negative. They may be made by contact printing, by a process camera, or by computer processing of a scanned and digitized input.

MASKING, ELECTRONIC Colour corrected separations may be produced by scanning a continuous tone image and then selecting from a set of programmed masks or generating a custom mask. The masking process may be completed in the computer, eliminating the need for separate photochemical masks.

MEAN In statistics, an average, i.e., a measure of the central tendency of a set of data. Two kinds of means are often used. (1) The arithmetic average, found by dividing the sum of the group of values by the number of items in the set. Such an average is used for numbers on an interval scale, such as weights, temperatures, and photographic densities, and is used as the central line in a process control chart. (2) The geometric average, which is the square root of the product of two numbers. This average is used to find the middle value for numbers on a ratio scale, such as shutter speeds, f-numbers, luminances and ISO arithmetic film speeds.

MEASUREMENT Photography is unique among the creative arts because it is the only one in which science and technology play major roles. From the transformation of raw materials into optical devices and photographic materials, through their application in the field, and to the viewing process, physics, chemistry, mathematics, and psychology are all important.

In each of these fields, securing data by means of reliable measurements is essential. In addition, everything must work together: one error in the entire process, such as an incorrect camera exposure, can be disastrous.

Even in an area as seemingly simple as temperature measurement, a long chain of data collection goes back from the user checking the developer temperature to thermometer manufacturer to the reference instruments at the bureaus of standards in various countries, and, finally, to the International Bureau near Paris.

In the United States, photographic measurements, such as the calculation of emulsion speed, are based on standards set up by the American National Standards Institute (ANSI), formerly called the American Standards Association (ASA). Similar organizations exist in other countries. All are related to the International Organization for Standardization (ISO) and to the Systeme Internationale d'United (SI).

MEDIAN A measure of central tendency used in statistics—the middle value when a series of numbers is arranged in order of size. In the set 10, 11, 11, 12, 15, 17, 90, the median is 12. Unlike the mean, the median is unaffected by extreme values.

MEGA- (M) A prefix denoting one million (10^6), as in mega-joule (MJ, 1,000,000 joules) or megahertz (MHz, 1,000,000 hertz).

MEGABYTES (MB) Loosely, one million bytes. More precisely, 1,048,576 (2^{20}) bytes.

MEMORY The active memory, or core memory, of the computer in which all data and instruction reside before and during processing. Data in memory is existent only as long as the system is operating. Once powered down, the memory becomes empty.

MENU A group of computer program alternatives from which one of the alternatives is to be selected to implement a command. Some menus are designed to be pulled down from a menu bar at the top of the display screen. Other menus are designed to pop up upon the stroke of a key or click of a mouse button. Menus are evoked by events and are a basic part of Graphic User Interfaces (GUI).

MERGE In electronic imaging, a function for overlaying two continuous-tone images so that both images are visible.

METAL OXIDE SEMICONDUCTORS (MOS) Efficient but costly photon detectors that can be used in place of Charge-coupled devices (CCD).

MICRO- (1) Prefix used in the metric system, meaning one-millionth. A microsecond is one millionth of a second. (2) Prefix meaning *small,* as in *microphotography,* which is the production of very small images, for example, in the manufacture of chips used in computers. (3) Also in the manufacture of chips, a term (without the hyphen) involving a dimension of less than 0.002 inches. (4) A prefix denoting the utilization of a microscope or the application of a technique on a very small scale.

MICROCOMPUTER A computer whose basic operating capabilities are on one chip. Using CISC technology, micro-computers are compact and powerful. The microcomputer has become known as a personal computer (PC).

MICROELECTRONICS That branch of electronics dealing with microscopic-sized components and circuits fabricated on a semiconductor chip. Microphotography is extensively used in the fabrication of these chips.

MIDTONE An area of an original scene or a reproduction that is intermediate in lightness between that of the highlights and the shadows—gray, for example, as distinct from white and black.

MINICOMPUTER A mid-size computer having processing power close to that of a mainframe, but at a lesser price while surrendering some of the mainframes key attributes, for example, supporting fewer temminals. Minicomputers have evolved into workstations optimized for specific applications. As processing power, RAM size, CPU speed, and bus speed/width increase for minicomputers and for microcom-puters, the distinction among the three levels of computers is difficult to characterize.

MINUS COLOUR Description of a colour in terms of the part of the spectrum that its colourant absorbs. For example, minus red indicates the absorption of the red part of the spec-trum, so that the colour is cyan. Similarly, minus green is magenta, and minus blue is yellow.

MIRROR IMAGE An image that is reversed either from left to right or from top to bottom, such as a reflected image seen in a vertical mirror or a horizontal mirror. Since the inverted image on the ground glass of a view camera is reversed both vertically and laterally, it is not a mirror image.

MIXED MEDIA A collection or exhibition made up of images produced with a variety of materials such as silver, pigment, or dye. May also refer to a presentation, with or without audio or text accompaniment, consisting of any variety of the following media: photographs or other art viewed by reflected light (opaque), by projection as still photographs on a screen, projection as motion pictures, digitized computer images, or in the form of television or other electronic image.

MODE For a set of numbers, the most frequently occurring value, a measure of central tendency in statistics. In a graph of a frequency distribution, the mode is the value associated with the peak of the curve.

See also: *Mean; Median.*

MODEL The term *model is* applied in several ways. (1) A scaled-down scene or object for display or photography that would otherwise be inconvenient or too expensive to achieve in full scale. (2) A person or persons included in a photograph to display fashions, represent a character, to complement a scene etc. (3) A nonworking mock-up of a product or article to represent its appearance. (4) Designation given to a particular piece of equipment such as a camera to distinguish it from other variations.

MODEM A modem (modulator/demodulator) is a device that converts digital data from a computer via a communications port into analog data for transmission via telephone lines. Modems also receive analog data and demodulate analog data into digital data for processing by the computer. A modem will convert binary data, 1's and 0's into two different harmonic frequencies or tones. In simultaneous transmission and reception, full-duplexing, modems use four tones, two tones assigned to incoming data and two tones to output.

MODULATION (1) The changing of the amplitude or power of an electronic signal of a beam of electromagnetic radiation. The change can be constant, such as with a neutral density or other lossy filter which decreases the amplitude or power of the incident radiation. The change can be a function of the wavelength or frequency of the incident radiation, such as with a bandpass or coloured filter. Or the change can vary over time as with the modulation of the carrier wave in a radio or television broadcast. Modulation that varies as a function of time is usually a result of the combination of a carrier wave and a signal. Amplitude modulation and frequency modulation are the most common examples of this type of modulation. The extraction of the signal from the carrier wave by a receiver is called demodulation. A distinguishing characteristic of modulation is that it is concerned only with the amplitude or power (which is the amplitude squared). Changes in phase alone are not generally considered modulation. (2) For a waveform, the ratio of the AC to the DC component, or the amplitude or power of the wave as compared to the maximum amplitude or power obtainable, usually expressed as percent modulation. (3) The ratio of the amplitude or power of a signal input to a system to the amplitude or power of the signal output, expressed as percent modulation. (4) The amplitude or power of a sine wave at a specific frequency.

MODULATION TRANSFER FACTOR The ratio of the output modulation to the input modulation for a system at a specific frequency, especially as related to the modulation transfer function, where the modulation transfer factor is just the value of the modulation transfer function (MTF) at a specific frequency. As such, the modulation transfer factor is a measure of the fidelity with which a system reproduces a given input. A modulation transfer factor of 1.0 means correct reproduction; a factor of 0.0 indicates a complete failure of the recording or transmitting system.

MODULATION TRANSFER FUNCTION (MTF)
The ratio of the output amplitude or power to the input amplitude or power for a system as a function of frequency. In photography, the input is a test target of known fixed contrast and increasing spatial frequency; the MTF is a plot of the contrast of the output versus the frequency. In optics, the MTF is the magnitude of the optical transfer function, a function that completely describes the output of an optical system as a function of the position and frequency of the input. The MTF is the Fourier transform of the point spread function (or impulse response). As such, it describes the ability of a system to reproduce high frequency components or small details. A broad, flat MTF corresponds to a narrow, tall point spread function, indicating that the system is capable of reproducing a wide range of frequencies with good fidelity. An MTF can be flat over some limited bandwidth, but must at some point go to zero due to the physical impossibility of reproducing signals of infinite frequency. The components and materials used in a very high quality audio systems are capable of producing MTFs that are relatively flat over the audio spectrum (20-20,000 Hz). In photography, the frequencies of interest are spatial. Whereas resolving power test targets use square wave (sharp edge) spatial patterns that have only two tones and measure only the limiting frequency of the image, modulation transfer function targets change gradually in tone according to a sine wave pattern and evaluate the image contrast over a wide range of frequencies. Separate MTF curves for individual components in an imaging system can be combined to produce an MTF curve for the system.

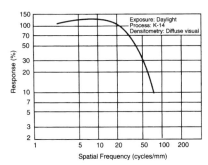

Modulation transfer function plot for Kodachrome 25 Film (from Kodak Publication P3-2E).

MODULATOR That element of a physical system (light, sound, radio frequencies, etc.) that alters its strength in accordance with another signal. In a photographic sensitometer, for example, the other signal is a step tablet or optical device that acts as the modulator to produce a series of light intensities.

MOIRÉ An artifact of an imaging system resulting from interference between two regularly spaced sets of lines. In printing, moiré occurs because of incorrect printing angles for lines screens; in video, moiré occurs when strong verticals are scanned.

MONITOR The video display terminal or monitor generally referred to as a cathode-ray tube (CRT) device, but the term is also used for other display technology such as liquid crystal displays (LCDs) and plasma screens.

MONOCHROME Identifying an image that consists of tones of a single hue, such as blue, or of a neutral hue (gray), or a process that produces such images.

MONOCHROME MONITOR A video display device that is only capable of black-and-white rastering. Monochrome monitors are not capable of continuous-tone display. Those black-and-white monitors that can display continuous tones are known as gray-scale monitors.

MORPHING In computer animation, the transforming of one shape into another in a set number of frames. The number of frames determines the speed and smoothness of the transformation. A number of motion picture special effects are achieved through this animation technique. Morphing is used interchangeably with *tweening,* an abbreviation for inbetweening. Tweening is vector-based approach to transforming one object into another; however, the two objects must share some common polymorphic similarities.

MORPHOLOGICAL FILTERING In electronic imaging, an image-processing approach based on the form and texture of the image and employing highly rigorous algebraic topology and geometry.

MOSAIC COLOUR SYSTEM Colour system in which the colours are formed by the additive mixture of light from adjacent areas that are too small to be resolved by the eye.

MOTHERBOARD In computers, the same as a logic board. In Microsoft MS-DOS systems the motherboard holds all the processing chips and circuitry necessary for the computer to function. The circuitry of the motherboard integrates all the bus slots, hard drives, display boards, and their controllers.

MOUSE In computers, a hand-held input device that controls the cursor when moved about. The mouse has become the most popular pointing device for graphic user interface environments.

MULTIMEDIA Originally, *multimedia* referred to the presentation of information using large projected images that combined a series of projected pictorial or graphic slides along with motion pictures and sound. From the presentation of individual sequential images, the development of electronic control equipment for projection systems allows the simultaneous presentation of multiple images. The number of individual images that make up a composite large screen display can be two, three, or a dozen or more. Often printed information, relating to the projected images, is used to reinforce or add to the depth of displayed visual information.

The development of large-screen projection television systems added the video medium to multimedia presentations. Educators, industrial trainers, and presentation specialists were eagerly looking for a more interactive form of presentation. The computer, as evidenced by the success of video games in the 1980s, provided an effective tool for interactive participation by the user.

Digital multimedia is now considered to consist of a single colour monitor display screen with interactive information that may include single pictorial or graphic images along with video images and sound. A valuable attribute of multimedia is the ability to create an interactive program—people learn more easily when they are part of the learning experience.

Multimedia, with its combination of technologies, offers great communication opportunities to industry, government, education, and the home. It offers the opportunity for computer software to easily use words, graphs, digital photographs, live video, and sound in a user-friendly way and present them within the spatial limitations of the personal computer environment.

Computer users have a variety of choices of computer systems for multimedia applications. The Apple Macintosh favors desktop presentation applications, while the IBM computer offers processing and storage power, and the Commodore Amiga is designed to input and output images that can be viewed using existing home television screens. Now, plug-in computer boards for sound, animation, and video enhance computer systems for use in multimedia applications.

Multimedia software has been developed for use with MS-DOS (Microsoft Disk Operating System) and OS/2, both standard operating systems for IBM PC and compatible computers. For these same systems using the Windows graphic interface, multimedia extensions are available.

System 7.0, Apple's operating system, introduced a software architecture that allows the seamless integration of dynamic media such as sound, video, and animation.

A number of other software programs exist for multimedia—some can produce complete multimedia programs while other programs produce the pictorial, graphic, or motion images or audio components of multimedia programs.

The Joint Photo Expert Group (JPEG) compression standard made it possible to use digital photographs and store and retrieve these images efficiently from mass computer storage media or transmit them more rapidly over existing communication facilities. Work by the Motion Picture Experts Group (MPEG) will soon complete a motion image standard.

Digital video interactive (DVI) technology for motion image compression is already available. DVI is based on proprietary compression/decompression algorithms and a video/graphics chip set that performs the decompression processing and display capabilities that result in real-time video images with sound.

Impressive interactive multimedia programs have already been created for industrial, medical, and educational applications. Future advances are expected to result in lower costs for the hardware, software, and storage media needed for the advancement of multimedia. Future multimedia offerings will be easier to use, while there will be more capabilities in both diversity of media elements and the methods used for presentation.

MULTIPLEX Process of transferring numerous related images from various imaging systems via optical systems to a common recording medium, e.g., the transfer of a multiimage slide-tape program onto videotape with retention of all visual effects.

MUNSELL SYSTEM A colour order system in which the colours are arranged with as nearly as possible perceptually uniform spacing. Colours are specified in terms of their Munsell hues, values, and chromas. There are five principle hues—red, yellow, green, blue, and purple—with intermediate hues in between. The value correlates with the lightness of the colours, value 10 being for the perfect diffuser, and value 0 for a black having zero reflectance factor. Chroma is 0 for achromatic colours (whites, grays, and blacks) and increases to values of about 16 for very strong colours. Munsell specifications are always given in the order hue, value, chroma; thus, SG 6/10 indicates that the hue is 5 green (a pure green), the value is 6 (a gray slightly lighter than a medium gray), and the chroma is 10 (a fairly strong colour).

NANO- (n) A prefix denoting one one-billionth (10^{-9}), as in nanosecond (ns, one-billionth of a second) or nanometer (nm, one-billionth of a meter).

NANOSECOND (nsec) In the metric system (SI), a unit of time equal to one-billionth of a second, which may be expressed as 10^{-9} second.

NATIONAL BUREAU OF STANDARDS (NBS) A branch of the federal government that is devoted to the improvement of quality of measurement in many fields. The photographic section is concerned with the measurement of characteristics such the edge sharpness and resolution of images and light intensity.

NATIONAL TELEVISION STANDARDS COMMITTEE (NTSC) The standards committee for colour television broadcasting for the United States, Mexico, Canada, and Japan. The standard is a composite luminance/chrominance system that allows for monochrome monitors to receive luminance information of a colour broadcast. Since computers are used to create video, any electronic imaging that will be passed through an NTSC system, such as videotape, must conform to NTSC standards.

NEGATIVE An image in which tonal relationships are such that light subject tones are dark and dark subject tones are light. Films that produce negative images are sometimes referred to as negative films, negative-acting films, or nonreversal films to distinguish them from reversal films that produce positive images.

Negative colour films not only invert the light-to-dark tonal relationship of the subject but also represent subject colours as complementary colours, so that a blue area in the subject is yellow in the image. The complementary nature of the image colours may not be obvious with colour films that have dye masking layers to improve the quality of the final positive print image.

NEGATIVE-POSITIVE VIEWER A viewer that permits a negative to be seen as a positive or vice versa. With one system, the image is projected by infrared radiation onto a fluorescent screen that is excited by ultraviolet radiation where the infrared proportionally quenches the fluorescence. Alternatively, the image is reproduced by closed-circuit television where the positive-negative polarity can be altered.

NEIGHBORHOOD PROCESS In electronic imaging, a filtering process that takes into account the neighboring pixels of the pixel to be filtered. The group of pixels is called a kernel. The spatial dimension of the kernel is a square composed of an odd number of pixels, 3 x 3, 5 x 5, 7 x 7, etc. Almost all electronic imaging manipulation programs use this filter for smoothing or sharpening an image.

NETWORK In computers, a group of connected computers sharing a common protocol for communications. These networks can be local or wide in area and can connect several to many thousands of terminals.

NEUTRAL (1) Colour name given to pure achromatic colours, that is, whites, grays, and blacks that are not tinged with any hue. (2) Colour name given to pure achromatic colour stimuli, that is, stimuli whose chromaticity coordinates are the same as those of the illuminant.

NO-BREAK A power supply system that automatically switches to an alternative source in the event of a supply failure, for example, a battery or a generator as a backup for the building electrical line current.

NODE One computer or terminal on a network.

NOISE (1) Noise refers to random variations, associated with detection and reproduction systems, that limit the sensitivity of detectors and the fidelity of reproductions, such as an unwanted humming sound in an audio system. By analogy, the same term is applied to nonaudio systems, such as the granularity of photographic images. (2) In electronic imaging, the presence of unwanted energy in the signal. This energy will degrade the image. This is comparable to photographic flare, i.e., nonimage-carrying energy.

NOISE FILTER (1) Usually a low-pass filter, sometimes made dynamic responding to the high-frequency content of program material. The idea is that if there is high-frequency program material it will mask high-frequency noise, so that there should be no filtering, but in the absence of high-frequency program, then the filter should be applied to attenuate noise that often takes on the audible character of hiss. (2) In electronic imaging, the degrading effects of noise can be removed by the application of a noise filter, for example, a Weiner filter or a fast Fourier transform.

NOMINAL SCALE A set of categories that are identified by names. In assessing the quality of photographic prints, for example, viewers might identify individual prints as being simply acceptable or unacceptable, a two-category nominal scale. An expansion of such a scale might include such labels as excellent, good, fair, and poor.

NONIMPACT PRINTER An electronic printing device such as a copier, laser, or inkjet printer, that creates images on a surface without contacting it.

168

NONINTERLACED In electronic imaging, the cathode ray tube (CRT) may be interlaced or noninterlaced. An unwanted effect of an interlaced scanning display is annoying and distracting flicker. Noninterlace monitors write every video line in sequence. The result is the disappearance of flicker.

NONLOSSY In electronic imaging, an image compression technique that is designed to save storage space and not lose any image data.

NONREVERSAL The term *nonreversal* may refer to a process or to a light sensitive material, either film or paper. It indicates that a positive is produced from a negative, or that a negative is produced from a positive. It is distinguished from a reversal film, paper, or process in which film from the camera produces a positive image after processing, or when a positive print is made directly from a positive original. Nonreversal applies most appropriately to intermediate steps in an extended process in which it is inaccurate to say *negative* or *positive.*

NONSILVER PROCESSES For the purpose of this article, nonsilver processes refers to a broad range of diverse photographic, processes that do not use silver salts for light sensitivity and that do not result in a final image consisting of silver. Besides this literal definition, since the 1960s the term *nonsilver photography* has become synonymous with *alternative photographic processes.* This implies that all processes other than silver become incidental and are grouped together without individuation. The result of this is an assumption of an ideal photographic convention being a straight or unmanipulated photographic print. It is not the purpose of article to debate the art/photography issue or to explain the historical implications of these arguments. It is important to understand the relationship of art photography to nonsilver processes because these processes are an important vehicle by which art photography breaks photographic conventions. Certain qualities of photographic processes are generally perceived as being inherently photographic. It was common, historically, that the commercially available support materials of the day defined the convention. The gelatin silver print holds that position today and, consequently, photography questions the inclusion of other kinds of imaging processes. It is particulary interesting to pinpoint exactly where in its history photography splintered the idea of process from that of aesthetic since photography owes it existence to the natural inclination—rooted in the nineteenth century traditions of science, chemistry, optics and philosophy—of creating an environment of experimentation and invention. So, historically, the photographic ideal was continually evolving and being rapidly redefined, predicted on each new invention and each new discovery. It was not until debates pertaining to the nature of art and photography and the examination of the expressive qualities of the medium after the beginning of the twentieth century, that the Pictorialists challenged the supremacy of painting over photography as art. The point of departure became the print itself, whether it extended the expressive potential of the medium by interpreting the negative through manipulation or remained faithful to the record. This controversy weaves a complex web around the very nature of the relationship of photography to art that centres the debate on the intrusion of the artist's hand upon the unrelenting mechanical eye of the camera, that influences the choice of process and the way the image is interpreted through the use of specific materials.

CONTEMPORARY TRENDS AND NEW TECHNOLOGIES The technological changes that have brought photography out of the darkroom and into the light via the computer and electronic imaging have not occurred suddenly or unexpectedly. These changes, in fact, continue the journey established early in the nineteenth century with the camera lucida, the camera obscura, and the camera. What started out based on the blending of light, alchemy, and paper to record, store, and transmit visual images is evolving into an electronic imaging system. Developing tanks, enlargers, and chemicals are being replaced by copiers, computers, software programs, and laser printers with an infinite range of possible manipulations that are based on nonsilver technology.

In their search to modulate the camera's precise and mechanical record, and in their struggle to glorify photography to the status of fine art where artistic influence was the ultimate creator of the image, the Pictorialists, which included Edward Steichen, Gertrude Kaesebier, Robert Demachy, Frank Eugene, Annie Brigman, and J. Craig Annan (to name but a few), reached its peak of popularity in 1910. The hand manipulated printing processes that were the signature style of the Pictorialists continued to be used into the 1930s but with less and less frequency. Photographers began to respond, in Europe, and America through Alfred Steiglitz's 291 Gallery, to the abstract forms of cubism and the chaotic challenges of the surrealists, leaving the manipulative processes behind in an attempt to serve this new vision directly through the camera lens.

The straight, unmanipulated image printed on a commercially available photographic paper prevailed from the 1930s until the early 1960s. Ansel Adams, Edward Weston, Paul Strand, Imogen Cunningham—all became a part of a enduring movement in photographic history that has become the photographic convention even today, that touted the clarity of the photographic lens and the objectivity of the *photographic eye*. The 1960s was a time of great social upheaval in the United States initiated by the Vietnam War. Photography in the 1960s was also defined by a rebellion against the traditional, dominant form of photography that generated a revival of the historic nonsilver photographic processes. This renaissance of print manipulation grew out of a desire to redefine parameters and blur the boundaries of photography and art. Based on their willingness to embrace popular culture, the Conceptual art and Pop art movements, which included artists like John Baldessari, Robert Rauschenberg, and Andy Warhol, used the photographic medium because of photography's powerful ability to define and perpetuate cultural myths and exploit the mass media. At the same time, influenced by these artists but interested in maintaining the inherent reality of the photographic image as a starting point, were photographic artists Betty Hahn, Bea Nettles, Robert Fichter, and Robert Heinecken, to name a few. Photography in the 1960s could be characterized by a radical transformation that was manifested by the willingness and insistence of artists to challenge and somehow interrupt or interfere with the accepted conventions of the medium. This period was one of great exploration that echoed the climate of diversity that had surrounded the discovery of photography itself. It differed, however, in that the struggle for recognition of photography as a fine-art form was no longer an issue. The relationship of painting and photography, specifically, and the relationship of photography to the plastic arts, in general, was less an adversarial role and more an interdisciplinary one than it was at the turn of the century.

Also at this time, a group of image makers began to explore the *new technologies* in an on-going attempt to broaden and expand the definition of photography. The straight photographer's acceptance of the limitations imposed by the mechanical nature of the camera came to be what defined the medium in its pure form, and their exploration of the expressive and metaphorical aspects is what helped establish photography's credibility as an art despite its dependency on a machine. By employing electronic-imaging systems and other commercially used processes, contemporary photographers like Sonia Sheridan, William Larson, Joan Lyons, and Sheila Pinkel continued to challenge photography's relationship to the machine through the use of nontraditional photographic materials. This reliance on the machine was no longer considered limiting or distasteful in the post-industrial society. Instead, it was seen as something with enormous potential for artistic expression. This mirrors the nineteenth-century distrust of machines vs. the twentieth-century embracing of them.

The office copier was invented to generate fast, inexpensive, and accurate reproductions of documents used in business. It is also a process that is available to almost everyone and is capable of transforming and manipulating images that can generate new visions. The use of these machines immediately brought into question the validity of photography to accurately describe what the world looks like. Copy machines for the most part act like a simple camera without a bellows adjustment. Therefore it produces a very flat, very limited depth of field that extends approximately one-quarter of an inch above the copier plane or copier glass. Black-and-white copiers use an electrostatically charged monochromatic toner that forms an image on paper and that is then fused or melted onto the paper support. The more recent development of the colour copier forms an image using the subtractive system (cyan, magenta, and yellow), with each colour made up of a thermoplastic powder, called a toner or pigment, that is electronically fused onto the paper. Laser copiers are the latest and most technologically advanced development in the history of electrostatic processes. This machine relies on a scanner that reads the image and converts it to digital signals which are then transmitted to a laser printer capable of subtle colour/tonal distinctions. This machine also uses the subtractive colour system with the addition of black, which creates a more accurate sense of colour and depth of field in image reproduction.

Chester F. Carlson, in the late 1930s, invented this new technology, called *electrophotography,* then sold the patent to the Haloid Corporation in Rochester, New York. Calling the new process *xerography,* it was put into practice in 1948. It did not, however, really become practically and commercially viable until 1960 with the introduction of the Xerox Copier #914 that remedied the early models' problems of being cumbersome, messy, expensive, and slow. The advantages of the present day machines are many, including:

1. Rapid, consistent, and relatively inexpensive duplication and production.
2. The ability to make a colour copy from a 35-mm slide or a 35-mm negative.
3. An amazing amount of colour control and manipulation, overall or specified areas only, of the colour reproduction, which includes a colour balance memory that can be programmed.
4. Contrast adjustment and control of reproduction.
5. Image size easily scaled up or down, including framing devices that allow the operator to frame, compose, obliterate, or segment the image and/or text, if desired, into as many as 16 segments.

Artists using copier machines to create art shattered the preconception that the copy machine's single function was to produce a facsimile of the original image. In 1979, a seminal exhibition of art created on copy machines entitled "Electroworks," curated by Marilyn McCray at the International Museum of Photography at George Eastman House in Rochester, New York, cinched the marriage of art and technology. The exhibition embodied work that combined *copier aesthetics* with every possible artistic medium including painting, sculpture, ceramics, printmaking, photography, video, film, animation, design, conceptual art, performance art, artists' books, mail art, and poetry. Installed along with the works of art were the machines themselves, with artists scheduled to generate art on them throughout the duration of the exhibition.

Due to the immovable nature of the copy machines, the photographic artist was once again relegated to the studio as the arena for the picture and art making. As in the nineteenth century when the subject was brought to the photographic artist who confined to the studio by slow film emulsions, bulky equipment, and process limitations, so the subject was brought to the machine in the twentieth century. Printing photographs on material other than sensitized photographic paper can also be traced to the second half of the nineteenth century when it was common for photographs to appear on glass, porcelain, tile, leather, and fabric.

Although called copies, the prints generated by the machines were considered original works of art conceived as unique objects, but due to the very nature of the machine art could be generated quickly, cheaply, and efficiently. This called into question the sacred artistic concept of the *original*. Artists had embraced a process that challenged the concept of creativity and brought into focus one of contemporary art's most curious paradoxes—technological processes designed for mass production but used to create singular works of art. The ability of the machine to rapidly generate images, however, is paralleled only by the use of electronic media such as electronic still photography and video.

Electronic Imaging: Present and Future Since the 1960s, computer technology has dramatically changed our understanding of photography. The way we read and process visual information has been challenged not unlike how copy machines altered our perceptions of *real* and *original*. Bridging the gap between technology and art, computer graphics offers a broad spectrum of manipulations and controls over the creation of visual images that dissolve the boundaries between real and fabricated. Computers have also dissolved the boundaries between one medium and another. The computer's astounding ability to assimilate or appropriate information seamlessly from one medium to another, disguising the origins of information, is unsurpassed in the history of image making. It destroys the idea of photographic truth. The implications of this are profound, affecting how pictures are made, stored, and disseminated. Our ability to detect image manipulation lessens as the sophistication of computer technology grows, the quality of image resolution improves, and accessibility to equipment expands. Photography, since its invention, has struggled with the mechanical nature of the medium. The nineteenth-century photographer's insistence of challenging this inherent quality of photography with the physical alteration of the image by the hand of the artist has become obsolete. Now, on the brink of the twenty-first century, artists have turned to embrace the mechanization that was once so abhorrent.

Electronic images are, for the most part, nonsilver imaging systems that artists can use to manipulate and reassemble images. Many of the artists who have used the historic nonsilver processes to alter colour, tonality, and print support material have turned to electronic imaging as a visual synthesizer that is simply another tool for artistic expression. The images achieved in this way are all but unattainable any other way. Images can be generated on overhead transparent projection material that is computer printed, and this piece of acetate is then used as the image support that is transferred to a final support material using a variety of alternative photographic processes.

NORMAL DISTRIBUTION (1) See *Gaussian distribution.*
(2) For a set of numbers, a pattern of variation about a central value caused by chance. The plot of such a pattern, often called, from its shape, the *bell* curve, is completely defined by the arithmetic average and the standard deviation.

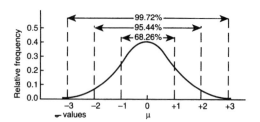

Normal distribution illustrating areas contained under the curve for
± 1, 2, and 3 standard deviations.

NUBUS A special high-speed bus found in Macintosh
computers. The Nubus is distinguished from other bus designs
by its protocol for moving data within the computer.

NYQUIST CRITERION Specification of discrete sampling
requirements of a continuous waveform; the minimum
frequency with which a continuous waveform must be sampled
in order for it to be accurately reconstructed from discrete
sampling data. This frequency is greater than twice the
maximum frequency present in the analog waveform. If the
waveform is sampled at a frequency lower than that specified by
the Nyquist criterion, the undersampled frequencies will be
aliased and the lower frequencies will be distorted.

OBJECT COLOURS Colours attributable to reflecting or transmitting objects, as distinct from colours attributable to light sources.

OFFICE COPIERS Early office copiers were designed primarily to make same-sized copies of printed materials. A number of different imaging processes have been used over the years, but the field is now dominated by the xerographic electrophotography system. Some of the improvements that have been made in office copiers, in addition to dramatic increases in the speed of reproduction, include the ability to (1) produce high-quality reproductions of continuous-tone originals, (2) alter the scale of reproduction, (3) copy on transparent projection materials, (4) control the density of the image, (5) copy both sides of a document, (6) collate and staple copies, and (7) make realistic colour copies.

OFF LINE In monitoring a process, a separation of the data analysis from the collection of data, which necessarily involves a significant time lag in finding and correcting an error.

ON LINE (1) In monitoring a process, an almost immediate analysis of the data collected, thus reducing the time lag between the discovery of an error and the correction of the process. (2) In computers, the term simply means that the computer is functioning. Sometimes *on line* is used to mean that the computer terminal is in communication with a host computer operating system.

OPERATING SYSTEMS (OS) In computers, a software program that supports the basic operations of the computer.

OPTICAL CHARACTER RECOGNITION (OCR) In computers, a software program that reads scanned text into a format that can be entered into a word processing or spreadsheet program for alteration.

OPTICAL EFFECTS Motion-picture special effects that are created by manipulating and/or combining images during the printing process. While some basic optical effects can be achieved in the camera or on a contact printer, the primary tool for making such effects is the optical printer, which is, in its simplest form, a motion-picture projector aimed into a synchronized camera, and to some extent can be thought of as a motion-picture version of a darkroom enlarger. Advances in video and computer technology are continually enhancing traditional optical printer procedures, allowing for greater efficiency and the ability to handle more complex imagery, as well as creating electronic alternatives to the optical printer.

TRANSITIONAL EFFECTS Often used when changing from one scene to another, to enhance visual vitality, to smooth over abrupt changes, or to indicate a change in time, location, or point of view. These effects include fades, lap dissolves, wipes, ripple dissolves, out-of-focus or diffusion dissolves, spin-in and out, zoom-in and out, and an unlimited variety of matted wipe shots. These effects can also be used to compensate for a variety of problems with the original footage.

FRAME SEQUENCE ALTERATION By eliminating or repeating selected frames from the original sequence, a variety of effects can be achieved, such as slow or fast motion, or the subtle altering of the speed of an action to enhance the sense of realism or visual vitality. Repeating a single frame over and over results in a freeze frame. Repeating a series of frames back and forth results in the creation of cyclic repetitive movements. Creatively applied, this technique can transform a shot of a cat walking, into a shot of a cat doing a series of dance steps, or allow a man falling off a roof to bounce back up again. Altering the original frame sequence can also create numerous expressionistic effects in terms of movement rhythm and visual complexity.

COMBINING IMAGES Images can be combined in innumerable ways, including superimposition, bi-packing (sandwiching of two film strips in the projector stage of the printer), split-screen, where several independent images are printed within the frame area, and through the use of travelling matte procedures. Travelling mattes are made on motion-picture film and bi-packed with original footage during the printing process, blocking selected areas of the frame from exposure. For instance, the appearance of a monster walking down a city street can be achieved by making a travelling matte that in each frame exactly matches the changing silhouette of a moving monster model shot in miniature. The matte is next bi-packed with the background footage and printed. The recording film is rewound and a second printing pass is made with the monster footage, in some instances using a reverse matte, combining the images into a new, seemingly realistic, film event.

CHANGE OF IMAGE SIZE OR POSITION Unwanted areas of the image can be cropped out. Closeups can be created for extra editorial cuts. Camera moves such as zooms and tracking shots can be imitated and action can be repositioned for dramatic effect or for use in further multiple exposure procedures.

OPTICAL MEDIA In electronic imaging, optical media are being used to store large image files that may exceed 20 MB. Unlike typical hard disks that are coated in a magnetically addressable medium, optical media are addressed by laser.

OPTICAL PUMPING the use of light (or electromagnetic radiation) to elevate the atoms or molecules of a substance to an excited state. Laser light is emitted from lasers as a result of optical pumping of the laser tube. Extremely powerful lasers can also be constructed by using a less powerful laser to pump the main tube. The concept of optical pumping also applies to some extent to the formation of the latent image in photography, although the term is not used because the result of the pumping is a chemical change rather than the emission of more light.

OPTICAL SCANNER See *Scanner.*

OPTICAL SYSTEMS An assembly of optical components such as lens elements, mirrors, prisms, and filters, suitably aligned and tested, for acquisition of an image for recording and evaluation.

OPTICAL TRANSFER FUNCTION (OTF) A mathematical expression of the extent to which an image-forming system conveys information. The OTF includes the modulation transfer function and the wave-phase shift, i.e., any change in position of the peaks of the waves.

OPTIMIZE In computers, the optimization of the hard drive causes contiguous sectors on the block to be available for storage, thus achieving faster reads and writes to and from the hard drive.

OPTOCOUPLER An electronic device consisting of a light source and a photosensor that uses light (or infrared) to couple two circuits without making an electrical connection between them. Optocouplers are useful in providing isolation between sensitive low-level circuits and noisy power circuits or between dc circuits and ac circuits. The light source is a light-emitting diode (LED); the photosensor can be either a photodiode or a phototransistor, with or without a transistor output amplifier. Input current through the LED causes it to irradiate the photosensor, which, in turn, causes output current to flow. The ratio of output current to input current, called the *current transfer ratio,* varies greatly from device to device. It can range from less than 1 to more than 100. The maximum voltage that can be applied between the input and output circuits without breakdown is usually 1000 volts or more.

ORIENTATION The relationship of an image to the viewer or to the image environment, for example, the position of an image (or a mount) according to its longer axis, i.e., *vertical* (long dimension perpendicular to the horizon) or *horizontal* (long axis parallel to the horizon). The vertical orientation is sometimes referred to as *portrait,* and the horizontal as *landscape.* The portrait and landscape designations are also used to define orientation of text on a page; landscape lines running across the length of the page, portrait across the width.

The term also applies to placing a negative or other image in a printer, enlarger, or projector with respect to the emulsion facing toward or away from the light source, the top of the image being positioned upward or downward, etc. It might refer to the axis or other reference of a photograph, such as the north-south axis of an aerial image.

Orientation might also refer to *right-reading* or *wrong reading* of text or image material, that is, whether it is a correct-reading image or a mirror image.

ORIGINAL The term *original* refers to the negative (or positive if reversal processed) that was in the camera when the object was photographed. It also applies to sound recordings on film, or video recordings. Originals are also materials from which copies are made, such as handwritten or typed documents, printed material, tracings, drawings, etc. The term might also apply to an original work of art.

OSCILLOSCOPE A useful test instrument that displays on a cathode-ray tube the variation of applied voltage with respect to time. The waveform is displayed on the screen of the CRT by moving a spot of light resulting from an electron beam (the cathode ray) striking the phosphors on the face of the tube. The spot can be deflected both vertically and horizontally. The vertical axis of the display represents the amplitude of the voltage applied to the vertical input terminals. The horizontal axis is linear with respect to time. The pattern on the screen, therefore, displays a graph of the variation of applied voltage as a function of time. The oscilloscope is generally used to observe two types of voltages: (1) those that are repetitive or cyclic in nature and whose trace is continuously displayed, and (2) those that are transient, where the trace appears on the screen only once (until triggered again). Some oscilloscopes can display two or more waveforms simultaneously. Although basically a voltmeter, the oscilloscope can also be used to measure current, phase difference, and frequency of cyclic waveforms. Certain physical quantities such as light, force, temperature, and distance can be converted to their electrical analog and can be displayed. One such photographic application is the shutter tester, where the relative amount of light passing through the shutter is represented by the vertical displacement of the CRT spot and time by its horizontal displacement. Oscilloscopes are capable of displaying exceedingly fast transient phenomena.

Photographing oscilloscope waveforms, cyclic as well as transient, provides a permanent record of the behaviour of the equipment under test and can be useful for later evaluation of the waveform, especially in the case of transients.

OUTPUT The terms *input* and *output* are interdependent, and they are commonly combined in the form of input/output to represent the beginning and end of a process. In the process of making a photograph, for example, the subject is generally considered to be the input and the photographic image the output.

OVERLAY (1) An assembly of transparent or translucent prints placed one over the other to form a composite image. (2) A drawing, tracing, or other transparent medium superimposed on another record or image to delineate areas or correlate them with other information. (3) In electronic imaging, the use of several images as pieces in the composing of a new image. The images are seamlessly pasted, and the resulting image is displayed without evidence of its being a composite.

PAINT In electronic imaging, the process of creating a specific colour, size, and shape, analogous to anually with a brush.

PAIRED COMPARISON (1) A method used in statistical testing when the measured values vary because of factors that are not under consideration. For example, in checking the performance of two densitometers, the recorded values will change markedly with the level of the sample density, and a comparison of the average readings over a range of densities would be ineffective. Therefore, the density readings from the two instruments are paired, and the differences in the pairs of readings are examined to detect a difference in the two densitometers. (2) A method used in statistical testing in which a set of items (for example, prints A, B, and C) are compared in all possible combinations of two (A and B, B and C, A and C) to determine if the results are consistent. If a person judged print A to be lighter than print B, print B to be lighter than print C, and print C to be lighter than print A, the responses would not be consistent, indicating that the person was guessing or influenced by some factor other than the actual tones of the prints.

PALETTE In computing, the possible number of colours displayed is a selection of colours from a larger possible group known as the palette. Thus a computer that can display 16 colours at any one time typically will select a group of 16 colours from a palette of 256 colours.

PANTONE MATCHING SYSTEM (PMS) A commonly used ink mixing and colour matching system.

PARALLEL PORT In computing, one of the two standard input/output means used by the computer to control external peripherals such as a printer. Parallel ports send data in groups, 16 or 32 bits at a time, thus allowing for a faster transfer.

PASCAL LANGUAGE A high-level programming language that is highly structured, that is, it requires that certain steps be followed absolutely and that certain lines of code be placed in specified locations within the program. Next to C, Pascal is the most commonly used language in computer imaging/graphics.

PASTEL (1) Adjective used to indicate that a colour is pale or desaturated. (2) Art work produced by crayons composed of chalk with other materials.

PASTEUP PROCESS A combination of two or more images, usually prints, on a single support, normally by the use of adhesives. Typically used to prepare material for publication in print. Distinguish from *collage,* which involves different media, and from *mosaic,* which involves the assembly of images of adjacent areas of a scene to form a continuous whole. In photomechanical reproduction, the assembly of text and graphics on a single support in preparation for reproduction.

PEAK WHITE In electronic imaging, the setting of useful highlight detail at 100 IRE units is called peak white. The difference between peak white and the pedestal is the contrast range of the system.

PEDESTAL In electronic imaging, the video signal that reproduces black at 7.5 IRE units. This black is elevated just above no signal black. Useful shadow detail is set at this level.

PERIPHERALS In computers, attachments that are connected through a variety of data input/output channels, for example, printers, scanners, and plotters.

PERSISTENCE In electronics, the tendency of certain phosphors to glow after the excitation has been removed. After the electron beam in a cathode-ray tube has passed over the fluorescent screen, the phosphor on the screen along the path traced by the beam may continue to glow for a certain time. Some phosphors, such as those used on high-speed oscilloscopes, have virtually no persistence, whereas other phosphors have long persistence to meet special requirements.

PERSISTENCE OF VISION The fusion of successive images, as in motion pictures, animation, and television, into an apparently continuous image without flicker. The duration of each persistent image is usually about 1/25th of a second, but it varies depending upon the luminance level and other factors.

PHI PHENOMENON The appearance of motion when a sequence of still pictures containing image elements that are systematically displaced in position are observed in rapid sequence, as with animated cartoons, motion pictures, and video.

PHOSPHOR A substance that emits light as a result of fluorescence or phosphorescence.

PHOSPHORESCENCE Electromagnetic radiation emitted from a substance as a result of the absorption of radiation incident on the substance. Phosphorescence is distinguished from fluorescence in that phosphorescence can continue long after exposure to incident radiation ceases.

PHOSPHOR PERSISTENCE In computing, the length of time that a phosphor within a cathode-ray tube (CRT) emits energy is determined by the chemical composition of the phosphor. There are various phosphor decay times. The selection of a particular monitor's phosphor decay rate depends upon the particular use that the computer operator has in mind. Monitors with long phosphor decay times would not be appropriate for an application that updates the CRT screen with new information with each refresh.

PHOTOBASE A computer network devoted to information about photographic education.

PHOTOCELL A solid-state electronic device that converts light into electrical energy or that uses light to regulate the flow of an electrical current.

PHOTOCONDUCTIVE CELL A photosensor, the electrical resistance of which decreases as light on it increases. The value of resistance at a specific light level is determined by the area of the cell, the configuration of the electrodes, and the type of photoresistive material used—most frequently cadmium sulfide (CdS) and cadmium selenide (CdSe). The spectral response of these cells is quite narrow Cadmium sulphide cells have a maximum sensitivity at about 515 nm (blue-green) and cadmium selenide from 615 to 735 nm (near infrared). Because of their spectral response, cadmium sulphide cells have been widely used in light meters and in cameras with automatic exposure control. At light levels of less than 1 footcandle these cells are exceptionally linear; that is, the current is directly proportional to the incident light. Disadvantages of photoconductive cells are that they need an external source of voltage to operate, unlike a photovoltaic cell, and their relatively slow response to changes in light level compared to the fast response of phototransistors and photodiodes.

Syn.: *Photoresistor.*

PHOTOCOPYING The process of making a reproduction of a document or other original based on the principle of light sensitivity, typically with an office xerographic photocopying machine.

PHOTODIODE A semiconductor *p-n* junction device whose reverse (leakage) current is proportional to incident radiant energy. Unlike the photoconductive cell, the photodiode is polarized and must be connected only in the reverse bias mode. The photodiode has a faster speed of response to a change in radiant energy than a photoconductive cell.

PHOTOELECTRON (1) An elementary particle bearing a negative charge. In photography, an electron freed from its normal position in a crystal such as silver halide by the absorption of radiant energy. Such electrons participate in the formation of the latent image. (2) An electron that is emitted from the surface of a phototube cathode when a photon strikes the cathode. The photoelectrons are attracted to a positively charged anode. The flow of electrons is frequently referred to as *photocurrent*. There is a linear relationship between the magnitude of photocurrent and the level of incident light.

PHOTOGRAPH An image of one or more objects produced by the chemical action of light or other forms of radient energy (gamma rays, x-rays, ultraviolet radiation, infrared radiation) on sensitized materials. By extension, an image formed by an electronic imaging system (electronic photography).

PHOTOGRAPHIC EQUIPMENT Photography,whether viewed as a form of artistic ,expression or technical discipline, is equipment dependent. From a photograph's initial inception to its final form, equipment is used extensively in each step. Although the word *equipment is* often used in an all-encompassing way, there arc many types of photographic equipment.

The evolution of photographic equipment has paralleled technological developments in many fields. Improvements or breakthroughs in mechanics, optics, and chemistry have all contributed to the rapid growth of photographic equipment and processes. later developments in electronics and computers have brought photography to today's highly sophisticated levels. In our world of computer-driven technology, many people feel that equipment has become so advanced that it takes away from the photographer's creativity. This could not he further from the truth. A camera or any other piece of equipment is just a tool that must be directed by the photographer. Rather than becoming distracted by, or even despairing over, advanced features, they should be seen as a way to free the photographer from mundane concerns. Technology will continue to advance whether greeted with open arms or fought tooth and nail.

Photographic equipment can be broken down into five basic groups: Cameras and accessories, camera supports, lighting, darkoom and processing equipment, and electronic imaging. Within each of these groups there are several subgroups. Camera equipment includes the various types and formats of cameras, lenses, and exposure meters. Camera supports refers to tripods, tripod heads, monopods, studio stands dollies, and motion-compensation devices. Lighting equipment covers tungsten studio and location lights, electronic flash, reflectors and diffusers, and stands and booms. Darkroom and processing equipment covers a wide array of items including sinks, processing tanks, thermometers, enlargers, safelights, driers, contact printers, and machine processors. Electronic imaging equipment includes computers, scanners, printers, software, and optical storage systems.

Electronic-imaging equipment is at the top of the list for the most modern technology. The debate over whether electronic imaging will ultimately take over photography is hotly contested in many circles. Needless to say, these new technologies will forever alter the photographic equipment world. Central to electronic imaging is the personal computer, or PC. The Apple Macintosh system took the early lead as the premier imaging platform. Recently, however, the IBM-compatible world has pulled into line with the Apple systems. The fast pace of development work on these imaging systems has brought prices down to a level that a typical professional photographer can afford. Electronic imaging is still closely linked with traditional photography. Current electronic-imaging cameras are not capable of producing the high resolution that is possible with silver-based film. Digital cameras offer the possibility of much higher resolutions in the future.

Scanners are the tools that allow photographers to import silver-based images into a computer imaging system. Transparencies, prints, and even negatives can be scanned and transformed into digital images that can be directly manipulated by software programs. High-quality scanners are able to resolve the image at near original levels. The ability to maintain the original resolution, colour, and density values of the image then becomes dependent on the hardware and software being used. The high-end standard for colour imaging is called 24-bit RGB colour. To achieve this level, each pixel is assigned twenty-four bits of colour information. A pixel is the smallest individual picture element that the system is able to resolve, and a bit is the smallest individual piece of computer information that can be assigned. In a 24 bit RGB colour image, each pixel is assigned 8 bits of information for Red, Green, and Blue. This combination allows for 16.8 million colours in an image.

Software packages for imaging offer an incredible number of features, allowing images to be manipulated in just about any fashion imaginable. Colour, density, and contrast can be altered or adjusted, and special effects such as posterization and image reversal are available. Sophisticated editing tools allow for cutting and pasting segments of images together. Other tools can take samples of colours or textures from one area of an image and reproduce them elsewhere. High-end imaging software can produce colour separations that can be electronically transferred to prepress for reproduction in the printing process. Once an image has been manipulated, it can be printed out directly by the computer or sent to a film recorder. Colour thermal printers are available that can produce near photographic quality prints.

Image storage technology and equipment are advancing rapidly toward mass availability. Eastman Kodak is pioneering the Photo CD system. This is a technology that allows photofinishing labs to place photographic images on a compact laser disc. The images can then be viewed with a Photo CD compliant disc player. Some see this as an answer to archival stability problems, laser discs are not subject to the same image degradation as silver based film and paper. Others may view this as the first step toward the eventual replacement of all silver-based products, but there is little doubt that photographic equipment as we know it today will continue to serve photographers for many years to come.

PHOTOGRAPHIC PHYSICS Areas in the general field of physics that are related to photography. To some extent this means that all physics is photographic physics, especially with the advent of electronic imaging. A more limited definition would involve the application of physics to photographic systems and problem solving.

PHOTOGRAPHY The age of the word *photography is* a good deal more certain than the age of the idea it represents. It has long been known that Sir John Herschel and the German astronomer Johann von Maeder used it in their mutual correspondence early in 1839, and Herschel used it in a letter to W. H. Fox Talbot dated February 28, 1839. Documentation that Hercules Florence had used the word *photography* in Brazil in 1833 was not discovered until 1973. The word *photography* was derived from the Greek roots meaning to write with light, and it immediately replaced Niepce's word, *heliography* (sun writing), and Talbot's phrase, *photogenic drawing.*

For 150 years, there was little question that the word *photography* referred to a variety of photochemical systems in which the agency of light alters sensitized materials in a camera. The materials are chemically treated to produce a visible image. Without a camera, these processes would produce photograms (which we do not alternatively call photographs) of the sort made by Talbot in the 1830s or Man Ray in the 1920s.

If the idea of photography is inextricably bound to the camera, then the idea can be traced back at least to the painters of the Italian Renaissance, who used lenses to project images in correct perspective on their canvases in darkened chambers. The images were made permanent in paint. If the idea of photography is fundamentally photochemical, then it is at least as old as the efforts of Wedgwood and Davy in about 1800 to record leaves and insect wings on paper, glass, and leather.

What, then, can we say about the systems of producing photographs that wed photochemical and electronic or digital processes, or that are purely digital? In all cases, light-sensitive receptors in electronic still video or digital cameras switch or produce currents that are electronically or digitally processed and stored. The pictures can be made visible by conversion from digital to analog for viewing on a monitor, or imaging to output devices such as a film recorder, a laser printer, or a thermal printer. The criteria of light-sensitive materials exposed in a camera, processed to produce a visible image are still met. These *imaging systems* are clearly, then, still doing photography and are properly referred to as photographic systems.

On the other hand, the lesson of modern lexicography is that usage determines meaning. It is pointless to try to legislate the continued use of the word *photography* if it is generally concluded that digital imaging systems are so radically different that they require a new name. For the foreseeable future, the word *photography* will appear both by itself and in hyphenated agglomerations and the hyperbolic phrases of advertising executives wishing to convince the world that what they offer is new, new, new, even as it follows the form and function of the tried and true.

PHOTOINSTRUMENTATION Photoinstrumentation is a field of photographic specialization that developed out of the military weapons and ballistic test ranges during the late 1940s and 1950s. The term was closely linked to the establishment of a technical group called the Society of Photographic Instrumentation Engineers, or SPIE, that developed around the activities associated with these ranges. This society thrives today, and while it kept its initials, it is now known as the International Society for Optical Engineering.

Eventually the subject matter that concerned this society, and indeed photoinstrumentation in general, expanded and eventually evolved to include a wide range of sophisticated applications of photographic- and electronics-based imaging techniques.

The field now encompasses any application of imagemaking instrumentation that is used to visualize events that are generally invisible to the naked eye or to standard cameras or photosensitive materials, the design and use of specialized photographic or electronic image-making devices, the making of records whose primary purpose is to serve as the basis on which measurements of an event under study are made, the use of cameras and image-recording materials in hostile environments, or any combination or extension of these factors.

Individuals who are able to operate successfully as photoinstrumentation engineers or technologists must posses a high degree of skill and knowledge obtained through on the job experiences and university-level education.

PHOTOMECHANICAL AND ELECTRONIC REPRODUCTION In the strictest sense, *photomechanics is* the term that applies to the operations of producing printing plates or image carriers. In the more general sense, the meaning of the term has been expanded to include as well all the photographic, colour correction, and image assembly operations before platemaking. It includes continuous tone-line, and halftone photography for the particular printing process; film processing; single and two-stage masking for colour separation; manual retouching with pencils, dyes, and airbrushing; manual colour correction with chemicals (wet dot etching); photographic masks for dry dot etching; opaquing; layout; stripping; plate exposure and processing.

PRINTING PROCESSES In the latest sense, the concept of photomechanics has been further expanded to include electronic reproduction. Ever since electronics and computers invaded printing, they modified and replaced many of the functions traditionally considered photomechanics. The impact of electronic reproduction has been so pervasive that the two technologies must be considered together to understand how images are prepared for reproduction.

Each printing process has proprietary characteristics that impose specific requirements and limitations on the types of images used for reproduction. Letterpress and flexography are relief processes that use halftone negatives to make original engravings and photopolymer printing plates. Gravure is an intaglio process that prints from cells in cylinders, mainly on roll-fed web presses. These have been made traditionally using positive continuous-tone images and chemical etching. Lithography is a planographic process with ink-receptive image areas and water-receptive nonimage areas. The printing plates are made from negatives or positives, depending on the platemaking system. Screen printing is a porous printing process in which the image carrier is produced on the fine screen either by manual or photomechanical means.

COPY PREPARATION *Copy is* the name given to text, line, and tone illustrations to be reproduced. The line and tone illustrations include diagrams, drawings, photographic prints, colour transparencies, and original art. They can be in single, spot, multi- or process colour. Copy preparation includes all the operations involved in getting the copy ready for reproduction. There are two basic steps: (1) the design or layout of the printed product; and (2) sorting, preparation, and assembly of the various job elements or components for reproduction. The layout is necessary before any of the other operations are performed. It can be a rough sketch, a loose comprehensive, or a tightly rendered comprehensive that looks like the finished product in all details.

For the text to be prepared for reproduction it must be typeset on a word processor or typesetting machine in the proper typeface or style and with the proper point size, letter and line spacing, column width, indention with hyphenation or justified; it must be set ragged right, ragged left, or as a runaround around an illustration, and proofread before photography or entry into a desktop publishing or prepress system. Line illustrations must be checked for size and examined for sharpness and density of lines. Photographs and colour transparencies must be checked for size and cropping and segregated according to type of reproduction, such as single colour, spot colour, or process colour, and tone reproduction such as normal, light, dark, high-key, and low-key originals. Photographs and colour transparencies are continuous tone and must be converted to halftone images for reproduction.

GRAPHIC ARTS PHOTOGRAPHY

Cameras Since graphic arts can involve the photography of large subjects or layouts with two or four pages, large darkroom process cameras are used. These are mounted on precision beds with spring supports to dampen vibration effects. The copyboard and lens board travel on precision tracks; the image back is stationary behind the darkroom wall and is connected to the lens board with a bellows. The image back is equipped with a ground glass for focusing and a hinged vacuum back on which the film is mounted for exposure. Vertical cameras that look like enlargers but are much larger are used for smaller images (up to 20 x 20 inches). These are usually used in a darkroom.

Lenses Lenses are coated to reduce internal surface reflections, thereby increasing image sharpness and resolution. Process lenses are usually of symmetrical design to decrease image distortion and produce a flat field for image sharpness over an image field of about 50 degrees. All process colour lenses are apochromatic, or fully corrected for the visible and near infrared spectrum. They have fairly small maximum apertures from $f/8$ to $f/11$ and have optimum apertures from $f/16$ to $f/22$ for best average sharpness over a wide field. Focal lengths range from 8 inches for wide angle lenses for 20 inch (vertical) cameras to as long as 48 inches for 40 inch cameras.

Lights and Exposure Controls High-intensity lights such as quartz iodine, pulsed xenon, or photoflood lamps are used to expose the slow-speed, high-resolution films used for graphic arts. Special point source lights are used tor contact printing. Computerized light integrators are used to control exposures in photography and platemaking. These integrate the total quantity of light received by the film by varying the exposure time inversely with the illuminance.

Graphic Arts Films Special high-contrast, high-resolution, slow-speed emulsions of silver halides in gelatin, coated on stable base polyester films, known as lith films, are used for line and halftone photography. Continuous-tone films are used for colour separations, masks, contact films, and gravure printing. Graphic arts films are colour blind (blue sensitive), orthochromatic (blue and green sensitive), or panchromatic. Special films are made for scanners, and they are films that can be handled in controlled daylight or yellow-filtered light made for stripping or image assembly.

Film Processing Special chemistries consisting of high-contrast developing solutions followed by a stop bath, sodium or ammonium thiosulphate fixing solution, and washing are used for processing lith films. The operation is usually carried out in an automatic processing machine that can also be used for processing continuous-tone films by changing the chemistry. Stabilization processing, used extensively for phototypesetting resin coated (RC) and film prints, speeds processing by eliminating washing through converting the unexposed silver halide to a moderately stable complex (that eventually stains after exposure to enough light). Rapid access processing uses continuous-tone type developers to process lith films exposed by electronically generated (laser) images.

Line Photography Line copy, including text matter, lines, figures, sketches, and drawings, that are to be reproduced, is placed on the copyboard of the camera. The image is projected at the correct size by adjusting the bellows extension and copyboard position, and the focus is checked on the ground glass that is on the image plane of the camera. High contrast lith film is mounted on the vacuum back positioned in the image plane. The lens aperture is set, the copy is illuminated by the high-intensity lights, and the exposure is made through the shutter, which is operated manually with a stopwatch or automatically by an electric timer or a computerized light integrator. The lith film is processed in a high-contrast developer in an automatic processing machine. The final product is a high-contrast negative image of the subject on the copyboard; i.e., the white areas on the original are reproduced by black and the black areas on the original are clear on the negative.

Contact Printing Contact prints, used extensively in graphic arts, especially for image assembly operations, are made by placing a negative or positive continuous-tone or lith film over an unexposed film of similar type but usually colour-blind in colour sensitivity, preferably emulsion-to-emulsion, on the blanket of a vacuum frame. The frame is closed and locked, the vacuum pump is turned on, the exposure is made to a point light, and the film is processed in the appropriate chemistry to minimize undercutting of the image by the light source. The product is usually a positive from a negative, or vice versa. Special duplicating film can be used to make negatives from negatives or positives from positives. Contact prints are also made on photographic papers, and contact or duplicate prints are made of colour transparencies.

Continuous-Tone Photography This includes photography on continuous-tone black-and-white and colour photographic films and papers. These are used as original or duplicate copies for reproduction. The photographic operations are similar to those used tor line photography and contact printing except for the photographic materials and the processing chemistries used.

Halftone Photography Halftone photography is done through the grid pattern of a halftone screen. In photography with a contact screen, the screen is used in direct contact with the film, with the emulsion side of the screen in contact with the emulsion side of the unexposed film. The variable density of the vignetted dots in the screen produces a wide range of dot sizes on the film, corresponding to the amount of light reflected or transmitted from the copy. The contrast of reproduction can be varied within limits by techniques known as flashing and no-screen or bump exposures. Flash exposures are used to reduce the contrast of reproduction, especially in the shadows, by producing a dot pattern over the whole film, and they are made by exposing the film to a yellow bulb or light. The bump exposure is used for increasing the contrast in the highlights and is done by removing the screen during a short part of the exposure. Contrast can also be increased by turning the screen over so the back side of the screen is in contact with the emulsion side of the film. Additional control of contrast is achieved by the use of magenta dyed screens and coloured filters during part of the exposure—yellow filter to reduce contrast and magenta filter to increase contrast.

Halftones can also be produced by the use of prescreened film. This consists of high-contrast photographic film that has been preexposed to a 133-line screen and packaged. During photography, the light areas in the original that reflect high levels of light produce large dots in the film, and darker areas that reflect lesser amounts of light produce smaller dots, so that when the exposed film is processed a halftone negative of the image is produced that contains dot sizes corresponding to the amounts of light reflected from the original. Halftones are made on electronic scanners by electronic dot generation. This is described in the section of this article on *electronic scanning.*

COLOUR REPRODUCTION Colour printing consists of the use of spot colour to emphasize or differentiate information or subjects; block colour as in cartoons, bar or pie charts, or other means of printing differentiating information; and four-colour process reproduction that produces quantities of prints that simulate colour photographs or paintings, or other colour images. Spot and block colour printing are like single colour except that a separate film and plate are needed for each colour, and reasonable care must be used to obtain fair register between the black text and spot or block colour images. Four colour process printing, on the other hand, is critical; it is dependent on the three-colour theory of light, which requires special colour separation techniques and inks with special colours and other printing characteristics; it demands very close register of images in platemaking and printing; and in lithography, it requires critical adjustment of ink and water in printing. Four-colour process printing involves three related processes: colour separation using the principles of the three-colour theory of light; colour correction and manipulation; and colour printing using transparent pigmented inks with colours complementary to the separation colours. The third process, printing, is not a part of the photomechanical process but will be described briefly since the printing materials and characteristics have an effect on the prepress and platemaking photomechanical operations.

Three-Colour Theory of Light Colour process reproduction is based on the three-colour theory of light and vision. It consists of three primary colours of light: blue, green, and red. In the physical sense, each wavelength of light differs in colour from every other wavelength. The human eye has two types of visual receptors: rods, which sense luminances, but not hues, and cones, which sense luminances and hues, but not at low light levels. There are three types of cones: those sensitive to a broad band of blue wavelengths of light; those sensitive to a broad band of green wavelengths of light; and those sensitive to a broad band of red wavelengths of light. This is the basis of the three-colour theory of light, which determines how colours are perceived. The three colours, red, green and blue (RGB) are called additive primaries because when lights of these three colours are added together in different proportions they produce an entire gamut of colours, including white light.

What a person sees depends on the health and condition of the cones and the experience of the viewer in addition to the nature of the stimulus and the viewing conditions. If the cones are abnormal, the viewer has a form of colour blindness that distorts the appearance of the subject colours. The appraisal of colour, therefore, is an individual, subjective experience. Difficult to measure in absolute terms, it is a comparative phenomenon that depends on the comparison of the reproduction to the original. This is why colour proofing is such an important part of colour reproduction.

Colour Separation The process of colour separation in colour reproduction is similar to the way the eye sees colour. The original photograph or artwork is separated into three records by photographing the subject through filters with light transmissions each corresponding to one of the additive primary colours—red, green, or blue.

Photographing the original with a red separation filter over the lens produces a negative record of all the red light reflected by or transmitted through the original. This is known as the red separation negative. A positive made from this negative is a record of the absence of red and its presence of blue and green in the subject. The combination of light blue and green light produces the colour called cyan. The positive made from the red separation negative is the cyan printer.

Similarly, photographing a colour subject through the green filter produces a record of the green in the subject. The positive made from the green separation is a record of the red and blue in the subject, which is called magenta. The positive made from the green separation negative is the magenta printer.

Photographing through the blue filter produces a negative record of the blue in the subject. The positive made from the blue separation is a record of the red and green in the subject. Red light and green light combine to form yellow. The positive made from the blue separation negative is the yellow printer.

The three colours cyan, magenta, and yellow (CMY) are called subtractive primaries because colourants of these colours absorb red light, green light and blue light, respectively. Cyan, magenta, and yellow are the colours of the printing inks used for process colour reproductions.

When the three positives made from the three separation negatives are combined or printed, the result is not a reasonable reproduction of the original. The colours other than the yellows and reds are dirty or muddy. There is too much magenta in the blues, greens, and cyans and too much yellow in the blues, magentas, and purples. The poor colour reproduction is not a fault of the theory but is caused by deficiencies in the colours and transparencies of the inks. To compensate tor the deficiencies in the inks, corrections are made in the separation negatives and positives. Even with these corrections the printed result lacks saturation and contrast.

To overcome the lack of image strength or saturation and contrast, a fourth printer, black, is added to the three colours, making colour reproduction a four-colour process. The black separation can be made using a special yellow filter or split exposures through the three filters successively. The black printer improves the contrast of the grays and increases the saturation of the shadows. It is used in a range of tone reproductions from a skeleton black to a full black. The trend is toward the use of full blacks, especially in high-speed magazine printing. The other colours are reduced proportionately so that inks transfer, or trap, properly. The operation of reducing colours and printing a full black in shadow areas is called undercolour removal. Gray component replacement is an extended form of undercolour removal in which black is used to replace the graying component, or the minimum third-colour combinations throughout the tone scale.

Colour Correction Corrections for the spectral errors in the inks are made by manual dot etching, photographic masking, or electronic scanning (described in the section on Electronic Prepress). These are also used to correct faulty tone reproduction caused by exposure errors in photography.

Manual Dot-Etching Manual dot-etching is used to increase or reduce colour in local areas, using chemical reducers such as potassium ferrocyanide to dissolve silver on the periphery of halftone dots to reduce their size. This is called wet or chemical dot etching. It is a delicate operation requiring very high manual skills. When the dot-etching is done on positives, it reduces colour by reducing the size of the image dots. When done on negatives, it increases colour by reducing the size of the nonprinting areas (black areas in the negative). Dry *dot-etching is* a method of colour correction in which dot sizes are changed by the use of computerized exposures and development.

Photographic Masking Photographic masking is the method of colour correction using low-density range continuous-tone negatives of the original made through special filters. The low-density range negatives are called masks and are placed in contact with the original, if it is a colour transparency, or in the back of the camera in contact with the unexposed film in the case of separating a reflection colour subject. The mask corrects colour in the separation negative according to the colours of the filter(s) used to make the mask and the filter used for the separation, and in proportion to the strength of the mask. Masks are also used to correct tone reproduction .

Image Assembly Image assembly is also called stripping. Before films can be assembled into page layouts they must be trimmed, checked for size, register, margins, bleeds, register marks, trim marks, etc., and touched up with special preparation, called opaque, to remove pinholes and other flaws or image defects in the films. This is where the page layout produced in copy preparation is implemented. This layout indicates the size and colour of each copy element and its exact orientation and position on the page. In addition, a plate layout is provided (by the press department or bindery) that indicates the exact position of each page on the printing plate to assure that pages after printing and finishing tasks such as folding will be in the correct or consecutive order. Also, fronts and backs of pages printed from separate plates must register so that heads, side and bottom margins, and page numbers (folios) line up. In label or forms printing, the labels or forms must be laid out so that they can be cut on a guillotine cutter without cutting through or destroying other labels or forms.

The stripper assembles all the films of the copy elements that print in the same colour on a goldenrod or red base sheet, called a flat, and cuts out windows for exposing images onto plates. A separate flat must be prepared for each colour. These are all manual operations that are very time-consuming and cost-intensive, as they require extensive and precise skills. This is an area where computer aided design (CAD) has been quite successful in reducing the time and cost and increasing the productivity of prepress operations (see the section on Electronic Prepress).

Colour Proofing The main purposes of colour proofing are to determine if all the image elements fit and are in the right colours and how the job will look when it is printed on the press. Colour proofs are usually made after colour separation, colour correction, page assembly, and sometimes after page imposition. They can be (1) press proofs, printed on production presses, which makes them slow and expensive to reproduce, (2) off-press proofs, which are made from colour separation films and are faster to make and less expensive than press proofs, but usually cannot be made on the actual printing paper or match the printing inks, and (3) digital proofs, which are made from digital information from electronic prepress systems.

Electronic Prepress The main objective of electronic prepress systems is to increase productivity by eliminating as many manual operations as possible by reducing the time required to process colour images. The first applications of electronics and computers in photomechanics were electro-phototypesetting in the period from 1949 to 1954 and colour separation by electronic scanning in 1950. Neither technology was successful until 1970, when the introduction of the video display terminal (VDT) and optical character recognition (OCR) made electrophototypesetting correctable and editable, and electronic dot generation and digital magnification made electronic scanners cost efficient and productive.

Practically all typesetting is done on electronic typesetting systems, which are so efficient they are called imagesetting systems, or more popularly, desktop publishing systems, using personal computers and software. These systems handle both text and graphics and have expanded their capability to colour reproduction.

Electronic Scanning Electronic scanning is the system of choice for colour separation and correction. The two types of colour scanners used are drum-type and flat-bed. The *drum-type scanner* uses a process similar to photographic colour separation. The original, mounted on a rotating drum. is scanned with light beam that is split into three beams after being transmitted by or reflected from the original, depending on whether it is a colour transparency or an opaque subject. Each beam is deflected to a photomultiplier tube or cell (PMT) covered by a filter corresponding to one of the additive primary colours, red, green, or blue, thereby separating each area of the original into its three colour components (RGB). Older scanners use analog computers to convert the voltages corresponding to the intensities of R, G, and B light to compute the amounts of yellow (Y), magenta (M), and cyan (C) in the separation films. A fourth computer is used to compute the black (K) from the RGB data. Also, colour correction is done by modifying the currents for each colour, depending on the effects of inks, papers, and other printing conditions on the reproduction of the printing colours.

An analog-to-digital (A/D) converter is used to convert the analog RGB data to digital CMY data needed for enlargement and reduction of images and converting the continuous-tone colour levels to halftone dot sizes by systems of electronic dot generation, which produce the correct dot size, screen ruling, and screen angles. Most newer digital scanners use digital computers, and these computations are assisted by the use of look-up tables (LUT) on computer boards. Also, they are modular so that input and output are in separate units and can be addressed by networks over a wide range of distances.

Flat-Bed Scanners Flat-bed scanners are less expensive electronic colour separation devices than drum scanners. They use special light and colour-sensitive electronic arrays like charge-coupled devices (CCD) to scan the image on a flat plane and record it as red, green, and blue separations. The main limitations of flat-bed scanners are size, resolution, which is dependent on the number of elements in the array, and dynamic range, which is equivalent to the density range of the reproduction. Most flat-bed scanners have dynamic ranges of about 2.0, while drum scanners have typical dynamic ranges of 3.0-3.8. The higher the dynamic range, the longer the scale of reproduction and therefore the more detail in the highlights and shadows. Several manufacturers have introduced flat-bed scanners for the conversion and reproduction of colour originals in single colour or duotone (usually black with an accenting colour).

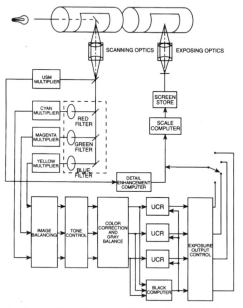

Electronic scanning. Schematic of an analog electronic colour scanner.

Prepress Systems Prepress systems were designed to process the information from scanners, retouch the image and combine it with other colour, text, and linework elements, and produce complete pages tor combining into assemblies or flats for platemaking. These systems consist of a scanner or scanner interface, digitizing tablet with cursor, mouse or light pen, computer storage, software, high resolution monitor, and an output device. These systems can input text, black-and-white and colour illustrations, page layout, and other image processing instructions; perform the functions of colour correction, airbrushing, retouching, pixel editing, cloning, type composition, page makeup with all elements in correct position, soft proofing on VDT terminals, and hard proofing on direct digital colour proofing (DDCP) systems; and output the digital information with electronic dot generation into digital data storage or into film recorders using lasers to produce colour separation films, and/or imagesetters to expose high speed printing plates.

Electronic Stripping Systems Electronic stripping systems use computer aided design (CAD) technology to perform the prepress image assembly (stripping) functions of producing layouts, shaping masks, dropouts, and undercuts for text, halftone, and screen tint images. After the mask films are cut, all the craftsman (stripper) has to do is crop the text, halftones, and screen tint films, and attach or strip them on the mask. These systems have enabled strippers to save more than 50% of total image assembly time. These systems have also been cost effective by providing new levels of mechanical accuracy for complex magazine and catalog pages with multicolour halftone images, screen tint backgrounds, and images that cross over on two facing pages.

Desktop Publishing Systems Although colour electronic prepress systems (CEPS) have been successful in minimizing and almost completely eliminating all manual operations and intermediate films and processing, they have been very expensive. They are all device-dependent systems with proprietary formats, or protocols, and interfacing between systems by different manufacturers is difficult, even with digital data exchange standards (DDES) approved by ANSI (American National Standards Institute).

Device-independent systems using personal computers (PC) and off-the-shelf software programs have increased in capability since they were introduced for typesetting in 1985. Called desktop publishing systems, their use for typesetting resulted from the introduction of the Macintosh computer, the Apple LaserWriter and Adobe's PostScript software program. PostScript is a universal standard page description language that enables typesetters or imagesetters by different manufacturers to interpret files from personal computers using available software programs.

Desktop colour prepress systems consist of a scanner to input colour transparency or reflection colour print images; a platform or workstation on which to view and manipulate the images as well as integrate them into pages, with the proper software for each function; storage capacity to store the pages electronically; a proof printer to see the pages as hard copy; and an imagesetter or other film recorder to output film negatives. All the components must be networked, or connected, together. Some systems

Color Publishing Systems

Features	Density/Creative	Desktop System	Mid-range System	High-end Prepress
Skill Levels	Low-moderate	Moderate	Moderate-high	High Proprietary
Hardware	Standard	Standard	Blend	Proprietary
Software	Standard	Standard	Blend	Proprietary
Productivity	Low	Low-moderate	Moderate	High
Quality	Low	Low-moderate	Moderate	High
Proofing	B/W laser	Color thermal	Color thermal	Traditional/DDCP
Storage Capacity	80 MB+	100 MB+	200 MB+	1 gigabyte+
Output	Proof printer	Imagesetter	Imagesetter	Film recorder
Cost	X	2X	4X	8X

have multiple workstations for different tasks such as scanning and retouching on one and page assembly on another. Also, the workstation requires a monitor and some type of calibration.

The four levels of colour electronic publishing systems are shown in the table.

Design/creative and desktop systems use similar equipment and software with the exceptions that design systems use lower cost proofers and output since they produce mainly comprehensive layouts. Mid-range systems use the same software as desktop systems but they use drum scanners in place of flat-bed, UNIX-based workstations instead of Macintosh or IBM compatible computers, and more sophisticated imagesetters. High-end systems are the expensive prepress systems with sophisticated drum scanners and film recorders. Many of the high-end systems have links to desktop or mid-range systems mainly to take advantage of the lower cost page assembly software. The most productive and cost effective use for desktop colour systems is for page assembly.

PLATE/CYLINDER MAKING The image processing operations for all the printing processes are essentially the same. The differences among the processes is in the making of the printing plates, cylinders, or image carriers and in how they are printed. Letterpress and flexography are relief processes that print directly from the plate to paper (or other substrate). Gravure is an intaglio process that uses cylinders almost exclusively and prints from cells, or wells, in the cylinder, using a fluid solvent ink and a doctor blade to scrape the ink off the nonprinting areas. It, too, prints directly from the ink-filled wells in the cylinder to the paper (or other substrate). Lithography is a planographic process that uses an ink-water balance to print viscous inks by the offset principle from the plate to an intermediate blanket-covered cylinder and then to the paper (or other substrate).

Letterpress Letterpress photomechanical plates can be made of three types: original photoengravings, moulded duplicate plates, and photopolymer plates. Original photoengravings can be either line or halftone. In the United States, line and coarse screen engravings are made on zinc or magnesium, and fine screen engravings are made on copper. In Europe, zinc is used for all types of engravings. Original photoengravings are made by coating the metal plates with special light-sensitive coatings, exposing the coated plates to negatives and developing the images. The plates are then processed in etching machines using special powderless etching chemicals.

The original photoengravings can be used for printing, but most generally are used to make moulds from which duplicate plates are made. The duplicate plates are (1) stereotypes, which have been used extensively for newspaper printing: (2) electrotypes, which are used for letterpress commercial and magazine printing; and (3) plastic and rubber plates, which are used for some commercial printing, books, and flexography for printing on rough surfaces such as envelopes, bags, tags, wrapping papers, corrugated boxes, and milk cartons.

Photopolymer plates are precoated and are used as original (or direct) pattern and wraparound plates. Plates coated on steel and mounted on magnetic cylinders are used for long run magazine printing. Photopolymer plates are also used for newspaper printing.

Letterpress has been declining in use because of the excessive time required for making the plates ready for printing (called make ready). The problem is caused by the variable pressure required by different size image elements (dots) to print properly. Highlight dots require less pressure or squeeze to print or transfer ink properly (without positioning the paper) than shadow dots, type, or solids. Evening out the pressure is a time-consuming manual task that has made letterpress too expensive for most printing markets.

Flexography Flexography, which is a relief process like letterpress, has avoided the make ready problem by the use of resilient plates that compress or distort during the impression. In addition, it uses solvent inks and a special inking system (anilox) that simplify ink transfer and eliminate the tack forces of viscous inks. Flexography uses rubber duplicate plates made with molds from metal original photoengravings, or special resilient photopolymer plates. Flexographic rubber plates and/or cylinders can be made by laser etching. Flexography has replaced letterpress in many of its applications, particularly newspaper, book, forms, and packaging printing

Gravure Gravure is an intaglio process in which the image consists of wells or cells in the surface of a copperplated steel cylinder that is chromium plated after imaging. The nonimage areas are kept from printing by a doctor blade that scrapes any excess ink off the smooth nonimage areas of the cylinder surface. Chemically etched gravure cylinders are almost obsolete because of the difficulty in controlling the etching process as a result of impurities in the copper. concentration of copper salts in the etch, local temperature effects, and other uncontrollable factors. Powderless etching, as used for letterpress engravings, has been used with variable results.

Practically all the gravure cylinders are produced by electromechanical engraving (EME). This process produces diamond-shaped cells in the copper-plated cylinder that vary in size and depth (volume) corresponding to the density of the prints scanned. The original prints can be continuous-tone or halftone negative or positive prints. A special reading head is used for halftone prints to defocus the halftone dots. The use of halftone prints makes it possible to use the same halftones for lithographic and gravure printing. After imaging, the cylinders are chromium-plated to increase image life on the press. When the chromium wears, because of abrasion of the doctor blade, the cylinders are removed from the press and rechromed. Gravure cylinders have been used for up to 100 million impressions.

Gravure is the first printing process to produce image carriers from digital information by going directly from the original copy to the press cylinder. Instead of using continuous-tone or halftone prints on electromechanical engravers, digital information is fed directly from the prepress system through an interface to the EME computer, which activates the diamond styli that engrave the copperplated cylinder.

Gravure is a long-run process capable of millions of impressions. It is also a very expensive process that requires large plating and polishing equipment to prepare the cylinders, expensive electromechanical engraving machines, and large expensive handling equipment to transport the cylinders between processing steps and mounting on the press. The plating chemicals and solvent inks are pollutants and require expensive anti-pollution controls and devices.

Gravure has been used to print large editions of mail order catalogs and long-run magazines for which it has been admirably suited. Changes in market conditions, however, are decreasing the need for long-run printing processes. Large mail order catalogs have been replaced by smaller speciality catalogs requiring shorter runs. Magazine runs have also been shortened by the trends toward demographic editions and target marketing. The new run lengths are within the range of lithographic print runs, which have encroached on gravure markets.

Photopolymer image carriers have been developed for gravure that make it a viable competitive process for shorter runs for publication and packaging printing. Precoated photopolymer plates on a steel base that can be mounted on magnetic cylinders after processing have been one approach. Another has been thin metal sleeves precoated with polymers or photopolymer coatings. The photopolymer coatings are exposed to films and developed in automatic processors similar to the way letterpress and flexographic plates are made. The polymer coatings can be imaged on electromechanical engravers.

Lithography Lithography is the leading printing process, accounting for almost 50% of all printing done in the United States. It represents about 75% of all commercial printing, which consists of advertising and direct mail printing, magazine and catalog printing, labels and wrappers, financial, legal and miscellaneous publishing, and general printing. It is a planographic process based on the principle that water and oil (grease) do not mix. Image and nonimage areas are essentially on the same plane with image areas that are ink receptive and water repellent, and nonimage areas that are water receptive and ink repellent.

Lithographic printing plates are relatively simple to make compared with plates or image carriers for letterpress, flexography, and gravure. Most lithographic plates have an aluminum base, usually anodized and sealed with a silicate solution to provide the plates with good water receptivity. They are all presensitized with diazo coatings for short to medium-long runs (over 100,000), or photopolymer coatings for very long runs (over 1 million). There are plates made for use with negative films, plates made for use with positive films, and a few plate types that can be used with either positive or negative films. Several plate types with silicone overcoatings can be run on the press without water. Most plate types use coatings that can be processed with water-based solutions, to avoid water pollution problems.

There are also four types of high-speed digital printing plates that can be imaged directly by digital data from electronic prepress systems, or desktop publishing systems without using intermediate films. These plates are: (1) silver halide based; (2) electrophotographic; (3) high-speed plates using special dye sensitized photopolymer coatings; and (4) nonphotosensitive, dry processed waterless plates. The first three types are exposed by lasers; the fourth is imaged by spark discharge. The spark discharge plate can be produced directly on the press since it does not require any processing except removing the debris from the discharge with a brush or cloth. While the plates are being produced, the press computer controlling the operation also computes the ink demands of each plate, by counting the printing dots, and automatically presets the ink fountains for each colour on the press. This reduces the make ready time appreciably and makes the plate profitable for short-run colour printing, a new market created by the availability of digital printing plates.

DIGITAL PRINTING SYSTEMS Besides digital plates, a number of other digital imaging processes can produce prints directly from digital data without the use of intermediate films or plates. These include high-speed copiers, electrophotographic, magnetographic, and ion-deposition printers, and inkjet printing.

High-speed digital office copiers use electrophotographic toner technology to produce imaging systems with speeds up to 135 pages per minute (ppm) for black-and-white prints.

High-speed colour copiers have been modified by the addition of intelligent processing unit interfaces with digital data from desktop colour systems to output digitally composed colour pages at the rate of 5 ppm. These systems are being used to produce short-run colour printing in runs up to 200 prints.

Electrophotographic printing is similar to high-speed office copier systems. It is a pressureless system that uses an electrostatic photoconductor that is charged by a corona discharge, imaged by lasers, driven by digital signals from a front-end system (DTP), developed by dry or liquid toners, and a system for transferring the toned images to a substrate. The system is used commercially on a special web press for printing business forms, checks, personalized advertising, forms, and other types of variable printing. The press is linked to an electronic page layout system and a data base of variable information. Speeds are slow—about 300 feet per minute (fpm)—resolution of images is about 300 dots per inch (dpi), and it can print two colours on one side of the paper, or one colour on each side.

Magnetographic printing is similar in principle to electrophotographic printing, except the photoconductor and toners are magnetic. It is a short-run process with a breakeven point with lithography of about 1500 copies. Its limitations are slow speeds (300 fpm), toner cost, as thick layers of toner are needed (up to 30 micrometers compared with 2 micrometers for conventional printing), and no light coloured or transparent toners, so it will not be suitable for process colour printing until such transparent toners are available.

Ion-deposition printing is similar to other electronic printing systems. It consists of four simple steps: (1) a charged image is generated by directing an array of charged particles (ions) from a patented ion cartridge toward a rotating drum, which consists of hard anodized aluminum maintained at a temperature of about 54°C (130°F); (2) as the drum rotates, a single-component magnetic toner is attracted to the latent charged image on the drum; (3) the toned image is transferred to plain paper and fixed on it by high pressure without heat (cold pressure fusing); and (4) most of the toner (99.7%) is transferred to the paper and the drum is readied for reimaging by removing the remaining toner with a reverse angle doctor blade.

Thousands of ion-deposition systems are in use for volume and variable printing of invoices, forms, tags, tickets, checks, letters, proposals, reports, and manuals. The system has not been used for colour printing because of the distortion in the paper that can be caused by the cold pressure fusing. A modified ion-deposition system for colour printing is in development. The process uses two unique materials that eliminate the deficiencies of previous processes. Among other features, the process will print continuous-tone images by varying ink densities on the image rather than by varying the size of image elements as in halftone printing. It will also have no image moire, 100% ink transfer, and instant setting and drying of the ink on contact with the substrate. Such a process could have print on demand capability as well as use for short- and long-run colour printing.

Inkjet printing is a nonphotosensitive printing system. Images are produced by fine droplets of aqueous dye solutions that are controlled by digital information from imaging systems. Two main types of inkjet printers are in use: continuous drops and drops-on-demand. There are also single and multiple jet systems. Inkjet printing is used mainly for variable printing such as addressing, coding, computer letters, sweepstakes forms, and other personalized direct mail advertising. New applications are short-run colour printing and the production of colour digital hard-copy position and verification proofs for colour reproduction. Multiple jet continuous drop ink jet colour proofing and printing systems have been developed that produce images with improved colour quality, saturated colours, and image smoothness without graininess.

PHOTOMONTAGE (l) A composite image, made by cutting and pasting or by projecting several images in sequence on different parts of the receiving photographic material, such as photographic paper on onto a video screen using cameras scanners and computers. (2) Any technique of making composite or multiple photographic images, such as multiple exposures in a camera or with an enlarger.

PHOTOMULTIPLIER TUBE A phototube capable of detecting and measuring extremely low levels of light. It is a transparent glass bulb containing a light-sensitive cathode, a series of electrodes called dynodes, and an anode. A resistance voltage-divider provides voltage for each dynode so that, proceeding from cathode to anode, each dynode is more positive than the adjacent dynode. A photoelectron emitted from the cathode is attracted to the first dynode with such energy that it causes more than one electron to be emitted from the dynode in a process called secondary emission. These electrons are attracted to the more positive second dynode, where they cause even more electrons to be emitted. This multiplication process is repeated through nine or ten dynode stages before the electrons are collected by the most positive electrode, the anode. Photomultipliers are used extensively in photographic scanners and in some densitometers.

PHOTOSENSITIVE Capable of undergoing a physical or chemical change as a result of the action of radiation, especially light. The term embraces latent-image formation, bleaching of dyes, change in solubility (as in photoresists), and change in electrical properties (as in photocells, TV image tubes, and charge-coupled devices.)

PHOTOTRANSISTOR A transistor responsive to radiant energy, used frequently as a light-operated switch. Unlike an ordinary bipolar junction transistor, the current through the phototransistor depends on the amount of light falling on the base electrode rather than on the amount of current flowing through the base-emitter junction. A phototransistor has a spectral response that peaks at about 800 nm but has some response in the visible range. Like the photodiode, the phototransistor has a very fast response to changes in light level. It is available in PNP and NPN configurations. Some phototransistors have an external connection to the base to supply bias current.

PHOTOTUBE A glass bulb containing a cathode coated with a light-sensitive metal, such as cesium oxide, and an anode to collect the electrons emitted from the cathode. The bulb may be evacuated or may be filled with an inert gas such as argon. With a dc voltage of 90 to 300 volts applied, the current through the tube is proportional to the light falling on the cathode. Phototubes are available with many different spectral characteristics, depending on the composition of the cathode coating. Phototubes have now been largely replaced by more rugged low-voltage semiconductor photocells.
See also: *Photomultiplier tube.*

PHOTOVOLTAIC CELL A light-sensitive device that converts light energy to electrical energy. The output current is proportional to the incident light when the cell is connected to a low-resistance load. Photovoltaic cells have an advantage over other photosensors in that they do not require an external source of power. Common photovoltaic materials include selenium and silicon.

The selenium cell consists of an iron disc coated with selenium, which in turn has applied to it a film of gold or platinum thin enough to allow light to pass through. In a light meter, the leads from the selenium and from the gold or platinum film are connected to a microammeter. The current generated by light falling on the cell causes the needle of the meter to deflect an amount dependent on the incident light. Even though the spectral sensitivity of selenium cells approximates that of visible light, a colour-correction filter is commonly used in light meters.

Typical silicon photovoltaic cells, also known as solar cells, have a peak response in the near infrared and are used primarily where efficiency of energy conversion is important. Special blue-enhanced silicon cells that have more sensitivity to blue light are commercially available.

PICA A unit of measure used by printers to measure lines. One pica is equal to 1/6th of an inch; 6 picas equal 1 inch.

Books: *Pocket Pal: A Graphic Arts Production Handbook.* New York: International Paper Company, 1976.

PICO- In the metric system (SI), a prefix meaning a trillionth, or 10^{-12}, as in *picosecond.*

PICTURE ELEMENT See *Pixel.*

PIEZOELECTRICITY Electricity generated by squeezing, bending, or twisting certain crystalline substances such as quartz, tourmaline, and Rochelle salt. Piezoelectric crystals are used in oscillators to maintain the precise frequency required for clocks, timers, and radio transmitters and receivers. The piezo-electric effect is also used in crystal microphones, strain gages, and as the energy source for specially designed flash bulbs. A piezoelectrical crystal will distort when a voltage is applied across it and can be used for micropositioning of photosensors, etc.

PIXEL Picture element, the smallest component of a picture that can be individually processed in an electronic imaging system.

PIXEL CLONING In electronic imaging, copying a pixel or group of pixels from an area of an image for the purpose of adding them to another area, in order to remove unwanted detail, for example.

PIXELLATION When the spatial resolution of an electronic, computerized image is low, the individual pixels or groups of pixels become visible. This *blockiness is* known as pixellation. The degree of visibility of these blocky pixels depends upon the viewing distance from the cathode-ray tube (CRT).

PLASMA DISPLAY In computers, cathode-ray tubes (CRTs) are only one form of display technology. As computers become smaller and more portable a limiting factor in achieving still smaller computers is the display. Plasma displays are flat-screen displays in which a wire mesh sits sandwiched between two sheets of glass in an environment of inert gas. Each crosspoint of the mesh represents a pixel that can be addressed by the computer.

PLATFORM In computer parlance, the term has come to

mean a specific type of computer system. The type of platform will determine what software will operate on the system.

PLOTTER In computers, an electromechanical device that literally draws with pens, charts, and graphics as determined by the software. Plotters are often used to provide high-resolution line drawings as required by computer assisted design (CAD) systems.

PLUMBICON In electronic imaging, video tube-type cameras use various types of pickup tubes to image a subject. The plumbicon tube is particularly noted for its ability to image under low lighting conditions. It has been used widely in the area of video surveillance.

POINTING DEVICE In computers, the graphic user interface (GUI) functions most efficiently through the use of a pointing device that locates functions, addresses menus, or launches events.

POINT PROCESSING In electronic imaging, a point process such as a histogram equalization is used to correct the brightness levels in an image in order to achieve a contrast change.

PORTRAIT ORIENTATION In computers, a page format with the vertical axis being the longer dimension, in contrast to landscape orientation, in which the longer dimension is the horizontal.

POSITIVE (IMAGE) An image in which the tonal relationships are such that light subject tones are light and dark subject tones are dark. Positive photographic images are commonly produced by printing camera negatives onto negative-acting (nonreversal, positive) printing materials. Positive images can be obtained without the printing process by using reversal-type film in the camera.

POSTERIZATION A photographic printing method by which details of the image are suppressed and tonal separation of large areas is exaggerated. The final image consists of a limited number of discrete tones, usually three to five. Separation negatives are made on high-contrast material, each negative recording a narrow range of tones, and are successively printed on the same sheet of positive material. A similar effect is accomplished electronically and almost instantly in a video system or with a scanned and digitized photographic image displayed on a video screen through a computer system.

POSTPROCESSING Postprocessing refers to manipulation of the negative or print after the normal steps of the process have been completed. In the case of ordinary monochrome photography, these normal steps refer to developing, fixing, washing and, sometimes, drying. The unmanipulated image has often been referred to as *straight,* while the treated one is called *manipulated, modified,* or *retouched.* Such steps as mounting, framing, packaging, display, and so forth are not generally referred to as postprocessing.

TYPES OF MODIFICATION The postprocessing treatments may modify or enhance the image or preserve the image without modification. They may, for example, change the physical characteristics of the article, thus making it more attractive to display, or to perform better in display equipment, projectors, and printers. The treatment may be such as to make the image more stable to the ravages of environment or time.

On the other hand, these treatments may be applied to the negative or print to modify the tonal nature of the image itself. Modifications of the negative will be translated to subsequent prints, while those made in the print affect that image alone (unless the print is copied to make a new negative for subsequent prints).

Physical characteristics may be changed by chemical or physical treatment. Image characteristics may be changed by optical, as well as by chemical and other physical methods.

Electronic Manipulation Black-and-white and colour photographic images may also be manipulated and/or retouched using electronic imaging methods. Photographic images can be entered into a computer using a video-type camera or scanner, where the image is digitized. It can then be manipulated by various methods that are available while reviewing the result on a computer monitor. When the desired result has been achieved, a hard copy can be produced by one of several printing methods.

POSTVISUALIZATION Photographic expression in which the image is manipulated in the conventional darkroom or an electronic darkroom as, for example, by combining photographs, parts of photographs, or other graphic material until a stimulating, unreal result is achieved, unlike that of a straight photography.

PREFERRED COLOUR REPRODUCTION Reproduction in which the colours depart from equality of appearance at equal or at different luminance levels in order to achieve a more pleasing result.

PREFERRED TONE-REPRODUCTION CURVE An s-shaped line on a graph of the tonal relationship between an original subject and a photographic reproduction where the line represents a photograph that would be judged to be of excellent quality even though it would not be a facsimile reproduction, which would be represented by a 45-degree straight line.

PRIMARY CELL/BATTERY Any of a number of electro-chemical sources of voltage that cannot be recharged.

PRIMARY COLOURS Sets of three colours that are used in colour matching or in colour reproduction. In additive systems, such as may be used in visual colorimeters and in colour television, the primary colours of light are red, green, and blue, in order to excite each of the three different types of cones in the eye as separately as possible. In subtractive systems, such as may be used in colour photography and in colour printing, the primary colours are red-absorbing (cyan), green absorbing (magenta), and blue-absorbing (yellow) colourants; in the past, in the printing industry, the cyan primary was sometimes called blue or process blue and the magenta primary was sometimes called red or process red.

PRIMITIVES In computer graphics, a set of instructions that allows the user to draw simple and complex shapes on the screen, such as circles, squares, and polygons.

PRINT A photographic image, usually made from a negative or positive image rather than directly from an original scene or the process of making such an image. Prints are made to be viewed or reproduced, and are typically positive images on printing paper for still photography and positive images on transparent film for motion pictures or to produce such images.

PRINTED CIRCUIT Electric wiring layout that is no longer produced by printing but by photofabrication techniques. A large scale drawing of the circuit is made and reduced to its true, miniature size. This image is projected on a blank laminated circuit board coated with a light-sensitive resin resist. The exposed areas are hardened, the unexposed areas are removed, and the copper circuit paths remain. Interestingly, the process is a relative of Niépce's heliography, introduced in 1822.

PRINTER (1) A device for exposing sensitized material to a negative or positive image on a transparent base, either by contact or projection, for example, contact printer, projection printer, optical printer, automatic printer. (2) A person whose function is to make photographic prints or photomechanical reproductions. (3) In photomechanical reproduction, an image-bearing plate that is used to make the final reproduction, such as the cyan, magenta, yellow, or black printer.

PRINTOUT (1) The production of a visible image on a sensitized photographic material such as printing-out paper by exposure alone. (2) A computer-produced image recorded on paper or other material. (3) An enlarged reproduction of a microfilm image.

PRINT QUALITY Attributes of a photographic print, such as density and contrast, that influence the appearance of the print with respect to the degree of technical excellence. Print quality is generally evaluated subjectively, but to the extent that subjective and objective measurements can be correlated, certain objective criteria can be established, such as appropriate minimum and maximum densities. Although the term may suggest that print quality depends entirely on the choice of materials and craftsmanship at the printing stage, it also depends on the quality of the negative being used and sometimes even such factors as the subject and the lighting.

PROCESSING Processing can be broadly defined as performing a systematic series of actions to achieve some end. In photography, processing refers to the actions taken after exposure of sensitized material to produce a visible, stable, and usable image. Processing of black-and-white films and papers normally consists of developing, rinsing, fixing, and washing, but may include additional steps such as presoaking film before development, using a washing aid between fixing and washing, and intensifying, reducing, or toning the image.

Dramatic progress has been made over the intervening years to shorten processing times, reducing processing costs, and improve the quality of the results. The use of resin coated printing papers, for example, has reduced the time required for fixing, washing, and drying to a fraction of that required for fibre-base papers. Roller-transport and other automatic processing machines for films and papers that provide dry-to-dry processing in a few minutes have revolutionized large-volume processing as required in photofinishing and custom-finishing labs and other large photographic organizations. Instant-picture materials produce finished pictures in seconds, and video and still electronic photography provide immediate viewing following exposure, without chemical processing.

In electronic imaging, processing refers to the electronic execution of programmed instructions as when digitizing, manipulating, storing, or retrieving an image or compressing image data.

PROGRAM (1) (verb) To write or specify a sequence of steps or commands that must be followed to achieve a particular result. This may apply to the programming of a computer or to the operation of processing equipment (2) (noun) The steps produced by this process (3) (noun) In education, an instructional sequence designed to create the conditions necessary and appropriate for students to acquire a specific body of knowledge.

PROGRAMMABLE READ-ONLY MEMORY (PROM) In computers, a chip that can be addressed to read a program and load it into memory so that accessing the program is quick because neither a hard drive nor floppy disk needs to be accessed.

PROJECTION Ever since humans first looked at and recognized shadows, we have been interested in projected images. Early in the prehistory of moving-image photography, there was a fascination with the process of image projection. The magic lantern was invented by Athanasius Kircher in about 1640. In his book *Ars Magna Lucis et Umbrae,* first published in 1645, Kircher outlines the principles of the magic lantern. His magic lantern was a rearscreen projection show, images projected against translucent fabrics. The projected images were transparent figures that were hand-painted on glass strips. The areas around the transparent figures were heavily painted and appeared opaque. By changing the glass strips, Kircher figures appeared and disappeared. When the lanternist moved the lantern closer to and farther from the projection screen, the images seemed to change their size and form, and when the lantern was dimmed or partially covered, the figures would seem to fade away. The exhibition/performance of magic lantern shows was considered entertainment, not much different than the motion picture today.

The phantasmagoria evolved from the magic lantern show. It too was a rear-screen projection entertainment event, with sound effects, fade-in, and dissolves. There were even X-rated striptease phantasmagoria. The use of concave mirrors and projected aerial images added to the idea of the fantastic and magical adventure. Peepshows, panoramas, and dioramas were extensions of the phantasmagoria and a fascination with perspective, lenses, light and projection. Some of the dioramas were elaborate room-sized camera obscuras displaying painted canvases manipulated with light projected on the canvas or through translucent painted images on translucent fabric. Unfortunately, the light effects were not always manageable or consistent because of natural ambient light. The attempt to mirror reality turned some of the exhibitions into "performance art." In Daguerre's *View of Mont Blanc* a real chalet and barn were introduced into the diorama, and for an added touch of reality a goat eating hay was included. This innovation was not an overwhelming success; it was perhaps a bit too soon for audience participation.

The magic lantern slide show evolved into a form of travelling entertainment, where an itinerant magic lanternist carried a hand organ and a magic lantern with slides and went door to door soliciting for places to arrange a private magic lantern show. In the early 1800s the Galantee show became a popular form of entertainment, an amusement similar to hiring a performer for a private party. The entertainment was provided by a team of two, one playing music on an organ while the other projected slides.

Long strips of hand-painted slides were passed slowly in front of the magic lantern lens and gave the viewer a sense of motion. Panoramic *comic strip* slides added to the levity of the entertainment, while slipping slides and lever slides continued the progress toward the development of a moving image. Rackwork slide projection could simulate movement and rotation and even simulate continuous movement, such as smoke rising from a chimney.

The magic lantern slide images were not always hand-drawn and hand-painted images. By the late 1850s magic lantern slides were also photographically produced and then often, but not always, hand coloured. The photographic process was becoming increasingly popular as a means of producing images for the magic lanterns. Drawings and engravings were also photographically reproduced as slides for the magic lanterns. The amateur photographers were encouraged to make their own photographic slides. So popular was the interest and production of slides and slide shows that the Crystal Palace presented slide shows daily throughout the 1880s and 1890s.

Two major slide publishers in London ran exhibition galleries where thousands of slides were available for viewing. Most slide publishers manufactured and sold hand viewers, usually constructed of mahogany with adjustable eyepieces, for looking at the transparencies so that they could be evaluated without the need to project them. The dealers sold the magic lantern slides either plain or coloured, and if the customer wanted to personally paint the slides, a set of transparent slide painting pigments could also be purchased.

The original, single-candle japanned tin lanterns gave way to more ornate models. The drawing-room version was made of mahogany with brass fittings on the highly polished lacquered doors. Some magic lanterns had multiple chimney arrangements. The single candle was replaced by oil lanterns, then by gas, and finally by electricity.

There were a variety of slide-changing mechanisms. The *Metamorphoser* allowed one slide to be withdrawn as another slide replaced it. Another device had a descending curtain-like object lower between the changing slides and an endless loop device projected rapidly changing panoramas. Stacked or multiple lens magic lantern projectors provided an early multimedia-style slide show. This was possible by turning up the flame of one lantern (brightness control) while lowering the flame of another; the images appeared to fade in and out from one to the other. A day scene turned into a night scene was the most common change. Second in frequency of occurrence was a black-and-white image dissolving into a full colour version of the same image. Live models were photographed in the real world or against a painted background scene, not unlike a Hollywood movie today. The use of photographic superimposition created a new visual vocabulary for the slide show, showing the audience a thought, an idea, either by projecting one image onto another or producing a multiple combination print and then converting it into a slide for projection.

The motion-picture projector came about through the evolution of image-projecting toys coupled with the magic lantern. The Projecting Phenakistoscope used a disk of images that revolved across a shutter-like device in front of a magic lantern, projecting a smooth moving sequence. This shutter-like device was a key to the smoothing of action in projected imagery and lead to the development of contemporary motion-picture projectors. The Thaumatrope, a disk containing two or more images placed around the centre that is twirled by two attached strings. The result is a single image that combines the separate images into one. By adjusting the tension on the string while the disks are spinning, the speed of rotation and the visual effect could be changed. The Zoetrope was another persistence-of-vision toy, capable of depicting the illusion of motion. A large, thin walled metal drum with slits in the sides, capable of revolving easily around a pivot point at its base axis, is spun around very quickly. Inside the drum is mounted a long, narrow strip of photographic images or drawings that simulate a sequence of some simple action. The viewer, looking through one of the slits in the revolving drum, sees a moving image.

Other devices somewhat similar to the Zoetrope added to the numbers of toys that projected or displayed moving images. The Praxinoscope Theatre is a toy with two concentric rotating drums and a strip of images rotating on the inside of the outer drum. These rotating images were reflected on pieces of glass in the centre drum, which also contained a stationary section that held little pieces of scenery. To the eye, the stationary scenery became the background over which the reflected moving images of the large drum danced. The Viviscope, and the Tachyscope were also based upon the Zoetrope. The use of instantaneous photography, when combined with the principles learned from the magic lantern projection devices and coupled with the persistence-of-vision toys, led to the development of the motion picture.

The projected image is a performance activity that is intended to communicate with an involve the audience. Unlike the single photograph, slide shows and motion picture provide, if viewing conditions are ideal, an intense, fully saturated colour image far superior to that of a photographic print. Coupled with sound, scale, and a visually captured audience (since there is nothing else to look at) projected images are an especially effective communication medium. But all projected images are not equal, nor are they necessarily works of art. An overhead projected image may assist in lectures and demonstrations, but it is not as compelling as a slide show or film. Projection in this instance is for presenting information in visual form, the sole purpose of the projected image is to reach a larger audience with less effort and at the least possible cost for the desired effect.

The sequential still image slide show and filmstrip had been the industrial and educational standard for many years, and although the multimedia slide show had been around, in one form or another, since before the turn of the century, it wasn't until the development of the sound tape/slide synchronizer that the multiimage slide show became popular. The early 1970s saw the introduction of the slide programmer, with the ability to do quick cuts and varied dissolves. The late 1970s produced the electronic programmer, which permitted more sophisticated effects, with easier and faster programming and with the ability to control several projectors at once with a single control.

As the programming became easier to control, the photo-graphic and projection techniques became more complex. The electronic programmer gave way to the microcomputer, which made it possible to control several banks of slide projectors, motion-picture projectors, lighting, and sound effects. These new more sophisticated multi-image shows with multiscreen projection began to take advantage of varied perspectives, closeup and panoramic vistas of the same subject side by side, essentially a multiveiw point show. Unlike filmstrips, video, and motion pictures, single image and multimedia slideshows can be edited instantly. For educational and commercial use, if something changes, a quick edit and the show is current at very little additional expense. In contrast, an entirely new motion picture, filmstrip, or video must be generated to include such updating. There are advantages and disadvantages of the various projection systems. The self-contained audio slide viewer permits the presenter to hand carry a slide tray, the projector, which has a built-in (usually 9 X 9-inch) rear-projection viewing screen and synchronized cassette tape player. These projection viewers make excellent point-of-purchase displays, sales promotion programs, and teaching tools, and, unlike most other projection presentations, the audio slide viewer does not need a darkened environment. Overhead projectors are useful for group presentation such as classroom lectures and business presentations, and are a necessary component for a personal computer LCD projection panel. These fan-cooled projectors can show large photographic transparencies (with subdued room illumination), standard overhead transparencies, and write-on projection films.

Computers are well on their way to becoming the major image-making, manipulating, and storage instrument. Interactive media puts the computer at the controls tor bringing together video, film, videodisc, electronic still video, and, of course, computer-generated imagery. Animation, paint, presentation, and hyper-card type programs allow images to be arranged, cut and pasted or sequenced, and shown on the computer screen, (a cathode-ray tube or colour monitor display), or sent directly to a LCD panel/overhead projector unit to be projected on a projection screen or sent to a video projection system for presentation on either a rear-projection screen or front-projection screen, or sent to a printer for a hard copy print.

The new Photo CD, a compact disc that contains photographic imagery as well as sound, text, and graphics, is bound to become a major force in multimedia presentations. Each disc can hold up to 100 images. Each image is represented in five different formats ranging from a thumbnail image for previewing, to a high-quality detail image file for photographic printing or TV viewing.

The laser disc or videodisc is another source of projectable imagery. Each disc can hold about 54,000 tracks, or frames, per side. This means that about a half hour of visual images can be stored and recalled. The recorded images can be played on a videodisc player and can contain sound as well as pictures. Coupled to a computer, with the proper software, the computer disk and player can become a random-access generator for high-quality colour video, still photography, or motion-picture film. The images can be projected onto large rear- or front-projection screens with a video projection system.

The more traditional computer-ware has evolved to encompass a virtual reality simulation system. Armed with a DataGlove and EyePhones, the viewer/user/player can now interact with computer-generated images by moving around in simulated worlds, complete with 3-D sound.

To ensure an ideal presentation, the projection equipment should be set up before the audience arrives, the sound tested, and the projectors focused and aligned, especially if more than one projector is to be used. Extra projection lamps, extension cords, flashlight, and gaffer tape should be part of the equipment carried to any projection location. If possible, the projectors should be isolated from the audience with a soundproof booth. If that is not possible, then the projectors should be as far behind the audience as is physically possible. With noisy equipment in the room with the audience, sound-absorbing partitions or screens should surround the equipment. For informational presentations that contain text and numbers, the audience should be no farther away than 8 times the screen height. If the text is larger than standard size or the program content is entirely pictorial, the screen-to-audience distance can be increased to 14 times the screen height.

PROJECTION SCREEN The most important characteristic of the projection screen is the reflective front surface. Projection screens are made from fabrics or plastics coated with substances that have highly reflective properties. Permanently installed theatre screens are stretched tightly over a frame in order to keep the screen surface as flat and wrinkle-free as possible. Projection screens that roll up like a window shade provide portability, and also flexibility in the use of wall space with installed screens. Many projection screens are custom fabricated to the individual needs of the user. Specifications such as the kind of coatings, that is, aluminized, pearlescent, smooth, embossed, lenticulated and nonlenticulated, matt, and textured will affect the reflectivity of the screen, the angle within which the audience can be seated, and how the ambient light affects the screen image. Manufactured reflective coatings produce brighter images (within a limited angle) than painted surfaces. Heavy gauge vinyl film screens are flameproof, mildew resistant, and in some cases washable.

There are several basic types of projection screens. *Beaded* screens reflect light back toward the source over a narrow angle, so that these screens are best suited for long, narrow rooms or rooms where the seating is within a 20- to 30-degree angle on either side of the projection beam. Because beaded screens concentrate light and produce very bright images, they are useful in rooms where there is a high level of ambient light. *Lenticular* screens have a regular or irregular raised pattern that act like tiny reflecting mirrors. These patterns are not noticeable from normal viewing distances and help to intensify the projected image by reflecting the projected image back to its source, the projector, which is in the direction of the audience. This same pattern helps to reduce image degradation from ambient lighting that falls on the projection screen from above or from the sides by reflecting the ambient light back to its source, which is away from the direction of the audience. Lenticular screens should be flat or slightly concave. The angle at which the projected image strikes the screen surface is important in that it controls the angle of reflection, and it may be necessary to aim the angle of the screen for the best results. *Matt* screens, also known as surface diffusers, reflect the incident light evenly in all directions. Regardless of where the viewer sits, the projected image appears equally bright. Unfortunately, this equally bright image is not as bright (for those sitting within a certain angle) as other, more directional types of screens. The matt screen is best suited for large widely spread out audiences.

Matt screens can be inexpensive, since any dull-surfaced, white-painted wall can be used.

PROJECTIVE TRANSFORMATIONS In geometry, a transformation of data plotted in one plane by projecting it onto another plane by means of lines emanating from a point suitably situated outside of both planes. Such transformations can be defined by sets of simultaneous linear equations. For any given colorimetric observer, all chromaticity diagrams are linear transformations of all others; hence, a straight line in any one such diagram will be a straight line in all other such diagrams.

PROMPT In a nongraphical interface environment, the graphical cursor is replaced by the prompt that simply locates the position of the text about to be entered or just entered. The prompt may be as simple as the sign ">" or as complicated as statement of disk drive and directory in use, "C:\HG>."

PROOF PRINT (1) A test print made to determine if anything needs to be changed in a picture setup or the procedure for making a photograph. (2) A print of a negative or set of negatives to serve as a file copy of the pictures and to facilitate selecting negatives to be used for quality printing.

PSEUDO-COLOURING In electronic imaging, black and-white images captured by video or scanned into the computer may be displayed in colour. The colour displayed will not have any relationship to the actual image, but rather will be coloured according to a look-up table that assigns colours according to group brightness levels within the image. For example, a pseudo-colouring program may divide the range of brightnesses within an image into eight levels each containing 32 brightness levels and then assign a colour to each level. The original black-and-white image will then be displayed in eight colours. In scientific imaging, pseudo-colouring is used to make subtle features of the image more visible, such as in radioangiography. The corresponding photographic technique of pseudo-colouring is posterization.

PSYCHOLOGICAL PRIMARY COLOURS Colours that do not appear to be mixtures of other colours, which include the hues red, green, blue, and yellow and the neutral colours black and white.

PSYCHOPHYSICS The scientific study of the relationship between the physical attributes of a stimulus and the perceptual response of the viewer. A goal of psychophysics is to be able to predict the appearance of a stimulus on the basis of physical measurements of the stimulus. For example, sodium vapour emits a narrow wavelength band of radiation at approximately 590 nm, and it can be predicted that viewers generally will identify the colour of the light as being yellow.

PULL DOWN/POP UP In computers, methods of displaying a menu.

QUALITY CONTROL A set of procedures used to monitor a process to detect departures from the desired result. Statistical techniques are often used, such as those involved in control charts. The phrase *quality control* is in fact a misnomer, because a process cannot be controlled in the ordinary sense.

Variability always exists, even in a manufacturing or processing system using the most reliable and up-to-date technology. Methods of quality control are intended to identify changes in the system that lie beyond those that are inherent. So-called assignable causes produce errors in the output that are correctable. Random, or chance, causes must be accepted, or the process must be redesigned.

Accurate test methods are essential to quality control. Calibration and routine testing of thermometers, densitometers, and so on, must be carried out.

The first stage of quality control requires extensive testing of a newly established process. A rule of thumb is that a large sample size must be initially obtained, *large* meaning 30 or more measurements. A plot of the frequency distribution will indicate whether or not the data probably come from a population having a normal distribution, i.e., one controlled by chance. The computed mean of the data will show whether or not the process average is sufficiently close to the desired result; the sample standard deviation is a powerful indication of the variation in the process, and thus the extent to which it meets specifications. Such a costly and time-consuming test procedure is reliable only if the process has operated normally, without detectable errors. If something has gone awry, the system must be corrected and the test procedure redone on the modified system.

Once the data indicate that the information has been obtained from a stable, correctly operating process, information is periodically obtained in order to detect future errors. Control charts are customarily used for this purpose. Usually, samples of small size are used, and the sample averages and ranges (differences between largest and smallest values) or standard deviations are plotted in sequence. Upper and lower control limits show the region within which plotted data will fall with high probability if the process continues to operate in an unchanged manner. Points lying outside the limits indicate the need to correct the process. Other indications of a needed process change are: (1) a sequence of points all lying above or below the process average (five or more such points are usually considered evidence sufficient to cause an examination of the process); and (2) a sequence of points all rising or falling, even though none of the points is outside the limits.

QUANTIZING In electronic imaging, the converting of

213

analog data into the digital domain. The continuous-tone information of the analog image is converted into a discrete number of bits, most typically into eight bits.

QUANTUM The smallest and basic indivisible unit of radiant energy; the amount of energy making up a quantum being dependent on frequency. The term *quantum is* used primarily where the basic concern is a transfer of energy. For example, exposure quanta are absorbed by a silver halide crystal; photons refract and interfere in an optical system to form an image.

QUARTZ CRYSTAL In computer imaging, a device for locking onto an analog video signal for the purpose of converting it to digital.

RASTER In electronic imaging, the scanning pattern of the electron gun across and down the cathode-ray tube (CRT) as it paints or refreshes the image. In computer graphics, a rectangular matrix of pixels.

RASTER GRAPHICS In computers, screen graphics are displayed by the cathode-ray tube (CRT) according to a raster pattern that is controlled by the deflection circuit of the electron gun and the circuit of the metal grid inside the picture tube. Graphic characters are created according to which pixels are excited by the electrons. Characters are composed of groups of pixels. The main drawback to raster-drawn graphics is the jagged appearance of text.

RASTER IMAGE PROCESSOR In electronic imaging, used to convert vector images to raster images in computers that use both kinds of image files.

RASTER UNIT In electronic imaging, the distance between the midpoints of two adjacent pixels.

READ In computers, the accessing of data or instructions from either a floppy disk or hard disk.

READ-ONLY MEMORY (ROM) In computers, a reserved location of chips that contain a set of instructions, usually a part of the operating system that cannot be altered or written to. ROM chips retain their instructions/data when the computer is off, unlike random-access memory (RAM).

READOUT The recall of stored information, from microfilm or a computer file, for example, in more usable form such as a print or a display on a monitor.

REAL TIME The representation of an event or sequence of events that takes essentially the same amount of time as the original event. It is particularly distinguished from a frame-by-frame representation. Film and video are real-time media. In computer managed imaging, enhanced microprocessor performance is bringing increasingly complex tasks into the real-time domain.

RECEPTOR General term for any surface on which radiation falls and which responds to that radiation, e.g. photoreceptor, photocell, photographic emulsion, photoresist, retina.
  Syn.: *Photoreceptor.*

RECIPROCAL (1) The result of dividing a number into 1.

Opacity is one measure of the absorption of light by a part of a silver image; it is the reciprocal of the transmittance. If the transmittance is 0.5, the opacity is 1/0.5, or 2. (2) Identifying a relationship between two variables by which as one increases the other decreases in proportion. To keep the exposure (H) constant, the needed light level (E) and exposure time (t) are reciprocally related, since $E = H/t$.

RECORD (1) A photographic image, especially one intended for use in data analysis, as compared with a pictorial image. (2) In colour photography, a separation negative or positive representing a primary colour.

RECORDING PAPER Photographic paper used in rolls to record the trace of a moving spot of light from a mirror galvanometer or other modulating device. The paper is moved continuously past the line in which the spot is focused. In some cases a direct print-out is obtained, amplified by controlled exposure to light of lower intensity. Colour recording papers in recorders with filtered, multiple writing beams can write several variables at once.

RECOVERY TIME The time required for the restoration of the ability of a device to function after performing an operational cycle. In a slide projector, for example, recovery time is the interval that passes between the advancing of one slide and the display of the next.

RED, GREEN, BLUE (RGB) In computers, a tri-stimulus colour system that displays colour as a spatially additive amount of red, green, and blue. Also, an acronym for the components of a colour video signal.

REFLECTION COPY Photographs and other images that must be viewed and copied with reflected light as distinct from transparencies. The term is used primarily in the graphic arts for images that are to be reproduced.

REFLECTION DENSITY The logarithm of the reciprocal of the reflectance of a print sample area. For example, if the sample receives 100 units of light and reflects 50 units, the reflectance is 50/100, or 0.50; the reciprocal is 1/0.50 or 2.0, and the density is the log of 2.0 or 0.30. Often the computation is performed with reference to the reflectance of the base taken as 1.0.

REFRESH RATE The speed at which the cathode-ray tube (CRT) updates the information displayed on the screen. The faster the refresh rate the steadier the picture appears.

REMOTE SENSING Remote sensing is a broad discipline that encompasses the specialized instrumentation and analytical techniques for observing and measuring an object or process without coming into physical contact with it. Thus, concepts as different as an explorer getting the lay of the land from a hilltop, observations of the Martian surface by space probes, and nondestructive testing of machine parts using video cameras (close range remote sensing) are included in the general definition. When most people talk about remote sensing, however, they are referring to that subset of the discipline that involves studying and measuring the earth using airborne or space-based sensors. In particular, a large component of the remote sensing field involves the development and use of aerial and satellite imaging systems.

Conventional photographic imaging systems (cameras) ranging from standard 35-mm cameras to exotic large format cameras (9 X 18 inches) using a variety of film types are commonly used. These cameras collect image data, which are then analyzed using remote sensing techniques to study many phenomena, including crop type and health for agricultural and forestry studies, water quality and extent for environmental and hydrological studies, land cover and elevation changes for transportation and engineering studies, as well as a host of other applications, including detailed mapping of topography and land cover features.

The large area coverage that can be obtained using images from airborne systems offers a perspective that often allows scientists an opportunity to study patterns and relationships that are not obvious in more localized studies. This was made dramatically clear when the first images from space began to show global cloud patterns as well as land cover and environmental conditions on national and even continental scales. The images from these early satellite systems were typically taken with the same film type cameras that were used for aerial photography. This approach is still the most common means of imaging on manned space missions. Over time, electro-optical imaging systems were also used for both aerial and satellite imaging. These systems have an advantage, particularly for satellites, because the image data can be sent down to earth where they can be processed on computers and printed out as photographs or displayed on computer monitors. The electro-optical systems have another advantage in that they can collect data at wavelengths where film is not sensitive. For example, many of the space-based systems collect data in the 8-14 µm (8000 14000 nm) region of the electromagnetic spectrum. In this region the energy that forms the image is largely caused by the temperature of the object viewed. As a result, the images carry information about the temperature of the earth. This temperature information can be used to study such phenomena as water circulation patterns and cloud heights. In addition, sensors using this wavelength region (for infrared) do not require reflected sunlight to form the image, and as a result they can image day and night. The low resolution version of some of these images are processed to form the moving cloud images shown with television weather forecasts. Higher resolution images from these same sensors are analyzed on computers and printed out as photographs for more detailed analysis.

By combining images from many spectral bands (e.g., red,

green, blue, near infrared), it is possible, using computer analysis, to identify land cover types and the condition of certain land cover features such as the amount of vegetation or biomass in a region. By combining satellite images of the same area taken over many days or seasons, it is possible to monitor very large scale processes such as the growth of the desert in central Africa or the deforestation in the Amazon basin.

Since the 1970s, advances in digital computing have enabled the remote-sensing field to draw heavily on digital image processing to increase the amount of data that can be extracted from imagery. This has included development of digital enhancement techniques to sharpen images for subsequent photo interpretation (e.g., to make the pyramids stand out in an image of the Nile valley from space), development of geometric correction methods so that images distorted by such effects as earth curvature can be removed, and development of methods to mathematically merge many different images together so that spectral or radiometric analysis can be performed to extract information that is often difficult for human analysts to see.

Increasingly, remote sensing has focused on developing improved ways to quantify the data extracted from imagery. As a result, more and more work is being done to directly measure environmental factors. This involves correcting for atmospheric degradation of these images and removing their effects on the final image brightness. Between dealing with the collection and correction of remote sensing images and the display and application of the data, a broad range of scientific disciplines are involved. Among the individuals developing or using remote sensing techniques are optical, imaging, and photographic scientists, as well as geographers, geologists, agronomists, foresters, environmental scientists, and archaeologists.

RENDERING In electronic imaging, the application of a textured surface to a wire frame object in a computer graphic. Rendering can be accomplished in two- and three-dimensional animation programs. In either case the computer power required to do rendering quickly and accurately is substantial.

REPRODUCTION An image that represents a copy of an object, scene, etc., such as a photograph, video image, drawing, painting, or photomechanical copy of an image.

REPRODUCTION GAMMA The slope of the straight line of a graph in which the densities of the final image are plotted against the log luminances of the original subject. Reproduction gamma provides information about the contrast of the midtones of the image in relation to the corresponding subject tones, but not about the shadow and highlight subject areas, which are represented on the nonlinear shoulder and toe portions of the graph, or the total contrast. Reproduction gamma can also be calculated by multiplying the straight-line slopes of the factors that determine the final image such as camera flare, negative material, printer flare, and printing material.

REPRODUCTION RIGHTS The right, arising from ownership of a copyright for a photograph, that permits the making of copies, in any medium. The owner of the copyright, usually a photographer, may license others to reproduce the photograph. The license is usually limited as to the medium and time. What the licensee receives is reproduction rights, not ownership of the photograph or the copyright. The licensee pays a fee to the photographer for the defined reproduction rights.

REPROGRAPHY A general term applied to photographic techniques of reproducing flat originals such as documents, drawings, photographs, and printed matter. Its scope includes silver halide and nonsilver copying processes such as microfilming and xerographic office copies, and photomechanical reproduction.

RESAMPLING In computer imaging, the resizing of an image to either larger or smaller dimensions. If the image is resampled to a smaller space, data are discarded. If the image is resized to a larger image, the data are either duplicated (pixel duplication) or interpolated.

RESCREENING Making a halftone negative or positive from a printed halftone, usually by placing a diffusion filter in front of the camera lens to eliminate moire effects.

RESISTANCE (R) The opposition to the flow of current by a resistor. Its symbol is R. The basic unit of resistance is the ohm (Ω).

RESOLUTION The act, process, or capability of distinguishing between two separate but adjacent parts or stimuli, such as elements of detail in an image, or similar colours.

RESOLUTION (DIGITAL IMAGES) In electronic imaging, the number of horizontal and vertical pixels that comprise the image. The minimum resolution acceptable for scientific image processing is 512 x 512 pixels. If the term is used to describe brightness levels (contrast resolution), then the minimum levels of brightness are 256.

RESOLVING POWER The ability of an imaging system or any of its component parts (optical system, photographic material, etc.) to retain separation between close subject elements, such as lines, in the image. Resolving power is measured in lines per millimeter, and is determined using a test target consisting of alternating parallel light and dark bars as an artificial subject. The width of a light-dark pair of bars in the smallest set of bars that can be distinguished in the image is used to calculate the number of lines per millimeter.

The resolving power of an imaging system is always less than the resolving power of any of the components. Thus, it is more accurate to determine the resolving power of a lens by examining an aerial image of the test target formed by the lens than to examine an image formed by the lens that has been recorded on film. Since it is necessary to use an optical system to form an image of the test target on film when testing the resolving power of the film, the optical system must have a much higher resolving power than that of the film to minimize distortion of the true value.

Two different mathematical formulas have been used in photographic references to represent the relationship of the resolving powers of the components of an imaging system to that of the entire system:

$$1/R = 1/R_1 + 1/R_2$$

and

$$1/R^2 = 1/R_1{}^2 + 1/R_2{}^2$$

Both formulas can be expanded to include additional components in an imaging system, such as an enlarging lens and printing paper. Substituting 100 for the resolving powers of a lens and a film in the two formulas produces a calculated resolving power for the system of 50 with the first formula and 71 with the second formula.

The resolving power of pictorial films tends to vary inversely with the film speed, and the resolving power of a given film tends to vary with the type of developer used and the degree of development. The resolving power also varies with the contrast between the light and dark bars in the test target, typically being between two and three times as high with high-contrast targets as with low-contrast targets.

It has long been known that whereas resolving power values for different images correlate well with perceived detail in a side-by-side comparison, the correlation is much lower with perceived sharpness of the images. Modulation transfer function (MTF) curves provide more information about image quality when both detail and sharpness are considerations, but sophisticated laboratory equipment and skills are required to produce MTF curves. Resolution with electronic imaging is sometimes expressed as dots per inch (DPI), spots per inch (SPI) or pixels.

RESOLVING POWER TARGET A set of patterns that normally consists of dark bars on a light background such that there are alternating dark and light areas of equal width. The targets are used to determine the resolving power of a lens or film or of an imaging system by determining the smallest set of bars that can be distinguished as being separate under the specified conditions. The measured resolving power varies with the contrast of the target and typically is two to three times as high with a 1000:1 luminance ratio high-contrast target as with a 1.6:1 low-contrast target.

RETOUCHING Photographic retouching is the process of applying transparent or opaque materials to local areas of negatives, transparencies, or prints, or removing density locally by physical or chemical means. The purpose of retouching is to correct flaws or to otherwise enhance the image. Skillful retouching can greatly improve a photograph, but clumsy retouching can destroy a photograph.

From the earliest days of photography, however, there have been purists who have objected—some vehemently—to any type of modification of the photographic image. Beaumont Newhall notes in *The History of Photography* (NY: Museum of Modern Art, 1982, p. 70), that despite these protestations and a lack of interest in retouching by most of the early photographers, "retouching became routine because sitters now demanded that the often harsh, direct camera records of their features be softened, facial blemishes removed, and the wrinkles of age smoothed away." Heavy retouching became the norm for still publicity photographs of Hollywood motion-picture stars during the 1940s and beyond, a practice also followed by many professional portrait photographers. Now the practice is to soften lines and blemishes rather than remove them.

Most professional photographers possess some basic retouching skills, such as retouching dust spots on prints, but the more difficult retouching tasks and large-volume production retouching are usually delegated to a retouching specialist.

Electronic digital imaging has raised retouching to a new level, where images can be altered on a pixel-by-pixel basis to produce undetectable retouching, in addition to making it possible to completely alter images, for example, by adding and removing objects and changing the colours of objects and backgrounds.

REVERSE POLARITY The result of the interchange of electrical terminals. In television, the use of reverse polarity can make a negative produce a positive image, and conversely.

RIGHT READING Identifying an image that corresponds to the orientation of the subject so that signs and printing in the original scene appear correct, in contrast to being laterally reversed. A negative exposed in a camera is right reading when viewed from the base side but wrong reading when viewed from the emulsion side.

ROOT-MEAN-SQUARE (rms) A geometric average of a set of numbers, found by squaring them, finding the average of the squares, and then taking the square root of the average. Such a calculation is used to find the standard deviation of a set of measurements, which is a useful indication of variability.

RUN In computers, the instruction to begin execution of a programmed task.

RUN TIME ERROR In computers, a program error that is other than syntax that causes the computer to crash. The error is not identified during compiling and manifests itself only at the time the program runs.

SAMPLE (1) In statistics, a part of a lot (the population) selected for study. In film manufacture, for example, from a very large roll of film (the population), a small amount of film (the sample) is tested. Similarly, in testing a 50-litre tank of developing solution for quality, only a few millilitres will be withdrawn for examination. Samples should usually be selected on a random basis. (2) In motion-picture production, a print made for quick examination for quality.

SAMPLING In electronic imaging, the analog image signal is sampled at given points in time prior to the actual quantizing.
Also see: *Nyquist criterion.*

SATICON In electronic imaging, video tube-type cameras use various types of pickup tubes to image a subject. The saticon tube is particularly noted for its ability to image at high resolution.

SATURATION The extent to which a colour deviates from neutral, corresponding to chroma in the Munsell colour system and purity in colormetry
Syn.: *Chroma.*

SAVE A computer instruction to store information on a magnetic disk or tape.

SCALE OF REDUCTION In image formation, especially in the copying and optical reduction of large originals, the linear ratio of object size to image size. An object reduced to a scale of 10:1 is recorded as an image of one tenth original size. It is the reciprocal of the scale of reproduction. The alternative use of scale of reproduction as the ratio of image size to object size is preferable and unambiguous. In optical work the preferred term is (optical) *magnification.*

SCALE OF REPRODUCTION In image formation by a lens, the linear ratio of image size to object size. For general camera work, this ratio is less than one as the image is a small reproduction of the scene. When subject and image are the same size, the scale is 1:1, also denoted S/S (same size). A larger ratio means the image is greater than the subject.

Because the scale is linear, it must be squared to give the area reproduction. A linear scale reproduction of 4:1 is an area reproduction of 16:1. In optical work, the term (optical) *magnification* is preferred.

SCALES Measurement systems used (1) to place items in separate categories (nominal scales), (2) to arrange categories of items in order on the basis of some characteristic (ordinal scales), and (3) to represent both the order of the categories of items and the magnitude of the differences between categories on a graduated basis (interval and ratio scales).

SCALING (1) The process of comparing the dimensions of a photograph or other image that is to be reproduced to the dimensions of the space allotted to the reproduction, including determining whether cropping will be required because of a difference in the height-to-width proportions of the original and the reproduced images. One method is to make a rectangular outline the same size as the original on paper, draw a straight line through two opposite corners, and add lines corresponding to the dimensions of the space available for the reproduction. (2) In photomechanical reproduction, determining the correct dimensions of an image to be reduced or enlarged to fit an area. (3) In electronic imaging, images are resized by percentage where 100 percent is the original input image.

SCANNER (1) A scanner is a device that can translate a transmitted or reflected light image into a digital form. Scanners include rotary drum scanners, flatbed scanners, handheld scanners, and dedicated film scanners. (2) In electronic imaging, a peripheral device that allows for the conversion of flat art, photographic prints, and transparencies into digital data that can be accessed by photographic imaging software.

SCHEIMPFLUG RULE An inclined subject plane is rendered sharp when the plane of the subject, the rear nodal (principal) plane of the lens and the film plane, all extended into space as necessary, meet in a common line. The depth of field about the subject plane is inclined in the same direction as the plane. (Theodor Scheimpflug, 1904)

SCHMITT TRIGGER An electronic circuit used to change random-amplitude signals with relatively slow rise and fall times into uniform-amplitude pulses with fast rise and fall times. Typical applications for a Schmitt trigger include improving the waveform of degraded digital signals in a digital computer and generating a square wave from a sine wave.

SCRATCH DISK In electronic imaging, many image manipulation programs require that a copy of the image being processed be held in storage so that operator errors can be undone. Because of the size of images, the copy image is usually held in a reserved area of the hard disk called a scratch disk. After the image manipulation is complete, the copy image is removed from the hard disk and that area is no longer reserved.

SCREEN DUMP In computers, when the data displayed on the cathode-ray tube (CRT) are sent to a file on a disk or are sent to a printing device.

SCREEN RULING In photomechanical reproduction, equivalent to the number of dot elements per inch or centimeter, usually expressed as lines per inch or lines per centimeter.

SCROLLING (1) To move lines of text up or down on a computer monitor or a motion-picture screen. The credits at the end of motion pictures are commonly scrolled. (2) Using cranking handles at the side of an overhead projector with plastic film roll allows a lecturer to present information for on-screen projection as it is written and then scroll to a clear part of the film to write additional information. Some lecturers write the notes ahead of time and scroll through them as they talk. (3) Using a microfilm reader, rolling the film to locate the desired frames. Using a microfiche reader, moving the flat plate card holder over the reading window. (4) In computers, the movement of text or graphics or images through a portion of the display screen called a window. Scrolling may occur in either a horizontal or vertical direction.

SECOND (1) A unit of time (1/60 minute) used, for example to identify a camera shutter setting. Exposure time is distinguished from exposure. (2) A unit of angular measurement (1/60 degree). (3) (adj.) Applied to an image made from an original camera image; commonly *second-generation*. (4) (adj.) Identifying a usable, but not first-class, photographic product or image.

SECONDARY CELL Any of a class of electrochemical sources, the energy of which can be restored by recharging it with electricity.

SECONDARY COLOURS Name sometimes given to the cyan, magenta, and yellow colours used in subtractive systems.

SECONDARY EMISSION The emission of electrons from a surface caused by the impact of incoming (primary) electrons. This phenomenon is used in a photomultiplier tube. Photoelectrons emitted from the cathode of the tube caused by impinging photons are attracted to a more positive electrode with such energy that they cause even more electrons (secondary electrons) to be emitted from the electrode.

SECOND-GENERATION With negative-positive processes, an original camera negative and a print made from the negative represent first-generation images. With reversal processes, an original camera transparency is a first-generation image. In other words, positive original to positive reproduction represents one generation or cycle. A second generation image is a copy or duplicate of a first-generation image, such as a duplicate negative, a reversal print made from a transparency, a duplicate transparency, or a copy negative made from a first-generation print or a print made from the copy negative.

SECOND-GENERATION ORIGINAL (1) In electronic imaging, typically a film output made from a computer data file of an original camera transparency or negative. (2) A second generation original results from the output of a digital image to a film recorder or imagesetter of such quality that the new image shows no apparent differences from the original image outside of image enhancement, image merging, or other electronic processing or manipulation.

SEMICONDUCTOR A crystalline material, the resistivity of which is between that of an insulator and a conductor. It was the development of semiconductors that made possible the invention of the transistor, integrated circuits, and the entire field of microelectronics. Semiconductors most commonly used are made from very pure silicon and germanium. To utilize the unique properties of silicon and germanium, however, trace impurities must be added to make *p*-type or *n*-type semiconductors in a process called doping. Semiconductors are also used in light-sensitive and heat-sensitive devices.

SEMICONDUCTOR CHIP An integrated circuit fabricated on a small semiconductor wafer that contains anywhere from 100 to more than a million circuit elements. Typically, the chips measure from 0.05 inches square to 0.50 inches square. They are called *chips* because they are broken off a much larger wafer that contains many identical chips.

SEMICONDUCTOR DIODE Any of a number of two terminal semiconductor devices that consist of one junction of *p*-type and *n*-type semiconductor materials. Like its vacuum tube counterpart, it allows electrons to pass through it in only one direction—from cathode to anode. The cathode end is usually identified by a band painted around the diode. Sometimes the diode symbol is painted on the unit to identify the terminals. Diodes may be specified according to their usage. A large diode might be referred to as a *rectifier* because it is designed to convert ac power to dc power. A small diode might be called a *signal diode* because it is used to process weak signals in electronic equipment.

SEPARATION NEGATIVES Both colour photographs and graphic arts colour reproductions are generally derived from exposures of the subject matter using red light, green light, and blue light. In the integral tripacks widely used in colour photography, these exposures occur in the differently sensitized layers of the materials. In graphic reproductions the three exposures are commonly made using red, green, and blue filters. In both cases, the initial stage is usually to produce negatives, and the three negatives are called *separation negatives*. Because in integral tripacks the negatives are not available as separate entities, however, the term separation negatives is generally applied only to photographic systems in which the three images are assembled, such as dye transfer processes, and to the graphic reproduction industry.

In photographic dye transfer processes, negatives of the scene, or more usually of a colour photograph of the scene, are exposed through red, green, and blue filters, and these are then used to produce positive images of hardened gelatin of varying thickness (the unhardened gelatin being removed by washing in warm water). The positive images are dyed with cyan, magenta, or yellow dye, as appropriate, and the dyes are then transferred in succession to a suitable support. For paper prints, a paper support is used; for motion picture films, a film support is used. This was the method used in the *Technicolor* motion-picture system. Before the availability of integral tripack colour negative film, the Technicolour system used a special beam-splitting camera in which the separation negatives were exposed on three separate films.

The major interest in separation negatives now is in the graphic reproduction industry. Although the original scene is occasionally used, as in the reproduction of artists' paintings, most separation negatives are made from colour photographs, and these are referred to as the *originals*. The filters used for making the exposures are typically similar to Wratten filter numbers 25 for the red, 58 for the green, and 47B for the blue.

MASKING Because the cyan, magenta, and yellow dyes or inks used to make the final positive image always have unwanted absorptions, good colour reproduction can normally be obtained only if corrections are made to the separation negatives. This can be done by *masking,* by which is meant binding up in register with a separation negative a low contrast positive made from one of the other two separation negatives. For instance, if a low contrast positive is made from the red separation negative and bound up in register with the green separation negative, the effect in the final images will be to reduce the amount of magenta in areas where cyan dye or ink is present; this reduction in magenta can then compensate for the unwanted green absorption of the cyan dye. Similar procedures can be used to correct for the unwanted blue absorption of the cyan, for the unwanted red and blue absorptions of the magenta, and for the unwanted green absorption of the yellow (the unwanted red absorption of the yellow is usually negligible). By making these masks slightly unsharp, useful improvements in the apparent sharpness of the final image can be obtained.

SCANNERS In the graphic arts industry, separation negatives are now usually made on *scanners.* In a typical scanner the procedure is as follows. The original typically consists of a photographic colour transparency. This is wrapped around a transparent drum on which a very small spot of white light is focused. The drum is rotated and advanced on a lead screw so that the spot of light scans the whole area of the picture in a series of parallel lines. The light is then split into three beams, one incorporating a red filter, another a green filter, and a third a blue filter. The three beams then excite three photodetectors, and the resulting electronic signals are used to control the intensities of three beams of light focused on three unexposed pieces of film or other photosensitive material, wrapped round further sections of the same drum. As the original transparency is scanned, the three pieces of film are exposed, and after processing, the separation negatives are obtained. Because of the difficulty of producing good blacks from cyan, magenta, and yellow inks alone, a black image is usually printed as well in dark and black areas of the picture, and another section of the drum can be used to expose a fourth negative from which the black ink printing can be derived.

In scanners, the information corresponding to the separation negatives is available in the form of electronic signals, and these can be manipulated to introduce various forms of correction corresponding to the older masking procedures; thus, corrections can be made for the unwanted absorptions of the cyan, magenta, and yellow inks, and the unsharp masking can also be achieved to improve the sharpness. Another useful procedure is known as *under colour removal* or *gray component replacement* (GCR); in this procedure, wherever all three coloured inks are present, the resulting gray colour can be replaced by the corresponding amount of black ink, and this can reduce ink costs, facilitate the drying of the inks, and improve sharpness.

Books: Hunt, R. W. *G., The Reproduction of Colour.* 4th edition. New York: Van Nostrand Reinhold, and Surbiton, England: Fountain Press, 1987.

SEPARATIONS In electronic imaging, the creation of four separate files one for each of the four process colours, cyan, magenta, yellow, and black. The software for separations may be machine specific or may have various look-up tables to maximize colour appearance for specific output devices.

SEQUENTIAL COULEUR A MEMOIRE (SECAM)

One of two European television broadcast standards. The chrominance signal is transmitted differently than either PAL or NTSC systems. The system is in use in France, the former Soviet Union, and in Eastern Europe.

SERIAL PORT In computing, one of the two standard input/output means used by the computer to control external peripherals such as a modem. Serial ports send data one bit at a time in a sequential string. It is a slower transfer than a parallel process.

SERVO Identifying a motor or mechanism that adjusts a process on the basis of feedback, such as an automatic focus mechanism, voltage regulator, and temperature control.

SHADE (1) A dark and unsaturated colour, as is produced by adding black to a more saturated colour. Maroon, a dark red of low saturation, is a shade. (2) An area that is protected from direct light from a source.

SHADOW MASK (1) A perforated metal screen that is separated from the geometrical mosaic of red, green, and blue phosphor dots on the inner face of a colour television tube and so positioned that it confines the passage of the beams from the R, G, and B electron guns to their corresponding colour emitting phosphor dots. (2) A mask used when the full shadow detail in a four-colour reproduction is desirably carried by the black printer. It is made from the black printer separation negative on a high-contrast emulsion and registered with the black printer positive when making the half-tone screen negative.

SHAPE The two-dimensional outline of an object or part of an object, as distinct from form, which implies a three-dimensional quality.

See also: *Form.*

SHARPNESS A perceived quality of an image that is associated with the abruptness of change of tone at the edge of an object or tonal area. The purpose of focusing a camera is to adjust the lens-to-film distance to obtain the sharpest image. Acutance is an objective measure of edge quality that is related to sharpness.

SHOULDER The high-density region of the characteristic curve where the curve diminishes in slope, becoming more nearly horizontal. This area is reached with increasing exposure for negative materials and with decreasing exposure for reversal materials. Subject tones exposed in the shoulder will have little or no detail in the image.

SIGMA (σ) Greek letter signifying standard deviation
See also: *Standard deviation.*

SIGNAL A general term for any desired input into a transmission, imaging, or other system that causes appropriate action with respect to the output. The term is commonly used in electrical, electronic, and electromagnetic contexts, such as the variation with time of a wave train by means of which information is conveyed in a transmission system. The simplest signal is a single pulse. Complex signals can carry sufficient information to build up a television image as a result of modulation.

SIGNAL-TO-NOISE RATIO (SNR) The quotient obtained by dividing the power associated with the desired input by the power associated with the random disturbance that may interfere with the desired record. In sound reproduction, the ratio of the loudness of the desired signal to the loudness of any unwanted sound signal. In a photographic image, for example, the signal is the mean average density of an image (D_I) less the mean background density (D_B), and the noise is the extraneous degradation introduced by granularity, normally expressed by σ. The signal-to-noise ratio is then $(D_I-D_B)/σ$. The typical SNR of photographic materials is about 4:1, but values ranging from 2:1 to 40:1 have been measured. In microcopying, a value of 11:1 is the minimum for a barely decipherable image.

SILICON-BLUE CELL (SBC) Identifying exposure meters that have a silicon photoelectric cell that is covered by a bluish filter to bring the spectral response of the meter into closer agreement with the spectral sensitivity of panchromatic films.

228

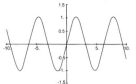 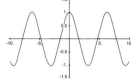

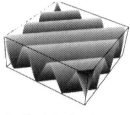

Sine Wave in two dimensions (rectangular coordinates).

A radial sine wave in two dimensions.

 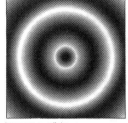

The same sine wave, with the amplitude indicated by the lightness, as in an image.

Image of a radial sine wave.

SINE WAVE A waveform, the amplitude of which is a sine (or cosine) function. The most common physical form for a sine wave is $A(x,t) = \sin(kx - \omega t + \phi)$, where $A(x,t)$ is the amplitude of the wave at position x and time t, k is the angular velocity of the wave, ω) is the angular frequency of the wave, and ϕ is the phase. Angular velocity and frequency are equal to the velocity (v) and frequency (υ) multiplied by 2π: $k = 2\pi v$, $\omega = 2\pi \upsilon$. They are used so that the angle of which the sine is taken will be in radians, a common unit. A cosine wave is a sine wave with a phase of π radians.

Sine waveforms pervade imaging—any image can be considered to be made up of a sum of sine waveforms with different frequencies and phases. Sine and cosine waves can also be subject to a wide variety of mathematical analyses. Most modern image evaluation techniques and a great deal of the more powerful image processing techniques rely on this fact.

SINE-WAVE TARGET An optical test pattern in which the

luminance varies gradually and periodically between maximum and minimum values, as distinct from a squarewave target where the luminance changes abruptly between high and low values, as in a bar resolving-power target.

SKEWED DISTRIBUTION In a graph showing the number of occurrences of different values in a set of measurements, the nonsymmetry whereby one tail of the graph extends farther along the horizontal axis than does the other tail. An example of a nonnormal distribution. Such a pattern usually appears in the graph of emulsion grain sizes.

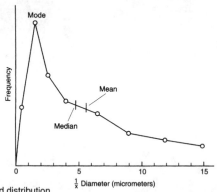

Skewed distribution.

SKIN TONE The appearance of an area of the face or other part of the body that is illuminated by the main light but does not include a specular highlight. When used as a standard for quality control purposes, it is assumed, unless stated otherwise, that the typical subject is Caucasian with a skin reflectance of approximately 36%, one stop or zone higher than the standard 18% reflectance gray test card, which corresponds to subject value or Zone V in the Zone System. Skin tone is sometimes used as a reference instead of a gray card when an accurate reproduction of the gray card does not produce an accurate or pleasing reproduction of the skin, or when a gray card has not been included in the scene.

SLOPE The steepness of a line graph over a given region or at a point. It is mathematically equal to the tangent of the angle between a straight-line graph and a horizontal line.

For two points on a straight line, the slope is $\Delta y/\Delta x$, that is, the ratio of the change in the output values to the change in the input values. For a point on a curve that is not straight, a tangent is drawn to the curve at the point and the slope of the tangent found.

For a characteristic curve of a photographic material, the slope is a measure of the relationship of the image contrast to the subject contrast.

SLOW SCAN In electronic imaging, the transmitting of video signals at a rate slower than real time is called slow scan. This is generally done because of bandwidth limitations. Slow scan video can be sent over radio frequencies other than those allocated for broadcast and over standard telephone lines.

SMALL COMPUTER SYSTEMS INTERFACE (SCSI) In computers, there are several means of accessing peripherals through a port that conforms to a particular protocol for data transfer. SCSI is one protocol that has become a de facto standard for data input/output in the Macintosh platform. Scanners and film recorders connected to a Macintosh exclusively use SCSI. Other peripherals such as removable cartridges and optical drives also employ SCSI.

SMOOTHING FILTER In electronic imaging, an electronic filter used to reduce the cross-hatch noise pattern that can appear with the use of charge-coupled devices.

SOBEL OPERATORS In electronic imaging, the use of a neighbourhood filtering process in which the values of the kernel are weighted in a directional orientation, for example north, south, northeast, etc. Such a filter allows for the easy visualization of subtle contrast changes that have a directional orientation. Sobel operators play an important role in enhancing medical and satellite images.

SOFT (1) Unsharp, either intentionally so, as with a soft-focus lens that is designed to be used when the reproduction of fine detail is not wanted, or unintentional unsharp, as in the resulting images when a camera, enlarger, or projector is inaccurately focused. (2) Low contrast, to describe an image that has less than normal contrast, a lower than average lighting ratio, a film, developer, or printing material designed to produce low contrast or compensate for high contrast elsewhere in the process, etc.

SOFT COPY The image on the video display of a computer or workstation.

SOFT-EDGE MASKING In electronic imaging, a process of sharpening soft edges by means of computer analysis of the pixels in the soft edges.

SOFT PROOF The image on a display terminal or CRT.

SOFTWARE Text material, illustrations, or other information to accompany or to be used with hardware (apparatus or equipment). In audiovisual contexts, software includes films, scripts, etc., and hardware includes viewing and projection devices. In computer and some video applications, software refers to a systematic collection of computer programs and their associated documentation as distinct from the equipment used to process and print the results.

SOLID An area completely covered with ink or a 100% dot area.

SOLID-STATE CIRCUIT Any electronic circuit, the active elements of which are semiconductor devices instead of vacuum tubes. Components used in solid-state circuits include semiconductor diodes, transistors, thyristors, integrated circuits, optocouplers, solid-state relays, and a variety of photosensors.

SPATIAL FREQUENCY (1) Frequency as applied to spatially varying (as opposed to temporally varying) waveforms; specified in cycles per unit length. Spatial frequency is particularly important in imaging as the input variable in modulation transfer function graphs and resolution tests. Image processing techniques are also frequently dependent on the spatial frequencies that make up an image, in the same sense that component sine waves can be combined to make a more complex temporally varying waveform. (2) In electronic imaging, a brightness value. The change of brightness values from pixel to pixel is referred to as spatial frequency change. If closely spaced pixels change brightness values rapidly, it is described as high-frequency information. Low frequency data are minimally changing pixels brightness.

SPECIAL EFFECTS Special effects includes a whole host of techniques that photographers use to create images that may or may not resemble reality but that usually have some unreal or questionable quality about them. Usually the purpose behind using special effects is to raise the impact or level of interest of an image or to produce images that only exist because of the use of such effects.

Special effects depend on the basic belief that photographs don't lie. They exploit this premise by presenting to the observer images that are seemingly impossible to achieve in reality or which enhance certain features of a subject beyond that achievable by normal photographic methods. In addition, special effects often enhance or modify reality for some ulterior purpose such as to enhance aesthetic merit, to convey information in a more effective manner than would be possible with a standard photograph, or to confuse or deceive the viewer into a false interpretation of reality.

Special effects and trick photography are sometimes considered synonymous but the word *trick* suggests that the photographs are intended to entertain viewers rather than serve more serious artistic and professional purposes.

A precise definition of what comes under the heading of special effects is difficult to give because some manifestation of a special effect can be found in most photographs. Although one can safely assume that *special effects* are not involved when the resulting photograph closely resembles the scene being photographed, when it is as accurate a record of the original scene as a two-dimensional representation of a three-dimensional scene allows, if it is an instantaneous and sharp record, if it was not manipulated after the image was recorded, and if it appears to be natural and unmanipulated, even in this case certain special effects could have been used by the photographer to achieve this look of naturalness and spontaneity. Also, a special effect that is used so frequently that it becomes commonplace tends to no longer be considered a special effect.

The advent of electronic-image storage, manipulation, and output has had a significant impact on the degree of sophistication and scope of special effects. Not only has this technology allowed for improved quality in creating traditional effects but it has made possible the creation of images that were totally impossible in the past. In spite of this, however, because computer-generated special effects require expensive computer equipment and computer skills, their use by photographers is limited. Only special effects produced by standard methods by still photographers will be considered here.

Special effects can be classified according to a variety of criteria. Some occur before the making of the photograph. Others are used during photography, and yet a third class of special effect is that which is accomplished by modifying the original image after the initial photograph is recorded. Special effects could also be classified based on the procedures used or the technology involved. The techniques can be optical, chemical, physical, photographic, electronic, or combinations of these methods. In fact, there are so many techniques that could be called *special* that it becomes impossible to attempt to list, classify, and discuss all of them.

ELECTRONIC STILL PHOTOGRAPHY Most of the special effects possible with conventional photography are performed more easily and better using electronic still photography. They can also be done in a lighted room with the press of a button. The changes can be seen as they appear on the screen and adjustments can be made as necessary. Instead of having to visualize what a composite picture might look like by adding or subtracting elements, the operation can be executed and the result observed on the screen. If the image is not satisfactory, it can be electronically erased or altered in a matter of seconds or minutes. A component of an image, such as a person's head, can be *lassoed,* using an icon of a rope that appears on the computer screen, dragged to any position on the screen, and then cloned by simply clicking on the mouse. If the position needs to be changed, this is easily done without disturbing the original image. The cloned head can be altered in size, changed in contrast, reversed in tone, made partially transparent, posterized, modified in colour, and so on. Software programs have been developed that have revolutionized both conventional imaging and special effects imaging in various fields, including photomechanical reproduction, motion-picture photography, video, and electronic still photography.

The convenience and simplicity of electronic imaging requires a considerable investment in equipment. A *scanner* is needed to input a photograph into a computer. Prints are scanned on a flatbed scanner and slides require a film scanner. After the image is manipulated it needs to be printed. There are a variety of *printers*—laser, ink jet, and thermal—each providing a different quality print. Near photographic quality is available with the best printers. Another concern, especially when working in colour and in large format, is that a large amount of computer storage memory is needed. This slows image processing, requiring more time and computer memory. For example, to scan in a 35-mm colour slide or negative at 200 dpi requires about 10 megabytes of memory.

Photographic special effects such as those easily and quickly made with a star filter using a single camera exposure would, using electronic photography, require the digitizing and super-positioning of two separate images. Effects such as Sabattier, solarization, and posterization that take considerable time to perform photographically are easily achieved electronically by simply pulling down an *image menu* making a selection, and clicking the mouse.

Books: Eastman Kodak Co., *Creative Darkroom Techniques.* Rochester, NY: Eastman Kodak Co., 1975; Evans, Ralph, *Eye, Film, and Camera.* New York: John Wiley, 1960; Hirsch, Robert *Photographic Possibilities.* Boston: Focal Press, 1991; Pfahl, John, *Altered Landscapes: The Photographs of John Pfahl.* New York: RFG Publishing, 1982.

SPECIFICATION A prescribed procedure or result, such as time of development or agitation technique in photographic processing, or necessary contrast index. Most specifications (specs) include tolerances, i.e., permitted variation in the specs.

SPECTRAL Having to do with the spectrum, especially variation in some response or output with wavelength (or frequency).

SPECTRAL COLOUR REPRODUCTION Reproduction in which the colours are reproduced with the same spectral reflectance factors, or spectral transmittance factors, or relative spectral power distribution, as the colours in the original scene.

SPECTRAL ENERGY DISTRIBUTION The energy output of a source as a function of the wavelength of the radiation. Spectral energy distribution plots are the most common means for indicating the output of a source as a function of the wavelength or frequency of the photons emitted. To obtain a spectral energy distribution curve it is necessary to use a spec-trograph or spectrophotometer that has been calibrated so that the actual energy output by the source can be calculated from the response of the instrument at each wavelength. Since the spectral energy distribution curve is a plot of energies, it is most closely related to radiometry. A similar, photometric plot could also be obtained by plotting luminance as a function of wave-length. Another plot of interest is the number of quanta emitted as a function of wavelength. Such a plot can be generated by dividing the spectral energy at each wavelength by the energy of a single photon at the corresponding wavelength.

Spectral energy distribution curves have long been the stan-dardized means for describing the output of a source. When they are used, however, to determine the response of a photographic material or electronic imaging detector, it is important to remember that the response will be given as a function of the amount of energy, and not the number of quanta, input to the detector.

SPECTRUM (1) A dispersion of some incident electromagnetic radiation, with the degree of dispersion depending on the wavelength and the device resulting in the dispersion, such as a diffraction grating or prism. (2) A graphical representation of the amount of electromagnetic radiation received by a detector in a spectrograph.

SPLIT SCREEN (1) By using a computer screen sizing box, the operator can adjust the computer screen so that two or more files or windows are open for inspection, modification, or transfer. (2) A projection area or screen divided into two parts, each showing a separately-projected image. Special split-frame or multiple-window slide mounts allow the photographer to place two or more transparency segments into separate windows within a single slide mount so that when the slide is projected the images are projected with a single projector. This technique is also used in television. (3) In motion pictures, two separate scenes or shots blended into one, as when a performer plays a dual role, two separate events are presented simultaneously, or full-scale and miniature sets are made to appear as one. A soft edge matte is often used for this purpose.

SPRAY BRUSH In electronic imaging, to add a specific colour to designated image areas, analogous to manual airbrushing with a colourant.

SPREAD FUNCTION (1) A curve representing the distribution of light or density in the image of a point (point spread function) or line (line spread function). Points and lines cannot be imaged precisely because of light spread due to diffraction and aberrations of the lens and light scatter in photographic emulsions. Spread function may also refer to image degradation produced by focus error, image motion, and other factors that affect image definition. Spread functions for separate factors can be summed to produce a quantitative record of the image degradation for the system. There is an inverse relationship between spread function and image definition. (2) Curve of intensity against distance in the image of a theoretical point source (point spread function) or an infinitely narrow line (line spread function). In the former it is a cross section of the Airy pattern. Because of diffraction and residual aberrations, a practical system cannot give an ideal image, and the spread function is a measure of degradation. Other elements in an imaging system, such as a photographic emulsion, development, defocus, vibration, and atmospheric effects, all contribute individual spread functions to the final total. The modulation transfer function is the representation of the spread function as shown by the degradation of patterns of sinusoidal intensity variation of different frequencies. Mathematically it is the

Fourier transform of the line spread function, and if this is asymmetric as in the case of a lens with coma, there is a nonlinear phase shift of the sinusoidal components at various frequencies, which is expressed as the phase transfer function component of the optical transfer function.

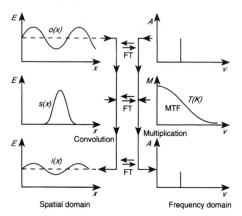

Spread function. Functional relationships in imaging. The linear imaging of a sinusoidal object. FT, Fourier transform pairs; $o(x)$, object function; $s(x)$, spread function; $i(x)$, image function.

SQUARE WAVE A waveform where the characteristic measure takes on two and only two values, usually with the amount of time or space at each value being equal. An example of a square wave is found when a set of dark bars is placed against a light background. The luminance abruptly changes periodically from a high level to a low level; as distinct from a sine wave which involves a gradual change. A resolution test target consists of a set of spatially varying square waves.

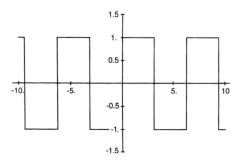

Square wave

SQUARE-WAVE TARGET An optical test pattern in which the luminance changes abruptly between maximum and minimum values, as occurs with a bar resolving-power.

236

STANDARD (1) A specification, test method, recommended practice or glossary of terms approved and published by a recognized standardizing body. (2) The basis of a set of measurements. The standard of length—the meter—was formerly the distance between two marks on a platinum bar kept in Paris. Now the standard of length for the meter is the distance occupied by a specified number of wavelengths of a specified colour of light. The standard for light emission—the candela (formerly candle)—is the light emitted by a black cavity of specified size at a specified fixed temperature. (3) A publication of the American National Standards Institute (ANSI) or the International Standards Organization (ISO), which describes methods of photographic processing, film and paper dimensions, testing procedures, and so on.

STANDARD DEVIATION (σ, s) The most useful measure of the random (chance-caused) variation within a set of data. It is the square root of the average of the squares of the deviations of the individual numbers from their mean (arithmetic average).

$$\sigma = \sqrt{\frac{\Sigma(X_i - \mu)^2}{N}}$$

where σ is the standard deviation Σ is the sign of summation (i.e., add all the following items), X_i includes all the members of the data set, μ is the population average, and N is the number of items. This formula implies that all possible members of the population are included.

Since the whole population can rarely be tested, the formula for the standard deviation found from a limited sample is slightly modified to read

$$s = \sqrt{\frac{\Sigma(X_i - \overline{X})^2}{n - 1}}$$

Now, s is the sample standard deviation, an approximation to the population standard deviation, $\overline{X}$ is the sample mean, and n is the number of items in the sample. The value of n is reduced by one in the calculation since theory and experience show that without this correction the sample standard deviation is smaller than the population value.

AN EXAMPLE OF THE COMPUTATION. Five temperature measurements of a processing bath—75°, 77°, 76°, 74°, and 75°—give a mean of 75.4°, and the following table:

$(X - \overline{X})$	$(X - \overline{X})^2$
0.4	0.16
1.6	2.56
0.6	0.36
1.4	1.96
0.4	0.16
	5.20

The value $5.20 \div 4 = \sqrt{1.30} = 1.14$ or, rounded off 1.1°F, the value of the sample standard deviation. Note that in the calculation of s the mathematical sign of the difference $X - X$ is irrelevant, and that the s-value has the same unit a the original data.

SIGNIFICANCE OF s If two conditions are met, the value of s is a good approximation to the population standard deviation σ and thus is a valuable measure of the variability of the data set. These conditions are: (1) s is computed fron a representative sample; i.e., the sample is properly selected and evaluated; (2) differences among the members of the population are caused by chance and not by any factor other than chance. Although both of these requirements are difficult to meet, they are often sufficiently well approximated. They can be tested by taking a large sample and plotting the data to see whether or not the pattern comes close to that of a normal distribution. If it does, then the following statements are true: about 68% of all the population data will lie between $+1s$ from the mean; about 95% within the $+2s$ interval; about 99.7% within $+3s$.

Referring to the temperature example above, if the data were properly collected and if the temperature in the bath varied only by chance, then the following inferences could be made: about 68% of all the temperature values lie between $+1.1°F$ from the mean of 75.4°F, or between 74.3° and 76.5°F; about 95% lie between 73.2° and 77.6°F, and 99.7% between 72.1° and 78.7°F.

APPLICATIONS

Conformance to Specifications The size of the process standard deviation must always be much less than the variation allowed by specifications. For example, suppose that processing directions call for a temperature of $75±1/2°F$. If the standard deviation is $1/4°F$, then the allowable temperature difference is $2 s$, and 95% of the bath temperatures will fall within the specified range but only if the process temperature is exactly centered on 75°F. Even then, 5% of the temperatures will fall outside the requirements. Only if the s value is less than 1/2 will the temperature error be less than 1 in 100 if the average is precisely on target. Clearly, process variation and specifications must be closely related.

Control Charts When a process is being monitored, successive measurements of the process performance are often plotted against time in order to detect undesired results. One method involves a graph showing the process mean and limit lines set at distances based on the process standard deviation. If $+3s$ limits are used, 99.7% of the data from an unchanged process will fall within the limits, and only 0.3% (i.e., 3 in 1000) will fall outside. Thus, if the decision is made that the process is awry when a point falls outside the lines, that decision will be in error infrequently. It is impossible to set the lines so far apart that *all* measurements from an unchanged process will be within the limits; thus, some risk of error is always present.

Tests of Hypothesis Many experiments are performed to see whether or not a change in manufacturing or other conditions causes a change in the results. If the measured exposure index changes to 110 from a previous mean of 100, for example, the apparent increase of 10 must be compared with the process standard deviation. Only if the s value is much less than 10 is it safe to suppose that an increase in the index has actually occurred. Many kinds of hypothesis tests are possible, depending on the process being tested and the nature of the experiment.

START-UP In photography, the opening stages of a digital or photochemical process in which normal operating conditions are established. Temperatures, chemical concentrations, and mechanical functions are checked. A computer checks its system files. When appropriate, test strips are run and the results are compared to process specifications. If necessary, changes are made to establish conformity, and regular operation is begun.

STATE OF THE ART The best currently available device, process, or system. The development of a better method advances the state of the art.

STATIC (1) Without movement or the effect of movement. Applied to a dull composition in still photography, design, or a shot in motion pictures in which the camera is not moved. (2) Short for static electricity.

STATIC ELECTRICITY Electrical charges at rest as distinguished from electrical charges in motion (current electricity). The ancient Greeks knew that amber when rubbed would attract bits of paper and other light objects. We have since learned that rubbing or simply separating two surfaces in intimate contact will cause a transfer of electrical charges from one surface to the other. One surface is charged with an excess of electrons (negative charges), leaving the other surface with an excess of protons (positive charges). To store the electrical charges the material must be a good insulator. Photographic film and paper are both good insulators and can therefore cause static electricity problems in a photolab.

When unprocessed film or paper is unwound from a reel, the separation of the surfaces can generate static electricity. If the voltage between the surfaces of the reel and the web is high enough, a spark will occur between the surfaces. This spark will expose the film or paper in an easily distinguishable pattern.

Electrostatic charges on negatives will attract dust and dirt particles, which if not removed before printing will degrade the quality of the print. The electrostatic charges on the film can be neutralized by the use of a static eliminator.

Walking across a carpeted room on a dry winter day can generate many thousands of volts. High electrostatic voltages can damage certain electronic components found in much modern photofinishing equipment. Great care must be taken when handling printed circuit boards that contain metal-oxide semiconductor (MOS) components because the high voltage can puncture the very thin metal-oxide film layer that insulates the gate from the drain and the source..

STATIC MEMORY The retention of information in semiconductor memory without refreshing or recirculating.

STATISTICS The complex body of mathematical theory and application that includes methods of data collection, analysis, and interpretation. Statistical methods are used, for example, in monitoring the manufacture of photographic materials and equipment and in processing plants.

KINDS OF DATA Objective data come from measurements. They include concentrations of materials used in processing solutions and characteristics of films and papers such as contrast and speed. Subjective data come from judgements made by observers concerning image quality. Although subjective data are difficult to obtain, they are basic to the assessment of the success of the entire photographic process, from manufacture to viewing conditions. Objective measurements of image quality must be shown to be equivalent to subjective judgements.

All kinds of measured data, however seemingly precise in nature, are subject to error. Therefore, the estimate of error is a fundamental part of the statistical analysis of data.

SAMPLING The entire set of possible measurements in a given situation is called the *population*. An example would be the entire production of a given lot of film, consisting of very many square meters of product. A sample is a small lot used for determining the quality of the whole production of a given kind.

The number of samples is, for practical purposes, necessarily limited. A sample of over 30 measurements of the same kind is usually considered large. Often judgements must be based on samples as small as 2 or 3 in size.

To avoid bias in the collection of the sample, random selection is often used. In taking a sample from a large roll of film, one is tempted to use only the ends or the edges of the roll. Such a sample may well not be representative of the rest of the product, unless tests show that it is. Various techniques are used to randomize the sample selection, such as tables of random numbers.

If there is reason to believe that the population is not well mixed, i.e., that it is stratified so that different portions of the population are significantly different from others, it is necessary to take random samples from the different strata. In a large processing tank, if the solution is not thoroughly stirred, there may be systematic or other differences in temperature or concentration from top to bottom. In this case, samples would have to be taken from different positions in order to avoid incorrect judgments.

MEASURES OF CENTRAL TENDENCY

1. The *mean is* the arithmetic average of a set of data. It is the most commonly used measure of the value around which the members of a data set are symmetrically distributed if they differ only by chance. For such a distribution, called *normal,* the mean lies at the centre, the highest point of a plot of such a data set.

2. The *median is* the value that divides a set of data into two parts having equal numbers of members. It is a useful measure of central tendency for a set of data that are grouped together except for a few widely separated ones.

3. The *mode is* the most frequently occurring value in a set

of data. It is used when many of the data have nearly the same value and others of the set are widely different.

If the data are representative of a population that is chance controlled, the mean, the median, and the mode very nearly coincide.

MEASURES OF VARIATION

1. The *range is* the difference between the largest and smallest members of a sample. Although simple to calculate, the range has limited use, in part because the size of the range is determined by only two members of the set. The range is often used for samples of small size and especially for the preparation of limit lines for control charts.

2. The most powerful measure of variation within a set of data is the *standard deviation.* It is found by determining the difference between the mean and each member of the set, squaring the differences, averaging them, and taking the square root of the quotient. The standard deviation gives equal weight to all members of the set. It is used in some control charts, in tests of conformance to specifications, and in tests intended to detect a difference between two populations, known as *hypothesis tests.*

STILL FRAME A motion-picture and video optical effect in which a single image is repeated in order to appear frozen in place, that is, stationary when projected.

STILL PHOTOGRAPH Identifying a single photograph, as distinct from a motion picture.

STILL VIDEO (1) See *Electronic still photography.* (2) An electronic method of recording individual images using 2-inch floppy disks that are capable of storing either 50 field images or 25 frame images.

STILL-VIDEO CAMERAS See *Camera types.*

STRONG COLOUR Adjective denoting high saturation or chroma.

STYLE A distinctive and consistent characteristic of photographs produced by a photographer, which, when they become familiar to viewers, can serve as the photographer's artistic signature. A range of characteristics have been used, separately and in combination, by photographers to establish widely recognized styles, including choice of subject, composition, lighting, camera lens, focus and depth of field, filters, print quality, and type of display. When a group of photographers share a common style, it is referred to as a school of style. Even though many studio portrait photographers have individual styles, there is a generic style to this area of specialization that distinguishes studio portraits from candid portraits, environmental portraits, passport portraits, etc. Schools of style also develop because of imitation of the style of an admired creative photographer, and commonalties related to any of a variety of factors such as age, education, economic status, geographic location, and from a historical perspective, the time period during which the photographers lived.

SUBJECT A person, object, or scene represented in a photograph or other reproduction or work of art.

SUBJECT ATTRIBUTES Particular properties of objects or scenes such as shape, size, depth, and colour. Certain subject attributes, such as shape and colour, can be represented quite accurately in photographic images. The size of an object can be represented accurately only with small objects (or with large photographs). Depth cannot be represented physically with conventional photographic processes, although the illusion of depth can be realistic, especially with stereoscopic images.

SUBJECT CONTRAST The relative luminance values of the highlight and shadow areas of a scene, usually expressed either as a luminance ratio, where the average ratio is 160:1, or as a log luminance range, where the average value is 2.2 (the logarithm of 160). A luminance ratio of 160:1 also corresponds to a seven-step or seven-zone range.

SUBJECTIVE (1) In visual perception, characterizing data obtained by visual examination of an image. Graininess, sharpness, and detail are subjective qualities of image structure. Compare with objective, implying instrumental means of obtaining data. Granularity, acutance, and resolution are objective measures of image quality that correlate with graininess, sharpness, and detail. (2) In motion pictures and video, the use of the camera as if it were one of the players by means of eye-level placement and by moving the camera as a person would be expected to move. (3) Any critique of a photograph, any event in which a human is making a judgement.

SUBJECTIVE COLOURS Chromatic sensations produced when black-and-white images are presented to a viewer intermittently at frequencies of about five per second, when certain black-and-white designs are rotated at appropriate speeds, and when certain black-and-white designs having fine detail are viewed continuously. In this case, the involuntary small-scale nystagmus movements of the eyes produce the necessary interactions in the visual-response mechanism.

SUBTITLE Written words added to a motion-picture or video image, usually along the bottom of the frame and usually to enhance, comment on, or add to information presented on the sound track. Most often used to provide translations for an audience not fluent in the original production language.

SUBTRACTIVE COLOUR PROCESSES System of colour reproduction in which the reddish, greenish, and bluish thirds of the spectrum of a white illuminant are modulated by varying the amounts of cyan, magenta, and yellow colourants, respectively. The subtractive colour process is used in colour photography and in graphic arts reproduction.

SUBTRACTIVE PRIMARY COLOURS Cyan, magenta, and yellow. Colourants having these hues absorb (subtract) red, green, and blue light, respectively.

SUNLIGHT Illumination (on a surface) coming directly from the sun, without admixture of skylight or other scattered illumination. In the open, sunlight is always mixed with other light. Brightly lighted portions of a forest floor will be lit primarily by sunlight. Daylight is a mixture of sunlight and skylight. As compared to skylight, sunlight is relatively warm in colour. The colour temperature of standard sunlight is 5400 K.

SUPERIMPOSURE The careful combination of two or more images so that both images are visible. Multiple exposure in a camera or from an enlarger, as well as sandwiching negatives in an enlarger, are ways to superimpose images. Names and subtitles can readily be added to an image by superimposure. With television, images can be superimposed by transmitting or recording two video images simultaneously.

SUPER VIDEO GRAPHICS ARRAY In computers, a cathode-ray tube (CRT) resolution of 800 x 600 pixels or above at 256 colours, minimum. This is the current standard for computer-based imaging. At this level of resolution, the CRT is noninterlaced and has a high refresh rate to limit flicker.

SURVEILLANCE PHOTOGRAPHY The use of photographic or electronic imaging systems to monitor and document activities and places, identifying persons and their conduct. The resulting images in the form of prints, slides, motion pictures or videotapes are most valuable as aids in any investigative process and can be used as supporting evidence in criminal and civil litigation proceedings. In some jurisdictions, the interpretations of the rules of evidence require that surveillance photographs cannot be entered as prime evidence without the testimony of an eyewitness.

Similar systems and methods are used in industrial manufacturing and retailing operations to observe, monitor, and record the activities of people and equipment for the purposes of safety, efficiency, and time-studies and to gather data for scientific investigations. Fixed installations are often used to monitor and control vehicular traffic at major intersections and on busy expressway routes. Aerial surveillance, conducted from aircraft at low altitude, is used in military operations and in scientific land survey studies. High altitude imaging systems, which include sophisticated electronic scanning from satellites and high altitude aircraft, are used for world and large land mass weather studies and mapping operations.

Systems can be *manned* or *unmanned, covert* or *obvious.*

Unmanned systems include continuous-running video cameras, intermittent motion picture cameras that make photographs using time-scheduled or triggered devices, or still cameras equipped with triggering devices. Surveillance for industrial and scientific monitoring and for traffic control situations frequently makes use of intervalometer controls, which actuate the recording system on a preset time schedule. Unmanned dummy cameras in plain sight are often used as deterrents to criminal activities or as control devices for group behaviour.

Close-range covert methods use autoexposure point-and-shoot miniature cameras, favouring high-speed films and lenses to overcome adverse lighting conditions. Innovative *camera-flage* devices that conceal the camera from the subject are often part of the system. Manned, covert methods call for the use of cameras with bulky long focal length lenses (traditional telephoto or more compact catadioptric style) positioned at a great distance to maintain some degree of concealment from the subjects under surveillance.

Covert camera methods and techniques include the use of long focal-length lenses to obtain identifiable images of individuals at great distances, the use of high speed films, infrared radiation sources and infrared-sensitive films, infrared or radio-triggered devices, and image-making with the aid of light amplification units.

Photographic concerns are: undesirable and low level lighting conditions, subject motion and focusing problems, camera and shutter vibrations, shallow depth of field, and the need for images that provide for accurate identification of individuals. Traditional cameras used for this are 35-mm single-lens reflex cameras with telephoto lenses in the 200 to 600-mm range. To obtain usable, identifiable images of individuals at great distances, lenses are chosen based upon the 1 *mm of focal-length for each foot of distance* rule. Thus, a 200 mm lens would be the required minimum focal length for a subject at 200 feet. Force-processed high speed black-and-white films (ISO 1600 to 25,000) are often used when low light levels are encountered. Camera vibration problems are minimized using portable clamp-mount devices, sandbags, etc. Supplemental light can include the use of focused telephoto flash units or remote-triggered illumination positioned close to the stake-out area. Aside from good identification of the individuals in the scene, information regarding the date, time of day, exact location, identity of vehicles, and the nature of the activity complete the surveillance photography assignment for law enforcement or civil litigation purposes.

Low-light level video camera systems have become the most popular method used for surveillance under adverse conditions. Combined with light amplification modules or equipped for infrared viewing, they make image-making possible under conditions where even the human eye cannot perceive details. Their ability to record sound and real-time elements are an added benefit. While conversion of these images to hard printed-out copy cannot produce the sharpness and resolving power of conventional photography, such systems have become the choice of most law enforcement agencies. Most modern-day courtrooms have come to accept video presentations as supportive to eyewitness testimony.

SYSTEME INTERNATIONAL D'UNITES (SI) The modern version of the metric system, more rational than its predecessor.

SYSTEM-MODULATION-TRANSFER (SMT) ACUTANCE A measurement that assesses the significance of the many factors that affect image sharpness. It is subjective in the sense that it involves human judgement. SMT acutance is expressed in terms of a scale on which 100 represents image perfection and 70 implies a just acceptable image.

TAPE In film and television, the term refers to nonperforated magnetic recording media, which may be supplied on open reels, or in a variety of cassette formats for audio and video tape in both analog and digital formats.

The term is also used as a verb in video productions to indicate what is called principal photography in film production, i.e., primary shooting before the cameras.

In double-system formats, where picture and sound media are separate, it is essential to provide a means of synchronization of the sound and picture tapes, since even the best professional recorders do not have absolute speed controls good enough to ensure lip sync throughout long takes without added controls. Most often today this is accomplished in film production with neo-pilot tone recording of crystal sync, and in video production through the use of SMPTE time code.

TAPE RECORDER/PLAYER A device for recording picture and sound or sound only on a moving strand of magnetic tape. Tape recorders as a general class may represent the signals to be recorded as analogs of the signal, such an analog being the strength of the magnetic field used to represent sound in direct analog magnetic recording, or the instantaneous frequency of an FM carrier as in analog video recording, or as digits in digital recording of audio or video. The essential ingredients of a tape recorder are a transport to move the tape past the magnetic heads, and record and playback electronics, usually used with record equalization and playback equalization to tailor the signal to be recorded to the tape medium.

TAPE SPEED One of a series of nominal rates of tape velocity past tape heads. For analog sound recording the speeds range across 30, 15, 7-1/2, 3-3/4, and 1-7/8 inches per second (ips), with the 15 and 7-1/2 ips speeds being the most common.

TARGET-OBJECT CONTRAST (TOC) The ratio of the reflectance (or transmittance) of the light and dark areas of a resolution test object. The ratio for black-and-white reflectance resolution targets is approximately 100:1. Low contrast targets may be as low as 2:1, and high-contrast transmittance targets may exceed 1,000:1.

TECOGRAPHY Category of image storage on reusable media, such as videotape recording of television images. The term also describes photochromism, photoplastic and thermoplastic recording, and various kinds of electrostatic imaging. In applied photography, unpredictable or intermittent occurrences may be recorded and analyzed in this way.

Tecography can be used to image on a cathode-ray tube

(CRT). A two-sided material is used, the front of which records an optical image and the back of which emits electrons in proportion to the image density on the front. The emissions are focused on a dielectric surface, forming an electric image of the subject that may be scanned or read and output to the CRT.

TELCINE In electronic imaging, a device that converts motion-picture images into video images.

TELERECORDING Reproducing a television or video presentation onto motion picture film.

TELEVISION SAFE AREA When projecting motion pictures for television, the central portion of the image that can be assumed will be seen on most home receivers. Because of transmission difficulties and variations in home receivers, some cropping of the original image is usual before it is viewed, and this cropping might eliminate up to 20% of the original motion picture image. It is therefore important, when filming in situations where television broadcast is likely, to keep all essential visual details, titles and subtitles, within the 80% of the motion picture image area that has been designated as the TV safe area.

TEMPORAL AVERAGING Computing the average of a quantity versus time, used especially when the level of the source used is not stable in time, such as with pink noise.

TEMPORAL FUSION The process by which successive images that are separated by a short time interval are perceived as being connected and continuous. The process is necessary in motion-picture photography to avoid flicker.

TERABYTE One trillion bytes, abbreviated TB.

TERMINAL In computers, a cathode-ray tube (CRT) that is directly tied into a host computer. The CRT is merely an input, accessing device and does not contain any "intelligence."

TEST (1) An experimental procedure used to obtain specific information about a material, process, or device, such as a lens resolution test and a chemical test of a developing solution. (2) In picture making, a preliminary trial to check the components of a system, such as exposing and processing a short length of film before beginning production on a motion picture.

TESTCHART An arrangement of letters, numbers, colour patches, etc., designed to provide information about an imaging system, such as the colour reproduction characteristics of different reversal colour films. The terms *test chart* and *test target* are sometimes used interchangeably.

TEST OBJECT A test chart, test target, or any object considered appropriate to serve as a subject for the purpose of conducting an imaging test.

TEXT The body matter of a page or book as distinguished from headings and graphics. Also, type, as distinguished from illustrations.

TEXTURE A relatively small-scale surface characteristic that is associated with tactile quality. Since a greatly magnified image of smooth paper can have the appearance of a rough surface, the small-scale qualification applies to the image rather than the subject with photographic reproductions. Some photographic printing papers are available with embossed textured surfaces. A texture screen placed in contact with a smooth printing paper during exposure produces a pseudotexture pattern.

THERMAL DYE TRANSFER An electronic printing method used to create continuous tone colour prints from computerized digital images or video analog images. Thermal dye transfer systems are an offshoot of similar devices used by the textile industry in the 1960s for printing on fabrics. The system consists of a cyan, magenta, yellow and black dye ribbon and a thermal printing head in intimate contact with the ribbon. When the printer is activated, the heated thermal head moves along the receiver paper (or transparency material) impregnating it with cyan, magenta, yellow and black dyes (C, M, Y, K). The heat causes the dyes to diffuse into the paper or transparency material. The spatial resolution of the image ranges from about 130 to 300 SPI (spots per inch) depending upon the original image, the quality of the paper or transparency material, and the particular printer used. Dye stability is comparable to other electronic printing systems. Printer speed is relatively slow. The quality from the best dye transfer printing system is near photographic quality.

THERMAL IMAGING DEVICE Identifying a photographic material that responds to infrared radiation.

THREE-COLOUR THEORY Theory on which colour separation and reproduction are based.

THRESHOLD In electronic imaging, a critical brightness value that determines a transition. In some applications all pixel values above a particular threshold may be assigned the maximum brightness value while those pixels below the threshold are assigned the minimum brightness value. The result is a high-contrast image containing only black and white pixels.

THROUGHPUT In computers, a measure of speed and efficiency that attempts to equalize all components of a system so that the ultimate criterion is how quickly the task is accomplished. For example, modems that have a baud rating of 9600 may actually have a throughput of 14,400 baud because of the use of compression firmware.

THUMBNAIL In electronic imaging, a collection of stored

images that may be visually displayed as a resampled series of 25 images per screen. These small thumbnail representations of the image allow for visually locating the desired image. Thumbnail images are often used when one wishes to arrange a series of images for presentation. In some ways a thumbnail screen display is similar to viewing transparencies as a group on a light table, instead of one by one in a projector.

TIFF In electronic imaging, images that are captured and saved to a storage medium as a file and are described according to some algorithm. The description is usually written prior to the image data in an area of the file called the header. Tagged image file format is one such header description widely used by electronic imaging programs. Others are TGA, VST, PCX, PICT, and PIC to name only a few. The proliferation of a multitude of image headers has caused serious porting problems. Many image manipulation software programs only read a limited number of header files. There are a number of commercial conversion programs that allow for the translation of one file format into another.

TIME-BASED CORRECTOR (TBC) In electronic imaging, video input from video tape recorders may contain time-based errors that make digitizing the images impossible. TBCs correct these timing errors.

TIME CODE Abbreviation of Society of Motion Picture and Television Engineers (SMPTE) time code. A method of encoding position into hours, minutes, seconds, and frames, along with other information, so that unperforated media, such as videotape, open reel tape, and so on, can be run in frame-accurate synchronization, by use of an electronic synchronizer. Time code occupies the space of one audio channel.

TINT A light and unsaturated colour, as is produced by adding white to a more saturated colour. Pink, a light red of low saturation, is a tint. The term is also used to identify base colours of photographic papers, including cold white, warm white, and cream white.

TITLE An identifying legend on a photograph, film strip, motion picture, video recording, etc. Titles in a motion-picture or video production include the main title of the production, followed by a cast title or titles identifying actors and the characters they portray, credit title for production and other staff, subtitles providing explanations where needed, and an end title.

TONALITY The overall appearance of the densities of the component areas of a photograph or other image with respect to the effectiveness of the values in representing the subject.

TONE (1) An area of uniform luminance or density in a subject or image. A high-contrast image might have only two tones, black and white, and gray scales have a limited number of tones, such as ten, whereas most subjects and continuous-tone images have many tones. (2) A slight hue in a monochrome image, such as warm-tone (brownish) and cold-tone (bluish). (3) (Verb) To chemically alter the hue of a photographic image.

TONE-CONTROL PROCESS The aim of tone control is to produce a range of densities in the final product that is either subjectively appropriate or objectively correct. To achieve this end, the original exposure may be biased to enhance highlight or shadow detail. The conditions of development may be altered, as may printing material and technique, and enlarger characteristics. Intermediate negatives and positives and masks of various types may be used to alter specific tonal values. Viewing conditions have a substantial influence on perceived tone representation.

TONE SEPARATION The degree to which different tones are distinguishable. Tone separation is dependent on four factors: (1) the densities of the tones in question, (2) the illumination falling on or passing through these densities, (3) the surrounding environment, and (4) the amount of noise present in the imaging system. Obviously, the smaller the differences in density between tones, the smaller the apparent separation will be. Also, the way the eye perceives luminance results in darker tones separated by some density increment appearing to be closer together than lighter tones separated by the same density increment. This effect is even more pronounced in dim lighting, or when the tones in question are surrounded by bright tones. At some point, when the lighting becomes too dim, or the surround too bright, it becomes impossible to distinguish between darker tones.

The effect of noise or grain on tone separation is also important. Tone reproduction studies are frequently conducted to determine the optimal reproduction of tones in an image, but it is important to remember that these reproduction studies do not consider the effect of noise. As the noise of point-to-point variation in the density of what is considered to be a single tone increases, the ability to distinguish that tone from another decreases. Optimum image quality is achieved by balancing optimal tone reproduction with noise considerations.

Books: Stroebel, Leslie; Compton, John; Current, Ira; and Zakia, Richard, *Photographic Materials and Processes*. Boston: Focal Press. 1986.

TOUCH SCREEN In computers, a type of cathode-ray tube (CRT) that serves as both a display device and input device. Touch screens enhance interactivity between the user and computer by rapidly accepting input when touch-sensitive areas of the display screen are pressed by the user. There are currently five types of touch screen technology in use: capacitive overlay, resistance overlay, surface acoustic wave, piezoelectric, and scanning infrared.

TRACKBALL In computers, a graphic user interface device

that controls the cursor when rotated. The trackball can be rotated 360 degrees in its cradle, causing the cursor to move to any position on the screen. Buttons on the cradle operate in the same fashion as buttons on a mouse.

TRANSCEIVER A device that transmits and receives signals, including those that describe images or documents, such as wirephotos and faxes.

TRANSDUCER (1) A general term for any device that produces one kind of energy from another kind, or that produces one type of signal from another type. (2) In electronics, a device that generates an electrical output, the strength of which is related to a physical characteristic, such as temperature, pressure, motion, etc. Transducers are used in automated control systems.

TRANSFER FUNCTION A function relationship between the input and output of a system. Examples include the Optical Transfer Function (OTF), Phase Transfer Function (PTF), and Modulation Transfer Function (MTF), which describe the relationship between the input and output of an optical or photographic system with respect to frequency. Sensitometric curves are also transfer functions in that they relate the input and output of a photographic system with respect to log luminance or density.

TRANSFORMATION EQUATIONS Equations by which colour matches made with one set of primary colours can be expressed in terms of another set.

TRANSITION EFFECTS In electronic imaging, the segueing from one scene into another through various procedures that are designed to maintain the attention of the viewer. Such effects are, for example, fade to black, fade to white, wipe vertical top down, wipe vertical bottom up, and shrink to a point. There are a umber of software packages that contain a large number of transition effects for graphics presentations.

TRANSMISSION DENSITY A measure of the absorption of light by a semitransparent sample, such as a film or filter. Transmission density is the common logarithm of the reciprocal of the transmittance.

TRANSPARENCY An image, usually positive, on a transparent or translucent base, intended to be viewed directly by transmitted light or indirectly as a projected image, or to be reproduced photographically, photomechanically, or electronically. Photographic images on transparency film have a considerably larger density range than photographic images or reproductions on white opaque bases, so that the luminance range of transparency images viewed directly or by projection, under the proper viewing conditions, is closer to that of the subject, thereby producing a perception of greater realism.

TRANSPARENCY VIEWER An enclosure that contains a light source, typically fluorescent tubes having a correlated colour temperature of 5000 K, under a diffusing panel, usually opal glass or plastic. Commonly used to examine negatives, slides, and transparencies, to display transparencies, and for layout work in graphic arts.

Syn.: *Transparency illuminator.*

TRANSPOSITION (1) The act of reversing the tonal values of an image from negative to positive or positive to negative. (2) The act of switching the relative positions of the left and right images in a stereophotographic pair.

TRIBOLUMINESCENCE The transformation of mechanical energy (such as friction) to light at low temperature (below those required for incandescence). A common example of triboluminscence is the light produced by removing some kinds of adhesive tape from surfaces in a darkroom.

TRICHROMAT Three colour. (1) Applied to a colour photographic process that comprises three sensitive materials, each sensitized to a different major region of the spectrum (red, green, and blue). The final image consists of varying amounts of three different dye layers (cyan, magenta, and yellow). (2) In colour television the red, green, and blue phosphors that constitute an additive system of colour reproduction. (3) Identifying a theory of colour vision that assumes the presence in the eye of three different sensors, each responsive to a different region of the visible spectrum.

TRICHROMATIC Adjective denoting association with the triple nature of colour or its reproduction.

TRICHROMATIC MATCHING Action of making a colour stimulus appear the same colour as a given stimulus by adjusting three components of an additive colour mixture.

TRILINEAR PLOT A graphical display used to show the direction and extent to which the colour balance of an image differs from that of an aim point, typically a neutral, using a grid containing three sets of parallel lines placed at angles of 120 degrees to each other. The three lines that radiate from a central aim point represent red, green, and blue additive primary colours. Extensions of these three lines beyond the aim point represent cyan, magenta, and yellow subtractive primary colours. The plot can be used, for example, for quality control purposes in colour processing and printing labs. Densitometer readings made with red, green, and blue light provide the data needed for plotting.

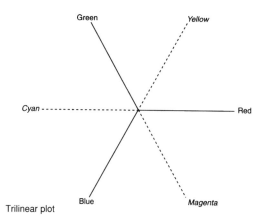

Trilinear plot

TRUE COLOUR In electronic imaging, the use of 16,777,216 colours for display description purposes. This standard is a 24-bit display system, i.e., 8 bits for the red channel, 8 bits for the green channel, and 8 bits for the blue channel. True colour is the equivalent of photographic quality.

TV CUTOFF That part of a slide, motion picture, or other image that will not be included in the picture area of a reproduction on a television screen.

UNDERCOLOUR ADDITION In photomechanical reproduction, the technique of adding yellow, magenta, and cyan (YMC) in dark neutral areas to improve the saturation of the shadow areas of the reproduction.

UNDERCOLOUR REMOVAL In photomechanical reproduction, the technique of reducing all three (YMC) colours on colour separation films in neutral areas and replacing them with an equivalent amount of black ink. This improves trapping and reduces colour ink costs.

UNDERSAMPLING In electronic imaging, the sampling of an analog signal at less than the Nyquist theorem.

UNDERSCANNING In electronic imaging, the displaying of a raster image so that the scanning raster is visible. Underscanning, although infrequently used, ensures that image data are not hidden.

UNEVENNESS Unevenness refers to variation of density in an area that represents a uniform subject tone or a variation of colour in an area that represents a uniform subject colour. While often less easily detected, it may modify areas of modulated density and colour.

Unevenness of a processed photographic image may be due to a number of causes. The defect is often masked by detail in images of scenes that do not contain large areas of uniform tone. Other subject matter may be very critical of this kind of defect. One cause of unevenness is improper agitation of the film during processing. Another cause might be the presence of a film of oil or other water-repelling material on the surface of the film at the time it is processed. A malfunctioning camera focal plane shutter may cause uneven illumination across the film plane.

When the film is printed, an improperly adjusted enlarger or contact printer may be the cause of uneven illumination of the sensitized material at the time of exposure.

UNIFORM CHROMATICITY DIAGRAM Chromaticity diagram in which equal distances approximately represent equal colour differences for stimuli having the same luminance.

UNIFORM COLOUR SPACE Colour space in which equal distances approximately represent equal colour differences.

UNIQUE HUE Perceived hue that cannot be further described by the use of hue names other than its own; there are four unique hues: red, green, yellow, and blue.

UNSHARP MASKING FILTER In electronic imaging, the digital counterpart of photographic unsharp masking. This digital equivalent uses a neighbourhood process to subtract an unsharp (smooth) image from the original image.

UNWANTED ABSORPTIONS In subtractive systems of colour reproduction, each of the three colourants should absorb only in the reddish third of the spectrum (in the case of the cyan colourant), in the greenish third (in the case of the magenta colourant), or in the bluish third (in the case of the yellow colourant). The dyes and pigments that have to be used as colourants in practice, however, also absorb in other parts of the spectrum. Cyan colourants usually have considerable unwanted green absorption and some unwanted blue absorption. Magenta colourants usually have considerable unwanted blue absorption and some unwanted red absorption. Yellow colourants usually have some unwanted green absorption but no unwanted red absorption. These unwanted absorptions, if uncorrected, make colours darker than they should be. In colour photography they are corrected by the use of coloured couplers and interimage effects. In colour printing they are corrected by the use of masks in making the separation images. These masks can be on photographic materials used in register with the images being used or their equivalent can be provided electronically in scanners. When film is used in television, electronic masking is used in telecine equipment. Telecine: equipment for replaying motion-picture film into a television system.

UNWANTED STIMULATIONS In trichromatic systems, ideally one primary should excite the long wavelength cones (ρ), another the middle wavelength cones (γ), and the third the short wavelength cones (β). Because the spectral sensitivities of these three types of cones overlap considerably, however, it is not possible to stimulate them separately. Thus, red light stimulates not only the ρ cones but also to some extent the γ cones, and blue light stimulates not only the β cones but also to some extent the γ cones. The worst case is for green light, which not only stimulates the γ cones but also stimulates the ρ cones considerably and the β cones to some extent. These unwanted stimulations mean that it is not possible to match the colours of the spectrum with mixtures of red, green, and blue light without sometimes having to add one, or occasionally two, of the matching stimuli to the colour being matched. When this is done, those amounts of the matching stimuli are regarded as negative. In colour reproduction, the unwanted stimulations caused by the primaries in additive systems, or by the equivalent primaries in subtractive systems, result in the reproduction gamut being limited, so that some colours can never be reproduced. They also result in the theoretically correct set of spectral sensitivity curves for the system having some negative lobes. The most important effect is that some blue-green colours cannot be reproduced, and the sensitivity curve required for the red channel or layer should have a considerable negative lobe in the blue-green part of the spectrum.

USEFUL LIFE The length of time during which a device or processing solution can be used with only unimportant loss of quality. For example, the useful life of a tungsten lamp is approximately half its total lifetime to burnout.

U,V DIAGRAM Uniform chromaticity diagram introduced by the CIE in 1960 but now superseded by the u',v' diagram.

$$u = 4X/(X + 15Y + 3Z)$$
$$v = 6Y/(X + 15Y + 3Z)$$

u´,v´ DIAGRAM Uniform chromaticity diagram introduced by the CIE in 1976.

$$u' = 4X/(X + 15Y + 3Z)$$
$$v' = 9Y/(X + 15Y + 3Z)$$

U*,V*,W* SYSTEM Obsolete colour space in which U^*, V^*, W^* are plotted at right angles to one another. Equal distances in the space were intended to represent approximately equal colour differences.

$$U^* = 13W^*(u - u_n)$$
$$V^* = 13W^*(v - v_n)$$
$$W^* = 25Y^{1/3} - 17$$

where $u = 4X/(X + 15Y + 3Z)$ and $v = 6Y/(X + 15Y + 3Z)$ and the subscript n indicates that the value is for the reference white; Y is the luminance factor expressed as a percentage. This colour space has been superseded by the CIELAB and CIELUV systems.

VALUE (1) In the Munsell system, a lightness scale where 0 represents an ideal nonreflecting black and 10 an ideal white having 100% reflectance. (2) In the zone system, a scale of relative subject luminances, subject values, using roman numerals from 0 to X where each higher number represents double the subject luminance, or a scale of corresponding print tones, identified as print values. (3) In the additive system of photographic exposure (APEX) system, scales for five major variables, identified as exposure value, (lens) aperture value, (subject) luminance value, (film) speed value, and (shutter) time value.

VECTOR A line whose length is related to the magnitude of a measurement and which has a specific direction. Vectors are used, for example, to show the pattern of light reflected from a surface.

VECTORGRAPHICS In electronic imaging, graphics that are displayed on the cathode-ray tube (CRT) as represented by a mathematical description. This mathematical description causes the CRT to scan the pattern as described and not according to a raster pattern. The result is a very high quality graphic without jagged edges. Vector graphics are displayed slowly because of the mathematical description.

VECTOR IMAGE See *Vectorgraphics.*

VECTORSCOPE An oscilloscope used to monitor the position (and direction from a neutral position) of the colours red, green, blue, cyan, magenta, and yellow. The video equivalent of a CIE diagram.

VIDEO CASSETTE RECORDER (VCR) An electronic device that is capable of recording television and related input onto magnetic tape in a video cassette (as distinct from reel-to-reel tape systems) and playing them or prerecorded video cassettes back through a television receiver.

VIDEO COLOUR NEGATIVE ANALYZER (VCNA) A closed-circuit colour television system designed to display a positive colour image of a colour film negative on a monitor. Calibrated controls for image brightness and colour balance make it possible to transfer data from the VCNA to a colour enlarger to reduce or eliminate tests when making a colour print from the negative.

VIDEODISC An audiovisual recording (of a television program or motion picture, for example) on a circular, flat, and rotatable medium, designed for playback on a television set.
  Syn.: *Laser videodisc.*

VIDEO FOR PHOTOGRAPHERS
THE PERVASIVENESS OF VIDEO IN SOCIETY

Nothing in human history save the great religious traditions has shaped the hopes, fears, and aspirations of as many millions of people as has the phenomenon of television. The medium gives us our news, informs our opinions on world events, persuades us what to buy and how to live, shows us lifestyles we can aspire to, entertains us with comedy and human adventure, takes us along to the theatre, the orchestra, and the opera, puts us *on the spot* for the repeated witnessing of the major events in our world, and, in general, offers us a complete vicarious existence on a scale that is unheard of in human history.

The core of what we call television is video, the relatively simple recording and playback devices with which we make these images in their myriad forms. Video is not just the technology of television, however, it is also a medium that has become widely and inexpensively available to millions of amateurs who use it to record important events in their lives. One can hardly think of a public event, a ceremony, or a popular vacation spot without envisioning dozens of people videotaping the action. More and more people are recording family snapshot occasions on videotape.

Correspondingly, and particularly with the availability of smaller, lighter, inexpensive, and user-friendly camcorders, video has been steadily taking over an increasing share of the traditional market for photography. This is true of both the amateur and the commercial markets. The public has come to accept—and frequently insist on—videotapes. Independent of how the photographer may feel about this new demand for video, becoming competent at producing it is now a necessity for surviving in the more competitive markets such as wedding and prom photography. The demand for, and expectation of, video have actually grown to the point that clients are now beginning to ask for two-camera, edited videotapes.

This growing demand is a major incentive for photographers to learn the basics of video production. There is almost no limit to the new markets for educational, documentary, advertising, and studio videotapes. As a basic strategy, photographers are advised to start by offering video products for the clientele and type of business they are already familiar with and then, after gaining experience, to consider exploring new areas. This makes the move to video a logical extension of present operations. Significantly, photographers already know the aesthetics and the business aspects of this kind of creative work.

This article will give a focused introduction of video. It begins by exploring what video is and how it works, describing the equipment and features to look for and telling how to set up a single- or multiple-camera operation. Following the equipment overview, how to visualize and plan video productions, how to make good videotapes, how to do basic editing, and then how to market this new product, will be covered. There is also a glossary of terms. All of this information is intended to help the photographer to actually begin making videotapes or to communicate with jobbers or production houses regarding clients' needs.

SIMILARITIES AND DIFFERENCES—PHOTO-GRAPHY AND VIDEO Photographers already know many of the fundamentals of producing high-quality video. The basic unit of video production is the shot: photographers are skilled in selecting or creating sets, positioning people and other elements within the frame and in relation to the background, creating interpretative lighting effects, and eliciting responses or poses from people being photographed. All of this is essential to creating a good shot in video. Photographers are also knowledgeable about the technical aspects of lenses, including f-numbers, focal length, and depth-of-field as they affect exposure, image size, depth illusions, and the selective uses of focus.

There are, however, two principle differences between still photography and video that must be taken into account when making the change-over: video is an electronic technology, and video is a motion medium. The first, the electronic nature of video is relatively easy to learn, and one can become quite competent at it in a short period of time. One way to regard this is to consider video equipment much like a home stereo (phonic) unit: there are components with different functions that hook together in specific ways to achieve the desired result. The other attribute, that video is a motion medium, is a bit more complex to master at the creative level. The "Video Production" section will provide insights into both of these characteristics and how they can be taken advantage of in order to get started with video.

HOW VIDEO WORKS Video is a system that converts the energy of light into an electronic image. The lens on a video camera focuses light reflected from a subject onto a photosensitive surface; relative amounts of light are registered as electronic impulses with different charges by an electronic gun (a magnetically controlled arc) scanning this surface. The electronic impulses generated by the optical image and sensed by the scan gun are, in turn, conveyed to either a recording or a playback device where the image is stored or the scanning process is repeated in reverse for playback. The electronic gun scans 625 horizontal lines on the photo-sensitive surface to make a complete picture. The scan pattern is from left to right, top to bottom, and the beam of the scan gun is on only during the left-to-right passes. There are two scanning cycles for each complete image of 625 lines. Scanning one-half of the 625 lines in this manner is called a *field*. For example, the first *field is* a scan of the 312 1/2 odd numbered lines and the second field is a scan of the remaining 312 1/2 even numbered lines. Two complete scans or fields make one complete image called a *frame*. The gun scan at a rate of 25 frames (50 fields) per second; (this explains why it is necessary to use a shutter speed of 1/25th or slower when photographing a television set or computer screen).

The photosensitive surface on which the lens focuses the optical images was historically the internal sensing surface of a vacuum tube. Generally speaking, the larger the tube or the more there were of them in the camera, the better the reproduction quality of the system. In the early years, tubes were large and expensive, especially on broadcast-quality equipment. Remember the pictures of the huge RCA studio cameras from the early years of television? Gradually, the big image orthicon (IO) tubes were replaced by smaller but very efficient vidicon tubes; these were generally replaced by saticon tubes, or some variation thereof, which are still in common use today. The field of video technology has, as is the case with all electronics, moved to smaller and lighter equipment without much sacrifice in image quality, and the cost of tubes has dropped from an IO tube costing thousands of pounds to a vidicon tube costing two or three hundred pounds. Even with the less costly tube technology, however, it is important to keep in mind that tube size should match the video format: use 3/4-inch or larger tubes for 3/4-inch videotape units. The use of smaller than format tubes, for example, 1/2-inch tube camera with a 3/4-inch deck, will result in a loss of image quality.

Tubes are now beginning to be replaced with charge coupled devices (CCDs). These are sensor chips with mosaic-like cells (pixels) that the camera's pickup system reads directly. They offer the potential of much smaller and lighter cameras without sacrificing reproductions quality. Formerly, with tubes, resolution was measured in the number of horizontal lines that could be reproduced (much like the line pairs-per-millimeter resolution tests for photographic lenses); now, with CCD equipment, resolution is determined by the number of pixels per unit of measure.

The video image, once it has been picked up electronically from the tube or CCD receptor in the camera, can be distributed in a number of ways or in combinations thereof: it can be transmitted via the airwaves (broadcast) or through cable (narrowcast), viewed directly on a monitor (a *monitor* is a television set that does not have a tuner to select different channels but that does have jacks on the back to accept video and audio inputs) or receiver (a receiver is a conventional television set with a tuner dial to select channels) or it can be recorded by a videotape recorder.

VIDEO EQUIPMENT CONSIDERATIONS
General Considerations

Format Selection During the early years of videotape, the late 1960s through the late 1970s, formats (the sizes of the tape and the means for encoding electronic information on them) were not standard. Each company that made recording equipment designed its own system. This meant that, while each one may have worked fine, tapes made on company A's machine could not be played on company B's deck. Buying into a system was risky: you took a chance on both the survival of the company and on the public acceptance of the format. Photographic film and plate sizes were like this well into the 1920s. Eventually, the early reel-to-reel video formats were standardized into U-Matic for 3/4-inch and EIAJ for 1/2-inch. With the advent of 1/2-inch cassette machines in the late 1970s Sony's Beta and Panasonic's VHS competed for market dominance. Many commercial and educational video users held off selecting one of these in anticipation of a new standard being developed for 1/2-inch cassette (one requirement of a new standard is that it not be an existing format). Eventually, however, it became clear that a new standard would not be forthcoming, and, in these early years, purchasers bought into both Beta and VHS. VHS gained almost all of this market over time and dominates the 1/2-inch cassette format market. VHS is also the most commonly used wedding format.

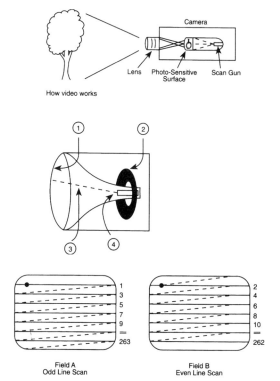

How video works

Video scanning. (1) Coated surface; (2) magnetic coil; (3) scanning arc; (4) scan gun.

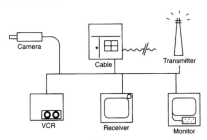

Video signal distribution.

The size and quality of video equipment selected should be determined by the intended end uses. As with photographic film, the larger the videotape, other things being equal, the higher the quality of the image, but large tape equipment is very expensive. Begin by ascertaining the minimum tape size that will do the job at the level of quality required. A size of 3/4-inch or larger tape is needed to achieve broadcast quality and is desirable for tapes that will be duplicated; beyond that there is a range of choices. The small 8-mm format is fine for home use or even some in-house corporate applications, provided the tapes will be used in direct video playback setups and that it will not be necessary to duplicate the tapes for distribution. The midrange of 1/2-inch formats includes a wide array of quality ranging from the standard VHS through Super-VHS, Beta-Cam, and the newer High-8, which, although not 1/2-inch, is becoming increasingly popular in this market. VHS is the most widely used of these formats, and there is a considerable range of price and quality in the available equipment. VHS is fine for nearly all direct video uses—that is one of the reasons it is so widely used. Also VHS equipment is priced from just a few hundred pounds to several thousand; it is possible to enter the videotape sales market with modest equipment in the VHS format and then, as business warrants, expand in modular fashion (but be cautioned about modularity and compatibility).

Beyond VHS in terms of resolutions and price, check into Super-VHS, Beta-Cam, or the new and modular High-8 format. The High-8 format features an interchangeable module (like a film back) that can be changed to convert the system from regular 8-mm to High-8. These higher quality systems, including 3/4-inch, 1-inch, and 2-inches, are very expensive and—although the principles given in this article apply to all formats—it is advisable to talk with someone versed in these systems (not just sales personnel) before purchasing one of them.

Tubes or Charge Coupled Devices? Most of the camera equipment on the market in the 1/2-inch or larger formats uses tubes rather than CCDs. CCDs are a new technology and they have been designed more for 8-mm and 1/2-inch video than for larger systems. Well made tube-type cameras offer excellent resolution and colour fidelity and will provide many years of service. CCD cameras promise to offer higher resolution for a given camera size, they are smaller and lighter than tube cameras, and bright lights do not burn an image into the CCD receptor plate as they can do with tubes (if video cameras with tubes are pointed directly at a bright light or reflected source, the light can burn a permanent image into the tube and a ghost image will appear in all subsequent pictures). The reader is advised to follow the developments in this new digital technology for the preferred format, as with any camera, silver-gelatin or electronic, use it under normal working conditions to see how well it suits your needs. Electronic specifications and technical sheets can provide general information, but only actual use can determine which camera is right for you.

Portability There is a truism in the trade that if it has a handle on it, it's portable. This was more humorous years ago because equipment was much heavier and bulkier than it is now. Later, we will suggest keeping video cameras on tripods insofar as possible. Even if used on a tripod, however, it is necessary to consider the size and weight of a system for the conditions under which it will be used. This consideration is particularly important for those who want to transport equipment frequently by air, especially into remote regions. Camcorders, especially CCD models, are the smallest and lightest of the configurations available.

Durability Some systems especially the Panasonic camcorders—have developed a reputation in the trade as being particularly durable and are in widespread use. Others have gained a reputation for being fragile or sensitive to humidity or other factors. One good measure of durability is the reputation a unit has with other users and with repair shops.

Standardization and System Adaptability Standardization and adaptability are especially important when buying or upgrading multiple camera operations. One chronic problem in video is that equipment does not tend to stay in production very long, at least not without being modified (improved). In addition, some cameras and accessory equipment use specialized versions of multipin connectors. Often, if a new or longer cable is needed for one of these a few weeks or months after being purchased, it may by then have been discontinued. This is a matter that can be checked out with local service people. An insurance procedure is to buy extras of these kinds of things at the time of the initial purchase.

Cost and Service Factors Video is such a competitive industry that cost will be determined more by the format and the type of camera than by brand differences alone. With electronics, and particularly with video electronics, you get what you pay for. While on this topic, it is better to invest in quality and simplicity than to buy a lot of gadgetry (see the section "Camera Features").

Service factors are important to business operations, and they are even more important when the business is highly dependent on (sometimes) temperamental electronic equipment. A good, local service centre for the brand of video equipment being considered is important. As with still photography equipment, arrangements should be made for backup emergency service and/or loan equipment. You do not want to have to send a camcorder to Osaka in the middle of a busy wedding season: plan for emergencies before they happen.

These general considerations will help you think through the broad questions regarding video formats and kinds of equipments. Next we will discuss the specific equipment features (some desirable, some not) that will be encountered when putting together a single-camera system.

Video System Design: Single Camera Systems Unfortunately, video cameras do not usually come as complete, ready-to-use systems. This is particularly true when moving in the high-end amateur and professional grades of equipment. Photographers should be somewhat accustomed to this: it resembles the way camera bodies are often sold independent of lenses. It need not be a problem provided one is aware of what comes with the equipment or—more importantly—what does not.

In considering the following features of contemporary video equipment, keep in mind, as with still photography, a camera is a box designed to hold the lens, image recording system, and a monitor/viewfinder. Beyond that, features become more and more discretionary, and at some point they can become distractions at best or systems that will need repair at worst. As with most crafts, tools are essential, but it is ultimately the videographers application of the tool, not extra features, that will create excellence.

Camera Features The new video cameras have a host of electronic features; indeed, there almost seems to be a new feature contest among manufacturers. Up to some point camera features can make your work easier. It is advisable to put your purchase money into the quality of the basic elements of the system before considering a lot of extra features. Simple, high-quality equipment will provide better and longer service than lower-cost equipment and/or versions with more complex gadgetry. To the argument that these are all space age electronics, remember that, in aerospace applications, there are three to seven backup systems for every function: here there are none.

Some things to check on a video camera for professional photography would include the following:

Manual White Balance Modern colour video cameras need to have the white balance set for the lighting conditions. This is analogous to selecting daylight (5500 K) or tungsten (3200 K) film for outdoor or studio use. There are two ways this is done with video. On older systems and on professional equipment, the white balance is set manually by turning the system on, holding a white card in front of the lens, and pressing a WB switch. For taping where the colour fidelity is important (every professional application), this is done every time the camera is turned off and on or moved to a different lighting environment. Some cameras have a WB memory: with these cameras you will not have to reset the WB unless you change the lighting situation. Newer and lower cost video cameras often have an automatic white balance feature. But this should be field tested under varying lighting conditions to determine if it will give consistent, professional quality hue and chroma. You may prefer to set the white balance manually.

Power Saving Mode Power saving mode is a small but useful feature. Basically, it turns off all but the essential electronics if the system has been left in *pause* or *standby* mode. The system draws very little electricity until the moment the *record* button is pressed, but the moment it is, it is ready to operate. This is particularly beneficial when operating in the *battery* mode in the field.

External Microphone Jack, Audio Monitor, and Gain Set Most of the video cameras in the 8-mm and VHS formats have built-in microphones, which are not very useful for professional applications. Unless the camera is very close to what is being taped and is situated in an acoustically dampened place, you tend to get more noise than signal with these systems. In a later section, we will talk about using microphones; meanwhile, look for a camera that has a MIC jack for an external microphone and a DUB or AUD[IO] MON jack for a small earphone so you can play back short segments in the field to check the audio track. It is also desirable to purchase a system that allows the audio record level to be set with a knob and a VU meter rather than having the equipment do it with something like AGC (automatic gain control). This may be hard to find on anything less than professional grade (expensive) equipment.

Fade and Dissolve Control Fades and similar shot transitions are best done during the editing phase, but many videographers find it useful to have a fade or dissolve feature built into the camera. This feature is usually simple to operate: press the FADE button and then RECORD and the camera fades up from black to the shot; or, conversely, press FADE with the camera running in RECORD and it slowly fades from the shot to black. The challenge is to know, as you are taping, just when to fade in and out of a shot.

Built-in Timers and Character Generators Most professional photographers getting into video productions will have little use for either of these features. The built-in time code displays—which record and then play back the date and time on the lower part of the taped image—can be useful for certain clinical or research applications where this visual frame referability is important, but for most people they are a nuisance. Users sometimes forget to turn them off while taping and ruin client tapes with this flashing clock overlay.

Character generators, small keypads with numbers and letters that can be used to add type to the leader, trailer, or the visual image on the tape, could be useful if the videographer wanted to add short titles or credits to a tape and did not have access to editing or other graphics capabilities. Some of these systems permit the user to superimpose letters and numbers over a previously recorded image, whereas others require the image and the text be taped simultaneously. There is a wide range of quality of the textual graphics and the options for applying them. Be sure to check the size, style, and legibility of the type, and look for user-friendly instructions. Most are not really complex, but they seem to intimidate the public—like the continuously flashing clock on home VCRs.

Lenses The standards that a photographer applies to the selection of lenses are all relevant to video lens selection. These standards include criteria for coverage, corrections, focal length, maximum aperture, contrast, resolving capability, and focusing distance. Coverage in this case would mean a lens is capable of covering the size of the tube or the CCD receptor plate in the video camera; corrections for chromatic and other aberrations would need to meet the standards of the productions anticipated. One important difference between lenses for still photographer and lenses tor video is that nearly all lenses marketed for video use have C mounts and zoom (variable focal lengths) design. C-mount has been the standard thread mount size in cinematography for many decades; it is now also the standard in high-quality video equipment. One new variation is that some companies now offer video cameras with bayonet mounts that are designed to accept the more popular 35-mm still camera lenses. This could be a way to use your own camera lenses on the video camera, but keep in mind that a normal lens for a 1/2-inch VHS video format has a focal length on the order of 25 mm; however 35-mm camera lenses on a 3/4- or 1-inch video system approximate the focal length effect they give the still camera.

Aperture The zoom lenses normally available for video offer maximum apertures in the $f/2.8$ to $f/4$ range, which are fine for most taping in daylight and under controlled lighting conditions. For frequent taping under low light conditions, look for a camera and lens specifically designed for low light use.

Auto-Iris Control Most of the equipment offered for sale today will have a lens with some kind of automatic exposure control. While this works well under certain conditions, it would be desirable to have a lock or manual override provision for those times when the automatic function fails to achieve the desired result.

Zoom Characteristics Lenses for video cameras come in variable focal lengths, with ranges from about 6:1 to 12:1, with the price increasing with the zoom ratio. For most professional applications, a range of about 10:1 should suffice. Again, the advice here is to test the characteristics under normal working conditions. For example, sports and wildlife photographers would want a longer focal length than someone who specialized in taping weddings.

Most of these zoom lenses are electronic, operating with a variation of the telephoto wide-angle rocker switch. When examining lenses, try to find one that allows the *speed* of the focal length change to be adjusted: many are fixed-speed and move too fast for a pleasing effect during general videotaping. If the electronic speed of the zoom cannot be adjusted, look for one that can be operated by hand when necessary.

One final lens feature, remote control, may be desirable for your operation. Remote control permits you to mount the camera on a tripod and control both the zoom and focus functions from handles located conveniently on the rear of the tripod head control arms. If the lens offers this option, there will be receptacles on the barrel for remote focus and remote zoom controls.

Autofocusing Autofocusing is a standard feature on most video lenses, and under a wide range of working conditions, it works fine. Professional equipment should, however, offer both a focus lock and a manual focusing capability.

Macro-focusing Most of the newer zoom lenses for video use offer some degree of macro-focusing. This feature is not usually a true macro capability of 1:1 (nor is it designed specifically for extreme closeup work or flat field reproduction), but it will permit closeup images of 1:4 or 1:6, which can be useful. There is normally a lock of some kind to prevent the lens from moving into macro mode during routine autofocus travel.

Filter Diameter Still-camera filters can be used on a video camera with step-up ring for glass filters or a fitted holder for gelatin filters.

Video Recorders Video recorders today are smaller and lighter and easier to operate than they were in the recent past. They have gone from being large, heavy units weighing 30 to 50 pounds and costing thousands of dollars through progressive miniaturization to about the size of a briefcase, and their price has fallen to a few hundred dollars. They have also become much easier for people to use without professional training.

Video recorders are devices housing the record/playback machinery and electronics, control switches, and often battery packs. Much of what used to be overly complex and problematic has been eliminated by design. Still, there are some features and characteristics the photographer would do well to consider during the selection process.

Camcorders vs. Separate Decks The choice of a type of VCR may be precluded by purchasing a system that only comes as a camcorder or as a separate camera and recorder unit; with others you may have the choice. The most popular configuration is the camcorder, which contains both the camera and the video recorder. These combined units, particularly those with the newer CCD type cameras, are smaller and lighter than were their equivalent format cameras just a few years ago. The reason for the popularity of the camcorder is understandable: there is less equipment to carry around and fewer wires and switches to contend with. For most photographers getting into the video market, a high quality VHS camcorder would be a good choice.

There is, in spite of the popularity of the camcorder, one real advantage to having separate camera and recorder units: if there is a breakdown in one piece, you don't have to send both of them in for repair. Having two separate cameras and two decks will provide a backup capability in the field.

Ease of Operation Ease of operation is partly a technical factor and partly a personal one. Do consider the relative clarity of control buttons and the simplicity or complexity of their operation with regard to your employees as well as yourself.

Power Sources All professional equipment should offer the choice of AC or DC operation, and accessory, rechargeable battery packs should be readily available. Although AC operation is always preferable, there are times and situations where it is necessary to operate the video equipment on batteries. Purchase the battery units (and their charger, if not a part of the system) *at the time you buy the equipment.* There are some unpleasant stories in the trade about someone buying into a particular equipment manufacturer's line only to come back a few weeks or months later to purchase an important accessory and finding out that the product had been discontinued.

Unfortunately, this is almost as true of the big names as it is of lesser-known ones: the electronics field changes rapidly, and companies, in order to try to stay competitive, are constantly changing product lines. Also, buy about twice as many of the rechargeable battery packs as you think you will need. Then study the literature that comes with them so you know how to keep them in good condition over time. Some, for example, require special kinds of deep discharging before recharging to counteract their charge memory.

Power Saving Mode As with the previous camera discussion, a power saving device can help conserve precious battery power in the field and is a desirable feature.

Audio Monitor Jack You need an audio monitor jack to play back and check the audio recorded in the field; the jack can be on the camera or on the recorder deck (it does not need to be on both).

Microphone and Audio Dub This input can be used to plug in an external microphone (MIC) or to plug in a sound source like an audio cassette player (DUB) to add music or sound effects to a tape, and you can do this either while you are making the videotape or at a later time. Read the VCR instructions carefully to determine what kinds of source audio can be used. Normally, a MIC jack will only take an unamplified signal (microphone), whereas a DUB jack will take an amplified one (audiocassette player). If you cross these, you will get a loud hiss or hum in the audio track.

Remote Operation Remote operation is a very desirable switch on a separate VCR unit. It enables the user to control all of the play and record functions of the VCR with the camera's control system. The recorder is set in *remote* and then activated with the controls on the camera body. The main advantage of this switch is that it permits the camera operator to stay with and be attentive to the camera during a recording session without having to go back and forth between the two units.

Receivers and Monitors The home television set is a receiver: it has a tuner that can be operated to select different frequencies (channels) for reception. A monitor is a television set without the tuner. It is wired directly to a video camera or VCR for playback; it also has a number of jacks on the back (this is called *Jeeped*) to accept cables for audio and video signals, in and out. Monitors are necessary for editing systems and studio applications, but you can get by with a high quality receiver for most other work. Receivers are considerably less expensive than monitors for comparable screen size and quality—this is why video professionals usually use small (8 to 10-inch) black and white monitors for editing and studio production and large colour receivers for client screenings.

Cables Cables can be problematic in video production in three ways: they are frequently too short—as supplied—for your needs, they do not have the right connectors, or they malfunction (like PC cords for electronic flash). The message here is buy cables that are longer than you think you will need, make sure they have the right connectors, buy extras of everything, and have a supply of connector adaptors on hand. Video is known for the numerous cables it requires to hook equipment together. Two recent trends have helped alleviate this problem: the all-in-one studio cable and the camcorder. Still, it is necessary to think ahead and be prepared.

There are several kinds of connectors in common use. The VIDEO and BNC pins are used for audio jacks; and the RF and

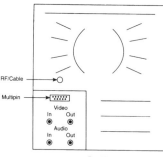

RF/Cable

Multipin

Video
In   Out
⊙   ⊙
Audio
In   Out
⊙   ⊙

Monitor jacks.

Rear View

MULTIPIN pins are used for composite signals (both video and audio). There are male and female adaptors for all of these (except some MINIPIN's that are specific to the make and model of equipment). PHONE and MINI connectors can be either stereo (the pin has two insulting bands near the tip) or monaural (the pin has one insulting band near the tip). Only a few of these connectors are needed for routine work.Talk to the dealer when purchasing equipment to make sure to get the right connectors or adaptors. All of these connectors are readily available from video dealers and repair shops except some of the brand-specific MULTIPINs: get extras of those (and longer cables) at the time you buy the equipment.

Electronic News Gathering Kits Electronic news gathering (ENG) kits are portable configuration kits for video cameras. Such a kit will usually include a should harness system for the camera, a small monitor (if the camera normally mounts a large one), extra-long cables, and a travel case. Some of them include luggage carts, which can be useful for rolling the unit around on location.

Pedestals and Tripods The large studio stands for cameras are called pedestals. These are hydraulically and/or electronically operated and provide great stability and mobility over a smooth, flat surface. Outside the studio, most video work is accomplished using sturdy tripods, sometimes with the legs inserted into a dolly (a rig with wheels under it). Any durable tripod used for still photography work fine for video, provided it will take the weight of the video camera or camcorder.

Heads and Movement Dampening The special heads made for video and cinema tripods normally offer pan and tilt movements, and they are dampened against jarring or shock. This dampening is done with springs or hydraulics, depending on the price, and it helps stabilize the camera during taping. Dampening is only marginally useful under calm and controlled conditions with prearranged shots; it is particularly valuable if taping is done under adverse conditions and/or if a lot of camera movement is required. Practice camera movement until you become proficient at doing it smoothly and then, if you still need dampening, investigate these heads for your tripod.

Dollies A dolly for your tripod will be useful if you need to move the camera around a lot within a confined area; the wheels will save the labour of picking up the camera and tripod for each move, which, at the end of a long day, can make an important difference in your fatigue level.

Microphones It is more important to use an external microphone that it is to be concerned about the type or brand. Built-in microphones usually pick up as much noise as they do signal. There are some characteristics you should be aware of.

Pickup Patterns Microphones do not *hear* all of the sound around them: they are sensitive to different patterns of reception (pickup patterns). These patterns range from the almost 360° sensitivity of an omni microphone through the heart-shaped patter of a cardioid to the extreme directionality of a shotgun model. The most useful microphones for general video use is the cardioid pattern, but do consider the kind of recording capability your needs dictate: for people sitting around a small table in a conference room, an omni-directional pattern would be best; for recording specific sound sources at greater than normal distances, a shotgun pickup pattern would better isolate the signal from the noise.

Styles Microphone styles are governed by their intended installation as well as their pickup patterns. There are three installation types in common use: *boom, hand-held,* and *lava-liere.* The boom microphones, as the name implies, are large and designed to be mounted on a stand; most of them have wide (omni) pickup patterns. Hand-held microphones are the most widely used type and come in a variety of reception patterns. These are the kind singers and television news people use on

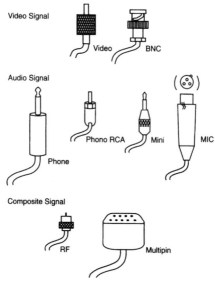

Cables. Cable connectors.

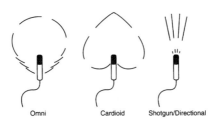

Pickup patterns of microphones.

stage or on location. The most readily available versions of hand-held microphones feature some variant of the cordioid pattern. Lavaliere microphones are the small *button* microphones that can be clipped to a lapel, commonly used by commentators on television. These, too, usually have a cordioid reception pattern.

Power Sources Microphones operate by converting sound waves to electronic impulses by means of a diaphragm; sound waves move the diaphragm, which, in turn, excites a coil in a magnetic field. The simplest of them, the ceramic microphones, are quite limited in their sensitivity. Dynamic microphones respond to a much wider range of sound waves (frequencies) and are a considerable improvement over ceramic models. Dynamic microphones are also very durable and are sensitive enough for most VCR applications.

Microphone sound pickup is greatly improved by adding an internal amplifier. The amplified microphones require battery or AC power, and they range in quality and price from the electret condenser through condenser models to the ribbon type. The electret condenser would be a good, high end choice for VCR use (particularly a lavaliere model). The frequently sensitivity of most condenser and ribbon microphones far surpasses the audio recording ability of VCRs, and their high cost would not be justified.

Microphone Cables and Wireless Models First a note on cables: as with video, microphone cables should be long enough to handle all anticipated needs. These cables are relatively inexpensive, so having extra and longer ones in your kit is sound practice.

The new wireless (transmitter) models have decreased dramatically in price in the past few years, and they can be very convenient to work with. This type can be clipped to a person in an inconspicuous way, the wire to the small transmitter box can be hidden under clothing, and the sound quality is excellent. They do have batteries to contend with (carry rechargeable spares), but there are no long cables to worry about. Always check the effective range of the transmitter to see that it meets the needs of the situation.

In summary, unless your working needs dictate otherwise, the least expensive means to obtain high quality audio would be to start with a condenser-type, hand-held microphone with a foam rubber windscreen over it to filter extraneous noise.

Portable Lights Most videographers find they work under conditions that, at least some of the time, require the addition of illumination to obtain satisfactory image quality. Here there is a wide variety of choice. The small, easily portable 500-watt quartz lights that operate on AC power are an inexpensive system if AC power is available on location and if they can be placed where they are needed. Obviously they would not work well at a wedding or a reception unless they are set up before the event. It might work to place just one or two at strategic locations, provided the celebrants would agree to being *hot lighted.*

The most widely used portable video lighting is a battery powered system that consists of a quartz lamp in a reflector, mounted on or near the camera, and a separate power source. It is better to get the light off of the camera to approximate studio main light modelling rather than that on-camera. Systems like this are priced from less than one hundred dollars to thousands of dollars. As with studio lights for still photography, the price directly reflects the quality of construction, output of the lamp, and the amp hour capacity of the power pack.

The power of the light required will depend on the lamp to-subject distance, and how large an area you need to cover will determine how many lamps are required. The duration of taping will dictate your needs for a power source (all lights should offer rechargeable batteries and an AC power option). It would be a good idea here to look into one of the major supplier's modular systems: you can start with a simple setup and then add to it later as your needs grow. You can learn a lot about portable lighting systems by talking to local wedding videographers, news people, and—if you live in a city—local video equipment dealers and their service technicians.

Multiple Camera Systems This section will cover the basic information required in order to set up a multiple camera option. If your needs dictate a more advanced operation than is discussed here, it is advisable to study what is required by reading books designed to cover studio operations and to retain the services of a broadcast engineer (call any radio or television station to find one) or other knowledgeable expert to advise you on the project. Keep in mind that most of what has been said regarding single camera systems is also applicable to multiple camera systems.

When, and for what purposes, should you consider using more than one camera? For many photographers who are getting started in video, one camera will perform adequately. Basically, as long as you can stop the event in progress and/or move the camera from one position to another to obtain the necessary shot, one camera is enough. Additional cameras are required when it is necessary to be in more than one location at a time, or when you want more than one view of a subject to select from later (during editing).

The progression of complexity and expense goes from single camera taping through multiple camera taping to *switched* operations. In multiple camera taping, two or more cameras are placed at different locations and each one records a separate videotape; these tapes can be edited into one product later. In the switched operations, two or more cameras feed their signals into a central control point, where only one of them is selected for recording (switched) at any given moment. Single camera and multiple camera taping make life simpler and less stressful: they require only an operator for each camera. A switched operation requires an operator for each camera plus someone at the switcher to make the critical selection of one of the multiple camera shots to record at any given moment and, for professional productions, someone to handle the audio recording. Note, too, that the switched effect can be achieved by taking the tapes recorded by more than one camera and editing their shots together after the event (things you do after taping are called *downstream* or *postproduction* in the video industry). By doing the shot mixing in postproduction, the chances of making uncorrectable errors during real-time recording are reduced: if you selected the wrong shot during switching, you would have to stop the event and have the action repeated to correct the mistake. During editing, on the other hand, you can preview the mixing and correct any mistakes. If possible, tape with separate camera/recorder units and create the editing effects later. Either way, using more than one camera on a job requires some additional equipment planning and consideration.

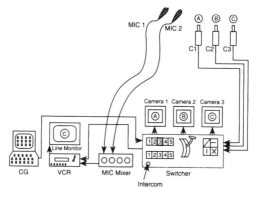

Multiple camera system. Studio equipment configuration.

It is beyond the scope of this article to go into a detailed discussion of studio operations, but a brief overview of what is entailed when designing a first-class industrial studio (as opposed to a full broadcast type facility) will provide a scheme to work from when putting together smaller-scale production capabilities. In a studio equipment configuration, all of the cameras cables come into a central switcher, each camera shot is visible on a monitor above the switcher, and only one signal can be selected to send to LINE/VCR. The basic controls on the switcher for selecting between the camera shots are CUT, FADE, SUPER[IMPOSE], or create SPECIAL EFFECTS. Audio is a completely separate system. The microphones are connected to an *audio mixer*. This mixer has several inputs: it can take audio from microphones and other sources like cassette tapes and it can then be used to select from among the inputs and/or mix the inputs at different levels (of volume) to send to the RECORD VCR audio track. A device called a *character generator* (CC) can be used to put titles on video.

The heart of such a complex system consists of some key components: the cameras, the switcher, the audio system, the character generator, and the facility itself (including lighting accommodations and acoustical treatments). A short discourse on these will provide general understanding of how studio equipment works, and categories to think about if you choose to assemble such an operation.

Cameras There are two important considerations regarding cameras: the cameras should be matched and, if their signals are to be fed to a switcher, they must have an *external synch[ronization]* feature. Any time you are using more than one camera on the same production, they should be matched. The easiest way to match cameras is to buy two of the same make and model at one time. It is striking how much the signals from two cameras can vary across models even within the same brand. (Did you ever try to match the colour and brightness of two or more slide projectors for a multi-image presentation?) Shifts in chroma are particularly troublesome when one is trying to create a professional product and the shots differ, even when they are properly adjusted on a waveform monitor.

External synch is required for multiple camera operations whenever a switcher will be used. This function of *external synch* is to allow the signal generator competent of the switcher to set the scan guns in each camera at the same blanking pulse which synchronizes the scanning. In the absence of this feature, the cameras will operate their scan gun's timing independently of one another; one may be at start while another is scanning mid-field. If the multiple cameras are not synchronized, the pictures on the LINE/VCR monitor will roll when you cut from one of them to another at the switcher.

Switcher A switcher is needed only when two or more cameras feed their signals into one VCR. A switcher is a device that receives video signals from multiple sources (camera and tape decks), synchronizes the cameras' scan guns, and enables the operator to select one signal as it is received or modified with special effects for recording. Switchers vary widely in capabilities and price. At the low end, there are simple models that accept two camera inputs and have buttons so the operator can cut back and forth between the different shots. At the high end, there are switchers that offer numerous inputs and literally hundreds of special effects that can be used in the process of cutting, fading, or superimposing shots. Most also offer an INTERCOM system for the director to communicate to the camera operators unobtrusively by using headsets. In the past, switchers were a combination of mechanical and electronic systems; now they have become almost completely electronic (some even operate with iconic menus and a mouse, like a personal computer).

Audio System All of the information on microphones cables, and connectors in the section on "Video Design System: Single Camera Systems" applies to audio for multiple camera and studio operations. Microphones used in studio work are most commonly either the lavaliere (lapel) or boom type (mounted overhead). Cables, of course, need to be longer than for most single camera operations, and it is important that they be laid out of the paths of action.

The *audio mixer,* often called a *mic mixer,* is the key component. Most of the units on the market today are well made and offer good quality sound. Quality does vary with price (as do the number of features or special effects); buy the most expensive and simplest mixer you can afford. A mixer should offer a sufficient number of high and low impedance inputs to accommodate what you need to *feed* it. The price of these units varies directly with the number of inputs in most cases—consider some margin for growth of your needs here. Next, the *potentiometers* (the knobs or dials used to set the volumes of inputs are called *pots)* or slide levers for each source should be smooth and easy to use; users vary here in their preferences and in their anatomy and dexterity: before purchasing a unit, test it by turning two pots or sliding two levers slowly and in synchronization with one hand *while* you operate a third pot or lever in the opposite direction with the other hand (this is what you need to do, for example, if you were fading two microphones in or out as you brought the music up or down). A good mixer will provide many years of service if it is not abused: take the time to find one that meets your needs as well as your budget.

Character Generator A character generator (CG) can be set up to operate during studio productions or downstream during editing. A character generator is a kind of electronic typewriter that has the capability of adding text to videotape. With the more costly ones, several pages of text can be created in advance and stored in memory to be recalled as needed; CGs can also offer many variations of fonts, type sizes, and lettering enhancement effects, and they can make the text crawl across the bottom of the screen or appear to scroll upward. Depending on the options available, this can be done on a black screen or superimposed over another picture.

The standard character generator is still being used by many production houses; recent trends suggest, however, that cards that allow personal computers to be used with video will gain a wide acceptance over the next few years. A major limitation to this alternative to the CG thus far has been the inability of the systems to achieve high quality text images on video at a price that is competitive. If this pattern follows that of electronics in general over the past few decades, this limitation will be overcome in the near future.

Studio and Control Room Facilities A studio for video production is similar to a studio for still photography: it should be a large, empty room with high ceilings so there is space to move things around, have adequate electrical amperage and multiple outlets where they will be needed, and it should offer good climate control for both temperature and humidity. Beyond the normal requirements for still photography, the video studio floor should be flat, to dolly cameras; the walls and ceiling should be acoustically dampened to a low reverberation rate, for good audio; there should be adequate storage space for props and sets, if they are used; and some kind of lighting grid should be installed in the ceiling. There are good commercial lighting systems on the market for small studios. If expense is a problem, a 4-foot grid of 2-inch *black pipe* will do nicely: any number of floodlights and spotlights can be clamped to the grid, and they can be moved around with little difficulty. It is convenient to have a lighting console (a panel with separate pots for each light) to select and to vary the brightness of the overhead lights without having to do it at each lamp head.

Control rooms adjacent to the studio contain things like the switcher and audio mix equipment. In the past, they had a large window so the director could look into the studio during taping; current thinking is that this is potentially a distraction: the director should be watching the cameras and *line* monitors during production, not the studio itself. If the director needs something done in the studio during a production, other than camera adjustments, there can be a person in the studio on an *intercom* headset (a floor manager) to make them. The control room can be small, but if the director is connected to the camera operators via an *intercom,* it needs to be acoustically dampened so noise or voice commands are not picked up by the studio microphones. If the control room has adequate space, it is also a good place to install the editing equipment.

VIDEO PRODUCTION

Production Planning This section provides some key strategies that can be used to make video programs or to communicate clients' needs to video production people. It is necessarily an abbreviated treatment. A complete discussion of all of the factors that could be considered in the creative and technical processes of making a video program would have to include most of the art and the history of cinematography along with all of the attributes that are peculiar to video as a small screen, electronic medium. What follows is a review of some of the more useful and cinematographically important variables and how they affect the final product.

Aesthetic Codes and Caveats of Video The primary aesthetic code, the technique and vision that make what people agree is good video, is the achievement of near-constant motion. Video rarely sits still. The camera, the zooming of the focal length of the lens, or the subject itself (or sometimes all three) are manipulated to be constantly in motion. Much in the same way that audio producers in radio dread quiet *(dead air),* video producers have difficulty with static shots of anything but the shortest duration. Video has become, partly by choice and partly because of the nature of the medium itself, our action medium *par excellence.*

Those of us who were trained in cinematography before moving into video think this presentation of near-constant and fast-paced motion is often overdone. Life and art both need *varied* pacing, and in many classic films the visually quiet and static moments provide dramatic pauses as a counterpoint to punctuate the ongoing dynamic grammar of film. One way to become sensitive to the difference between the aesthetics of video and those of film is to carefully view many examples for both. This, plus the nature of your client's needs, the kinds of videotapes you produce, and your creativity, will help you achieve a reasonable balance between motion and effects for their own sake and the other extreme of static dullness.

Videotaping certain kinds of performances often presents conflicts between the aesthetic codes of the performance and those of the video medium. For example, a ballet is choreographed on the assumption that there is a fixed optimum point of view for the audience that is near the centre, about one-third back from the orchestra pit. From this perspective, our ideally situated viewer sees the principal dancers (figure) set against the movements of the supporting dancers (ground).This viewer attends to figural movement and background movement alternatively, but with primary attention of the whole bodies of the principals. All of this is done unconsciously and is taken for granted. Note what happens, however, when the ballet is videotaped. Multiple cameras jump around visually in various closeups and relocations. No longer is the code of an ideally situated viewer operating; rather, the viewer is in many places almost at once and sees so many rapidly-paced closeups that orientation to the dance as a holistic event is lost. At best, the videographer would move in perfect synchronization with the naturally patterned movement of the eyes of an informed viewer; at worst, the videographer jumps around visually (cuts from one shot to another rapidly) in order to achieve the best shots, independent of their meaningfulness to the particular ballet. There is no easy resolution of this conflict of the aesthetic codes of the video medium and performances designed for the stage or theatre. Choreographers would place a camera where the best seat is located and just let it tape the performance. No cuts, no zooms. Videographers would tend to cut from one camera to another and use a fast-paced series of medium and extreme closeups. Although these tensions exist, you can minimize their negative effects by carefully studying both video aesthetics and the aesthetic demands of the kinds of performances you will frequently tape. It also helps to the candid about this and make the potential conflicts clear to the client. If your videotapes of things like theater and dance are to be used for educational purposes, it is important that the audience be made aware of how seeing the video differs from what they would experience at a live performance.

Screen Conventions and Symbolism There are certain conventions and symbols that have developed over the history of cinema that are available to video producers as design elements. Some of them can be effective when used thoughtfully and judiciously; as with any effect, overuse of such visual symbols and camera psychology can seriously reduce the production value of a video program.

Time Passage A sense of the passage of time can be created for the viewer by using such common cinematic conventions as the pixillated movement of the pages of a calendar, a sunrise, sunset, or moonlight scene, a slow fade from one scene to another, or by footage that indicates a change of season.

Screen Direction Alternating shots between two moving subjects can indicate movement toward or movement away from one another. The faster these alternating shots are cut and the more progressively they change from medium shot to closeups, the greater will be the power of the impending contact or collision of them in the viewer's eye.

Viewer Relocation The setting of a video can be moved around from one place to another by the use of travel motifs like scenery passing by the window of a moving vehicle, showing a vehicle moving across the land, or even a cut to some geographic marker (like a city limits sign) that indicates a different location.

Camera Psychology It is commonly known that, in portrait photography, for example, camera height in relation to the sitter's eye level can be neutral (camera at eye level), can increase the effect of the power and importance of the subject (camera below eye level), or can decrease the power of the sitter (camera above eye level). Medium, closeup, and telephoto shots have a similar effect, image size and camera level are particularly powerful when used together. For example, a person would really appear small and insignificant, or lost and lonely, if filmed with a wide-angle lens at a high camera angle. Also, things placed at the edge of the frame appear to be moving off camera, while things near the centre are perceived as being stable.

Depth and Focus Shift Video is a two-dimensional medium; depth can only be suggested by the use of conventions. Long shots (wide views) convey depth. Objects in the foreground help provide a sense of near and far for the viewer (provided they do not obscure the shot), and the use of overlapped objects gives the visual effect that one is behind (farther away than) the other. This depth of viewer awareness can also be manipulated by shifting the focus alternately between near and far objects.

The Language of Video Some terms have specific meanings when applied to video production. You can use language defined more fully in the Glossary at the end of this article—to plan your own productions or as a way to communicate your ideas to a subcontractor. Some of the most commonly used design terms and their screen effects are the following.

Screen Change Effects

> *Cut:* an instant switch from one shot to another; used to indicate spatial or temporal continuity of action.
> *Fade:* a slow change from one shot to another; used to indicate the passage of time or a change of location.
> *Jump cut:* a bad switch from one camera position or lens focal length to another that is so similar to the preceding shot that the image appears to jump slightly.
> *Insert:* when a second, smaller-sized picture is inserted into a primary shot to add background interest or information (as when a news commentator has a picture appear over to one side).

Super (imposition): when one shot, most often titles or credits, is layered over another. Graphics that are to be *supered* over another picture need to be made with light lettering on a dark background.

Wipe: works like a fade from one shot to another but done in a specific direction like left to right; screen effect is similar to a fade.

Camera Directions

Arc: to roll the camera to the left or right in an arc (as though it were tethered to centre stage).

Dolly: to roll the camera in (toward the stage) or out (away from the stage).

Pedestal: to physically raise *(pedestal up)* or lower *(pedestal down)* the camera on the tripod/pedestal.

Tilt: to point the lens (front of the camera) up or down.

Truck: to roll the camera to the left or right.

Lens Directions

XCU: extreme closeup; to include a person's face or part of face only.

CU: closeup; to frame a person's head and upper chest tightly.

MCU: medium closeup; similar to a bust in portraiture.

MS: medium shot; a full-length image of two or three people.

LS: long shot; people, as in a small group, make up less than one-third of the image area.

Focus: to adjust the lens for more or less image sharpness; to focus video camera zoom lenses, the standard practice is to zoom in tight (telephoto) and focus.

Zoom: to change the variable length of the lens toward wideangle (zoom out) or toward telephoto (zoom in).

Ways of Planning Video Productions Given that you cannot just go out and point a video camera at an event (if you want a quality product), you need to think about planning for video as a motion medium. There are at least three different ways to conceptualize the making of videotapes, and these ways are often used in combination. One way is to plan each shot in advance, much in the same manner that major films are made. This method, discussed in detail in the section on "Scripting and Storyboarding," gives the most control over taping, but it requires absolutely compliant people, situations, and events. The second method is one wherein you can exercise some control over the participants and the action but otherwise have to follow the known structure of the event. A wedding would be an example of semiplanned videotaping: you can arrange the people for a few of the key shots, but otherwise you have to follow the unfolding structure of events. The third method, as we move from structured to spontaneous videotaping, is when you have to work without control over the talent of the action. Here you need to rely on your positioning and your sense of timing.

Even in those situations in which you have only positioning and time to rely on, you can intelligently anticipate how the event will unfold and where the action will be. Most public ceremonial behaviour is culturally patterned even when it appears to be random. Imagine the plots of the stories people tell of commonly shared events: the story outline is a potential shot structure. If you reflected on this, you could sit down and write a rough script for things like family reunions and birthday parties. Even newly popular boudoir portraits follow a stereo-typical, pop-cultural pattern for glamour. Some time spent considering the spontaneous event you have been hired to videotape will greatly improve the likelihood that your final choice of camera positions and your timing will be good if not optimum. We are also an image-conscious people. Often the participants in what is normally an uncontrollable event will gladly posture, pose, or otherwise make accommodations to see that you get good footage of them.

The more complex and/or the more expensive a production is, the more important it becomes to plan it as tightly as possible: script, storyboard, and rehearse everything. Also try to work under conditions where you are not subject to variables such as weather. These factors are reasons that the motion-picture industry quickly built huge studios after moving to California to take advantage of the weather, and they are also the reason video production houses systematically do complete story-boards for major productions: planning and control save money and ensure a good product. It would be good discipline to do a full storyboard for each production if you are new to video or if you are familiar with video but will be taping an unfamiliar event. It is also a good way to train your assistants in the language, conventions, and discipline of the trade and in your personal style. After you become comfortable with video/or with the new subject matter you tape, you will not need to do a complete storyboard for routine productions such as weddings. There will also be cases where you will not have the time or the control over the performance to plan as tightly as you would like; in those instances, plan your basic shot coverage as well as you can and then try to think through the cultural pattern inherent in the ceremony. This will help your intuition guide you regarding your camera positions and timing. Remember that all commonly repeated marker events (life's major thresh-olds) are culturally patterned, and follow the suggestion to sketch out the screenplay beforehand. A note here: if you are working with ceremonies or events that have their origins in other cultures, it would be advisable to go to a few of them before videotaping one or to have a member of that culture or ethnic group explain the story to you.

The next section provides the plot for tight production plan-ning: start with it, but never be so locked into a shooting plan that you are not open to special opportunities for improved shots that happen spontaneously once you are on location. The more experienced you become, the safer it will be for you to deviate from a fixed plan.

Scripting and Storyboarding Storyboarding, the process of sketching visual and narrative information on cards as a way to plan video productions, has evolved out of the motion-picture industry, where it is still used extensively. Film studios frequently have walls covered with tracks to hold the storyboard cards to that an entire production can be put up and looked at as a whole. While it remains a key planning process within the domain of cinematography, storyboarding can be used effectively for the design of video productions of all kinds.

Storyboards are divided into a visual component (the left side) and a narrative or text component (the right side). It is an unsettled matter within the field whether one is to begin with the visual images in mind and then fill in the script or do the listing of themes or ideas and the writing of the script first. Probably, Fellini works in the former mode and most producers work by alternating between the two. It may have some connection to one's right or left hemispheric brain dominance as well. One significant characteristic of the process is that it works well either way, or as a dialogue between the two as one progresses.

The model itself is quite easy to use. There are four basic steps to guide you through the critical verbal and visual choices that will ultimately determine the videotape's effectiveness or appeal to your client.

1. Write on Notecards Take a stack of notecards (size is your choice, but most production houses prefer the larger ones, on the order of 5 x 7 inches). Write each separate thought, key idea, or essential point on a separate card. List this verbal information on the right half of the card, and remember, 'at this point, these are terms to organize your thoughts with—writing the precise narrative comes later. For those who are right-brain dominant, it would work just as well to begin with sketching the key shots on the left side of the card and then adding the narrative later. During this process, be sure to consider the use of music and any environmental sound that would enhance the production. When you have finished this process, you will have a stack of index cards that are, in effect, notes for the key elements to be videotaped. So far, this is not greatly different from what you would do on sheets of paper to begin outlining. Notes on paper, however, have to be rewritten every time you want to reorder or change them; herein lies one of the real advantages of the card system: cards can be rearranged over and over until you are satisfied with the flow. This makes the next step enjoyable rather than tedious.

2. Play Solitaire with the Cards Sit on the floor or at large desk and lay out your cards; sequence and resequence them until you are fully satisfied with their order. This is also the time to look at them, topic by topic, to make sure that they contain enough (but not too much) information on each subpoint. Add to and subtract from them as needed to balance the unit. Limit your unit size by focusing on the key themes or ideas. When you are fully satisfied that you have dealt with all essential points and eliminated all nonessential points, number all the cards in sequence.

The two steps that follow can be done in any order or in a back-and-forth kind of dialogue; this makes further allowance for how each one works as an individual (especially visual or verbal dominance) and how small production groups normally divide planning responsibilities.

3. Visualize the Production Go through your stack of cards and note what, if any, visualization would be effective or necessary. Sketch in a rough picture of the shot on the left side of the card. If there a need for greater communication than your sketch affords (or if someone else will be doing the visual production), make notes in shorthand under the image, for example "CU KEYBOARD FUNCTION KEYS." Keep in mind that not every card will necessarily need a visual, and that some cards may require several pictures. In the latter case, add the cards in and number them subordinately (such as, "12A, 12B"). In this step, consider carefully the visual sophistication of your clients and design the pictures to be interesting for them. When you are finished with this step you have what the trade calls *shot cards*.

Shot cards are the sketches the video production people work from—just like in the movies. These *numbered* cards can now be sorted by type of image: those requiring graphics and titles to go into one stack, those to be shot on a job site into another, and those with studio closeups of equipment into still another: each type of shot is done at one time. Doing all of the like visuals together saves an enormous amount of time and labour in setting up and taking down equipment for each image.

4. Write the Script This step could be done before step 3—it depends on your style. When you have finished sequencing and expanding or reducing your cards and then numbering them in order, you have completed the content outline. All that remains is to go back through the cards and write the script from the key themes. Here, as with the visuals, consider your audience's language ability and vocabulary when writing. Also consider viewer fatigue; there's no hard rule here, but as a profession, we have tended in the past to attempt to do too much in our programs. Several short productions can frequently by much more interesting and effective than one long one.

As you write from the brief notes on your cards, your use of formal English may get in your way. Most producers are well educated and most of that education has called for written performance. Productions via audio track call for a spoken instead of written style. It is not hard to tell the difference. When you have your narrative written out from the cards, read it aloud with the correct emphasis and intonation as though you were taping it: those places where you trip over your tongue or over extended adjective constructions or vocabulary are where this difference lies. Find these places and smooth them out until they flow like normal conversation (this usually means simplifying the sentence construction or the vocabulary).

The planning strategy outlined in the foregoing steps will give you a good start toward becoming accomplished at video design. Most commonly, producers use a combination of structured, semistructured, and spontaneous methods. Much will depend on the nature of the events to be taped and on your personal style and experience. In addition to the matter of planning strategy, there are some pragmatics of video production that you should give thought to before pressing the RECORD button for a client, time spent on these kinds of preparations will help ensure high-quality and profitable video operations.

Production

Preproduction Considerations There are some things you should consider before videotaping: permissions, test sessions and rehearsals, and cinematic etiquette. The kinds of permission you need to obtain will depend on what and where you are taping. Some people and sites are more agreeable than others. For example, it is common practice to discuss photographing a wedding with the minister who will preside over the ceremony, but you rarely need to obtain permission to make pictures in the church itself. On the other hand, if you need to videotape an event at a famous place or building, you will often have to request—and sometimes pay for—permission to do so. In those instances, be sure to get signed model or property releases. The best guide here is, if in doubt, ask.

Test sessions, going on-site and setting up the camera, lights, and microphones, and recording some videotape under what will be the actual working conditions will yield valuable visual and audio information in the form of problems that can then be corrected before you tape the actual event. This is particularly valuable for the beginning videographer; it is less so for the seasoned professional. Ideally, you could do one test session on the unoccupied side to determine the best camera positions and then another one during a staged rehearsal. It is one thing to work out your camera placements and lighting in an empty architectural space; it is quite another to do this with people there. The client is not interested in your problems with working in an unfamiliar place or with a ceremony or event that is new to you: the client want results. It is up to you to do whatever is required to provide them. Sometimes you can build in a slight margin in your fees for rehearsal or for on-location testing. Keep in mind that these test sessions and rehearsals are excellent opportunities to train your staff.

Finally, the matter of etiquette is a delicate one and one about which it is hard to give general advice. The central proposition is to balance your need to be assertive enough to get good footage with the needs of the participants that you be unobtrusive to the dignity of the ceremony or event. Clients and their trends will remember how you treated them, so protect your reputation. On the one hand, you cannot stand meekly in the back of the church behind Uncle Fred; on the other, you cannot crash onto the altar like a wire service photojournalist at the site of a terrorist bombing. Much of this "etiquette tension" can be avoided by planning where you will be during key moments of the event and letting the participants know what to expect.

Videotaping Events

Image Quality With videotape, as with cinematography, you need to think on two levels simultaneously. First, you need to envision the flow and the on-screen effect of the video as a whole. This *gestalt* has two levels in itself that require you to "see" what you will tape and how you will frame it. What to tape is often based on the client's need or on the structure and flow of the event. Even when the content images are predetermined, however, you should still consider the value of some embellishing footage. This background ("B-Roll") footage could include images of things like the place where a wedding couple met, their favourite activities, close friends, the honeymoon site, or the like. Obviously, the wedding is the focus of the tape, but judicious inclusion of meaningful B-Roll images can enhance the final product.

Beyond the content, with or without B-Roll, there is the visual question of the tape as a film. This raises questions of *shot variety* (the mixture of wide, establishing shots, medium shots, and closeups), *pacing* (how fast the shots will change on the screen), and *sequencing* (may be fixed by an event like a wedding, but if not, this determines what is seen in what order).

Secondly, there is the shot itself. Once you have decided on a shot mixture, your vision as a still photographer can be used to make each shot a good picture. Here are the considerations of camera placement, framing, selective focus, lighting, a background all need to work together. As with still pictures, the shot is the basic unit of video product. With video, particular attention needs to be paid to subject placement, the quality and direction of light, focus, and the steadiness of the camera (use a tripod). The goal is to produce clear, effective images. It is extremely beneficial to pay particular attention to the background. As Edward Weston once said, "Take care of the corners and the rest will take care of itself." Not literally true, of course, but it is all too easy to overlook background distractions during the excitement of taping an event.

Beyond the videotape as a film and the quality of the individual shots, there are a few caveats particularly applicable to a still photographer who begins to produce videotape. One is that video, relative to film, is a crude resolution system with inherently high contrast and a small screen problem. To accommodate the low-resolution capability, try to avoid very fine detail in the images, and, if seeing details on small objects is important, move in tight, focus carefully, and light for the effect. Video's inherently high contrast means that you should avoid trying to achieve subtle tonal differentiation in visual appearances of hue or the reflectance of the subject matter. The small screen problem of video means that, compared to film, video favors bold, closeup, fast-paced action over slow subtle, mid-distance imagery. As an aside here, video also tends to prefer *hot* (loud and fast) audio effects over more subdued ones.

Another caveat concerns the overuse of the zoom lens. In my first cinematography course some years ago, the professor had each of us load a 16-mm camera and take it out and expose an entire film magazine while constantly running the zoom lens in and out. This may seem like overkill, but he made his point: more film and videotape is ruined by neophytes over using the zoom lens than by any other problem (a close second is the failure to use a tripod). The zoom lens can be used sparingly if zoomed slowly, but resist the urge to overuse. Thinking like a cinematographer might help: imagine that you have a three lens turret on the camera with a wide angle, medium, and telephoto lens mounted on it. Plan your shots with specific focal lengths rather than zooming in and out while seeking the best frame.

All of the contemporary video cameras have automatic iris diaphragms. As with still cameras, this is a mixed blessing. Most do not do a good job of compensating for side- or back-lighted subjects. Be sure to do a test of these on location before making your final tape.

The final potential trouble area has to do with camera stability (or the lack of it). Buy a good tripod (one that is sturdy enough for the weight of the camera you plan to use) and use it. Hand-held work may be necessary under emergency conditions, but it will produce rough and inferior shots. Pay attention to the selection of a head for the tripod. Get one you can pan and tilt with smoothly. Videographers vary a great deal on this: some can work with inexpensive heads while others really need fluid-dampened ones.

Setting Up on Location It is beneficial to go through the story-board and design process, to consider the attributes and aesthetics of good video, and to do on-site test sessions. There are also some things you can do when you arrive at the taping location that will help achieve professional results.

As with location portraiture, if you are using AC power, arrive early enough to locate the circuit breaker panel (especially if you will be operating lights on AC) and to run your power and microphone cords neatly and safely. The cords should be out of the flow of traffic insofar as possible and, to ensure a good signal as well as to minimize your liability, they should be taped to the floor with duct tape.

Try to situate the camera away from temperature extremes or excessive dust. Video recording heads are particularly sensitive to humidity, changes in temperature, and dust. Be attentive to letting your equipment warm up to room temperature after is has been used outdoors during cold weather or transported in a cold vehicle (note: the baggage compartments on modern jet aircraft can reach temperatures of -50°C): condensation on the heads will create a bad picture or no picture at all. It also helps to clean your VCR heads before each job. Establish the habit of recording a short test segment before each recording session; this will let you know whether or not you are getting a good signal. Do this for the audio track also. While you are doing these tests, it is a good time to make your final decisions about lighting and audio recording. Check the direction and the quality of the lighting *on the recorded segment of tape:* just as with still photography, there are nuances and subtleties you can see through the lens that are not apparent when you look directly at the scene.

Audio testing is important and often overlooked during video production. Pay particular attention to the quality of lip-synchronized sound (where the speaker's voice is heard as his or her face is seen on screen). Nonsynched sound (called *wild sound)* can always be narrated or dubbed in later, but unless you have a major production house at your disposal, get high quality synch sound at the time you tape the image. Microphone selection (external to the camera; wireless?) and placement (as close as possible to the sound source) are important variables in getting good audio. Also try to position the camera and the talent away from background noise, and instruct the talent not to handle or nervously fidget with the microphone cord during taping. Some microphones, particularly the lower priced ones, pick up a bumping noise each time the cord is touched. If in doubt, rehearse and test.

Making People Look Good There are several things you can do to enhance the appearance of people on camera. Some of these are similar to what you would normally do for portrait sittings; others are specific to video. The goal is that the individuals (figure) be tonally separated from the setting (background), that they look attractive, and that clothing and other accessories not be visual distractions. Beyond the classic portrait advice of light for a pleasant, sculpting, mainlight effect, use a short lighting ratio for modest contrast, and focus carefully on the eyes, high quality video further requires that the talent not wear bright white (it glares), small checkered patterns (they create a *moire* effect), or excessive amounts of jewellry (especially if the hands are to be shown in a closeup shot).

Soft, pastel garments, simple backgrounds, and shots that are framed tighter than you normally would for still photography will produce pleasing video images. If you do makeup, you will find a slightly more exaggerated effect (more separation between the base and the accents) works nicely. This would be a good opportunity to make a "Looking Your Best on Videotape" flyer that you could give to your clients well in advance of the taping session (if you do not already have one printed).

In-Camera Editing If you are working with one camera and do not have editing capability, try to plan the shots as tightly as you can so they all go together well in the finished tape. In-camera editing is really careful planning and taping. The more the action will be predictable, and the more you can storyboard the production in advance, the more likely you can successfully edit as you videotape. Be careful here how you stop the camera: some cameras will create a glitch in the picture if you turn them off and on; others will do this when you use the pause feature. This would be good thing to test before you purchase a system.

Postproduction If you videotape an event with one camera using in-camera editing and if you record your audio as you make the video, or if you do studio productions where the visuals, audio, titles are mixed during recording, there is no requirement for postproduction. More commonly, however, there will be something further you want to do to improve the quality of your work that needs to be done after the initial taping.

Graphic and Titles Graphic and titles for video can be recorded during studio production or downstream. At either point, they can be made with lettered cards positioned in front of a camera or they can be typed in electronically with a character generator. Independent of where they are accomplished during the production process, titles for video need to be simple and bold. Use as few words per screen as you can, and make the lettering large and distinct. Letters that contrast with the background are easy to read on-screen. Video does not pick up fine detail, so avoid small or ornate text with serifs.

There is also a standard from broadcast television that should be kept in mind: it is safe to assume that many viewers' receivers will be out of alignment vertically or horizontally, thus clipping off one edge or another of the picture. Because of this, it is standard practice to leave an unused safety margin around the edges of a title or product shot (particularly in advertising, where seeing the product or the product name is critical). This standard, called the *must see area,* leaves approximately 10% of the outer extremes of both dimensions unused.

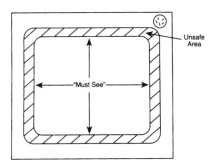

Graphics and titles. "Must see" area.

Editing A basic editing system consists of a *source VCR,* a *control module,* and an *edit VCR.* All of the normal VCR operations for both decks (play, record, fast forward, rewind pause, and stop) are controlled by the module. On the editing module, these controls are present in their customary form as buttons and switches; the functions of *fast forward, still frame* and *rewind* are also present in the form of two large knobs (one for the source VCR and another for the edit VCR), and each knob has a fast and slow mode that can be set to look at images either frame by frame or quickly. Turning a knob to the right in the normal mode gives a fast forward effect, whereas turning it to the left makes the tape rewind. The slow mode does the same thing but at a much lower (frame-by-frame) speed; in either case, you can observe the images on their monitors as you move the tape.

It is customary to go through recorded tapes and to make an *edit log* of the frame-counter addresses *(in* and *out)* points) of the various shot segments before beginning the editing process. This log, along with the label on the tapes, saves time and keeps things organized.

At the risk of oversimplifying what can be a complex stage of the video production process, editing can be thought of as a controlled way of copying segments of separate videotapes onto a single tape. There are two ways to do this: *insert* and *assemble.* To understand these terms, you first need to know that videotapes with images on them also have a *control track*. This is the electronic pulse laid down by the camera or the switcher at the time of the a tape is recorded—in many ways, it resembles the sprocket holes in a piece of motion picture film; the control track regulates the timing of the images. Some editing systems will put the control track on a blank tape by just running the deck in record (with no video signal being used); others require that you put a control track on with a camera and recorder. Check your equipment manual: the edit (blank) tape has to have about 5 seconds of a control track in the beginning in order to take any edits, and it needs to have it within the tape to take insert edits. You can check for a control track by putting a tape in either editing deck and putting it on play: if the footage counter on the control module runs without interruption, you have a good control track. *Insert editing* is transferring the visual and/or audio recording from the source tape to the edit tape while leaving the control track on the edit tape intact. *Assemble editing* is taking the picture, audio, and control track from the source tape and transferring them to the edit tape.

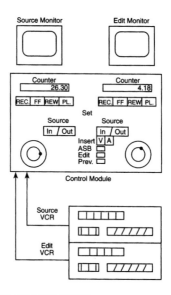

Editing decks and control module.

To accomplish an edit, the tape containing the footage you have recorded is placed in the source deck and a blank tape with a control track is placed in the edit deck. It is good discipline to get into the habit of rewinding all tapes and resetting both tape counters on the control module at the start of each editing session. As you play the source tape, when you come to a segment you want to transfer to the edit tape, you set its beginning as the *in point* on the module and its end as the *out point*.

288

Then cue-up the edit tapes to where you want the new segment to come in and set this as its *in* point. Note: you cannot make an edit at the very beginning of a tape: both decks have to rewind about 5 seconds to synchronize the edit transfer. You can then preview the way the edit will look *(preview)* or make the edit.

Editing can be accomplished with the control module cuts alone, or you can run the signals through a device called a post-production effects generator to enhance the transfer of images and audio. This machine operates just like the switcher discussed earlier: during the edit you can cut, fade, wipe, or add a special effects; it also has audio inputs for microphones and other sources that allow the mixing of sound during editing. It is also possible to add titles during editing by feeding a signal from a character generator into the effects generator.

There are also new editing special-effects computers on the market that you can use to create many effects that were previously obtainable only on very costly broadcast-grade studio equipment. Foremost among these as of this writing is the "Video Toaster." Ask your local dealer for a demonstration of the impressive capabilities of this device to alter images.

Inserted Segments and Music There may be times when your own creative ideas or the demands of a client make it desirable to include video footage from programs someone else produced or to use music for a particular effect. Both of these matters raise serious copyright problems. To use video footage, contact the producer of the video and arrange for permission to use the segment. This may range from being simple to do to being next to impossible, and from *gratis* to extremely expensive. There are several variables: the producer, the nature of the product, you, and your intended use (commercial uses demand higher usage fees).

The same thing applies for music. Normally it is not desirable to use popular music in video—you can never know what reactions your client may have had to it. Most producers prefer music with a soft melody line so it does not overpower the visual imagery. Commercially recorded music copyright litigation is one of the largest sections in most law libraries: be extremely careful here, and be even more careful if you plan to show your video for admission fees or use it for advertising. A copyright lawyer can advise you on any particular questions you have. There is one nice alternative with music: there are companies that provide copyright-free music for this purpose. These companies offer either a subscription service (for high-volume producers) where set fees are paid on a monthly basis and the subscriber receives updated music regularly, or (for low-volume users) they offer a service with a lower fixed expense where you pay for the music as you use it ("per needle drop"). They are listed in the trade publications.

MARKETING VIDEO SERVICES Marketing video services is very much like what you already do to make the best possible presentation of your studio and your pictures. It is important to have a clean, bright, and professional setting in which to do business. Beyond what you already do for your still photographic operations, you will need to set up a screening room for clients to see videotapes.

A screening room can be part of a room that you use for other purposes, but is should be one you can darken tor optimum video viewing. Use good equipment here: a fourhead VCR and the largest colour receiver you can afford. The receiver should be mounted no more than 5° above nor 15° below a line connecting the centre of the screen with the eyes of a (comfortably) seated viewer. Photographers show proofs instead of contact sheets: show a carefully edited tape to the client rather than excessive and/or unwanted footage. It is also a good idea a show a copy rather than consume a master tape for screening and other purposes.

SUMMARY Video is a powerful communication medium and one that is steadily demanding a larger share of the conventional studio photography business. It is not overly difficult to move into the production of videotapes, but there are differences between video and still photography that you must take into account when doing so. So, too, are there similarities that can help ease the transition. The primary differences lie in video being electronic in nature and in its being a motion medium. Some of the basic electronics must be mastered, but these are not particularly complex. By studying how video works and by following the suggestion outlined, this part of the learning should be accomplished in a short period of time. The other difference between video and still photography, that video is a motion medium, can be handled using the information in this article and from critically viewing films and tapes: it will take longer to fully master, but that will be time well spent. The payoff will be in technically proficient and creative programs that will please you and your clients.

It will save you a lot of valuable time and energy if you will study the section on "Video System Design" carefully. Video equipment needs can be confusing, particularly since the modular nature of video hardware resembles that on the market for computers more than it does equipment used in still photography. Wrong choices can be costly to your business. Knowing what capabilities you need in a piece of equipment will go a long way toward insulating you from being sold things you do not need and at prices you may not be able to afford. On balance, though, it is often preferable to pay more for a good device than to save a little on what will turn out to be an inferior one. Just be sure of what you are getting.

Finally, taking the time to go through the test sessions, and the on-site set-up advice will help prevent some of the most commonly made video mistakes. It does take some practice and study to become accomplished at video production, but the suggestions given in this article will make your time work to maximum advantage. It would even be a good idea to develop short checklists for preproduction and on-site use: these are used by major producers to systematically double check everything. Against the argument that checklists look amateurish, remember that veteran airline pilots use them for every take-off and landing. It looks far more professional to use checklists than it does to forget some critical item or step in a commercial production. Use the similarities between still photography and video to ease your transition into the new medium. Video production is an enjoyable and rewarding process: photographers are creative people and video adds another dimension—motion—to that potential. As you begin to produce video, word will get around, and you will find growing markets for your services. Take your time, allow yourself the practice and study, and think of video production as adding to, rather than subtracting from, your still picture market.

TIPS FOR PRODUCING BETTER VIDEO
- Plan for motion and shot sequences
- Light well
- Use a tripod
- Minimize zooming in and out
- Frame shots tightly
- Watch background distractions
- Use an external microphone
- Record wedding background audio separately (dub in later)

GLOSSARY OF SELECTED VIDEO TERMS

A & B roll editing A procedure where two or more videotapes are fed into a editor and mixed onto the edit tape.

Address The location of a segment of tape on a reel given by its frame counter in and out points.

Arc To move a camera on a dolly in a left- or right-hand direction while keeping the same distance from centre stage (as though it were tethered to that point).

Assemble edit The transfer of video, audio, and control track signals from a source tape to an edit tape during editing.

BNC A video cable connector with a locking collar.

Boom A microphone stand with a long horizontal arm that is counterbalanced; used to position a microphone above the set.

Camcorder A video camera and videotape recorder combined into one piece of equipment.

Cathode ray tube (CRT) The large picture tube on a receiver or monitor.

Character generator A kind of electronic typewriter that is used to add text to videotapes.

Coax[ial] A type of video cable with a thin single strand of wire inside a plastic tube that is wrapped with a woven wore and covered with insulation; like the antenna for cable television.

Composite signal A combined video and audio signal.

Control track An electronic signal on a videotape that provides a timing reference for the electronic sensing of the visual and audio imagery; like sprocket holes in motion picture film.

CU (closeup) A video shot that, for a person, covers the area of a head-and-shoulders portrait.

Cut To switch instantly from one shot to another with a switcher or effects generator.

Dolly To move a camera toward *(dolly in)* or away from *(dolly* out) centre stage. A tripod platform with wheels.

Dropout A place on a videotape where the magnetic coating is worn or damaged; this causes a white fleck in the picture.

Dropout compensator An electronic device in a receiver or VCR that replaces dropout flecks with the last bit of imagery scanned in order to give the visual effect of continuity in the quality of the picture.

Dub To add sound to video after recording the visual imagery. To copy video or audio tapes.

Editing log A list of the shots on a videotape recorded by their address on the frame counter.

Effects generator A device used in editing that permits the use of special effects (different kinds of fades and wipes) when making a transition from one shot to another. Can also be used as an audio mixer. Similar to a switcher but does not have a synchronization generator.

Electronic News Gathering (ENG) The use of a camera outside of the studio and in a portable configuration.

Establishing Shot A long shot.

Extreme Closeup (XCU) Very tightly framed image—usually less than 3 feet—used to show small detail.

Fade; dissolve To move slowly from one shot to another with a switcher or effects generator.

Field One-half of the scan of a picture. See also: *Frame.*

Focus To adjust the lens for image sharpness.

Format The size of videotape. Also used to indicate a type of program.

Frame Two scans (fields) of a, picture m,aking one complete image (frame). Scan rate is 50 fields, 25 frames, per second.

Insert To add a portion of one shot into (usually an upper corner of) another; adds background interest or information.

Insert edit The transfer of either video or audio signals, or both from a source VCR to an edit VCR without the transfer of the control track.

Key; chroma key An editing or switching effect that cuts one image into another; used to add titles and graphics. Chroma key uses colour (normally blue) to drop background from the shot to be keyed in.

Lavaliere A small microphone that is worn attached to the lapel.

Long shot (LS) A wide-angle picture that includes more background that it does figure; used to establish context.

Medium shot (MS) About the equivalent of a three-quarter pose in portraiture.

Medium Long Shot (MLS) Similar to a full-length portrait or small group shot.

Microphone Mixer/Audio Mixer; Mic Mixer A device that accepts multiple audio inputs, has volume controls for each, and feeds one signal to record.

Pan To move the camera lens to the left or right in a

Pedestal To raise *(pedestal up)* or lower *(pedestal down)* the camera, or to move it around. A large, studio-type camera stand with wheels that is operated hydraulically or electronically.

Pixillation An effect used to make inanimate objects appear to move around; achieved by repeatedly running a short segments of tape and moving the object around in the shot. When played back, the object *moves* as though under its own power.

Pot[entiometer] A volume or gain knob (coil) on a microphone mixer, switcher, or lighting control board.

Preroll The distance a VCR rewinds a tape before an edit in order to synchronize it with the other VCR; usually 5 seconds.

Radio Frequency (RF) A means of video distribution via a coaxial cable with multiple composite (video and audio) signals; requires a receiver.

Safety Shot In multiple camera operations, one camera is kept on a complete view of the scene that can be used if one or more of the other cameras fail during taping.

Skew An adjustment of the VCR's tape tension, used to stabilize the upper portion of a picture.

Source VTR(s) The VCR(s) used to feed video signals into the edit VTR.

Super[impose] To layer one shot atop another by means of a switcher.

Switcher A device that accepts multiple video inputs, synchronizes the scan cycles of the cameras, has an intercom for studio crew communication, and offers multiple special effects in the process of cutting or fading to the signal that is sent to record.

Synch[ronization] The aligning of the travel of equal scan guns on two or more camera so the pictures are timed together and can be mixed by a switcher without rolling.

Tilt To move the camera lens up or down.

Time Base Corrector (TBC) A postproduction device used to filter and strengthen *(clean up)* the control track signals on tapes made with different pieces of equipment.

Tracking An adjustment of the VCR used to stabilize a picture.

Video Toaster A microprocessor that generates computer graphics and special effects for video applications.

Truck To move the camera to the left or right parallel to the front of the stage.

VCR/VTR Video cassette/tape recorder.

Videographer An image maker that uses video.

White Balance (WB) To set the video camera for the colour temperature of the lighting being used; similar to selecting daylight (5500 K) or tungsten (3200 K) film for still photography.

Wild Sound Audio that is recorded independently of the video.

XCU (extreme closeup) Very tight framing; full-face of a person or details on small object.

Zoom A type of lens with variable focal lengths. To adjust the focal length from wide-angle to telephoto (zoom in) or from telephoto to wide-angle (zoom out).

References:

Adams, Michael, *Single Camera Video: The Creative Challenge.* Dubuque, Iowa: William C. Brown Publishers, 1992.

Bunch, John B., "Aesthetic Education and Educational Media." *Journal of Aesthetic Education 20* (Fall 1986): 81-92; "Developing Audio Productions for Effective Listening." *Training & Development Journal 36* (December 1982): 30-39; "The Effective Utilization of Video as a Training Technology." *Video Handbook. Volume Two.* Alexandria, Virginia: ASTD Press, 1987; "New Approaches to Video as a Training Technology." *Video Handbook. Volume One.* Alexandria, Virginia. ASTD Press, 1986; "Professional Advice on Videotaping Instruction." Performance & Instruction Journal 29 (January 1990): 16-21; "The Storyboard Strategy tor Planning Visual Communications." *Training & Development Journal 45 (July* 1991): 69-71; "Video as a Simulation Technology for Teaching Photography." *Educational Technology 22* (May 1982): 14-16.

Burrows, Thomas D., Wood, Donald N., and Gross, Lynne Schafer, *Television Production: Disciplines & Techniques,* Fifth Edition. Dubuque, Iowa: William C. Brown Publishers, 1992.

Zettl, Herbert, *Television Production Handbook,* Fourth Edition. Belmont, California: Wadsworth Publishing Company, 1984.

VIDEO GRAPHICS ARRAY (VGA)

In computers, the colour display of the cathode-ray tube (CRT) is driven by a video card or board according to a standard established by the card's classification. VGA superseded CGA and EGA boards. Industry standards for VGA are 640 x 480 pixels at 16 colours and above.

VIDEO RANDOM-ACCESS MEMORY (VRAM)

In computers, a specialized form of RAM that can simultaneously write data to the display monitor as it is receiving data from the central processing unit (CPU). This form of dual-port chip greatly speeds up the displaying of images on the cathode-ray tube (CRT).

VIEWING DISTANCE

Viewing distance is the spatial separation between an observer and an object or a photographic or other reproduction. The retinal image size of an object or a reproduction is inversely proportional to the viewing distance. The correct viewing distance of a photograph for normal appearing linear perspective is equal to the camera image distance for a contact print, or equal to the camera image distance times the magnification for an enlargement. For example, if a 10 times enlargement is made from a negative produced with a 2-inch camera lens, the viewing distance for correct perspective is 20 inches. Depth of field also varies with the viewing distance of the image.

VIRTUAL IMAGE The image seen after refraction by a diverging lens or after reflection in a plane or convex mirror when the light rays diverging from an object point cannot then be brought to a corresponding image point. The virtual image is seen by looking at the subject via the mirror or through the lens at the subject and cannot be received directly on a screen or film surface. It can however be treated as a *virtual subject* and reimaged by a lens capable of giving a real image from a real or virtual object. Virtual images are usually upright, unreversed, and bright and formed for visual convenience in many optical instruments such as microscopes, telescopes, and rangefinders.

VIRTUAL INSTRUMENTS In computers, the use of fast graphic user interface (GUI) computers to imitate laboratory and test equipment in a transparent fashion. Virtual instruments can be created via software and an input/output port with many different platforms. A computer can be programmed to function as a pH meter, oscilloscope, sine-wave generator, or frequency counter, to name only a few instruments.

VIRTUAL REALITY In electronic imaging, a form of intensive computer processing and specialized display and input peripherals that create the seamless illusion of an alternative reality. Research into virtual reality has taken place in the areas of medical diagnosis and treatment, space exploration and georesource mapping, and amusement and entertainment activities.

VIRUS A computer program designed to disorient, slow down, or "kill" the computer's operating system or data files or the hard disk's directory.

VISUAL AID A projected image or a displayed image or object that is used for educational or informational purposes.

VISUAL ANGLE The angle subtended by an object at the front nodal point of the eye.

VISUAL COMMUNICATION

Distinctions and Definitions Two distinctions are essential to any understanding of visual communication:

1. not all visuals are communication, and
2. not all communication is visual.

The first distinction is conceptual and the second is perceptual.
The first distinction refers to the fact that not everything we see is communication. We may look at something that is not a message from another human, that is, it does not possess any means of human expression. On the beach, the rocks, by themselves, have nothing to say. Objects do not "intend" to commu-

nicate. In fact they do not and cannot intend anything; that separates them from subjects. For our purposes, only human subjects are possessed of the willful powers of intent that are essential to communication.

Communication in general can be defined as a circulation of expression and impression between two or more individuals with or without the use of a medium such as stone, wire paper, canvas, polymers, or any other substance. It is important to distinguish visual communication and visual observation because there are different mental compartments for the two, and if there is a mismatch, the system error can be very serious.

Sight and Hearing Seeing may be believing in the objective realm of observation, but in the subjective realm of communication, seeing is evaluating. Evaluation takes into account the pre-existing relationships with the communicator, the form, and the topic, all of which may substantially reduce the "believing" that follows the "seeing." Still, seeing is not hearing.

It is because we believe that the primary sense that processes the expression leaves its mark on the resulting internal impressions that we bother to make the perceptual distinction between visual and nonvisual communication.

Communication, in whatever form, may address any combination of senses: touch, smell, taste, hearing, or sight. For whatever reason, in most cultures, including our own, hearing and sight are singled out for the great majority of adult communications. The communications addressed to these senses may be called aural if addressed to the ear, or visual of addressed to the eye.

Visual communication would include any form of human expression addressed to the eye alone or to the eye in combination with other senses. In most cases, where the eye is one of a combination of senses, the eye becomes the dominant sense.

We shall not embark on a lengthy physiological description of visual observation or vision outside of the communication process except to say that as a means of perception, vision distinguishes itself from the other primary sense, hearing, by its speed relative to the cognitive process. It has been demonstrated that the eye can put sense data together faster than the cognitive processes can abstract meaning from that sense data. Where as with hearing, cognition may find itself waiting for the sequential linear code. With aural perception, before meaning can be derived the auditory sensations must be processed one pulse at a time. With the eye, parallel rods and cones are firing simultaneously, bringing in nonlinear simultaneous patterns. This makes vision less time-dependent than hearing and therefore more spatial. Vision's nonlinearity or simultaneity makes the internal visual impression appear to be all there, all at once. This unchained, spatial freedom of visual communication is its hallmark.

Dynamic and Static Communications Although these words were written for the eye of the reader, they could have been delivered electronically in a passive or interactive dynamic display. The advent of computers has added new wrinkles to the analysis of visual communication at both ends of the circulation: dynamic production tools and dynamic displays. These very words could have been generated more or less by software and sent instantaneously as electronic mail for example, or recorded for noninstantaneous delivery on disk.

Despite all the variations of delivery systems afforded by the information age, there seems to be a constant place for the traditional static display of text—*hard copy*. Why?

Some readers have suggested that it is the resolution of ink on paper, others feel that holding the text in one's own hands lends a level of control and comfort. It could be added that the static display, which holds the text still for the eye for as long as it likes, makes this otherwise tricky path more surefooted. While one is trying to decipher, chain-stepping through the line of symbols and side-stepping out to references, all at the same time, knowing that the text on this page will wait for the eye for split seconds or centuries, provides a level of assurance or comfort which seems to defuse the pressure. That is not to say that one cannot read and comprehend from electronic media, but it takes much longer. The knowledge that the text might have been corrupted accidentally, that, by some mystery of hardware or software, it might not be on the disk next time, or that the power might go off, adds sensory insecurity that slows the process clown. It is also true that in a delivery system that has the enormous capacity for dynamic images and sound, each of which requires much less pretransactional initiation, text seems to be lost in the enormous channel capacity, and so the static display is preferred where the text seems to fit more snugly.

Not all visual symbols are text, but in their static display there must be an overarching convention about their order. Mathematical or musical notation too must abide by static display conventions. Pictographic alphabets, which are also symbolic visual expression, allude to meaning via images. They are, nevertheless symbols and not images. As such they too must adhere to the more rigid static display conventions for symbols (following vertical rather than horizontal lines in Chinese for example).

The static display conventions for all symbols are more rigid than the static display conventions for images, because of the precision and abstraction to which the symbols aspire. Beyond the lines that order the symbols, the visual effects of page layout and type font can affect the interpretation process of this text.

This text is an example of visual symbolic expression made by dynamic electronic tools but coming to you by way of a static display—a book. Conventions for such static displays are well settled by years of consensus. In the case of the English language, the alphabetic symbols are designed to represent the sounds of the words—they are a phonetic alphabet. As such, convention dictates that they be read from left to right, with pausing points marked by commas, periods, and paragraphs. Not too long ago these symbols would have been penned with ink from a well, then with continuous flowing ink from fountain pens, ballpoints, typewriters, and now computer word processors. Clearly, stopping to dip for ink affected the preparation time and the boldness of the stroke, both of which affected the expression, and, of course, eventually, the impression of the text as well. This so-called "charm" of pen and ink added overtones to the primary meaning in the expression content, just as the easily selectable variety of type fonts offered by the word processing programs can shade the meaning of this text. Words can be made **bold** or *italicized* or <u>underlined</u> with a single keystroke, changing the emphasis in the expression represented by the printed words.

No effect of the static display of text or any other form can supply any of the missing steps or links in the decoding chain, but within the limits of the code, the static form can affect the content. The same visual symbolic expression couched in the form of a hand-written note, or a formal business letter or a published book or a telegram will each have a slightly different impact.

The dynamic capacity of the electronic display, monitors and TV screens, has been harnessed by two opposing conventions. One passive convention leads the eye in a preordained path, while the other, interactive convention, offers to follow the eye in its own unique path. These display dynamics apply to both pictures and symbols.

Whether static or dynamic, two-dimensional visual images may be *wrought,* that is rendered by hand, and/or they may be *captured.* In either case, the help of some tool is required, which implies a technology. Perhaps the information age represents the coming together of Lewis Mumford's stages of development: man the tool maker and man the symbol maker.

In addition to being wrought or captured, images may be sent and displayed as single *static* images ur *dynamic* sets of images. Here again, the dynamic images may be *passive* or *interactive* (responsive). Once again any image may be static or dynamic, and if it is dynamic, it may be more or less under the control of the viewer, which we are characterizing as passive or interactive.

The Static Image The static image, whether wrought (put together by hand) or captured, is the most independent from time and timing; it allows the eye to proceed in its own path at its own pace. This of course means that no single path is the correct one. The myriad of possible visual paths is the hallmark of the form and also the feature of the form that the visual communicator works against to lend impact to the visual expression. Compositional patterns and chiaroscuro (use of light and dark) are some of the techniques at the visual communicator's disposal to trap the emancipated eye of the beholder. To the extent that the freed-up eye is trapped back into the subtle patterns, a second, unannounced, imprecise level of communication occurs in the *bulge* of the form by content. Like the more abstract overtones of harmony in musical expressions, this esthetic bulge may delight the viewer without any precise understanding of the reason. Not only is the subject or object identified by eye but a more abstract pattern sings a harmony or counterpoint for the eye, the total effect of which is greater than the sum of its parts.

In this connection, the skilled wrought-image communicator

has more work to do, but, by the same token, more can be done. There is more control and therefore a deeper channel capacity, if not a broader one. The relationship of figure to ground, shapes, distortions, shading, colours, and the combinations of all of those factors can extend the image beyond the reality of everyday objects. The wrought image can afford to be more the direct offspring of imagination and intent, more internal, more subjective. It can speak about interior consciousness as well as external reality.

The captured static image on the other hand (the photograph) is limited by the size and shape of the object that happens to be in front of the lens at the time; even if the object happens to be the physical body of another subject, it is a light-reflecting object where the captured image is concerned. Much interpretation can be done with lighting and processing, but the reflected light from a real figure or figures is the basic ingredient of the form. Here again the great content pushes against this limitation and bulges the line in the direction of the neighbouring wrought image.

The fact that the wrought image preceded the captured image historically has some communication significance. The initial coding for imagic communication was dictated by the wrought image. Probably life experience itself originally linked *brooding* to heavy clouds, but it was the painter who set that into esthetic code. It was the wrought-image esthetic code that influenced the esthetic sensibility of the photographer. These pre-established wrought-image codes had to be addressed if the captured image was to communicate on any deeper level, and then they had to be exceeded if the captured image was to establish itself as an independent form. This is a challenge for each new captured image.

One feature of form that helped distinguish the captured image was its speed. Even with the long exposure time and tedious processing of early captured images, the overall rendering time was shorter than it was with wrought images. And so image capture pushed the technology for greater and greater speed and facility of process in order to underscore its differences and establish itself as a distinct form. Eventually galloping horses and hummingbird wings could be captured mid-stroke for the eye to peruse at its leisure. These figures could never have posed for the painter. This assured the form of static, captured images a secure place in the hierarchy of visual communication.

The speed also meant that the single visual communicator could make more images in a day or in a career. A broader range of subjects and objects could model for this visual expression. Instances that would have been lost to the painter could be brought home in the camera. Needless to say this changed the course of the wrought image as well as the captured image. It forced the hand of the wrought-image maker further toward imprecision, that second voice, or second level where the camera's speed had no advantage. Modern so called *nonobjective* or *impressionistic* or *abstract* art can be viewed as the reestablishment of the wrought image with new levels of subjectivity in the underlying code.

Still the forms could not settle down each to their own turf. Once the static wrought image became less objective, more subjective, the static, captured image followed suit.

Now with electronic imaging tools, the lines become blurred both at the expression or production end and at the display and impression end. The fact is that visual expression can now be partially wrought and partially captured. And the *bastard* image can show itself in a static, dynamic-passive, or dynamic interactive display. In other words, one can take a photograph with film or electronic camera; one can then scan the photograph into image-processing software and use computer graphics to change it in an almost infinite number of ways. The product of this mixed compound process can now be printed on paper as a standard static display, or it can be compressed and transmitted and displayed electronically as a still image across the world, or it can be animated so that it becomes part of a dynamic passive display or it can be pieced into a more elaborate responsive display that purports to be interactive.

These mixed forms have yet to establish their own codes so that viewers' perception and conception processes know what to expect and how to respond. Instead the old codes are still in effect and the new images must make their way as photographs or paintings to the viewer's interior.

There are, however, collateral effects of the new imaging processes. With the new-found processing and transmission speeds, the visual communicator can compete with transmitted text and voice for time-dependent subjects such as fast-breaking news.

A second effect of the new imaging processes has to do with the veracity of the captured image. Traditionally the captured image didn't lie. At least we assumed that it didn't lie because it was so directly related and close to visual observation. It seemed to be much harder to lie with the camera than the brush or pen. Some semblance of what was in the photograph had to have occurred in front of the lens. The truth might have been exaggerated by focus; it might have been staged, but even in the staging there were limits. Now subjects and objects that were not and could not have been together can he seamlessly pieced together in the captured image. This dramatically punctures the line between captured and wrought images. On the positive side, the subjective intentional energies of imagination can and will make a wider variety of statements in the neo-captured image format that heretofore might have been reserved for the wrought image. On the negative side, collateral technology or laws or canons of ethics will be necessary to reinstate the veracity.

A third effect of this compounding of captured and wrought images has to do with the cost efficiency of the production and publication. Publishers traditionally created a necessary super-structure that served as a topical bottleneck. The visual expression had to pass through editors before it was disseminated. That is no longer the case. You can desktop publish your own work, eliminating the superstructure with whatever good or bad effects that had on delivery. This is an information age by-product that affects all expression, not just visual expression. The heralds of this democratization of the communication hegemony hope for a demassification of audiences, resulting in a broader range of topics serving the broader range of interests. At this point, however, it is only a hope.

Books: Ciampa, John *A., Communication: The Living End.* N.Y.: Philosophical Library, 1988.

VISUAL LITERACY Having or showing knowledge of the process of communicating by means of pictorial images, as distinct from the ability to communicate with written and spoken words.

VOICE ACTIVATION In computers, an advanced form of user interface that directs the computer through a sophisticated software package with a hardware peripheral that recognizes and acts upon voice instructions.

VOLTAGE REGULATOR—DC An electronic device that maintains a constant value of output voltage despite changes in the input voltage or the output load current. DC power supplies usually have voltage regulator circuits that maintain the output voltage within a fraction of 1% of nominal voltage. The complex circuits of a precision voltage regulator are available in a single IC chip. A less precise voltage regulator can be achieved with a single zener diode and a series resistor.

WARM-UP Refers to the time required for equipment or material to reach a stable condition before use. Depending on the size of film and paper packages, several hours may be required to reach room temperature after removal from refrigerated storage. Some electronic densitometers may need a 30-minute warm-up time for all of the components to stabilize at a constant operating temperature.

WASHED-OUT Identifying an image or area of an image that appears to have too little density. Thus, a washed-out highlight would lack detail, and a washed-out print would appear to be too light in all areas.

WAVE A travelling, periodic, oscillatory motion, or a combination of such motions.

WAVEFORM (1) A mathematical representation of the form of a wave. As such, it is a functional plot of some characteristic of the wave as a function of space and/or time. One of the most common characteristics plotted is the amplitude or magnitude of the wave, such as the height of the surface of the ocean at a particular time as a function of position, or at a particular position as a function of time. Other characteristics plotted are the phase, power (magnitude squared—this makes all values positive), and the real and imaginary parts (most waveforms are represented using complex numbers). Since waves are periodic, waveforms are periodic functions. (2) One periodic of a waveform function as defined in (1).

WAVELENGTH The distance on a waveform from one point to the corresponding point in an adjacent period. For convenience sake, wavelength is usually measured from the maximum or minimum amplitude point on a wave to the similar maximum or minimum amplitude point on the next period. All waveforms have wavelengths, but wavelength is of particular significance in specifying electromagnetic radiation. The nature or category of a particular type of electromagnetic radiation is specified by broad wavelength bands, such as light being electromagnetic radiation with wavelengths between approximately 400 and 700 nm. The specific characteristics of the radiation are specified by the specific wavelength, such as radiation with a wavelength of 550 nm being a specific colour of green light. The changes in wavelength that electromagnetic radiation undergoes when passing through materials with different indices of refraction determines the indices of refraction of the materials. Because of this effect, wavelengths specified on spectral plots are the wavelengths of the radiation in a vacuum, which has an index of refraction of one.

WEAK COLOUR Adjective denoting low saturation or chroma.

WHITE Name given to colours that are very light and exhibit little or no hue.

WHITE LIGHT Light that is made up of photons with a sufficient variety of wavelengths such that the light appears neutral to the viewer. The rigor of the term *white light* varies enormously depending on the viewer, the viewing conditions, and the requirements of the situation. Metamerism can make almost any nonmonochromatic spectral energy distribution appear relatively white. Several blackbody curves with colour temperatures between 3000 and 6000 K have been defined as standard sources of white light for various applications, but these sources are not interchangeable, and appear to be different in colour when compared. Also, one blackbody curve can contain absorption bands and be indistinguishable from a similar curve with no absorption bands, yet the rendition of certain sample colours can be significantly affected by the bands.

The most useful application of the term *white light is* in distinguishing from specifically non-neutral light in a specific application. For example, colour enlargers sometimes have a lever that moves the colour correcting filters out of the light path. When this is done, it is said that the image is being projected using white light. In a studio, a photographer might combine *white light* exposures with exposures through different coloured filters. Both of these examples use the term *white light* to indicate light from an incandescent or flash source that is not filtered, and this may be about the best practical definition. It is important to remember, however, that the exact nature of the light source must be considered when designing new systems or conducting tests on equipment and materials.

WHITENESS (1) Attribute of a visual sensation according to which an area appears to contain more or less white content. (2) Attribute that enables whites of different colours to be ranked in order of increasing similarity to some ideal white.

WIENER SPECTRUM The result of the analysis of a complex waveform into an equivalent set of sine waves, displayed as a plot of wave amplitude versus frequency. The method is used in the study of the grain size distribution in processed photographic images.

WINDOW (1) In computers, a frame or frames in the cathode-ray tube (CRT) that display different processing operations, for example, one window may display a spreadsheet while a second window on the same CRT displays a word processing document. Window environments are a form of graphic user interface (GUI). (2) In computers, a proprietary graphic user interface (GUI) operating system for IBM and compatible platforms by the Microsoft Corporation.

WIRE FRAME In computers, a graphical approach to sophisticated drawing in that the object is drawn as a composite of polygons in the form of a wire frame, thus saving time and space. Upon completion, the wire frame object will be rendered.

WORD PROCESSING In computers, a software program that allows the user to enter text for the purpose of writing a document. The text may be edited and sent to a printer for hard copy.

WRAPAROUND In computers, word processing software allows for an automatic line feed so that text characters that reach the end of a line automatically wrap around to the next line without the entering of a carriage return. Also, in electronic imaging, the manipulation of a brightness value above 255 or below 0 automatically wraps around to the higher or lower brightness value, for example, the next value after 255 is 0, and the next value after 0 is 255. This type of image brightness wraparound is undesirable.

WRITE In computers, to store data on a floppy disk, hard disk, or optical disk.

WRITE ONCE READ MANY (WORM) In computers, a storage device that is written to by a laser. This system allows for a large amount of data to be stored. Optically based, this approach can only write once to a given sector on the optical platter. However, the data can be read from the platter as often as necessary.

WRITE PROTECTED In computers, hard and floppy disks can be physically and virtually manipulated to prevent writing over important data that exist on the disk. Writing over data has the same effect as erasing data.

WRITING RATE In photorecording such as oscillography, the velocity of the spot of light across the sensitive material when the trace is made.

YIQ In video, NTSC standards abbreviate chrominance as I and Q, and abbreviate luminance as Y. I and Q refer to hue and saturation. Y refers to value or brightness.

YOUNG-HELMHOLTZ THEORY The hypothesis that there are in the retina three different sensors, each of which is sensitive to a different primary colour of light, specifically red, green, and blue. Physiological evidence in favour of the hypothesis involves the discovery that such sensors do exist.

YOUNG THEORY Young visualized a triangular outline for representing pure spectral colours, with red, green, and blue at the apexes and white in the centre, in place of the circular arrangement suggested by Newton. Mixtures of red and green, green and blue, and red and blue were placed on the straight lines connecting the pairs of colours. This suggested that the visual system required only three types of colours sensors, a concept stated more explicitly by Helmholtz in the Young Helmholtz theory.

ZONES (TV) Circular divisions of a television screen around the centre where the diameter of zone 1 is 0.8 times the height of the picture area and the diameter of zone 2 is equal to the width of the picture area. The zones are used in the evaluation of picture quality.

APPENDIX

Exponents, Factors, Logarithms, *f*-stops, Zones

(Base 2)			(Base 10)			*f*-stop	Zone
Exponents	Factors	Log₂	Exponents	Factors	Log₁₀	change	change
2^0	1	0	10^0	1	0	0	0
2^1	2	1	$10^{.3}$	2	.3	1	1
2^2	4	2	$10^{.6}$	4	.6	2	2
2^3	8	3	$10^{.9}$	8	.9	3	3
			$(10^{1.0}$	10	1.0)		
2^4	16	4	$10^{1.2}$	16	1.2	4	4
2^5	32	5	$10^{1.5}$	32	1.5	5	5
2^6	64	6	$10^{1.8}$	64	1.8	6	6
			$(10^{2.0}$	100	2.0)		
2^7	128	7	$10^{2.1}$	128	2.1	7	7
2^8	256	8	$10^{2.4}$	256	2.4	8	8
2^9	512	9	$10^{2.7}$	512	2.7	9	9
2^{10}	1024	10	$10^{3.0}$	1000	3.0	10	10

Logarithms are exponents to some base, such as 2 or 10. Some variables in photography (and computer memory in bits and bytes) are based on exponents (logarithms) to the base 2. This means that as the exponents increase by one, the factor doubles. (Computer memory chips having 1024 bits, have 2^{10} bits.)

In photography, all factors representing a doubling or halving of exposure, such as full f-stops, shutter speed settings, light values, exposure value numbers on most exposure meters, and zone numbers, are based on logarithms to the base 2. However, neutral density filters, density, and log H are based on logarithms to the base 10. As exponents to the base 10 increase by one, the factors increase 10 times. In practical terms, a 0.30 neutral density filter can be thought of as a 1-stop filter, a 0.60 filter as a 2-stop filter, and so on. A log exposure increase of 0.30 is a doubling of exposure. Further, each 0.10 log change in exposure is equivalent to 1/3rd of a stop.

An average outdoor scene has a brightness range of about 126 to 1 (factor), or 2^7, 7 *f*-stops, 7 zones, or a log luminance range of 2.1, which is $10^{2.1}$. Film has a log exposure (log H) range (latitude) of about 1000 to 1, or $10^{3.0}$. Photographic paper has a reflectance density range of about 2.0, a factor of 100 to 1, or 10^2. (Note: Exponents to base 10 have been rounded off for simplicity, more correctly $10^{.301} = 2$.